Education

D0934987

ED

ED

# Counseling the Adolescent

# Contributors:

LEO H. BARTEMEIER

FRANK M. BUCKLEY

MRS. EDMUND D. CAMPBELL

PAUL J. CENTI

EDWARD V. DAUBNER

IRENE DAVIS

ROSE MARIE DICKSON

JEANNE G. GILBERT

GHISLAINE D. GODENNE

HAROLD F. HILL

LEO KANNER

ROBERT J. MCALLISTER

JOHN R. MCCALL

RAYMOND J. MCCALL

JOSEPH D. MCGOVERN

DESMOND P. MCNELIS

ARTHUR G. MADDEN

LAWRENCE R. MALNIG

MOTHER M. STELLA MARIS

CLARE O'DWYER

JOHN F. O'GRADY

HENRY V. SATTLER

ALEXANDER A. SCHNEIDERS

ABRAHAM SHUSTERMAN

SARA L. SIEBERT

# Counseling the Adolescent

Alexander A. Schneiders
*Boston College*

and Contributors

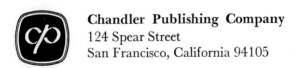

**Chandler Publishing Company**
124 Spear Street
San Francisco, California 94105

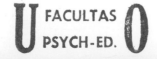

Previously published and copyrighted materials are reprinted with the permission of authors, publishers, or copyright owners as listed below:

Aldrich, C. Knight. *An introduction to dynamic psychiatry,* pp. 171–173. Copyright © 1966 by McGraw-Hill, Inc. Copyright © 1955 by the McGraw-Hill Book Co., Inc. as *Psychiatry for the family physician.* Used by permission of McGraw-Hill Book Company.

Allport, Gordon Willard. *Pattern and growth in personality,* p. 560. Copyright 1937, © 1961 by Holt, Rinehart and Winston, Inc.

Arbuckle, Dugald S. *Counseling: an introduction,* p. 139. Copyright 1961, Allyn and Bacon, Inc., Boston, Massachusetts. Reprinted by permission of the publisher.

Curran, C. A. *Counseling in Catholic life and education,* pp. 19–21. Copyright, 1952, by The Macmillan Company.

Engel, George. *Psychological development in health and disease,* pp. 147–148. Philadelphia: Saunders, 1962.

Ginsburg, S. W. *A psychiatrist's view on social issues,* pp. 67–68. New York: Columbia University Press, 1963.

Hand, H. C. *General education in the American high school.* Copyright © 1942 by Scott, Foresman and Company.

Hechinger, Grace, and Fred M. Hechinger, *Teen-age tyranny,* p. 17. New York: William Morrow and Company, Inc. Copyright © 1962, 1963 by Grace Hechinger and Fred M. Hechinger.

Hobbs, N. "Some notions about guidance." *Peabody Journal of Education,* 1952, 29, pp. 229–231.

Hutchins, Robert M. *A conversation on education,* p. 11. Santa Barbara: Center for the Study of Democratic Institutions, 1963.

Josselyn, Irene. *The adolescent and his world,* p. 25. New York: Family Service Association of America, 1952.

Josselyn, Irene. *Psychosocial development of children,* pp. 89–92. New York: Family Service Association of America, 1948.

Mosher, Ralph L., Richard F. Carle, and Chris D. Kehas. *Guidance: an examination,* pp. 77–78. New York: Harcourt, Brace & World, 1965.

Pearson, G. H. J. *Adolescence and the conflict of generations,* p. 99. New York: W. W. Norton & Company, 1958.

Remmers, H. H., and B. Shimberg, *Examiner's manual, SRA youth inventory,* pp. 12, 15–28. Copyright 1949, Science Research Associates, Chicago. Used with the permission of the publisher.

Ruesch, J. *Therapeutic communication,* pp. 22–23. New York: W. W. Norton & Company, Inc., 1961.

Ruesch, J., and G. Bateson. *Communication: the social matrix of psychiatry,* p. 19, New York: W. W. Norton & Company, Inc., 1951.

*This volume
is sincerely dedicated to the
youth of America who
challenge our understanding
in every age.*

# Contents

▲▲▲▲▲▲▲▲▲▲▲▲▲▲▲▲▲▲▲▲▲▲▲▲▲▲▲▲▲▲▲▲▲

## PART I

### Perspectives on Adolescence

## PART II

### Discipline and Rebellion in Adolescence

## PART III

*Critical Choices and Goals in Adolescence*

## PART IV

*Adolescent Feelings and Emotions*

## PART V

*Mass Media and the Adolescent Mind*

## PART VI

### The Counseling Process

## PART VII

### Counseling the Adolescent

## PART VIII

### Principles of Mental Health and Mental Hygiene

# *Preface*

▲▲▲▲▲▲▲▲▲▲▲▲▲▲▲▲▲▲▲▲▲▲▲▲▲▲▲▲▲▲▲▲▲▲

For the past five years, beginning in June of 1961, Mount Saint Agnes College, an institution of higher learning for women, has offered a series of workshops on Mental Health, Adolescent Development, and Counseling, all of which were of particular interest to teachers, counselors, and administrators. The first two workshops, in 1961 and 1962, were organized around problems in mental health, and the third and fourth workshops, in 1963 and 1964, centered around the problem of the teen-ager in American culture. The final workshop, in 1965, rounded out some of the ideas expressed in earlier workshops and bore the title, "Guidance and Counseling in Schools and Colleges." Each workshop extended over a five-day period, and was attended by more than 200 participants from many different parts of the country. This volume is a compilation of selected proceedings from each of these five workshops.

The forty-five selections presented in this volume represent a variety of viewpoints, theories, and empirical studies which have been organized into eight parts. This organization was determined by the topics rather than by the chronology of the papers. The eight areas include: Perspectives on Adolescence, Discipline and Rebellion in Adolescence, Critical Choices and Goals in Adolescence, Adolescent Feelings and Emotions, Mass Media and the Adolescent Mind, The Counseling Process, Counseling the Adolescent, and Principles of Mental Health and Mental Hygiene. It will be readily seen by the reader that the title of this volume, "Counseling the Adolescent" corresponds closely to the content of the material. The reader will also note that the various contributions were written by persons well qualified in their respective fields. A brief glance at the short biographies (pp. xiii–xv) will indicate readily the qualifications of our contributors for participation in these workshops. The range and depth of the topics can be easily discerned from a brief study of the Contents.

I wish to express my appreciation to all those persons who made both the workshops and this publication possible. To Sister Mary Cleophas, R.S.M., the President of Mount Saint Agnes College, to Sister Mary Magdala, R.S.M., Dean of the College, and to all of the other staff personnel who fulfilled countless tasks during the period of the various workshops, I am most deeply grateful. To the contributors who made each workshop a significant intellectual and pedagogic experience I express my sincere thanks. And finally, to my wife, Glen Elizabeth Schneiders, to my secretary, Miss Martha McLaughlin, and to my assistant, Miss Rose Marie Dickson, whose unremitting help in the preparation of this volume was a source of constant encouragement, I offer my deepest gratitude. Without the help and dedication of all these persons, this volume could not have been completed.

ALEXANDER A. SCHNEIDERS

*May 1, 1966*

# Contributors

▲▲▲▲▲▲▲▲▲▲▲▲▲▲▲▲▲▲▲▲▲▲▲▲▲▲▲▲▲▲▲▲

LEO H. BARTEMEIER, M.D., is Director of the Seton Psychiatric Institute in Baltimore, Maryland, and past President of the American Psychiatric Association, The American Psychoanalytic Association, and the International Psychoanalytic Association.

FRANK M. BUCKLEY, Ed.D., is Professor of Psychology and Chairman of the Department of Psychology and Education at Assumption College in Worcester, Massachusetts. He is also Consulting Psychologist, Department of Psychiatry, Massachusetts General Hospital in Boston.

MRS. EDMUND D. CAMPBELL, M.A., is a graduate of Columbia University and President of the Greater Washington Educational Television Association and a member of the Health and Welfare Council of the National Capitol Area.

PAUL J. CENTI, Ph.D., is Director of the Counseling Center at the College of the Holy Cross in Worcester, Massachusetts, and a certified psychologist, and Associate Editor of *The Catholic Psychological Record*.

EDWARD V. DAUBNER, M.A., is a graduate of Fordham University in New York and an Associate Professor of Education at Loyola College in Baltimore, Maryland.

IRENE DAVIS, A.B., is a Phi Beta Kappa graduate of Goucher College in Baltimore, Maryland, and Assistant Registrar for the Johns Hopkins University.

ROSE MARIE DICKSON, M. Ed., is a graduate of Loyola University in New Orleans, Louisiana, and a graduate fellow in Counseling Psychology at Boston College.

JEANNE G. GILBERT, Ph.D., is Director of Research at the Mount Carmel Guild in Newark, New Jersey, Adjunct Associate Professor of Psychology at Fordham University, and a practicing psychotherapist.

GHISLAINE D. GODENNE, M.D., is a graduate in Medicine from the

University of Louvain in Belgium and is presently Assistant Professor of Mental Hygiene and Instructor in Pediatrics at the Johns Hopkins University in Baltimore, Maryland.

HAROLD E. HILL, M.S., completed his Master of Science degree in Mass Communications at the University of Illinois and is presently Vice President of the National Association of Educational Broadcasters in Washington, D.C.

LEO KANNER, M.D., is a graduate in Medicine from the University of Berlin, author of the classical text in Child Psychiatry, and a recipient of numerous awards and Professorships at universities in the United States and Europe.

ROBERT J. McALLISTER, M.D., Ph.D., is a psychiatrist in private practice in Washington, D.C., lecturer at the National Catholic School of Social Service of The Catholic University of America, and a consultant to the Child Center of Catholic University.

JOHN R. McCALL, S.J., Ph.D., is Professor of Psychology and of Pastoral Psychology at Weston College, a School of Theology for the New England Province of the Jesuit Order. He was formerly Director of Guidance at Fairfield University in Fairfield, Connecticut.

RAYMOND J. McCALL, Ph.D., has doctorates in both Philosophy and in Psychology, and is Director of Clinical Training at Marquette University in Milwaukee, Wisconsin. He was formerly Chairman of the Department of Psychology at Marquette.

JOSEPH D. McGOVERN, Ph.D., a clinical psychologist in private practice in Washington, D.C., is also Assistant Professor of Psychology at Georgetown University Medical School and a visiting staff member at the District of Columbia General Hospital.

DESMOND P. McNELIS, M.D., is Director of Medical Education at the Seton Psychiatric Institute in Baltimore, Maryland.

ARTHUR G. MADDEN, Ph.D., studied at Columbia University and completed his work in Philosophy at Fordham University. He is Chairman of the Division of Philosophy at Mount Saint Agnes College in Baltimore, Maryland.

LAWRENCE R. MALNIG, Ph.D., studied at Columbia University and at New York University, from which he earned his Ph.D. in Psychology. At present he is Director of Guidance and Testing at St. Peter's College in Jersey City, New Jersey.

MOTHER M. STELLA MARIS, R.S.M., is Vicar General of the Sisters of Mercy of the Union, which staff Mount Saint Agnes College in Baltimore, Maryland.

CLARE O'DWYER was educated at The Catholic University of America and is the Director of the Catholic Youth Organization of the Archdiocese of Baltimore.

JOHN F. O'GRADY, L.L.B., is Master in Chancery of the Circuit Court of Baltimore City in the Division of Juvenile Causes. He has had wide experience in working with juvenile offenders.

HENRY V. SATTLER, C.SS.R., Ph.D., was Assistant Director of the Family Life Bureau of the National Catholic Welfare Conference and is the author of several popular books on sex education and marriage.

ALEXANDER A. SCHNEIDERS, Ph.D., is Professor of Psychology and Student Counselor at Boston College, and the author of several widely used texts in adolescent psychology and the psychology of mental health.

ABRAHAM SHUSTERMAN, Ed.D., is Rabbi of the Har Sinai Congregation of Baltimore, Maryland, and President of the Clergy Brotherhood of Baltimore.

SARA L. SIEBERT, B.L.S., is a graduate of McGill University in Montreal and is presently coordinator of the Work with Young Adults of the Enoch Pratt Free Library of Baltimore, Maryland.

# PART I

## Perspectives on Adolescence

▲▲▲▲▲▲▲▲▲▲▲▲▲▲▲▲▲▲▲▲▲▲▲▲▲▲▲▲▲▲▲▲▲

# 1. The American Adolescent— Needs, Problems, Tasks

ALEXANDER A. SCHNEIDERS

## A Portrait of the Adolescent

It is not easy to draw an accurate portrait of the contemporary teen-ager, partly because of wide individual variations and partly because he is in a stage of cultural transition. All of us feel at times that today's youngster is basically no different than his counterpart of a generation ago, and we recognize that our perception of him can be distorted to an appreciable degree by the psychological presbyopia of advancing years and by the paramnesia that invariably occurs whenever we retrace our steps and go back to the somewhat nostalgic past. As Pearson emphatically points out in his well-known book, *Adolescence and the conflict of generations* (1958), a certain amount of repression and distortion occurs with respect to our own adolescence because it would be too disagreeable to remember what it was actually like. It is a gen-erally accepted principle that the mind represses that which it does not wish to recall.

Yet is is difficult to escape the impression that the youth of today are different from their earlier counterparts. The contemporary teen-ager is too often more deeply disturbed than the situation warrants. He often lacks zest for the challenge of adult responsibilities that seemed to characterize previous generations. He does not seem as sure of his values and his goals as he should be in order to face the conflicts and difficulties of adult life. There is often a lack of direction to his strivings and a looseness of personal integration that stand in the way of a resolute confrontation of basic issues regarding himself and society. The contemporary teenager seems unsure about his vocation, the role

3

of military service in his life, the value of an education, his obligations to or relations with his family, or what he is willing to fight for.

This lack of direction makes it difficult to capture the image of the contemporary adolescent. The image does not hold still long enough; it shifts from day to day and from year to year. In much the same way that the individual adolescent is in a period of transition from childhood to adulthood, so the concept of adolescence is in a period of cultural transition and has not yet crystallized into a solid image that can be described with accuracy. The events of the past fifty years have so disrupted the main currents of life that the adolescent can be readily pardoned for his uncertainty and inconstancy. The values of his world and the general shape of things have changed so radically that the contemporary adolescent does not know exactly when or how he fits into the picture. The world has become a threatening place in which to live, and there is no longer the complacent certainty of existence that characterized human life prior to the outbreak of World War I. It was then that the world began falling apart, and ever since it has continued to do so at a rapidly accelerating rate.

The teenager of today senses the impact of two massive, frighteningly destructive world wars, a nearly disastrous economic depression, the ever-present threat of total annihilation, and the enforced disruption of daily living by the demands of military service. These things have so thoroughly disengaged human values and so completely altered the perception of reality, that the adolescent feels like he is treading air rather than walking on solid ground. Psychologists and psychiatrists refer to this state of affairs when they speak of *universal anxiety* and point out the existence of the constant stress and threat of our contemporary existence which breeds that anxiety (Banary, 1948).

This world of anxiety is what the adolescent must face; and he knows with deep certainty that it is a world created by the generation that preceded him. Because of his own anxiety, he does not trust this world, nor does he trust the generation that created it. And therefore he is in constant conflict with those persons in his life who are part of this preceding generation. He does not see eye to eye with his parents regarding many things of importance. He scoffs at the things that they feel are important and valuable. He ridicules their jaded morality, especially when he finds that in practice it involves many contradictions. He often develops an open and sometimes violent rebellion against traditions, standards, and the values of a society that by its own admission is somewhat decadent. In many instances this rebellion flares into full-scale delinquency, and the adolescent becomes an outcast in a society that callously prepared the way for his downfall (Greeley, 1961).

## The Adolescent Problem and the Adolescent's Needs

The problem of the contemporary teenager stems to a large extent from the social-cultural matrix within which he has developed and within which he must function as an adult. This problem is not easy to solve because no one has yet discovered a formula for changing the dynamics or the structure of contemporary society. Thus the teenager —whether in school, at work on some job that offers neither dignity nor promise, or drifting aimlessly about in an effort to find himself in a world whose shifting values offer little hope for personal identity (Wheelis, 1958)—is caught between a bleak past and an even less promising future.

But we cannot understand the contemporary adolescent by the simple expedient of defining his relationship to the social order. The portrait needs a great deal more depth. Just as important as the impact of society are the adolescent's fundamental personality needs, those driving forces within him that shape his personality from the very beginning, determine his relationship to the people around him, and give character and form to his individual approach to reality. There are at least four such categories of needs: (1) existence-safety needs; (2) reality needs; (3) self needs; and (4) self-other needs. The first two categories of needs are basic to the adolescent's existence, whereas the third category of self needs is directly related to the self-actualizing process, and the category of self-other needs determines the degree to which the adolescent becomes more distinctively humanized and is fitted into the social structure.

We need not dwell long on the first category of needs because their relationship to the total welfare of the adolescent is too obvious to require explanation. Nevertheless, they stand out prominently as the prototype of human needs. Their structure and their dynamics are such that they demonstrate with unmistakable clarity the basic proposition that human needs must be gratified if the welfare or the stability of the human organism is to be maintained. This fact is the very core of need-dynamics. Needs do not tolerate frustration, at least not for an indefinite period. Sooner or later they break through whatever barrier exists and force a response, whether it be good or bad. We see this dynamic action exemplified in the functioning of physical or viscerogenic needs. Hunger, thirst, rest, and other such physical requirements of the human organism soon demand gratification, and their strength is such that almost any barrier will be overcome in one way or another. Other such basic needs, including freedom from threat and harm and freedom from noxious stimuli, function in pretty much the same way. As a typical example, note the frenzy with which an individual strives to eliminate such a simple stimulus as an itch, or how anxiously he reacts to the threat of disease or illness. Physical integrity and well-being are a fundamental requirement for the human organism, and therefore the needs that serve these qualities are among the most powerful we encounter.

The human personality, at any level of development, is also dynamically influenced by other reality demands, what we call *reality needs*. The adolescent particularly, because of the constant changes going on in his personality and also because of his tendency toward idealism, needs to develop a healthy orientation to reality. He needs to develop a realistic view of people, events, and the world in which he lives. He needs also to acquire a life philosophy, that is, a system and a scale of values, of truths, and of beliefs that will enable him to understand reality, to confront it courageously, and to cope with it. We are all aware of how important a philosophy of life is to mental health and to wholesome adjustment; and, for obvious reasons, the adolescent with all of his frustrations, conflicts, and anxieties needs this value system more than anyone else. For the same reason, he needs spiritual succor, a religious orientation that will bring him into contact with God and enable him to develop a personal religious relationship that will bulwark his life philosophy and his orientation to reality.

The fourth category of needs are the *self-other needs* of affection and love, acceptance and belonging, approval and recognition, participation and partnership, conformity and similarity. These needs, more than any others, enter into the socializing process, the process whereby the egocentric child becomes gradually converted into a sociocentric adolescent and adult. It is the gratification of these needs that generates such important personal qualities as friendliness and compassion, neighborliness, loyalty, altruism, other-mindedness, and a host of similar traits that enable a person to live effectively and creatively in a social environment. It is the gratification of these needs that leads to social adjustment.

By the same rule, the frustration or blocking of self-other needs can interfere with or even seriously damage personality growth. In the absence of affection and love, acceptance and belonging, or approval and recognition, the traits most likely to develop are self-rejection; a sense of worthlessness; deep-seated shame and guilt; scrupulosity; a sense of sinfulness; feelings of rejection, hostility, and hatred; destructive aggressiveness; jealousy; envy; and similar characteristics. We must remind ourselves constantly that man is by nature a social being, and that he cannot achieve full humanity or mature adult status unless the socializing process begins early in his life and culminates in other-minded adulthood.

However, at the same time that this socializing process is going on, the teenager, like the child before him, is being determined in his behavior by a group of *self needs* which are organized and function within the structure of the personality so as to assure self-actualization. These important and powerful needs include independence, self-identity, achievement, security, and experience. When these needs are adequately gratified, as they should be particularly during the adolescent period, there is every likelihood that the individual person will achieve not only maturity and adulthood, but even more importantly, selfhood. The adolescent-becoming-adult cannot survive in the demanding and threatening world of today without a clearly defined selfhood. In the course of growing up he must come to grips with himself. He must find out who he is, what he is, where he is going, and why. He must achieve a certain measure of independence and security, and he must develop a sense of achievement through worthwhile experiences. The frustration of these basic needs can only generate uncertainty about oneself, indecision, massive anxiety, defensive and withdrawal symptoms, and a general inability to cope with either self or reality. In the absence of this type of need gratification the end result must eventually be gross maladjustment or mental disorder. If, as we have seen, man is by nature a social being, he is even more definitely an individual being; and therefore the self-actualizing process is basically necessary to the achievement of personality in the fullest sense of that term.

## The Adolescent's Problems

The social condition, the conflict of generations which it breeds, plus the needs of the adolescent together create the adolescent problem; and they also play an important part in determining the problems of adolescents. In one way or another the adolescent problem has always been with us—although wearing different masks—because the period of adolescence contains within itself the seeds of disruption. As we all know, it is a period of rapid and profound transition and therefore breeds instability and discord. It is a time of deep-seated change in every aspect of personality, including basic physical structures as well as those complicated psychic mechanisms that determine the adolescent's behavior and personal relationships. We all know that during adolescence the physical organism is undergoing constant change that results in considerable anguish and anxiety and that sets a limit to ego development. Sexual impulses and temptations, fantasies and guilt feelings hammer away at the bastions of conscience and morality until the adolescent no longer knows right from wrong. The vital interests of today become tomorrow's shadows, with nothing left but a fading memory of the joys once experienced. The simple friendships of the preadolescent period are stormed out of existence by the demands of newer interpersonal relationships. The superego of childhood is replaced by the tortured conscience of the adolescent seeking to formulate a reliable moral code. The religious beliefs that seemed so certain and unassailable are corroded by doubts, conflicts, and contact with the scientific and economic world that knows little of God and often cares less. This period is one of transition, and in many instances it leads the teenager down a path of disorganization and even despair.

Not only is the adolescent tortured and confused by the internal changes that are taking place, but he must also cope with the conflicts between himself and the society in which he lives. Conscious of a strong desire to conform to the rules and regulations of the social order, he nevertheless feels strong impulses toward rebellion (Hechinger and Hechinger, 1963). Keenly aware that he did not create the values, traditions, mores, and practices he is supposed to accept, he understandably revolts against them, even though he desperately wants to find his place in the scheme of things and even more desperately wants to belong.

The adolescent's conflict is, in literal truth, a conflict of generations. His rebellion against society has a clear analogue in his relationships with his own family (Greeley, 1961). It is the same rebellion, the same aggression, but in a different setting. His rebellion against his family is spurred on by the same needs and impulses that cause his rejection of the social order, but in this case directed against persons he is supposed to love and who are supposed to love him. Society is something of an abstraction for the adolescent, but his family is real, it is close, and it is immensely important. His own rebellion frightens and alienates him, and at the same time he feels that without it there can be no independence, no self-identity, no self-respect, no style of life that he can call his own. The warm, comfortable security of the happy childhood is gone, and in its place comes turbulence and confusion, conflict and uncertainty, doubt and indecision. Longing to achieve independence, the adolescent feels strong impulses toward emotional succorance. Anxious for psychological weening, he still yearns for the warm milk of mother love. This conflict is at the heart of the adolescent problem and one of the primary sources of the many problems of adolescence. In somewhat broad strokes, it is also the portrait of the contemporary adolescent which we can use as a background for a discussion of other teenage characteristics.

Looked at from a long-range point of view, therefore, the typical adolescent is beset with the adolescent problem which we have just defined and with a number of problems that grow out of this central problem. The adolescent encounters problems at home and at school, problems with girls and boys, dating problems, money problems, moral problems, religious problems, and sexual problems. He shows signs of maladjustment, deep and pervasive mental conflicts and confusions, and an overriding anxiety. Many of these problems disappear with growing maturity, and some adolescents are hardly aware of them at all. But we know from many sources and from personal experience that countless adolescents stub their toes on numerous conflicts and frustrations during their journey to adulthood, and that often they need a great deal of help before they reach the plane of maturity.

These problems stem from many different sources and are closely tied to the adolescent's basic needs. It is when needs are continuously frustrated, or lead to conflict with the social order or the demands of others, or to conflict with the moral order, that difficulties begin to arise. Other people, the environment, and reality itself create threats and stresses for the adolescent, who usually feels already unstable because of the continuous transition that is taking place within his personality. Add to this instability the fact of personal limitations and the demands of the developmental process, and it is easily understood why the adolescent problem looms so large. As we noted before, the contemporary adolescent lives in a much more complex society than existed a generation ago, and this complexity also contributes a great deal toward increasing the magnitude of the adolescent problem (McIver, 1961).

## The Adolescent's Tasks

We have taken a long, hard look at important aspects of the adolescent's life—his needs and his problems—and this type of exploration is one of the surest paths to an understanding of the adolescent. But we need also to take a close look at his responsibilities, the tasks that confront him as he moves away from childhood and comes closer and closer to maturity. Without knowing what these tasks are, what responsibilities the youngster must confront as he moves toward the goal of maturity, we cannot possibly understand what is going on between him and other persons in his environment. The nature of these tasks, incidentally, will vary to some extent with the social and cultural matrix of adolescent development. Here again we see why the adolescent problem of today is not the same as it was a generation ago and certainly not what it was a hundred years ago.

The basic and most important task of the adolescent is *to grow up and to mature*—physically, emotionally, intellectually, socially, morally, economically, and spiritually. As simple and as trite as this statement sounds, it is nevertheless the most profound truth regarding adolescent development. Without a compelling urge to grow up, and to the extent that he fails to do so, the adolescent cannot become the mature adult he must be if he is to assume unavoidable responsibilities, form satisfying relationships, fulfill the roles that will be expected of him, or achieve important goals that he has defined for himself. Maturity is the *sine qua non* of manhood and of womanhood, and thus the achievement of maturity is the primary task which the adolescent must face.

All of the tasks of the adolescent are in some way bound up with the achievement of maturity, simply because maturity requires the completion of these different tasks. Thus, a second principal task of adolescence is the *achievement of independence,* which includes independence of thought, of decision, and of action. It also involves independence of feeling and emotion (Schneiders, 1963). To become an adult, the adolescent must free himself from the dependence of childhood, since to remain dependent in this way is to be childish. It is particularly important to achieve emotional independence, since the adolescent will not become free to develop emotional relationships with others, particularly persons of the opposite sex, unless and until he frees himself from emotional involvements with his parents. Thus a man of 25 who still clings emotionally to "mom," is guilty of "momism" and will find it impossible to build a healthy emotional bridge between himself and a potential sweetheart or wife. Similarly, the failure to achieve intellectual or volitional independence will interfere with sound judgment, the making of important decisions, and the realization of personal ambitions and goals.

The third great task confronting the adolescent is the *development of a deep sense of personal responsibility,* particularly responsibility for self. There must also be a corresponding *willingness to accept responsibility.* This task is obviously linked to the achievement of both independence and maturity. One of the most basic distinctions between the child and the adult lies in the depth and range of their responsibilities. We do not demand a great deal of responsibility from the child, simply because he is immature and does not possess the self-determination necessary to full-scale responsibility. We do not allow the child to drive an automobile, handle large sums of money, get married, vote for political candidates, or decide for himself which school he will attend. We recognize that this would be too much responsibility for the young child. On the other hand, when a person grows up and passes through the transitions of adolescence, we do expect him to be responsible for his decisions and his behavior, and we do invest him with adult responsibilities. The irresponsible person of twenty or twenty-five years of age therefore has failed to fulfill this supreme task and is lacking in maturity.

The development of responsibility involves the *achievement of self-discipline.* Here again we see how sharply a child differs from an adult. In early childhood rules of conduct are externally applied, and the child is made to do what the parents regard as morally good or socially correct. This approach to behavior is defined as external discipline, as distinct from internal discipline—which the adolescent is expected to acquire as he moves toward maturity. Internal discipline is commonly referred to as self-discipline, or self-determination. This discipline involves a slow, gradual, and sometimes painful process which in many instances is far from complete when the teenager reaches the threshold of adulthood (Phillips, et al., 1960). However difficult to achieve, self-discipline is the springboard of responsible action and one of the surest signs of independence. It has always been recognized as the core of character formation, and the indispensable ingredient of responsible selfhood. It enables the possessor to accept challenges, to defer gratifications when necessary or desirable, and to regulate the course of his own destiny—in other words, to act as a mature person. Apart from the achievement of this task maturity is impossible.

Self-discipline helps the teenager to face another important task, and that is the *development of worthwhile goals,* including an education suited to his personality, and the *acquisition of a dependable set of values.* Goals and values are so closely allied that the development of one is fundamentally related to and dependent upon the other. Sooner or later the adolescent must determine the direction of his strivings and decide what he is going to become. Should he go to college? Should he take a pre-med course? Should he follow in the footsteps of his father and become a lawyer? Should she embark on a career and defer marriage for an indefinite period or should she attempt to combine both?

These questions are all goal-directed—questions to which the adolescent must find answers in order to embark on the serious business of adult living. Answering questions like these will enable him to project himself into future roles of manhood or womanhood, fatherhood or motherhood, of doctor, nurse, priest, or lawyer. In this process the adolescent's moral, spiritual, and social values—which have been shifting and taking new forms during the adolescent period—will impinge directly or indirectly on his choice of a vocation, his attitudes toward marriage, his decision to enter or not to enter the religious life, and his aspirations regarding future achievements. The development of a value system, therefore, becomes a primary task of the adolescent.

Finally, the adolescent must confront the task of *achieving selfhood and self-identity* and thus locate his position in the world. This is perhaps the most important psychological development of the adolescent period. Without self-identity, the adolescent remains confused, indecisive, and immature. He finds it difficult to assume responsibilities, to be independent, or to utilize self-discipline effectively. He fumbles in his effort to formulate clear-cut goals and finds it equally difficult to project himself into future roles. His values remain ill-formed and murky, and the future is perceived as a threat rather than as a challenge. Without self-identity the boundaries of the ego are obscure and poorly defined, with the result that the youngster's relationships to reality become vague and uncertain. Self-identity is the steppingstone to selfhood, without which one cannot adequately cope with any of the tasks of the adolescent period.

## The Adult's Role in the Drama of Adolescence

The above are the needs, problems, and tasks that confront the growing teenager, all of which reflect as well as influence the dynamic, changing relationships between him and the important adults in his world, particularly his parents and teachers. Parents and teachers, and more broadly the family and the school, are the primary social determinants of the socializing and self-actualizing processes that go on during the adolescent period. They will also determine the adolescent's attitude toward reality and toward adult responsibilities. Parents and teachers have countless opportunities to help the adolescent fulfill the tasks that confront him. They can help the adolescent learn how to discipline himself; they can create models of responsibility for the adolescent to imitate; they can help him in the definition of values and goals; they can offer him the support that he needs and at the same time create opportunities for independent decision and action. In a thousand different ways, the alert parent and teacher can help the teenager achieve a higher level of adjustment, promote mental stability and health, and pave the way for the adolescent's achievement of maturity. To the extent that parents and teachers fulfill their responsibilities to the adolescent, the adolescent will fulfill his responsibilities to himself and to society.

# 2. The Adolescent and His Peer Group

JOSEPH D. McGOVERN

Although the Adolescent Peer Group (PG) abounds with dynamic factors and conditions which are not only fascinating but also worthy of detailed and comprehensive consideration, my purpose in this essay is to present only a schematic presentation of this topic. The presentation encompasses three major areas: structural characteristics, functional characteristics, and the dynamics of the peer group. An attempt will also be made to translate the essential points of this presentation into suggestions and recommendations of interest to counselors, educators, and researchers who are intimately concerned with the adolescent in contemporary society.

### Structural Characteristics of the Adolescent Peer Group

One way to delineate the structure of the peer group is to distinguish it from other groups in adolescent society. For example, the peer group differs from the adult-sponsored adolescent group insofar as it is not initiated by, associated with, or supervised by an adult socializing institution such as the church, home, or school. By definition, the adolescent PG excludes adults from affiliation and participation. The adult-sponsored adolescent group is organized around mutual formal interests, whereas PG is usually bound together by informal attitudes and interests.

Although the peer group is similar to the adolescent gang in that both are primary, transitional groups which are characterized by discontinuity with the formal social structure of adult society and exhibit withdrawal, secrecy, compulsive conformity, and conflict with

14

authorities, PG differs from the gang in respect to the following five features:

1. *Size of membership.* PG has no less than three and no more than fifteen members, whereas the gang may have a large interlocking membership which numbers in the hundreds.

2. *Degree of organization and formality of hierarchical structure.* The status-role structure of PG embodies an informal rank order of functional leadership which is determined by the members' relative capacity to fulfill, clarify, and concretely represent group norms, expectations, and goals, and appropriately satisfy the relevant needs of the membership. However, PG has no explicit standards or methods of recruitment, selection, induction, training, or withdrawal. It has no elected or appointed leader or formally recognized hierarchy of leadership structure. It has no explicitly stated functions, no specifically avowed purposes or goals, and no regular time or place of meeting. In all the above respects, the gang is much more formal and organized than PG.

3. *Socioeconomic class representation.* PG membership generally reflects the social, cultural, and ethnic rankings of adult middle-class society, whereas the gang reflects the values of the lower-class culture, particularly its delinquent subculture.

4. *Type of activities preferred.* PG emphasizes social, avocational, and recreational activities, whereas the gang engages in predatory activites and is the institutional medium for juvenile delinquency preparatory to adult criminality.

5. *Norms and sanctions.* Both PG and the gang require compulsive conformity of members to the norms, values, and goals of the group. PG sanctions and influences include manipulation, control, avoidance, rejection, and "levelling," but not the gang methods of physical coercion and abuse. PG transmits middle-class norms, values, socialization patterns, and training for adult middle-class roles, whereas the gang consistently opposes middle-class culture to the point of crime and delinquency.

Another way to delineate the structure of the PG is to describe its component parts or phases of development. We note first that it is composed of *two distinct subgroups* which appear in overlapping sequence and which perform institutional functions in different ways. The first phase of the PG is the *clique* which (1) emerges in childhood during the latency phase of development; (2) ranges in size from two to fifteen members; and (3) is monosexual in membership. Clique norms institutionalize sex cleavage for the purpose of reinforcing sex-related differences in attitudes, emotions, and behavior. The clique members are not indifferent to the opposite sex but are usually antagonistic to it and may resort to exploitation and ridicule of the opposite sex. Also in this phase PG (4) is class-selective; (5) is transported through puberty and links the childhood and adolescent periods; and (6) is finally absorbed by, coexists with, or is subordinated to the *crowd,* when affect of the members is transferred from clique mates to members of the opposite sex.

The second phase of the PG is the *crowd,* which may include several cliques but is larger than any one clique. The crowd serves as a *transitional* structure which, from puberty to courtship, permits movement from monosexual to heterosexual relationships by sponsoring and encouraging heterosexual interests and activities. The crowd functions as a tentative, exploratory, and experimental normative agent which provides both approval and opportunities to practice the behavior and rituals of group dating. When the group dating process evolves into paired dating, couples begin to break off from the crowd. The crowd is finally abandoned at the courtship stage.

All PG members know each other and communicate, interact, and relate to one another on an intimate, informal, face-to-face basis. Relationships are based on common needs, norms, and affectional ties; and attachments are maintained over a relatively long period of time. This atmosphere is that of the *primary group,* as distinct from that of the *secondary group* (the club or clique).

Relationships in the group are *equalitarian.* Contrasted to the adolescents' dependent and subordinate relationships with parents and other adults, members of PG are more on a par with one another insofar as they are approximately of the same age, intelligence, socioeconomic class, and the like; they share similar needs, interests, attitudes, feelings, and ideas; and they participate in group activities and functions which are based on common values, norms, and goals.

There is a *dynamic* character to PG. It is an open group, that is, a continuous system of *overlapping membership.* Candidates join and members leave the group without disrupting it. Group functions are mutually related, interdependent, and discharged through a complex process of interaction and communication. Group structure and functions are relatively fluid and vary according to situational factors and conditions. The group operates as *a functional and structural whole* which develops in time toward levels of greater complexity, integration, and differentiation.

PG represents a distinctive *subculture* in contemporary society which is relatively *autonomous* and lacking in integration with the adult culture. It is fairly independent of external supervision and control. Its members withdraw both socially and psychologically from the family, church, and school; but they do not withdraw physically because of their economic dependence which requires satisfying material needs through adult society. Therefore, PG is not a genuinely autonomous group. It is a subculture. By consent and indulgence, the family generally provides most of the materials, facilities, and conveniences for PG activities, such as money, clothing, telephone, family car, refrigerator, and meeting place. Although PG uses these materials of adult society as a means, it invests them with peer symbols, and these symbols reflect adolescent values, aspirations, and perceptions.

PG has its own idiomatic "slanguage" which changes to some degree with each succeeding generation. The normative content of this idiom is oriented toward heterosexual and competitive interests and relationships. It is also an instrument of sanction when it is directed toward making invidious distinctions among persons and events. PG "slanguage" enables the members to think in certain ways and to communicate shared feelings and attitudes. It establishes a sense of group identity separate from adult society and creates a "we-feeling" which intensifies group unity or cohesiveness. It also imposes a communication barrier so as to exclude outsiders. The communication power of "slanguage" is indicated by the awkward attempts of adults (including researchers) to imitate and comprehend it.

All groups are characterized by their degree of exclusiveness and PG is no exception. A particular PG can be identified not only by the kinds of candidates admitted to membership but also by the kinds rejected or avoided. *Selection criteria* are usually combined in a holistic manner. The total personality and behavior of the candidate, the structure and functions of the particular peer group, and environmental factors and conditions are all relevant to the selection process. In short, PG does not maintain separate explicit criteria, but evaluates the total personality and behavior relative to the particular group situation.

If the members perceive that a candidate's personality and behavior patterns approximate theirs and if it is predicted that he can contribute to the enhancement of the group, he is accepted even though some of his patterns differ significantly from those of the group. The members may even unconsciously distort their perception of the candidate to make him appear to suit their needs more than he actually does.

As regards specific selection criteria, apparently there is no direct relationship between intelligence and PG acceptance and status, except that the members are generally similar in intelligence. Also, because the PG has its own achievement symbols, academic achievement is not an index of individual acceptance or status. Nor is there a one-to-one relationship between any single objective variable of family background and PG membership. Members of the same socioeconomic and ethnic class generally choose each other on a sociometric basis. PG selection of members reflects the same degree of importance that adult society attaches to socioeconomic position and ethnic background. PG draws selectively from middle and upper classes. Skills, however, are a major selection criterion. One must have competence to belong, and affiliation provides certain necessary experiences for additional skill development.

Finally, we may note that peer groups vary according to cohesiveness, that is, degree of organizational solidarity and movement toward goals. Some peer groups are highly cohesive, others are more disruptive. Cohesiveness is a complex phenomenon because it is a function of codes, customs, roles, sanctions, affectional ties, need satisfaction, goal achievement, leadership, and the sentiment-binding capacity of a particular group.

## Role Dynamics and Structure

A *role* is an organized pattern of attitudes and behavior in an interpersonal setting. Individual roles combine to form the role structure of the peer group. Role playing is essential to the interaction process, to cohesiveness, and to goal achievement. Each PG has a specific role structure and process which is a function of its special needs, the self-concepts of members, situational conditions, and the like. Generally, the role repertoire of PG is rich and diverse.

The PG observer can identify various roles in action. There is, for example, the Spark Plug, Operator, Idea Man, Arranger, Clown, and Daredevil. There are also those who supply information or materials, who set the pace or style, and who act out egocentric roles.

PG norms are organized so that roles are accorded different degrees of status. For example, the Style Setter or Fashion Leader may achieve high status in a particular suburban, upper-middle-class group, whereas the fearless defier of adult authority may enjoy high status in an urban, lower-middle-class group. Thus, role behavior is functional for each group and situation.

In addition, roles which may have high status in one phase of a group's existence may lose value as the group matures because other roles become more important. For example, the individual who plays the role of the Clown—which is highly valued in the clique—may be relegated to low status in the crowd because the role may no longer be appropriate. Thus, to obtain and maintain status the individual must continually satisfy the group's needs and conform to group expectations.

A role in PG is not simply granted to anyone who wants it; it must be merited. For example, the leader achieves and maintains his status position by demonstrating his capacity to meet the demands of a situation and satisfy certain needs and expectations of the membership.

Membership in PG provides experiences and opportunities for learning and revising roles. Some individuals, by virtue of personality and experience, have a rich and varied role repertoire, whereas others have a limited number of roles, are less skilled in role behavior, and find conflicts in the organization of roles in their personalities. PG provides varying situations for the members to explore, experiment with, refine, and discover new and effective roles, satisfactory and appropriate to the individual and group needs. Once the individual becomes familiar and competent in a particular role system, he may transfer it from one group situation to another.

Role playing potentially leads to *interpersonal conflicts* because no one can have his own way all the time. Someone has to get and someone has to give. When role conflicts occur, tension rises and certain defenses and problem-solving mechanisms are automatically brought into play. Roles must also be revised to enhance compatibility and to reduce tension. If role conflicts are not adequately resolved they continue as acute or chronic discomforts which may force the individual to withdraw from PG.

Adolescents with clear concepts of self and of others are generally able to meet the group demands regarding role assumption and enactment; or they may decide that the roles are not worthwhile. If the individual has inner-directed strength, values, and positive self-regard, he is less likely to conform in order to gain group identity and status. He may leave the group and seek affiliation with another PG whose values are more similar to his. On the other hand, the adolescent with a limited perceptual field—because of paucity of experience or emotional insecurity—is inclined to be more rigid in his role playing. He may settle for low status so long as he can continue to belong. This type of other-directed adaptability by which the member sacrifices his uniqueness and overconforms for the sake of belonging is one problem of interest. All PG members gain identity and status through affiliation and participation, but not in the same way or to the same degree as does the overly dependent and overly submissive member for whom the group is the center of existence.

## Group Norms and Sanctions

PG is fundamentally a sentiment-binding group whose structure is based not only on role relationships but also on a code system. This code system is so comprehensive that no area of behavior is free from group influence. The group dominates appearance, dress, language patterns, selection of friends, and even dating partners. Some groups require discussion of dating and sex experiences. The group also controls attitudes towards adult persons and institutions, identifying them as friends, as enemies, or as unimportant.

The purposes of the code system are to protect and enhance the cohesiveness and influence of the group; to distinguish the group from other institutions by significantly modifying formal adult norms and perpetuating its own values to guide behavior; to permit the members to reach their goals and realize their purposes by defining what behavior is approved and expected; and to protect the integrity of the group by opposing or evading adult authority and sanctions.

PG membership involves the coercive requirement of rigid conformity to the norms, values, and goals of the group which induces the members to think, act, and believe in a similar manner. In exchange for affiliation, participation, and status, the members are rigidly required to accept and abide by group expectations. If the interests of PG conflict with those of other reference groups, the authority of PG is so rigorous that it takes precedence. This rigid conformity is intensified by the partial withdrawal of the members from the family, school, church, and other adult socializing institutions. As a result of this withdrawal, obstacles and barriers are created to adult supervision and control, and conflicts arise and are exacerbated between PG and the adult culture.

The norms and sanctions which PG initiates and perpetuates effectively preempt the loyalty of the members and manipulate sentiments and behavior. PG also teaches and approves certain behavior which is tabooed by adult norms. In effect, these group-approved norms and sanctions significantly modify the influence of formal adult norms.

Some peer-group norms are judged by adult norms to be undesirable, incompatible, and therefore unacceptable to adult society. For example, competitive dating, a major institutional device of PG, is initiated and perpetuated by elaborate group norms, sentiments, and sanctions independent of, and even conflicting with, adult norms. The incompatibility of competitive dating norms with courtship and marital norms is such that the more "successful" the individual is in dating, the less prepared he may be for marital adjustment. The prescribed adult sex norms include premarital chastity, monogamous marriage, mutual affectional commitment, romantic love, and family life. In contrast, the norms of the competitive-dating phase of adolescent culture emphasize concurrent or sequential relationships, no mutual affectionate commitments, mutual exploitation, and premarital intimacy.

If parents and other adults attempt to intervene, adolescents of both sexes try to evade such supervision by avoidance and concealment. For example, petting is particularly subject to adult censure because it violates moral and social laws. Consequently, petting is conducted by adolescents only in privacy and in secrecy, both of which are maintained by silence about such behavior and by avoidance of adult observation. The automobile is particularly valued by the adolescent because it provides the necessary privacy, mobility, and anonymity for sexual experimentation.

The norm of secrecy which amounts to a conspiracy of silence with nonmembers is not unique to the adolescent peer group; it is a universal phenomenon of group dynamics. However, its influence is significant in PG because it combines with the adolescent's withdrawal from adult socializing institutions as well as with the peer group's relative autonomy and isolation from the adult culture. The result is a significant lack of influence, communication, and interaction between adolescents and adults.

The norms which differentiate the PG subculture and the adult culture predispose PG members to perceive and to respond to the same institutions, situations, and individuals in different ways than adults do. These disparate perceptual frames of reference serve to separate adolescents and adults and to block the lines of communication between them. As a consequence, most adults are largely ignorant of PG dynamics. Even those adults who attempt to study PG complain that norms impede their observations and exclude their participation.

By setting up barriers to interaction and communication, PG excludes all nonmembers and thereby provides a safeguard from external sanctions. The concealment of PG behavior from adults not only provides relative freedom from adult supervision but also modifies the effect of operation of adult norms. The norm of secrecy also adds the obsessive element of the sacred and the mysterious, which reinforces the compulsive conformity of PG members. The mystique of secrecy and mystery are reflected in the idiomatic "slanguage."

The adolescent who feels threatened by adult sanctions develops skill in concealing his disapproved behavior. PG assists him in this secretiveness by providing mutual confidence, support, training, and insurance of privacy by rigorously excluding nonmembers and informers. Deception, selective transmission of information, and protective lying are also typical modes of adjustment employed to avoid overt conflict with adult authorities. In many situations these tactics are approved by PG to secure goals disapproved or denied by the adult culture. PG may also conceal its norms and behavior behind a facade of apparent conformity to adult values.

The deception and evasion practiced by PG members are learned by observing the behavior of adults in various situations. Thus, these tactics are more a function of situational learning than they are a function of basic character traits of the adolescent. For example, many adolescents initially learn the conspiracy of silence from parents who withhold certain facts of life and who are disinclined to discuss matters of sex. When they learn about sex from their peers and older associates, they keep this information a secret from their parents for fear of punishment. With the onset of heterosexual relations, adolescents subsequently assume an attitude of outward conformity to adult formal norms which they may violate in secret. United against the adult culture, PG then protects its members from adult sanctions. Thus, the conspiracy of silence is initiated in the family by the parents; is incorporated in the earliest peer associations in the juvenile era; is perpetuated and reenforced in the heterosexual phase; and is intensified by PG. The purpose of this norm is to avoid adult disapproval and sanctions.

PG is able to enforce its norms by powerful sanctions in the form of positive rewards which include status, approval, acceptance, praise, emulation, support, honor, recognition, identity, social visibility, protection, and other satisfactions of group life. The punishments largely involve verbal manipulation and control in the form of censure, sarcasm, scorn, abuse, mocking, smearing, ridicule, and use of value-loaded epithets; gestures in the form of pantomime, winks, titters, or horse laughs; the silent treatment; and actions in the form of ostracism, avoidance, isolation, rejection, reduction of relative status, and with-holding of full membership. The adolescent's fear of rejection and humiliation is combined with the group's constant, public, ruthless, and calculated pressure toward conformity.

These types of sanctions are effective control devices because the individual's needs for acceptance, approval, identification, conformity, affiliation, and status are intensified in adolescence and represent con-venient and powerful handles for group manipulation. The average adolescent is vulnerable to group pressure and is too uncertain, inse-cure, and self-conscious not to conform to group pressures. It is very difficult for the average adolescent to be a conspicuous and solitary holdout against the group's authority.

The individual becomes dependent on PG once he has withdrawn from formal socializing institutions and is ego-involved in PG. If he is rejected by PG, he has few places to go for group life. He can with-draw into individual pursuits, but these are generally less satisfying.

Group pressure is continuously, ruthlessly, and publicly applied. The informal sanctions are designed in a calculated manner to mercilessly and explicitly induce feelings of shame and humiliation in the presence of peers. PG is also a form of influential authority for its members because it is relatively autonomous, anonymous, and enjoys freedom from external supervision and control.

## Functions of the Adolescent Peer Group

PG spontaneously attempts to substitute or compensate not only for the apparent discontinuities between the adolescent and adult societies but also for the dysfunctions of adult formal socializing institutions such as the family, church, and school. These discontinuities and dysfunctions are principally caused by the adult society's lack of ade-quate institutional devices to provide structural continuity in the ado-lescent phase of development and to ease the difficult transition from childhood to adulthood.

Familiar examples of these formal discontinuities and dysfunctions in contemporary society are:

a. Lack of an explicit cultural model for adolescence.
b. Lack of bench marks to delineate adolescent phases.
c. Lack of widely recognized and accepted ways of inducting ado-

lescent individuals into adult culture, for example, ceremonies, rituals, observances, and rites of passage.

d. Failure to provide timely, adequate, and appropriate sex education.

e. Generation conflict due to rapid social change and vertical mobility in society. This conflict causes adults and adolescents to be mutually out of contact and to lack knowledge about and to fail to understand one another. Generation conflict contributes to parent-youth conflict, which may develop into serious crises as tensions, exasperations, distortions, and resentments accumulate and disrupt communication and interaction.

f. Prolongation of adolescence and dependency upon adults. Extended education for adult vocational roles is necessary to prepare the individual to achieve economic independence in our complex, industrial, urban, technological society, which prolongs adolescence and extends dependency.

g. Competition and conflict of authorities in adult society such as incompatible parental standards within the family and among families; different norms and lack of relatedness among the family, church, and school; ethnic, racial, class, regional, economic, political, and religious differences; inconsistencies between what adults say and do, that is, between formal ideological standards and actual behavior.

PG arises spontaneously and attempts to compensate for these discontinuities and dysfunctions *by providing its own institutional devices* to achieve structural continuity and to facilitate the difficult transition from childhood to adulthood. Perhaps the only discontinuity which PG does not combat is that of economic-role development. PG does not directly provide guidance or experience in fulfilling adult economic roles.

PG functions chiefly as a series of *socializing institutions* which provide devices for social development. Adolescence is considered second in importance only to infancy in the socialization process. It is the last phase of intensive socialization prior to adulthood. After adolescence, personality and behavior patterns are generally fixed.

The social development of the adolescent takes place in a transactional field in which the family, church, school, society, and PG present their expectations and also attempt to demonstrate to the individual how he should behave and what he should become. These institutions cooperate and compete with each other in the situational field which surrounds the adolescent.

Most adolescents feel that if they belong to the right PG and behave in the expected way their needs will be satisfied. PG distinguishes between friendship and status-prestige relationships. It values the individual for himself and his capacity to share affection, not for what he has done or achieved. These affectionate ties are important for security and satisfaction in the adolescent phase and for realization of the full measure of maturity. PG also functions as a bargaining and pressure instrument in adolescent transactions with adults in order to gain privileges, status, equality, and independence from adult control. Through its individual representatives PG is in constant transaction with the adult world.

Although PG is subordinate to adults, it has strength in numbers. A member's influence with his parents is increased when he contends: "All the other guys in the crowd are doing it." A parent may find it difficult to be a lone holdout against such importunings, especially if he is regarded as a monster who is causing his child to be a group deviant and a martyr to outmoded standards. Generally, the adult is anxious and takes the easiest way out because he is not certain whether he is right or wrong.

Generally, the transactional relations between adults and adolescents are strained. Each attempts to manipulate the other according to certain norms. The tactics may include those of peaceful coexistence, cold war, open warfare, or underground guerrilla warfare. Conflict is probably inevitable and salutary. Adults and PG work out their own resolution of the conflict. Both learn from each other and also modify the other's behavior.

The PG is primarily an activity group which operates in the medium of social, recreational and avocational activities. These activities are usually informal, free, and unsupervised, and pervaded with emotional overtones because they are related to basic needs. The diverse activities include just being with the group and "fooling around"; going someplace and "having fun"; participating in endless discussions; enjoying spectatorship activities, shows, sports, TV, and records; partaking in group dating, which is more cultural than biological; and pursuing hobbies of all sorts.

Another primary function of PG is to provide sex education, that is, to prepare the individual for a durable, monogamous relationship in a procreating family. It cooperates with adult institutions insofar as it dichotomizes, differentiates, polarizes, and reinforces psychosexual and sociosexual roles and complementary role behavior. It accomplishes this important developmental task by: acting as a medium for the transmission, reception, interpretation, and feedback of sex information, particularly adult-tabooed information; teaching and approving norms of sexual behavior; fostering and encouraging the initiation of heterosexual relationships and behavior; providing opportunities for exploratory and experimental experiences in heterosexual relations; fostering the movement of the individual from the clique to the crowd stage and further to the courtship stage; attempting to resolve the confusion and conflict about what constitutes masculinity and femininity. Much time and activity are directed toward exploring and endeavoring to master masculine and feminine roles as they are envisaged by contemporary society.

Authorities claim that most adolescents first learn about sex in PG. The majority of adults credit PG with the dubious distinction of providing more sex information than any other group or institution in society. Much of this information is accurate and relevant, but some of it is distorted.

One of the primary needs and developmental tasks of the adolescent is to establish a clear and stable self-identification—a definition of who he is, what he has done and can do, and what he truly thinks and feels. The adolescent needs to become a person in his own right who is capable of deeply felt relations with other individuals distinctly perceived as individuals. PG assists the individual in this process of individuation by:

a. Helping him analyze, understand, and resolve conflicts within himself and between himself and others. Conflict is dialectical and inherent in adolescent development. In a society where there is no conflict there is no adolescence. The responsibility of PG is not to be nice to its members but to be real to them by providing an interpersonal process and relationship structure which amounts to a "here-and-now" conflict-resolving situation.

b. Emphasizing and teaching respect for competence. Competence is the foundation of maturity and autonomy. Because competence is real and is not based on fantasy, the adolescent almost compulsively strives for competence and PG assists in its achievement.

c. Teaching one another and also learning from one another in an experiential manner. Members learn through identification, clarification of experience, and development of self-esteem. If the individual does not clearly and specifically understand his behavior and experiences, he has no true basis for self-esteem. PG provides a continuous feedback on personality and behavior which permits him to evaluate himself on specific grounds by consensual validation.

Another major developmental task of adolescence is the social and emotional emancipation from the family of origin and the gradual movement toward membership in a family of procreation. PG participates in this emancipation process by acting as an authority which transfers dependency to itself and by providing outlets for dependency needs without discouraging independency strivings in relation to adults. Thus, PG serves to balance the individual's needs for both independency and dependency in the emancipation process. In this process, the adolescent does not merely exchange dependency on adults for dependency on peers. In PG he is a peer, not a subordinate. For most adolescents, compulsive conformity to PG norms in exchange for self-enhancement and independence from adults is a "good deal."

In contemporary society the adolescent is expected by adult institutions to surrender his established and familiar derived status of an emotionally dependent child and to strive simultaneously for primary adult socioeconomic status to which developmental factors and conditions are inducing him. In essence, the adolescent has the full status of neither childhood nor of adulthood. He is not completely without status, but his adolescent status is vague, ambiguous, changing, marginal, and transitional.

Thus, PG offers the individual a structure, situational opportunities, and institutional devices to acquire status roles denied him by society. The status offered by PG is more certain and predictable because it is based on values and expectations the individual understands and can fulfill by playing appropriate, group-centered roles. Thus, PG is not only a membership and an activity group but is also a *reference group* which consists of significant others, that is, persons of importance to the individual and to whom he psychologically relates himself. The individual compares himself with other members in evaluating his status. PG is thus a frame of reference of both self-evaluation and attitude formation. Membership and participation in this reference group helps the adolescent develop a more mature and expanded self-concept.

## Summary and Conclusions

Although the research effort is expanding in quantity and quality, there is a notable hiatus of relevant experimental investigation on PG. Granted that difficulties and complexities abound; but there is still a need for more scientific investigation of PG phases, institutions, dynamics, devices, principles, methods, structures, functions, and relationships in contemporary society. More and better hypothetical constructs and theoretical models need to be formulated which are amenable to direct testing and which can be unequivocably related to empirical data.

There is a particular need for cross-cultural and cross-class investigations to determine and to cross validate PG hypotheses and operational constructs. There is also a need to investigate various parameters of PG, and its members to understand individual-group causes and effects.

Finally, there is a need to establish and maintain a holistic, eclectic, and dynamic approach to PG in contemporary society which takes note of relevant and significant motivational, psychological, sociological, and cultural factors and conditions.

The present viewpoint asserts that PG is not a myth but a noteworthy facet of the adolescent culture in contemporary society. PG has a widespread and significant influence on the majority of urban and suburban adolescents of the middle and upper classes. Individuals who participate in PG subculture significantly experience its dynamics and accept it as a dominant influence in their lives because its values, norms, goals, and services are functionally and structurally relevant to the needs of adolescents.

# 3. The Adolescent and His Problems

## ROBERT J. McALLISTER

▲▲▲▲▲▲▲▲▲▲▲▲▲▲▲▲▲▲▲▲▲▲▲▲▲▲▲▲

The teenager is a complex of lofty ideals and lowly weaknesses. He is caught in conflict with himself and in deep discord with his environment. Childhood still envelops him, for the things of a child are not yet put away and the thoughts of a child still influence his behavior. And all the while, adulthood is being forced on him by his growth from within and by the expectations of the world around him. In his eagerness to meet this challenge of maturity, in his wish to grasp the gauntlet of adulthood, he sets out to solve the mysteries of life when he cannot even solve the mystery of himself. The wide-eyed wonderment of childhood with which he viewed the world is replaced by an inner anxiety as he anticipates his place in a world which now belongs to him. He is suddenly confronted with the choice of what he wants to become before he is certain of who he really is. His physical growth and physiological development unleash powerful impulses within him. He most certainly cannot control that inner development, but he most certainly must control the behavior toward which it pushes him. He is expected somehow to control these bursting impulses before he can be expected to understand them.

Adults sometimes are more concerned with the problems teenagers encounter with them than they are with the problems teenagers experience with themselves. Adults worry about how early the adolescent should be home at night, about his friends, about his success in school, or about whether or not he should drive. These parental concerns are important, but they are a nearsighted view of adolescents. For youth has concerns of its own. To concentrate on their behavior without recognizing and appreciating their needs is like mopping up

29

the puddle on the floor when it rains without attending to the hole in the roof. Parents look for a set of rules to regulate their teenagers, but what they need is a set of attitudes with which to approach their adolescent sons and daughters. Parental restrictions form an irregular patchwork to mend the fabric of adolescent failures. The original garment of personality is fashioned from the needs within the youth himself.

There are four basic needs from which the fabric of youth is woven. These four needs around which adolescent development occurs are: the need for identity, the need for individuality, the need for integrity, and the need for independence. It is impossible to give parents and teachers a set of absolute rules to apply to adolescent problems. New situations are always arising. There is always the unexpected, the unforeseen, the unpredictable. Circumstances change and individuals vary. But rules are rigid. It is not that rules are unnecessary; it is only that adult attitudes are more important. The rules of adults can be accepted and obeyed, or rejected and broken. And teenagers take either path fairly easily. However, the attitudes of adults cannot be so quickly rejected, so quietly ignored, for teenagers learn something about themselves from the attitudes that others have toward them. Although it is necessary for adults to tell them what to do, it is also necessary for adolescents to know what adults think of them, particularly when they do not do what they are told.

Adult attitudes are determined by their understanding of the inner conflict, the restless struggle, the incessant confusion that marks teenage life. It is these four needs of youth, namely, identity, individuality, integrity, and independence, which I intend to discuss in this paper, with some concrete examples of how they are manifested in adolescent behavior and how they are fostered or thwarted by the adult response.

A youth's *need for identity* introduces him to the concept of self. The child knows himself as belonging to a certain family, living on a certain street, having certain friends, going to a certain school. The adolescent begins to ask that more searching question, "Who am I?" He is thrust into a new role as he searches for new ways of establishing his identity. He must play a part which separates him from childhood. He must find a niche which is near to adulthood but separate from it.

The extreme of this attempt to establish identity is seen in the black-jacket garb, the unkempt haircuts, the switchblade weapons of certain juvenile gangs. It also appears in the teased hair and eye shadow of many teenage girls, the peg pants and open collars of teenage boys. The identity which once revolved around home and family is changed for a set of styles all their own. Hair fashions, clothing fancies, dietary whims, dance fads, music manias—all take on the characteristics of a cult; and teenagers take on an identity as they follow the march of the Pied Piper who is a creation of their own need. Sometimes their styles shock us, their fads frighten us. It is important to understand that these things are not the goal of life, even though teenagers may act as if they are. They are means by which the teenagers attempt to achieve an identity of their own.

Another identity which teenagers must establish if they are to become healthy adults is sexual identity. Early adolescence is a critical period in determining later adaptation to one's sexual role in life. There are a few general principles which affect sexual identification at this period. First, the parent of the same sex must have some contact with the budding teenager in order for that teenager to have an image of the sexual role with which to identify. Second, that parent must be a person worthy of some respect and also human enough not to preclude imitation by son or daughter. In short, a father who spends most of his leisure hours on the golf course with his buddies instead of at home with an adolescent son is not only depriving that son of his companionship, but even more important, is depriving him of the opportunity for identification with the masculine role. Similarly, the mother who resents her role of housewife and spends her time at bridge clubs or social engagements to the neglect of a young teenage daughter is depriving that daughter of a feminine model with which she can identify.

Similarly, the wife who degrades her husband in front of their sons is running the serious risk of impairing their proper psychosexual development. The same is true of a husband who belittles his wife and thus raises a question in his daughter's mind regarding her role in life as a woman. If mother or father is absent through divorce or death, a boy should have the opportunity to have some contact with a male figure and the girl with a female figure. Teenagers reach the proper sexual identity through the cooperation of both parents. The parent of the same sex provides a prototype, a model; the parent of the opposite sex, by respect for the spouse, provides a healthy background for proper sexual identification.

Finally, in regard to the sexual identification of the teenager, there is no place and there is no excuse for the father who raises his daughter in a masculine role or for a mother who forces her son into a feminine role. Teenage tomboys and seventeen-year-old sissies become social misfits and psychological cripples.

In the process of achieving his own identity, the adolescent separates himself from his family. Identity with the family unit should not be dissolved too quickly, for if it is, the adolescent may find himself alone on the open field of life without a stable place on which to stand. Family ties may be loosened but they should not be lost. The adolescent should still be brought within the intimacy of the family circle, even though he approaches it reluctantly. I have had teenagers in treatment who have not eaten at the family table for months and sometimes for years. Dinnertime is the most likely time for the family to be together. The importance of some special effort on the part of every family member to be there and to behave cordially toward others cannot be sufficiently stressed. We often hear that it is a dangerous policy to drink alone. I think, perhaps, it is just as dangerous emotionally and even physically to eat alone, particularly for the teenager. The dietary aberrations will pass more quickly if they occur at the family table.

Special family celebrations, vacations, or certain trips should involve the entire family, including the somewhat unwilling and partially protesting adolescent. He may not be certain that he wants to go with the family, but he needs to be certain that they want him to go with them. He has not yet decided where he belongs in the world. It is gratifying to have a part of that world tell him he belongs in it.

Another source of identity is career choice. The teenager begins to think seriously about what he wants to be. If his parents are antagonistic to his desires, they may destroy his plans; but more importantly, they may disturb his sense of identity. If an eight-year-old is laughed at because he wants to be a garbage man, he may be embarrassed, but he isn't destroyed. If a fifteen-year-old is laughed at because he wants to be a race-car driver, his feeling of identity may be shattered.

The *need for individuality* may seem to be an unlikely need in a group which so often appears to follow some primitive herd instinct. Much of adolescent behavior, most of their fads, have an assembly-line quality. Sometimes it seems that only their names differ. However, the individual teenager resents the suggestion that he does not think and act in his own individual way. Teenagers even resent the lack of individuality that is accorded them when they are grouped together as teenagers.

Adolescents want to participate with their peers; they want to be companionable with the crowd. Yet, each one wants to be judged on his own merits. They resent being compared with others, either in the same family or with teenagers in the same school or in the same neighborhood. Each wants his due as an individual. A girl does not want her parents to believe that she likes the Beatles because other teenagers swoon over them. She wants them to believe that her liking the Beatles is an individual decision and has nothing to do with the mass hysteria which accompanies their performances. She believes it is her private, personal good taste.

This need for individuality is more apparent in the teenager who turns the tables and violently dislikes something about which all other youngsters are wild. It is often the youth whose individuality is seriously threatened who takes this latter course; he is constantly opposed to his peers and to their sacred icons.

Teenagers expect to be treated as individuals. This expectation is one of the reasons that a community code of behavior is not always successful. The more rigid the rules of home or of school, the more the adolescent resents them. Some adults believe that making an exception is a breach in the rampart of discipline. Yet, I think we grow uneasy with high-speed electronic computers which are beginning to sit in judgment on our income-tax returns, our bank accounts, our mortgages, our insurance, our population problems, our international decisions, and perhaps someday, our medical symptoms. These machines don't make exceptions. Everyone's little punched card gets the same treatment. We resent the loss of individuality. Even worse than making no exceptions, these whirring wizards don't make any mistakes. There is something very reassuring about mistakes, particularly other people's!

The adolescent may gain an important sense of individuality from steady dating. Going steady has a meaning for adults which is far removed from the interpretation of teenagers. I cannot believe that the average adolescent sees going steady as an opportunity for sexual misbehavior. In fact, I would even make the suggestion that going steady, if it is properly controlled, may prevent many teenagers from indulging in sexual misbehavior. I think that steady dating is often the help an adolescent needs to stop a habit of masturbation or to prevent one from starting. I also think that steady dating may prevent many adolescents from coming into close contact with those misguided youths who believe that playing the field really means sexually seducing as many partners as possible. When we attack the concept of steady dating, we may be fighting a fundamental need; not the need for sexual stimulation which we are so worried about, but the need to be regarded by others and to regard oneself as an individual.

Being an individual also means being allowed to progress in one's own way, with one's own limitations and abilities, and being accepted as one is. This includes accepting and respecting a daughter even though she isn't popular with the boys or even if she doesn't do well in school. It means accepting and respecting a son, even if he isn't a great athlete or even if he doesn't want to go to college.

The *need for integrity* is critical in the adolescent period. There is much that threatens the sense of personal integrity at this time. Let's face it: we are suspicious of our teenagers. We are more afraid of their impulses than they are aware of them. We are afraid they'll cheat, afraid they'll misbehave sexually. And they do these things—or at least some of them do, and to some degree. So we are suspicious of them, and we cast a shadow over their sense of integrity. Our attitude is replete with innuendo, and we make them wonder about themselves. Our doubts are difficult for them to ignore and suggest to them the weakness of their youth. Rash judgment is most tragic when directed against adolescents.

Adolescents have a mounting need for privacy. It becomes something of a symbol of their integrity. It is a time when a separate room at home is important if it is at all possible. I had a fifteen-year-old girl as a patient who had been physically ill for weeks. She was admitted to a local hospital where extensive and expensive tests were conducted. Nothing was found. During her psychiatric interview, it was easy to ascertain that her physical complaints had begun shortly after her grandparents moved in with the family. This made it necessary for her to give up her room, something which meant a great deal to her. The emotional disintegration with the concomitant physical symptoms was her way of expressing the loss of integrity that she felt in giving up her room. I am not saying that this girl's attitude was a proper one, only that it was present and that it had a deep influence on her.

It is not always possible to give a teenager his own room. But it is always possible to give him an adequate amount of privacy. There are parents who read their teenager's letters. I had a twenty-one-year-old patient whose mother still opened her letters and read them before the daughter came home from work. Parents sometimes search their teenager's rooms, snoop in their books, sift through their waste baskets.

Of course, if they find something—a note about some boy, a bad word, a critical remark about themselves or about the teachers at school— they feel justified. If they don't find anything, they always hope to the next time. I cannot see any justification for such gestapo techniques. There are few teenagers who would be foolish enough to leave something around for their parents to find if they really didn't want them to find it. There are few teenagers who do not become aware of snooping parents. You may be sure they will police their secrets when they become aware of the secret police.

The use of the telephone is another area in which the teenager deserves some privacy. He has a right to receive calls and to make calls without his little brother teasing him, his father timing him, and his mother listening in on the extension (or in the same room if his sister is already listening in on the extension). I think teenagers are gratified when they can receive a phone call, talk privately for fifteen or twenty minutes, and not have someone ask them afterwards, "Who was that?"

One area which has an intimate bearing on the adolescent's sense of integrity is the area of punishment. There is no room for and no good reason for physical punishment of teenagers. Such punishment is a direct attack on their physical and therefore their emotional integrity. Verbal abuse is almost equally as destructive. Restrictions that are reasonable and limitations that are logical allow the adolescent to maintain his self-respect. Punishment that destroys his self-respect will cause him to lose respect for those who punish him.

Teenagers are sensitive because their emotional balance is precarious, their inner turmoil is acute. Any process, any situation in which they are held up to ridicule, may leave an indelible scar on their personalities. A youth who is belittled publicly, who is degraded in front of his classmates, who is shamed before his peers is deeply and needlessly hurt. At times their behavior may seem to invite public criticism, and their attitudes may suggest that they look for ridicule. If this is true, it is only because their sense of personal integrity is already seriously shattered, and they accept the loss as their due.

Another source of threat to integrity is physical illness. Adolescents often become preoccupied with their bodies and the illnesses that befall them. Colds may be interpreted as tuberculosis. Swollen glands mean leukemia. Stomach cramps signal appendicitis. A headache may be a brain tumor. Their outward manner may never reveal their inner anxieties when they are ill. A sympathetic and reassuring attitude on the part of adults is the best insurance against their "immediate" demise. If parental fears increase their panic, if the physician's lack of decisive reassurance increases the anxiety of the parents and teenager both, an appendix may be removed heedlessly, a diagnosis of possible rheumatic fever may keep a youth in bed for months, a lengthy hospitalization with consultations, examinations, and laboratory analyses may be necessary to bring everyone back to the reality of a simple, nonsignificant physical pain.

The fourth need of teenagers is the *need for independence.* Unless they achieve emotional independence, they cannot acquire the stature of maturity. Their quest for independence is often interpreted by adults as rebellion against authority. Their sporadic separation from the family circle is often interpreted by parents as lack of love and failure of gratitude. It is not so much that they are growing away; they are growing up.

There are little ways in which independence can be encouraged. One of the important commodities that life entrusts to each of us is time. One's emotional health is greatly dependent upon one's ability to use time effectively, to enjoy it enthusiastically, to appreciate it leisurely. It is excellent training for an adolescent to be given the independent use of time. This training can well begin with the purchase of an alarm clock. A high-school student should certainly be able to get up with the help of an alarm clock of moderate value and of some self-initiative, which is of great value. This situation is much healthier and much easier on parents than the method of having mother call constantly from the kitchen or father bang belligerently on the bedroom door. If a teenager can come to accept and to appreciate the importance of getting up on his own, he should be able to learn that it is important to go to bed at a reasonable hour; and this hour can then be regulated entirely by himself.

Teenagers' use of time should also involve a great deal of latitude. Telling them when to do their homework, when to clean their room, when to go to the library, or when to go to confession leaves them little room for independent action and oftentimes little room for independent thought. Parents may expect their teenagers to do these things but should give them some freedom of choice as to when they are to be done and in what manner.

We must learn to spend time wisely if we are to pass the test of life. We must also learn to spend money wisely if we are to pass the test of livelihood. Teenagers often prefer not to have an allowance because they do not want the responsibility of managing their money, and they correctly surmise that they can usually get more by their well-learned emotional maneuvers which somehow relax the parental purse strings. However, a reasonable allowance, given on a monthly basis, provides them with some financial independence and also gives them an opportunity to learn that responsibility is on the other side of the coin of freedom. Part of their allowance might well cover some of the necessities like school lunches and bus fare; a portion of it should be theirs to use without restrictions or parental criticism.

Another area where adolescents can be given some freedom involves the question of the key. It seems appropriate for an adolescent to have a key to his own house, and in addition, to be allowed to use it. I had a fifteen-year-old boy in treatment whose parents had lost nearly all control over him. He stayed out as late as he pleased, which was frequently one or two o'clock in the morning. However, they absolutely refused to allow him to have a key to the house. Consequently, he rang the doorbell when he returned from his nocturnal wanderings, and his father dutifully let him into the house. Items of responsibility such as his own key help an adolescent feel independent and also increase his sense of responsibility. Even as adults, we feel that our sense of independence is somewhat dependent upon knowing the time of day, having some money of our own, and possessing a key to our own house.

Also necessary to the need for independence is the opportunity to make some decisions, the chance to make some choices. The teenager is not an adult and does not expect to be treated as one, even though he acts as if he does. He is well aware that limitations must be placed on his freedom. Parents and teachers not only have the prerogative, they also have the obligation to guide teenagers in their behavior. The school may properly forbid a girl to wear a strapless formal to the prom, but her parents may allow her to choose her own dress within the rules of propriety. Parents may decide which high school their son or daughter will attend, but the adolescent may be allowed to decide on elective courses. Parents and teachers may encourage a teenager to go to college, but the choice of going to college as well as the choice of career must ultimately be an independent choice of the individual.

One can remain independent and still accept the suggestions of another. In truth, it is only the independent person who is at liberty to listen to advice, to take suggestions, and to accept the ideas of others. The more one becomes authoritarian with adolescents, the more one has to control them with commands, and the more their basic need for independence is challenged. Adults must try to teach them that independence is born of initiative, nurtured by good judgment, and enlarged by wise counsel.

These four basic needs of adolescent development, namely, identity, individuality, integrity, and independence are the four strong corners of healthy personality development and happy maturity. This super-structure of needs may be embossed with the effects of learning, ornate with the trappings of success, plain with the simplicity of limitations, or rough with the results of labor. But whatever the superstructure may be, it will be determined by how well adults understand these needs.

# 4. The Problem Adolescent

ROBERT J. McALLISTER

Adolescence can be defined as the time of life between the ages of twelve and twenty-one—or it can be related directly to that period between the onset of puberty and the end of physical growth. The boundaries of the adolescent period can be set rather clearly, either by reference to chronological age or by reference to physical development.

## Defining the Problem Adolescent

Boundaries for defining the problem adolescent are not so easily drawn. Who is the problem adolescent? Is it the young juvenile delinquent who breaks probation for car theft by stealing another car? Is it the mentally defective fifteen-year-old girl who doesn't understand much about life or people, but whose impulses and whose impulsiveness have brought her to a home for unwed mothers? Is the problem adolescent the youthful criminal who has confessed to multiple, premeditated murders? Is it the young schizophrenic girl whose greatest pleasure is kicking her feet in the leaves in her back yard and living her fantasies of being a Japanese princess? Or is the young boy who quarrels with his mother and fights with his younger siblings a problem adolescent? Is "problem adolescent" the appropriate label for the sixteen-year-old boy who drops out of school because he is more interested in cars than in education? Or is it the proper label for the fourteen-year-old girl who has come under a doctor's care for treatment of gonorrhea?

Shall we group all these together—the juvenile delinquent, the mentally defective, the school dropout, the precociously demented, the quarrelsome teenager, the sexually promiscuous—shall we gather all these under the one label of "problem adolescents"? Obviously not, for the only homogeneity they may have is based on the factor of age—their adolescence—but not on their problems.

### Statistical Picture of the Problem Adolescent

The stark reality of adolescent problems is etched in the black of some scattered statistics. The rate of juvenile delinquency has tripled in the past twenty years. Some 265,000 juveniles are brought before our courts each year. Every ten minutes a new case of teenage venereal disease is reported. Of all cases of venereal disease, 22 per cent occur in teenagers. The highest incidence of venereal disease in females is at age 18. Suicide is the fifth most common cause of death in the 15-to-19 age group. Of attempted suicides, 12 per cent occur in teenagers. Of teenage deaths, 50 per cent are due to accidents, and over one half of these deaths are due to auto accidents. One baby in every seven is born to a teenager.

One study revealed that 87 per cent of the marriages between teenagers who were both in high school began with an illegitimate pregnancy. Twenty-five per cent of 18-year-old girls are married, and 16 per cent of 17-year-old girls are married. Recently, in one year, there were 133 children charged with murder in the United States. There were 11 deaths in New York City juvenile-gang wars in one summer alone. Over 43 per cent of adolescents seeking medical care have functional disorders. It is estimated that 10 per cent of public-school children have emotional disorders needing treatment. In one major study of alcoholics, it was found that nearly 50 per cent of them began abnormal drinking patterns during their adolescence.

These statistics tell us some stark facts about the period we call adolescence. Let us look behind the cold figures for some knowledge about the people we call adolescents. Teenagers have a keen desire to grow, to experiment, to learn, to do, and to do for themselves. The number of teenage accidents tells us of this need. Auto deaths tell us of the rush they feel within them, for time is something with which they grow restless, and hurry is sister to activity. The incidence of venereal disease tells us of their warmth, their passion, their feeling for life and for one another, their need to shut out the loneliness of living. The suicide rate points to their sensitivity to hurt, to wrong, to injustice, and the depth of their despair. The number of teenage marriages and the frequency of illegitimate pregnancies remind us of their impulsivity, their lack of self-control, their struggle with the growing powers within them. The rate of juvenile delinquency and the frequency of youthful murders speak for the resentment and rebellion that can grow within them like a ticking bomb, exploding when time runs out.

In contrast to the disturbances highlighted by these statistics, the great majority of teenagers exhibit intellectual, social, or psychological problems which are of mild degree. There are some adults who would call even this group "problem adolescents." Many parents have forgotten too quickly the shortcomings of their own adolescent years and condemn today's teenagers, including their own teenage sons and daughters. Occasionally, society and social agencies, in haste to quiet their own guilt over their group neglect of adolescents and their needs, brand them with big letters, JD—juvenile delinquents, and so relegate them to an outcast status. Some teachers, some lawmakers, some clergymen, and some physicians place all teenagers in one large group and consider them all to be problems.

## Kinds of Adolescents

Because of my own struggle to delimit, for myself, this group of problem adolescents and because of the natural grouping which seemed to appear in the workshop program, it seemed appropriate to divide teenagers into the following trichotomy: the normal teenager, the problem teenager, and the pathologic teenager. All three of these groups have the same drives, the same goals, the same conflicts; yet, they do not have the same patterns. Of course, I would not suggest that these groups are sharply separated from one another; rather, they lie along a continuum. However, there are some lines they must cross to pass from one group to another.

In labeling one group as the normal teenage group and the second group as the problem teenage group, I do not infer, and I am sure that Dr. Schneiders has not led you to believe, that the average or normal American teenager is free of problems. Perhaps the teenager is the one member of our society about whom we ought to worry if there are no problems present. There are many competent authorities who feel that freedom from problems in teenagers is a serious symptom of psychopathology. The teenager who is not, at times, in conflict with his parents or some other authority figure is having some difficulty in his emotional growth. The teenager who doesn't have some rather strong mood swings just "isn't with it." The teenager who doesn't have some struggle to control his impulses, both sexual and aggressive, has something the matter with his motor. The teenager who isn't sometimes confused and frightened by the world of adults, and who, consequently, doesn't retreat into Zen Buddhism, beatnik attitudes, a Hollywood fad, or a diet kick of his own, just isn't properly "tuned in" on that adult world in which he must soon live.

Adolescents have problems. But, *having* a problem and *being* a problem are two different fields of interest. The teenagers who merely have problems are not difficult problems for the counselor; the problem adolescent is a problem; the pathologic adolescent is a very demanding problem.

The pathologic adolescents are seriously disturbed. They are not just problem adolescents; they are ill. They have pathology which is serious, which is deeply rooted, and which is almost certain to bring them into severe and continued conflict with their environment. At the same time, this pathology may not be superficially apparent. This group includes the psychotics, the criminal psychopaths, the grossly defective, the severely neurotic. They are adolescents who frequently need institutionalization. They need the intensive care of professionals. They need the control of an environment which cannot be controlled by them.

Paradoxically, one might say that the problem adolescent includes the characteristics of the other two groups; for one finds him at one moment moving quietly along the path of healthy adjustment, and then, in a flash, he is seen precariously dashing about on the brink of serious behavior which could lead to destruction and disaster. The problem adolescent is dutifully mowing the lawn one moment and the next he is drag racing in his father's automobile. The problem adolescent is genuinely religious during the week, but on Saturday she is doing her usual petty shoplifting. These teenagers move easily and quickly from the area of healthy adjustment to the area of frank pathology. A boy may change overnight from being an A student, interested in geography, to a D student interested in pornography. A girl may win a debating contest during the day and find herself passed out from alcohol at some party that night. Sunday's shining altar boy may be picked up for peeping-tom activities on Monday. The boy who showed tremendous athletic promise may find himself transferred from the basketball court one day to police court the next day for stealing a car and going joy-riding. The girl who was most popular among her classmates in an all-girl high school may be forced to drop out of school because she is pregnant.

These are problem adolescents. These are the teenagers who beguile us one moment and cause us to envy them their charm, their enthusiasm, their vitality, their youthful success; and the next moment, they shock us by their crass unfairness, their frank rebellion, their deliberate lawlessness, their irrational delinquencies.

One important fact must be kept in mind. These changes in behavior, these alterations of attitude, are a thoroughfare with two-way traffic. Unless we put up roadblocks to the teenager who has taken the wrong course, his trip back to normalcy is almost as easily and as quickly completed as was his excursion into error. This possibility of quick reversal can be too quickly forgotten when we find the problem adolescent on the wrong side of the bridge, outside the law, beyond the boundaries of society. If we condemn him when we find him there, we weaken the bridge over which he can travel back to healthy adjustment. If we punish him too severely, we destroy the road over which he can return. If we are too severe or if we are only vindictive, we make our side of the chasm less pleasant, less inviting. If we give him a stony ear instead of listening to him, if we do not offer the hand of encouragement even when he holds both of his defiantly behind his back, we may alienate and anger him to the point where he will tear down the bridge that could bring him back to normality and thereby isolate himself from us on the side of criminality or psychosis. It is really his easy accessibility to us and the easy accessibility of healthy behavior to him that keeps the problem adolescent out of the area of real pathology. When his maladjustment is made fixed by the rigidity of adult responses, when his withdrawal is made complete by the coldness of adult responses, when his rebellion is increased by the vindictiveness of adult responses, then the pathology of his position rises up to engulf him. He is then no longer just a problem adolescent.

### Difficulties in Understanding the Adolescent

In my work with adolescents, I often note a remarkable psychological fact. It seems to me that if there is one period in our lives for which we have the most repressed memories, it is the time of our own teens. Isn't it possible that the inaccessibility to consciousness of our own adolescent period makes the adolescent with whom we deal inaccessible to us now? In adult therapy we work for an anamnesis of early childhood experiences, and we are often secretly proud, I think, when a patient recalls some early memory. If we could induce parents and those who work with teenagers to remember the facts and feelings of their own adolescence, I am sure they would have a wholly different attitude.

I suggest that the memories of adolescence are among the most painful memories we can uncover in the dark recesses of our unconscious. I can think of two reasons. First of all, many of those events were painfully embarrassing, hauntingly terrifying, seriously disturbing to our own sense of identity, our own sense of personal worth. Remembering them might still be very unpleasant. Secondly, I suspect that the wild wandering of adolescents, their aspiration to high achievement in stark contrast to the depth of their frailty, their indecision, and their inability to effectively pursue that which they idealize tell us too much about ourselves. These youths remind us that once we too stood on the open plain and saw the world stretched out before us; we looked to the mountain peaks and the stars beyond and said, "These shall be ours." And then we descended into the valleys and caves and sought for that to which we had never aspired. Isn't this the story of adult life, this conflict between ideals and weaknesses? Don't we see it outlined in the problem youths around us? In fear lest they awaken some residuals of our own agitated adolescence and pry open the Pandora's box within us all, we stand horrified at their conduct and attitudes and shout so loudly at them that we cannot hear the voices whispering within ourselves.

One reliable study has shown that ninety-nine per cent of nondelinquent persons have engaged in the same type of offenses for which delinquents have been committed by the courts. Does the figure of ninety-nine per cent sound shocking? On the contrary, I'm wondering how that other one per cent escaped the universality of adolescence!

Occasionally, a parent is candid enough to admit that as a teenager he did things he would "beat the daylights" out of his own teenager for doing. Maybe we should divide parents into two groups—those who have completely repressed the transgressions of their teen years and thus can understand nothing of their children's conflicts; and those who comfortably remember the turmoil of their own teens and, still unable to accept their own limitations, are determined that their sons and daughters are not going to make the same mistakes.

## Characteristics of Adolescent Development

There are two processes that take place in producing a healthy teenager, or in turning an average teenager into a problem teenager. One of these processes takes place within the youth himself, the other within his environment. The process within the adolescent is essentially a process of growth. The physical, physiological, and psychological development of the adolescent forces him into a condition of change. If attempts are made to thwart this natural change, then some distortion takes place in personality development. If one keeps a cast too long on the growing arm of an adolescent, a deformed arm will result. In the same fashion, psychological growth cannot be rigidly contained within the same set of rules and attitudes that fitted childhood. The teenager has grown out of the slacks or skirts of gradeschool days. The teenager has also grown out of the parental restraints which suited him in earlier years.

The vivid curiosity of the human mind lies somewhat dormant during the latency period. In the adolescent it bursts forth again as sharply as when he was two or three years old. There is a new surge of interest in the immediate and the remote. The world takes on new horizons as it expands rapidly before his curious mind. It expands so quickly that he cannot understand it all; brief periods of confusion and bewilderment are the result. The teenager who asks why Communism isn't a good form of government is not unlike the five-year-old who wonders why the moon doesn't shine like the sun. But the teenager expects an answer and can be critical of that answer.

The youth of fifteen or sixteen who is confronted with the strong sexual urges of his developing glandular powers is, I suspect, much more deeply involved and more precariously balanced than is the child of five with his oedipal concerns. Parents who worry about the dating practices of their adolescent sons and daughters are hardly worried because of their own oedipal conflicts. They are concerned because they know, from their own experiences in life, the danger of drive-ins and of prolonged parking, the siren song of soft lights and sweet music, the intimacies that accompany intoxicants.

The curiosity of teenagers is dangerous for two reasons. First, it involves some very basic issues; for example, what is sex really about, what is it like to drive a car at ninety miles an hour, why should one obey *any* laws, how does it feel to beat up on someone, is there *really* a God, how powerful is a gun? Second, their curiosity is dangerous because it is coupled with another characteristic teen trait—the need for independence. Children are usually satisfied with adult answers to their questions, but teenagers are not. *They don't want answers; they want experiences.* They are not satisfied with answers that are given to them; they want conclusions that they themselves find.

This process is one of psychological growth. Curiosity drives the ado-

lescent forward, and the need for independence calls him to maturity.
If this curiosity is not kept within limits, it brings him into situations
which he cannot master, it brings him knowledge for which he is emotionally unprepared, and it pushes him into experiences which he
cannot understand. If his drive for independence is not directed and
allowed to unfold gradually, it brings the teenager a freedom which
is frightening, a liberty which is confusing, and a latitude which may
be overwhelming.

The second process involved in teenage development takes place
within the environment. Parental answers that satisfied a six-year-old
don't satisfy a sixteen-year-old. In the same way, parental attitudes
that managed a seven-year-old cannot manage a seventeen-year-old.
The parent-child relationship changes radically with the onset of
puberty and subsequent teen years. Parents who cannot make the adjustment to this change turn normal children into problem teenagers.
Adults who are frightened by adolescent curiosity and independence
erect a barricade, as ignominious as the Berlin Wall, between their
sons and daughters and the realities of adult life. Like the enslaved
of East Germany, some of these youths break through the barricade
to escape from parental domination, but frequently show scars of their
escape to freedom. Consider the young, unmarried mother from a
home where sex was taboo and dating was looked upon as worse than
wicked; the youthful car thief from a home where cars were a symbol
of superiority and teenage drivers were condemned; the youthful delinquent from a home where religion was worn like a suit of armor—
rigidly, conspicuously, and unrealistically.

Adults are often bewildered by the eagerness of youth to do things.
Especially incongruous are the parents who always pushed their child
forward, but cannot understand their adolescent's desire to push himself forward. Some parents push their child to be toilet-trained early,
to tie his shoes before the neighbor's children learn to do so. These
same children are pushed into nursery school at age three for social
interaction, into ballet at age five for the attainment of grace and
poise. They are shuttled off to camp in summer for the development
of healthy civic attitudes. They are crowded into advanced classes for
intellectual stimulation. They are encouraged to have mixed parties
when they are in fifth grade in order to foster heterosexual ease at
about age ten! These same parents are absolutely shocked when their
twelve-year-old girl wants to go steady with some high-school senior,
when their fourteen-year-old boy comes home drunk from a little

neighborhood party, when their sixteen-year-old boy insists on having a car for dating, when their seventeen-year-old girl runs away and gets married. Children can be pushed too rapidly in the social area, in the sexual area, and even in the intellectual area. Parents who want their children to be intellectual wizards at eight, star athletes at nine, and popularity winners at ten rob them of their childhood; and in return, they get back the hollow response of uncommunicating teenagers.

## Parents and Their Adolescents

What must parents give to their teenagers to keep them from becoming problem youths? The old lamp of authority grows dim, and parents must trade it in for a new lamp of trust if they are to light the way along the road of adolescence. The simple formula of trust is not so simple for many. They say, "How can you show someone you trust him when, indeed, you don't; and most assuredly, you can't?" On the other hand, how can a youth trust himself when no one else trusts him? It is the duty of parents to bring their children to adulthood, but until they can give the treasure of trust to their teenagers, they will remain as children. Trust does not mean lack of guidance. There must still be guidelines within which the adolescent can move with freedom and self-confidence.

Even though they have no serious pathology, problem teenagers often need psychiatric care. This psychiatric care can serve two purposes. First, the psychiatrist can attempt to alter some of the parental attitudes. Let me give a brief example from practice. A fifteen-year-old boy is condemned by his mother, criticized by her for nearly everything he does, and is frequently restricted by her from recreation suitable to his age. The boy sees his mother as rejecting and dominant, his father as a nice person but ineffective. In this case, the father was advised to put his foot down at home and to take this boy's side against his wife, even if it led to open argument in front of the boy. In fact, I felt an open argument between father and mother in which the father defended the boy might do the boy a world of good. In this case, I felt the father was really capable of winning the argument. If he lost, the boy might be worse off. But I'm not so sure of that either because I believe very strongly that what most of these problem teenagers need is someone who stands up for them, someone who doesn't condemn them, someone who believes that they aren't always wrong. Their champion need not even understand them. I doubt if any of us, as therapists or as parents, really understand the adolescent, especially when he gets to be a problem adolescent. In fact, the gift of understanding other humans probably remains the domain of children, for only they possess the simplicity and lack of prejudice that are precursors of understanding. So we need not always understand teenagers; indeed, we cannot. What we need to do is to give them the benefit of a hearing, the courtesy of a discussion, and the respect of our honest attention.

When the psychiatrist cannot alter parental attitudes, more drastic measures may be in order. I recently insisted that a boy live elsewhere than with his father before I would take him in treatment. This boy is eighteen years old. His father beats him with a rubber hose across the naked back until he bleeds. The parents brought him to me because he had contracted syphilis as a result of a homosexual contact. Not long ago, I hospitalized a fifteen-year-old girl because her mother persecuted her so thoroughly that a behavioral disorder of some magnitude was almost certain to result. These youths do not have pathology. Drastic measures must be taken to prevent pushing this problem adolescent across the line into psychosis, into severe neurosis, or into criminal behavior.

The other purpose of psychiatric care for these problem adolescents is to lend them an ear that really listens; to reach out with a hand that really wants to help and with a heart that really cares and believes in them. It is a belief that within them, as within each human being, there is some untouched island, some hidden battlement, some sacred spot which no outside evil can reach and which the darkest night cannot destroy—a belief that from this inner self they can launch, if only they have hope and courage, their own campaign for responsible living, for health, for success, and for happiness.

My goal in therapy with teenagers is not to win them back to parental dominance. It is my goal to set them free of parental influence, to move them toward maturity, to bring them to a self-confidence, a self-respect, a responsibility for self which adults cannot destroy or take away from them.

In the steady glow of maturity we may wonder at the holocaust that is youth. We would do well not to put out its fire.

# 5. Special Aspects of Adolescent Problems

CLARE O'DWYER

ROBERT J. McALLISTER

IRENE DAVIS

## The Early Dating Problem
(CLARE O'DWYER)

The tragedy, and I use the word with care, is that the majority of people adversely affected by the detrimental consequences of early dating do not realize that the early dating was the problem and that it caused the difficulties now blighting their happiness. Here I am referring to both the youth involved and to their parents.

But what do we mean by "early dating"? For our purposes, I would limit it to the pairing off of youngsters in their early teens, that is, those fifteen and younger. That there will be recreation together in this age group is perfectly understandable. Mixed youth groups at dances, picnics, and house parties are certainly permissible, but when they pair off at this age level, then we have "early dating." For example, John, 14, asks Mary, 12, to go to a movie unchaperoned and without any of the rest of the crowd. Incidentally, today we can just as easily reverse the above and have Mary asking John, for girls have long since given up the idea that they should be sought after, and now they themselves do the seeking with a tenaciousness and guile that make us wonder how the male hunter was ever successful in his masculine simplicity.

In a more general sense the problem of early dating also includes

49

the many headaches that arise from the present youthful trend of going steady. By this latter term we are referring to the association between one boy and girl to the exclusion of all others. This association is usually a natural outgrowth of early dating as previously defined. Whatever conclusions will be drawn from the problem of dating at the early teen level will certainly apply to the vast numbers of youngsters who are going steady.

That early dating has caused and is causing a problem will not be denied by any person engaged in the study of human behavior. Youth workers, marriage counselors, clergymen, sociologists, and educators are all concerned with the myriad problems caused by the American phenomenon of dating by grammar-school youngsters as though they were in their late teens and ready for marriage. Further, the age for dating apparently keeps moving downward, and it would be a rash person indeed who would say where it is going to stop. In a society that is leaning more and more toward such customs as graduation ceremonies—complete with academic gown and mortarboard—for children successfully completing kindergarten, it is possible that our ingenious American minds may yet figure out how youngsters can date before they can walk.

The causes for early dating are many, though I would single out three as having the greatest weight in foisting this unnecessary problem upon the American scene.

1. *The drive to be a success.* Competition is woven all through American life, and where dating is concerned, it boils down to a simple formula: one must be a success; one cannot be a success unless one is popular; but one cannot be popular unless one dates; and unless one dates the world will suspect one has no charm, initiative, or social grace. As a whole, we are terribly concerned with what other people think; so we carefully choose and use words and actions in order that we may be well liked. Apparent popularity is possible for all youth if they employ the accepted means: constant use of the telephone, preoccupation with and planning of their social life, and obtaining of money, usually through a persistent campaign against their parents. Thus, though all cannot be star athletes nor star personalities, all can set up a way of living that would indicate popularity to the superficial viewer and thus also success. "John is always in demand with the other boys and girls," says the happy father. "I guess he's just a born leader." Our contented mother is in her heaven when she can purr to neighbors

and friends, "My Mary is on the go all the time; she certainly is popular."

2. *Group pressure.* A second cause of early dating is group pressure. The greatest weapon youth possesses is the time-honored phrase used by millions of young people to break down adult authority: "Everybody else is doing it." The strange part about this approach is that though this method has been used by youth through the years, individual parents react to this argument as if it were brand-new. What has happened to their memories? Which parents cannot recall the hundreds of times they made use of the same weapon when they were young? In the majority of cases, their parents had answers that held youth in check even if these answers were as basic as that of the father who said to his small son, "You'll do what I tell you for the simple reason that I am bigger than you!"

3. *Mother.* A third cause of early dating is the mother's attitude. Here we encounter mother's consuming passion to relive her own youth and see to it that her daughter is successful in achieving the great feminine goal of acquiring a husband. Finding a husband is a pretty serious business, and mother feels it is never too early to begin developing in her daughter the necessary feminine wiles. True, mothers were made to worry. They worry that their daughter is too popular— or not popular enough. However, it does seem that they are apt to worry more about the latter than the former. Now, a worrying mother exerts formidable pressure, and it would indeed be a rare youngster who could withstand mother's decision that her child is going to be popular. After all, "Mother knows best."

These three factors plus youth's desire to seek all possible privileges and to become an adult, whether he is ready or not, has led to behavior that has had and is having disastrous effects on our young people. In the main, the effects of early dating are the following:

1. The breaking down of youth's morals by wittingly or unwittingly overemphasizing the role of sex. Immature healthy boys and girls are bound to become preoccupied with sex, for the proximity effected by early dating will break down barriers and leave the youngsters shorn of natural defenses.

2. The artificial shortening of the time between childhood and adulthood. Too much dating at too early an age will ultimately lead the youngster to attempt to act as an adult before he is ready. Suddenly,

our youth is an adult; but having arrived too fast and taken too many shortcuts, he is not ready to take his proper place in the adult world. Steak seared may look as though it is cooked, but it is not. Similarly, John's big physical frame and occasional reflections on mature subjects may lead one to think he is a man, but inside he is a boy.

3. Marriage at an early age. If one has raced through his youth, what big adventure remains except marriage? To the immature, marriage is the panacea for all their problems. They will have freedom from parental authority; they will have bliss in legitimate sex relations; and they will have status in their crowd, for they have proved their maturity by taking the big step.

Briefly, and I am sure with much too much oversimplification, we have seen the causes and detrimental effects of early dating. What can we do to solve or control this particular problem? There is no simple answer. I can only present some generalities that might be helpful.

First, there can be no substitute for love and good example. Selfish parents should not be surprised that they spawn selfish children. The nagging, self-pitying mother and the do-as-I-say-but-not-as-I-do father should have no complaints about their rambunctious children. Indeed, they should thank God if they turn out reasonably normal. Nor should the parents make the mistake of substituting material gifts for love. Love seeks the good of the child despite the personal sacrifice involved; and there is a great deal of sacrifice involved in taking the time and trouble to supervise the child's pleasures, oversee his friends, and listen to his troubles.

Second, parents should try hard to understand the difficulties their teenagers are experiencing. Can we not all recall our own teenage uncertainties? The agony of pimples, clothes that did not fit, wondering whether or not we were really loved by that new girl in the neighborhood, and not having the money for the latest fad—these problems caused moments of great crisis. Other people died, went bankrupt, or went off to war, but what were these troubles compared to our own massive adolescent problems? Thus it is extremely important that parents make every effort to treat sympathetically and seriously the problems of their children, even though to adults these problems may appear to be unimportant.

We must understand, too, the adolescent's need for acceptance in the peer group. This age is one of budding independence from parents and from home; but within, there is fear and uncertainty. Being a member of a group gives to the adolescent the necessary assurances that all is right with the world. Parents should do all that they can to steer their youngster into a group that has fairly high ideals.

Regarding the specific problem of early dating, parents must be made to realize that such practices can be seriously harmful. Parents should make the rules for their children, which is not only their pre-rogative but also their duty. These rules will gain more acceptance if parents give logical reasons for insisting on certain modes of behavior. If the child will not listen to reason and ignores affection, then it must be pointed out that final authority rests with adults, because it is rea-son that differentiates children from adults.

Lastly, parents should teach their teenagers that privileges bring responsibilities. If youth insists on acquiring certain privileges, then youth must also accept the responsibilities that go with them. The use of the car means the acceptance of such tasks as driving a younger member of the family to a boy- or girl-scout meeting, helping with the shopping, and so on.

Adulthood is not something that can be either grabbed or rushed into; rather, it is something one grows into. Nor can parents surrender their obligations regarding their children to religious or civic organi-zations. True, these organizations do help youth bridge the difficult gap between childhood and adulthood, but there never was nor can there ever be an adequate substitute for good parents. Personally, I have trust in our youth. I believe they will accept difficult and even severe challenges if these challenges are reasonable and have worth-while goals. Thousands of young people died in the Hungarian revolt; thousands of boys and girls endangered themselves, rightly or wrongly, in student riots in South America; thousands of young Negroes today are chancing personal injury in their fight for social justice. We adults must challenge youth to accept responsible roles in the moral-ethical-religious revolution now under way.

## A Study in Adolescent Guilt and Scrupulosity
(ROBERT J. MCALLISTER)

In going through the records of adolescents whom I have treated, I found only one case which I felt suitable for presentation today. This discovery surprised me a little. Certainly, adolescents with obsessive-compulsive difficulties are not unusual. Furthermore, I had among my case records of adults a sizable percentage of patients whose symptomatology had begun with a severe case of scrupulosity during their adolescence. I considered these fifteen to twenty adult cases more carefully and found that very few of these adults had received psychiatric evaluation or care during their adolescence. In most of the cases, their scrupulosity remained their confessional secret for years until more obvious symptoms brought them under psychiatric care. Some were considered only to be unusually religious. I think that the parish priests, the Sisters at the school, and sometimes the relatives of these children may have realized that something was wrong; but they found it difficult to recognize the problem as an emotional one and saw it rather as a quasireligious one.

I would imagine that priest-psychiatrists and priest-psychologists, as well as Catholic guidance clinics, have more than a few referrals of children and, for that matter, adults—whose predominant symptoms include scrupulosity. Certainly, Father Thomas Vernor Moore's writings would indicate this fact. In 1960, an article was published by the Medical Director and a staff psychologist of the St. Charles Child Guidance Clinic in Brooklyn, New York. The staff psychologist was a Jesuit priest. Their article reported on a study of twenty-three adolescents referred to the clinic over a ten-year period because of "continuous and chronic scrupulosity" (Weisner and Riffel, 1960). The frequency of referrals for this symptom was certainly not high. Although there are no statistics available at the Child Center of Catholic University for the three years I have been there, I do not recall any case that was referred because of scrupulosity or any case in which scrupulosity appeared as a major problem during therapy.

I suspect that unless specifically, and perhaps persistently, asked about guilt, confession, and religious practices, an adolescent in therapy would not be willing to volunteer information concerning this area. In fact, because of the nature of the symptom, it is natural to resist any suggestion that other than a sensitive conscience and a deep sense of religion are present. Therefore, unless the neurosis spreads to other areas or unless it becomes grossly incapacitating itself, it is not likely to become subject to psychiatric intervention.

Such was the situation in the case I am going to present here. Larry was an eighteen-year-old boy referred to me by his doctor, who told me during our initial telephone conversation that Larry was a chronically ill boy who was quite withdrawn and showed signs of a long-standing, schizophrenic illness. Let me again refer, very briefly, to the study mentioned above. Psychiatric evaluation was done on eighteen of the scrupulous adolescents, nine of whom were seen "as having an underlying schizophrenic matrix or functioning on a pre-psychotic level" (Weisner and Riffel, 1960, p. 316). The doctor's evaluation of Larry recognized the social withdrawal and somewhat bizarre thinking in this young man, and he decided that schizophrenia was involved.

Larry's parents were both Catholic. The father was forty-five, the mother forty-three. His father had been a policeman for over twenty years. His mother was a housewife. Larry had an older brother, aged twenty-four, who was an electrical engineer, married, with one child. There were two younger brothers, ages thirteen and eight, both in Catholic schools. Larry had completed Catholic grade and high school and was, at the time of the initial interview, enrolled in a local junior college and living at home.

Larry's presenting symptom, and the one which had been the reason for his doctor's visits for the preceding eight months, was his fear of ringworm. The doctor had repeatedly explained the nature of the disease to him and had constantly reassured him that he did not have it and was quite unlikely to contract it.

History regarding this symptom was as follows. Larry remembered that in the sixth grade he had put on another boy's hat at school and one of the boys remarked, "You'll get ringworm." Larry had been aware of the disease prior to that but could not recall when or how he became aware of it. His real concern about ringworm began in the first year of high school. It bothered him a great deal during his first and second years of high school, subsided during the third and fourth years, but had returned with renewed intensity since his college enrollment.

He worried about seeing people wearing stocking caps and about seeing stockings lying on the ground. He was afraid of touching the stockings and would frequently wash his shoes after walking outside. He had read that athletes' foot might be caused by a fungus associated with ringworm, so he washed his hands carefully after putting on or touching his shoes and socks. He always had his hair cut in a crew cut and washed it immediately afterwards. In addition, he changed all his clothes and put them in the laundry after a visit to the barber. He washed his hair every day and more frequently if anything touched his head.

Larry had acquired two books in the first year of high school which contained small articles on ringworm and which he read often. One was a book on general health, the other an insurance handbook. Larry kept these books in a big box with other books in the basement and would go down alone and read them without anyone knowing about it.

Such was the situation which caused Larry to seek help, first from his doctor and later from me. Now, let us look back a few years and see when and how Larry's difficulties developed.

As was mentioned earlier, when Larry was in the sixth grade, someone told him he would get ringworm from wearing another boy's hat. This wasn't all that happened in sixth grade. Following a day of spiritual meditation at school, Larry had gone to Confession and had begun to think that every sin was a mortal sin. I believe this type of religious experience or the preparation for first Holy Communion or for Confirmation often triggers scrupulosity. In sixth grade there was a group of neighborhood boys and girls who improvised parties at which they played, among other games, spin-the-bottle. Larry had played this game many times without giving too much thought to it. Then one night in late sixth grade, he began to feel scared, nervous, and uneasy during the game. He spent a good bit of time in the dark room where they did their kissing with the girl who had invited him. There was another boy present who also liked this girl and also spent considerable time in the dark room with her. Larry was angry at him. Following this experience, his concern about impure thoughts became more severe, and everything he did seemed to be a mortal sin.

At the end of the seventh grade, the Sisters took the class to church for Confession. Larry's examination of conscience was torture. He began confessing that he had made bad confessions. Shortly afterward, he bought, in the narthex of the church, a book entitled "How to Make a Good Confession." When he mentioned this book to me, he spontaneously commented, "This is the second or third time I've bought a book to get out of something and I've only gotten in deeper." He said he was referring to the books on ringworm, which in fact he had not bought, and to a magazine for men which he had found in his older brother's room when he was in the first year of high school. This magazine contained some seminude poses which he had secretly looked at from time to time. In his comment about the books, Larry linked the two principal areas of syptomatology, namely, Confession and ringworm, with the area about which they both revolved, namely, sex. His other interest in books came during his second and third years in high school when he bought or borrowed from the library every book he could find on astronomy. One might certainly consider this a sublimated sexual curiosity, as well as a defense against his sexual drive—

an attempt to devote his attention to an unemotional, scientific subject.

The night before his eighth-grade graduation, Larry could not sleep at all because he was so worried that he might have an impure thought that would keep him from going to Communion the following morning. At about this same time, he was thinking seriously of being a priest. His best friend from grade school later entered the seminary.

In high school, cheating was a common practice. Larry considered cheating a mortal sin but he participated wholeheartedly.

At the time therapy began, he was going to Confession and Communion only at Christmas and Easter. He found it so difficult to keep out of mortal sin from Saturday night until the next morning that this period became one of tremendous emotional stress for him. For example, he could not watch television because it would excite impure thoughts. He felt an extreme urge to commit a new mortal sin as soon as he had gone to Confession. Once he did so, he felt relieved and was no longer so sorely tempted. This neglect of Confession and Communion seems to be a usual pattern among scrupulous patients, particularly by the time they have turned to psychiatry for help. Prior to psychiatric help, I suspect they make up that group of scrupulous individuals who go to Confession repeatedly in a short space of time. Those who have turned away from Confession seem to do so because it imposes on them the burden of being good, which they know they cannot carry.

Larry denied—and I feel quite honestly—ever having masturbated. Nocturnal emissions were regular and caused him no moral concern. They were without remembered dreams. His only concern regarding nocturnal emission was that the seminal fluid might get on some girl. He would not read a library book in bed or in the bathroom for fear that seminal fluid might be carried on the pages and picked up later by some girl. If that occurred, something would happen to the girl. When I insisted on knowing what he thought might happen to her, he admitted that he feared she might become pregnant. However, he made an exception of his mother and felt no concern about her changing his bed or washing his sheets. Similarly, he made an exception of his mother's stockings in connection with his concern about ringworm; he had no fear of them as he had of all other women's stockings.

During high school, Larry began to wash his hands after touching almost anything. This was to protect himself from contracting ringworm. He even became fearful that he might catch ringworm from touching his own penis while urinating. At about the same time, he was so concerned with impurity that he began to think that it was sinful to go to the bathroom because he had to touch his genitals to do so.

There are a few other interesting aspects of Larry's obsessive-compulsive problem. When he was four, his family moved because of Negro neighbors. From an early time, he associated ringworm with Negroes. He had seen them wearing stocking caps and he felt they did not keep clean. At the time of therapy, Larry's parents were once more surrounded by colored neighbors, and they were anxious to move but unable to do so.

Larry had been very fat in the upper grades of elementary school and in high school. He was often teased and embarrassed by his appearance. He stated that he was worried about ringworm because he thought of how ridiculous he would look wearing a stocking cap. People would laugh at him as they had when he was fat.

Larry had been a good athlete. His baseball pitching apparently showed real promise. He had been jeered by the fans as "Porky Pig," and during one game he had tried to attack the father of one of the boys on the opposing team. Once, playing football while in eighth grade, he had shooting pains in his left chest and was hospitalized overnight. In his first year of high school he pitched on the varsity team. One Saturday morning he had to go to practice on the bus because his father would not get up from bed to take him. During practice that morning he became nervous and tightened up. He had been unable to pitch well ever since. Larry said that his father wanted him to do well in sports as well as in school. He was failing in his junior-college work.

Larry stated that he used to be able to get quite angry but he had not been angry for several years. Any show of anger was now a mortal sin.

Something further should be said about Larry's parents. His father was, as I mentioned, a superego personified—a policeman. He was a large, red-faced man who looked like and was an alcoholic. He seldom drank very heavily; he just drank fairly constantly. He did not like to get up in the morning when he was drinking. Perhaps when he refused to take Larry to baseball practice, the son was more angry about his father's alcoholism than he was about his own inconvenience. Larry allowed his father to make most of his decisions for him. In Larry's own words, "I feel better when someone else tells me what to do. I always have preferred that to making up my own mind." This is the characteristic indecisiveness of the obsessive neurotic. At the same time, Larry considered his father a weak man because of his alcoholism, and he was ashamed of him. His father had spanked him when he was younger, but as he grew older, his father just talked to him. He would talk for two or three hours at a time, repeating the same thing over and over and over again. If his father admonished him, and if Larry tried to explain his position, his father would say, "Don't talk back to me." Inwardly, Larry resented this attitude deeply.

Larry's mother was an anxious little woman whom Larry described as a great worrier. The parents were considering buying a new home, but Larry's mother could not decide on one. She worried about her eight-year-old son crossing the street, or falling in a stream, or going into the woods. She had had the same concern about Larry who was not allowed to cross a relatively quiet street alone until he was ten. He also remembered some special soap she had used to clean his hands, and this washing evidently became somewhat of a ritual which his mother performed. His mother now worried constantly about the hydrogen bomb as well as about her own personal health. She would not consult a doctor regarding her health. She would never allow Larry's younger brother to play with Negro children because she considered them dirty.

Larry's story of morbid guilt and scrupulosity presents the major characteristics of this kind of emotional problem. His father dominated the household, but not because of strength of character or others' respect. He was an alcoholic, a weak man, but one who exacted payment for failure by his lengthy, repetitive lectures, and who proved himself unreasonable by his use of the phrase, "Don't talk back to me." Larry's superego was the image of his father. It dominated him, yet it was somehow weak and perverse. It exacted its toll in compulsive, repetitive acts. Finally, it gave no ear to reason.

His mother provided his ego with a pattern of behavior. She was fearful, a worrier. She was afraid of streets. Larry became afraid to go into the streets because of the women's stockings he might see there. His mother was afraid of Negroes because she considered them dirty. He associated Negroes with ringworm and became afraid of ringworm.

So his superego and ego were primed for the stirrings of his id. In time these stirrings came—first in sexual impulses, later in aggressive impulses. His guilt over his sexual awakening at a spin-the-bottle party caused his extreme and somewhat bizarre avoidance of his own sexu-

ality. His avoiding behavior, however, only emphasized the reality of
sex. His concern about urinating epitomized his pathology. He wanted
to avoid touching his penis because he might catch ringworm from it.
At the same time, touching it seemed to be a mortal sin. His sexual
drive, no doubt, made him want to touch it more. In this one act,
one sees the operation of id (the sex drive in this case), ego (fear of
ringworm), and superego (fear of mortal sin).

Sex was all too obvious for Larry. He not only had to protect himself from masturbation by not touching his genitals at all, from impure
thoughts by not watching television, from heterosexual interest by
avoiding girls and even their stockings; but, in addition, he had to protect girls from his own sexuality, his seminal fluid, by not allowing his
sheets to come in contact with anything girls might touch. One might
certainly consider the possible oedipal origin of his denial of his
mother's sex. It was all right for her to wash his sheets, and her stockings did not disturb him. It was as if she did not belong to the group
of females whom he must avoid.

Larry is still in treatment. He is slowly extricating himself from the
iron cobweb which he has spun around himself. He is young; he is still
flexible; he wants help. With encouragement, this David may someday find his Lisa, and she, in turn, will complete the work of bringing
him outside of himself, outside of his shell, into the freedom of loving
another more than oneself.

### The Case of Tommy:  An Academic Misfit
(IRENE DAVIS)

In November of his senior year in high school Tommy Miller's counselor told him that he ought to go to college. Tommy was doing well
in his courses; his test scores showed ability, and the year before he had
received honorable mention at the countywide Science Fair. A few of
Tommy's friends who had graduated from high school had gone to
college. Tommy knew the time was coming when he would have to
make some plans for the future, but his ideas were vague. The counselor suggested several colleges, gave Tommy some catalogues to read,
and told him to talk to his parents.

The idea of college for Tommy had been mentioned several times
at home. Mrs. Miller had gone back to work as a secretary several years
ago after the younger children entered school. She told herself and
her friends that she was working to put the children through college.

Unfortunately, her bank account was not growing very fast because of extra clothes, lunches at the company cafeteria, transportation costs, and a cleaning woman one day a week. Tommy's mother did not know exactly what it would cost the family to keep Tommy in college for a year, but she felt sure that he was bright enough to win a scholarship, and she would, therefore, have to pay only for his room and board, his books, and his vacation trips home. She indicated that if Tommy wanted to join a fraternity he could pay for that himself by summer employment or a part-time job on campus.

Mrs. Miller's family had not been able to afford to send her away to college. She was determined to give Tommy the chance she had not had herself—a chance to have a good time, to make nice friends, and to get ahead in the world. Day dreaming on the bus on her way home from work, she could see herself as a young, pretty freshman coed, flirting her way through fabulous dances and imaginary football games or walking hand in hand across the campus with a boy who by now would be a rising young surgeon in the big city. Returning home from these reveries she was usually annoyed by her husband's lack of enthusiasm for higher education. His talk of mortgages on the house, installment payments on the car, life insurance, automobile insurance, fire insurance wearied her. Wasn't it enough that she was willing to work? Wasn't it her money? If she wanted to spend it on Tommy in her way, wasn't that her business?

So Tommy applied and was accepted at the state university. He was also offered an engineering scholarship at another university. Mr. Miller was in favor of the engineering program, having decided that if Tommy was going to college he ought to study something practical and not waste his time just reading books. The counselor, knowing the family situation, mentioned to Tommy that he might attend the local junior college for several years, but Tommy did not even discuss this suggestion at home. If he were going to be an engineer he would have to go to one of the universities sooner or later, and going sooner meant the chance to make varsity teams and to join a fraternity. Tommy was, after all, the son of his mother as well as his father.

June came and Tommy graduated tenth in his class of 175. The principal announced that 45 of the graduates were going to college and that they had won scholarships valued at $60,000. It made him proud to say this, and it was at least theoretically correct, because $15,000 a year for four years would certainly amount to $60,000. He knew from experience, however, that not half of the students would complete four years of college, and he also knew that each one of the students would have to supplement scholarship funds with loans, family funds, and hopefully, part-time jobs. Hopefully, because jobs for teenagers were scarce indeed.

As the summer wore on and Tommy received various bits of information from the university, a few small worries and irritations developed. For one thing, the business manager was asking for payment of the first-term dormitory bill in September. Mrs. Miller could not meet the payment and still buy Tommy some new clothes. Tommy had picked up a few odd jobs during the sumer, but an old car which he bought cost more than he earned and he was by now $50.00 in debt to his older sister. Mr. Miller had promised Tommy that for a high-school graduation present he would give him the money for his books. He was surprised to learn that the books plus supplies might total $100.00, which was about twice as much as he had expected. In his opinion much of this was foolishness anyhow; it did not make sense to him that Tommy's freshman program should include English literature and political science. Tommy could not explain why these courses were included, and he knew better than to tell his father that he was on the whole rather pleased about the program himself. He had had a first-rate English teacher in high school and he had enjoyed her classes. This interest was his well-kept secret, however, because he would have received some heavy kidding if he had let it be known that he was attracted to such a "girlish" subject. He had enough trouble with the fact that he had graduated with honor. In his group, it was the athletes who won the real honors and usually the girls too.

During the first few weeks of the freshman year Tommy's elation knew no bounds. He had been told by all of the speakers in the orientation program that he was now free, free to make decisions and free to plan his own time. He was free to make his own mistakes, too, it turned out. When the first marks appeared he was in danger of failing mathematics, and he was behind in his laboratory work in chemistry. The chemistry did not worry him because he was sure he could make that up, but he was angry and annoyed about the mathematics. He had been a star pupil in mathematics in high school, but down here at the university they were teaching things of which he had never heard. In derision he and other students called it "magic math" and made fun of the professor.

Tommy's social life was much more satisfying. He was rushed by three fraternities and received bids from two. He was a promising athlete, a good-looking boy, and it was known that he had a scholarship and therefore could be counted on to increase the scholarship average of the chapter. Tommy was flattered and desperately anxious to accept a bid, but how was he going to pay the fees? Paying fraternity fees was to have been his responsibility, but he had not been able to get a job. In fact, his advisor told him he should not try to work during his freshman year because he would need to devote 40 to 50 hours a week to his studies. Tommy thought this advice was foolish because he had never studied more than five or six hours a week in high school.

When February and the grades came, Tommy had a failure in mathematics, a failure in chemistry laboratory, and a D in the lecture part of the chemistry course. He passed political science with a C and received a B in English. Tommy was sure that he had almost passed the mathematics and he thought his chemistry grade was very unfair. He had to admit to his adviser that he had let his work slide to some extent, but he had stayed up all night studying for the final chemistry examination. If the professor had not changed so many of the questions from the previous year's exam, Tommy would have done much better. One of the advantages of belonging to a fraternity would be to have access to a file of examination questions.

When Tommy's parents received his report they were shocked because he had never before failed anything in school. His mother was sure there had been some mistake; his father grumbled about the fraternity and lectured Tommy severely about girls and late hours. Tommy, with his new-found wisdom, assured his parents that everything would be all right, that he could take his math course over again and make up his chemistry failure in the summer school. He might as well study during the summer, he argued, because he couldn't get suitable work anyhow. He had found that he could borrow money under a government loan program. He felt sure that he could do better work in the second semester now that he had caught on to the ways of college life. He tried to impress upon his parents the great difference there was between college life and the life of a young boy in high school. He felt very adult. During the examination he had gone for a week without shaving. He toyed with the idea of letting his beard grow, but the baseball coach vetoed this idea.

Tommy embarked on the second half of the freshman year having patched up his academic program and his financial situation. Compared to the strain of January, the month of February was pure bliss.

Tommy went to classes regularly, missing only a few of those that were scheduled early in the morning and on Saturdays. Everybody except the "spooks" cut Saturday classes and Tommy was certainly no spook. He was treasurer of his class, a member of the freshman baseball team, and he was engaged. It was a wonderful spring when spring finally came, but there was only one thing to mar it, the final examinations. This time, Tommy was certain he was going to "crack" the exams. On several occasions he took advantage of the opportunity to discuss his work with his teachers. He was still having trouble because he could not see the relationship between his courses and the field of engineering as he understood it. He thought he was not getting a practical education. His adviser discussed the program with him. Some of the boys told him that he should have attended the Dean's orientation lectures during which the professors from different departments had discussed their branches of engineering and had told about new developments in thermodynamics, electronics, energy conversion, circuit theory, operations research, fluid mechanics, solid mechanics, and transportation phenomena. Tommy had skipped these lectures because his fraternity brothers had told him that they would be a waste of time unless a student intended to go into research.

As Tommy grew more and more confused about his professional goal, he found his real satisfaction in his English classes and in a course in introductory psychology which he had started in February. The satisfaction did not help much, for Tommy did not know anybody who earned a living as a psychologist, and the only people he knew who made money from English literature were school teachers. Obviously, he was not going to be a school teacher. Equally obvious was the fact that he was going to have to start making a living pretty soon, even sooner than he had expected. His girl was not interested in waiting three years to be married, and Tommy could not face the possibility of losing her. She wanted to get married and help him with her earnings. If he gave up engineering, however, he would lose his scholarship; in fact, he would probably lose it anyway because of his low marks. His first year had been a financial struggle even with a scholarship, and it would be impossible for him to return for another year without it.

That June Tommy became one of hundreds of Tommys who start college in the fall and leave it the following June. For some this break in studies marks the end of their higher education. I am happy to report that it was not so in the case of Tommy. Tommy had a good mind and basically a good set of values. As he grew older and gained some work experience, he gradually cast off the unreal dream of college which his mother had carried over from the years before World War II. As he assumed the duties of fatherhood, he began to appreciate the provision which his own father had made for him and gained new respect for mortgages, installment payments, and insurance. After service in the armed forces, Tommy returned to his civilian job, and he and his wife began to look ahead to the time when they would have to send their own children to college. The company for which Tommy worked gave him a chance to go to night school and offered to pay part of his expenses if he made satisfactory grades. Today Tommy is not an engineer, but he has found a use for his mathematical ability as a member of a management team in a large corporation. He has continued his studies in psychology and has not lost his love of literature. If some people consider his interest in literature sissy he no longer cares, because he realizes that some of his old friends will probably be teenagers all their lives. Tommy, the misfit, recently received his bachelor's degree. He blames himself for his youthful folly, but as we review the case we must conclude that the blame must be shared. When the boy doesn't fit, do we alter the boy or the situation?

# PART II

## Discipline and Rebellion
## in Adolescence

▲▲▲▲▲▲▲▲▲▲▲▲▲▲▲▲▲▲▲▲▲▲▲▲▲▲▲▲▲▲

# 6. The Meaning of Discipline

LEO H. BARTEMEIER

The term "discipline" is derived from the word "disciple." A disciple is one who received instruction from another, especially one who accepts the doctrines of his teacher and assists in spreading them. Such a person is a follower—specifically, a professed follower of Christ in his lifetime, especially one of the twelve Apostles. The Disciples adopted the teaching, the beliefs, and perhaps even the manners of Our Lord and devoted their lives to teaching the Saviour's Gospel. The Apostles became identified with Jesus and subsequently became teachers themselves.

To discipline is to educate, to develop by instruction and exercise. Education includes training to accept those rituals, those restraints, and those checks and balances which all children need to develop in the years when they are becoming socialized.

When we turn to the *Dictionary of word origins* we learn that a leader or teacher sets down the precepts for his disciples. Those who spread the precepts are the disciples. The fact that disciples are given instruction suggests to us that one of the meanings of the word "discipline" is education. Education, however, means much more than the acquisition of knowledge, far more than the development of the intellect to which we have mistakenly directed an almost exclusive attention.

The parents are the first teachers of children. They also learn from their children as school teachers learn from their pupils. To teach is always to learn from those whom we teach. What and how we teach is always an expression of ourselves. No two teachers ever teach the same way, just as no two physicians ever practice medicine in the same fashion. All teaching and training is tinted, colored, and channelled by our previous life experiences, and is invariably an expression of our

69

attitudes, our prejudices, our beliefs, and our feelings toward those whom we teach. It is, therefore, necessary to recognize that our teaching of any subject is always woven in the fabric of our individual personalities. From these preliminary remarks we may understand that the basic factor in the disciplining of children is our personal influence as it is perceived by pupils in the course of our teaching. This influence is conveyed almost unknowingly and unintentionally and is usually beyond a teacher's awareness.

The word "discipline" also means a special department of knowledge or a branch of instruction; we speak of the teaching profession as a discipline, or of biology, or mathematics, or theoretical physics as disciplines. However, on this occasion we are not concerned with these definitions. At the same time we recognize that we have disciplined ourselves to become teachers, mathematicians, or theoretical physicists. In this connection we need to consider what we mean by a well-disciplined person apart from his having acquired a specialized field of knowledge. A well-disciplined person is the product of a wholesome upbringing by his parents, his teachers, and other significant persons during the years when his character was in the process of formation. He possesses a built-in function of control over his impulses which operates more or less automatically and often beyond his field of awareness. As early as his second and third year of life, his parents exercised a relative control over some of his behavior. They permitted him an optimum gratification of his impulses and simultaneously restricted him in other satisfactions of his primitive strivings. During that period of his early childhood he was dominated by his impulses, and his behavior could be controlled in a wholesome fashion only by external authority.

All children need the love of their parents and all children fear the loss of this love. It is through this most powerful influence that the external controls of parental authority find their meaning. Little children who admire their parents want most of all to be like them. They imitate their fathers and mothers and somewhat later come to identify themselves with them. Through this gradual process of identification the previous external controls gradually become internalized within the psychic life of the child. Whatever was previously forbidden by the child's external authorities now tends to be forbidden by an internal authority which we describe as the superego. This internal authority, however, is not yet firmly established at the age of five or six, and teachers and others in the school function as continuing controls over his behavior and simultaneously assist him in strengthening his developing superego.

Irene Josselyn (1948, pp. 89–92) has had the following to say on the subject of discipline and I wish to quote her at length:

Insight into the reasons behind behavior patterns in children has caused considerable confusion about the question of discipline. When less was understood about the meaning and motivation of children's behavior, discipline, primarily in the form of punishment, was taken for granted. It was the accepted way to make a child into a desirable adult. A swing of the pendulum followed as a result of popular awareness that behavior was an expression of the child's feelings. There followed, as a result, an attitude espoused by parents and child experts that discipline in all forms was unjustified and wrong. Unfortunately a child under such a regime may fail to develop a superego and often has not even a conscious check on his impulses. Sometimes, as another extreme, the child feels so unprotected that he inhibits his own behavior much more severely than a wise parent would.

The child who fails to develop control of his behavior is a confused and unhappy child. A child is bombarded by many impulses, some of which can be properly gratified with parental approval. Other impulses cannot be easily or completely gratified and the child must develop adequate controls and sublimations. If he is not helped to find a satisfactory balance between control and satisfaction, his behavior becomes random and unpredictable. He is thrashing about for some way to gain gratification and has no pattern to follow. Wise discipline offers the child guidance toward optimum gratification with minimal expenditure of emotional energy in developing suitable controls. The child who, under a non-disciplinary regime, controls his behavior too severely does so because of anxiety. One child who had never been corrected in anything he did was, at the age of 10, incapable of any spontaneous behavior. Every move he made was in imitation, and consciously so, of very proper parents. When questioned concerning this he stated his problem very clearly. He felt like doing certain things and not doing others. He recognized that his parents did not do the things of which he disapproved. He was not certain how safe it would be to do things his parents did not do, since they never told him what was safe behavior and what was not. His only safeguard therefore was to imitate his parents rigidly without allowing his own impulses any freedom. Actually this child was a healthily aggressive child. It was his aggression that he feared and that he maintained under such rigid, artificial control. The whole process of living was a matter of walking on what he feared was thin ice. No one helped him to evaluate the ice so that he could recognize where it was safe and where it was not. Wise discipline gives the child a sense of security and, at the same time, of freedom. The child is aware of limits placed upon his behavior which, if accepted by him, assure him of the reward of emotional security. Within these limits the child is free to express himself, gain certain gratifications, and not jeopardize his basic relationships. It assures him further that he is protected by those limitations from carrying out impulses which might destroy what he wants to preserve.

It is difficult to define too specifically what wise discipline is. Part of the wisdom is based upon the adult's intuitive capacity to recognize the child's ego strength. Discipline should be geared to the individual child's capacity to tolerate frustration without being overwhelmed by it. When it is not so geared the child may be "over-disciplined," in which case he may have to become passively accepting of restrictions placed upon impulses that should have some mode of expression . . .

Punishment is at times necessary in order to sharpen the necessity for conformity in regard to important issues. There is no "best" form of punishment. Punishment is most meaningful to the child when it is in proportion to the misdemeanor rather than in proportion to the parent's irritation; when, if possible, it has some relationship to the behavior that necessitates it; and when it is carried out consistently once it is imposed. Parents are often extremely unimaginative in their use of punishment. One mother complained that her 4-year-old daughter always caused her to be late in meeting her husband at the train. The events leading to her tardiness had all the implications of a family ritual. She would call her child to come and clean up. The child would delay coming, obeying only after repeated calls from the mother. When the child came in the mother always spanked her for being late. She then tidied the child and took her to the train, to be greeted by an angry husband and father. Actually, all the mother had to do was to leave the child home with the maid for a few evenings. . . . There is no reason for parents to apologize for setting certain requirements for the child to meet as long as the requirements are reasonable and within the child's capacity to meet. Parents with conflict about their own adult status often need to be reassured that they are not only more powerful than the child but that the child looks to them to exercise a protective parental authority.

Parents can impose certain demands and at the same time be generous in allowing the child discretion in making less essential decisions. Most children accept reasonable restrictions if they have the repeated reassuring experience of having their own desires considered when major decisions are not at stake. It is important, however, that the parent's approach to the subject at issue be clearly defined so that the child knows whether the final answer rests with him or with the parent. It is of equal importance that the child not be forced to assume the responsibility of making decisions until he is capable of doing so. Children are as aware as adults are that they do not have the capacity to judge values in an adult world. They are frightened and confused if required to form judgments in matters beyond their ability, but they gain a sense of well-founded confidence if they can be free to make decisions in matters that are a part of a child's world.

Teachers are expected to maintain discipline in their classrooms. The children of some teachers are relatively well behaved because they love and respect their teachers. In other classrooms, pupils are well behaved because they are fearful of their teachers. In still others, their teachers exercise little or no influence over their pupils, and this lack of discipline becomes a factor in many school dropouts. We may begin to see that the health or ill health of school teachers, the favorable or unfavorable influences they exert in the lives of their pupils may be important factors that determine whether some children continue their schooling or leave their education prematurely. If attending school could be made into a fascinating and exciting experience, it is likely that the present percentages of dropouts would diminish considerably.

The adolescents and young adults whose behavior is characterized by the absence of internal controls and whom we describe as undisciplined are more frequently sentenced to prison for their antisocial behavior than to mental hospitals for reeducation and rehabilitation. It is their unbridled aggressiveness which makes them unsafe and unfit for society, but unfortunately the prisons to which they are so frequently sentenced are not correctional institutions. We know from our years of clinical experience that many of these unfortunate young people are amenable to treatment in suitable hospitals and can ultimately become well-disciplined persons. It is encouraging, indeed, that an increasing number of adolescents are being admitted to such institutions.

Discipline is not to be confused with punishment, nor is it to be related to severity, nor to rules and regulations. The meaning of discipline derives from disciple, and the disciples of today are your pupils and students in your schools. They are disciples insofar as they accept your instructions, but the instructions you give them cannot be separated from yourselves as persons. The medicines prescribed by physicians for their patients are invariably identified by the sick as the doctor's medicine, and for many patients the physician himself is their best medicine. You and your teaching function are one and the same. To the extent that you have the love and the trust and the respect of your pupils they will accept and profit by your teaching and become educated. Education and discipline have the same meaning. In becoming teachers you have identified yourselves with the teachers of your youth. You have followed in their footsteps in the selection of your profession. With our present shortage of teachers in our schools it is of paramount importance that many of the children and young people you are teaching seek to become identified with yourselves and follow the life choice you have selected. Youth cannot learn anything from you unless they first accept you, and this acceptance depends so importantly on the kind of person you are.

# 7. Dynamics of Adolescent Rebellion

JOSEPH D. McGOVERN

Adolescent rebellion is an organized and forceful pattern of resistance to, or defiance and renunciation of, internal or external authority and norms for the purpose of achieving adaptive changes in the structural, dynamic, and economic relationships within the personality and between the individual and the environment.

A popular assumption in adolescent psychology is that rebellion is peculiar to adolescence and is a necessary phase of emancipation and maturation. However, rebellion also occurs in other life phases. It is not the only means available to many adolescents in contemporary society. Not all adolescents rebel. Many conform to ideals of freedom and independence. Some overconform to values of adjustment and authoritarianism.

Adolescent rebellion typically has multiple causes and cannot be sufficiently explained in reductionistic terms of a sovereign or single cause. No extant explanatory system adequately encompasses the distinguishable kinds and degrees of rebellion observable in adolescence.

Because rebellion is understandable only in terms of its referents, it is necessary to characterize rebellious attitudes and behavior relative to authority, freedom, normative standards, group dynamics, developmental tasks and problems, and psychological, familial, social, sociological, and cultural factors and conditions. Rebellious attitudes and behavior can be delineated in terms of:

a. The quality of motives and the quality of goals, for example, whether they are intense or mild, rational or irrational, real or fantastic, compulsive or voluntary, conscious or unconscious, positive or negative.

b. The ways and means by which rebellion is expressed, for example, whether these means are substantial or symbolic, active or passive, chronic or intermittent, overt or covert, direct or indirect, productive or unproductive, partial or complete, successful or unsuccessful.

c. The direction of the effects or consequences of rebellion upon the individual, group, or society, for example, whether these effects are constructive or destructive, reversible or irreversible, functional or dysfunctional, relevant or irrelevant, significant or insignificant, progressive or regressive.

d. The cathected images of persons, objects, or situations which the rebel invests with his vital energy and attention, for example, whether these images are actual or symbolic, central or peripheral, internal or external, beneficial or harmful.

e. The content, structure, and function of the rebellious causes which provide phenomenological and objective bases for understanding.

f. Affiliation with membership and reference groups, and the kind and degree of identification with members, norms, values, goals, practices, and expectations.

## Kinds of Rebellion in Adolescence

The kinds of rebellion are here discussed under the heads of: (1) productive nonconformity, (2) pathological rebellion, (3) compromised insurrection, (4) innovative rebellion, (5) ritualistic rebellion, (6) rebellious retreatism, (7) rebellious resentment, and (8) regressive revolt.

### Productive Nonconformity

Productive nonconformity is positive-constructive rebellion against both internal and external factors and conditions and is expressed in a spontaneous, affirmative, efficacious manner to realize developmental and evolutionary aims; to nourish factors which should be preserved; and to revise or eliminate dehumanizing conditions. It neither vitiates itself, the individual, the group, nor society because it does not function negatively, destructively, randomly, or purposelessly. Its purposes and products are individuation, acculturation, and creative socialization.

The productive nonconformist is one who successfully surmounts, primarily by his own initiative, personal limitations and environmental restrictions. In the process, he usually experiences an identity crisis, the resolution of which permits him to continue his personal development and contribute to the evolution of his culture.

The adolescent who exhibits productive nonconformity is remarkable, extraordinary, and rare, because he expresses his potentialities in an exceptional manner and to an exceptional degree. He is also a catalytic change agent who energizes and recruits others to his cause. He is psychologically successful because he accomplishes his mission. He is able to sustain his psychic equilibrium despite severe stresses of both active and passive resistance on the part of others. He is not masochistic or sadistic because his motives, means, and goals are positive, constructive, and productive.

His developmental history reflects freedom, independence, and achievement training; parental respect, support, and encouragement for decision making and action taking; and opportunities to test the natural consequences of behavior. He has been reared to draw upon his resources, to actualize his capacities, and to exploit potentialities for the benefit of all concerned. His attitudes apparently derive from internalized, integrated values and standards.

He accepts authority as a fact of life, but his relationship to authority is one of critical respect rather than of unreasoning servility. He conforms to cultural values, but when he differs on important issues he can maintain his deviant position despite significant pressures. However, he is willing to entertain and to consider alternatives. Nonconformity as an end in itself he regards as pointless. His typical approach is that practically all situations can use constructive restructuring. Because he can appreciate various facets of an issue, he may occasionally have trouble reaching decisions, but he usually can and does get things done. He is familiar with anxiety because he realizes that society tends to discourage, suppress, and even punish individualism. Nevertheless, he has an urgent need to express his personal qualities altruistically, that is, to alter situations and relationships for the betterment of all concerned. He is also tense and alert because he recognizes discrepancies between actuality and potentiality. He is restless and discontent with the status quo and is determined to participate in progressive change. His readiness and tension motivate him to live a fuller, richer, better life.

He is committed to life rather than being simply engaged in an occupation or vocation for the sake of utilizing his energies. His absorbing commitment consists in a constant and conscious dedication to the ongoing process. He is devoted to a breakthrough into the next dimension of advancement, whatever it may be. He invests himself to the fullest extent and capitalizes—when, where, and as he can—upon his creative and productive capabilities. In such a noble experiment he discovers his own identity and the meaning of life in his era.

He is also a skeptic who nurtures the rational habit of inquiry. He refuses to passively accept testimony or tradition. He has been taught to be skeptical by self-disciplined adults who allowed him opportunities to examine and validate their authoritative communications. His skepticism is a unique quality which signifies a secure sense of personal freedom.

He is also a "field-independent" person who actively attempts to master and reorganize situations. He is concerned both with his subjective life and with the modus of others' behavior. He strives for achievement, independence, leadership, special skills, and competencies. He expresses himself with spontaneity and responsible self-direction and self-control. He is comfortable both when alone and in intimate, non-exploitative relationships.

## Pathological Rebellion

The pathological rebel is one who typically acts out his impulses in an impulsive, uncontrolled, negative-destructive manner without appropriate cause or productive purpose. He apparently rebels for the sake of rebellion, that is, for the immediate gratification of instinctual urges which are acted out in an overt, nonrationalized way. He lacks insight into his own responsibilities. Whatever interferes with the satisfaction of his needs is attacked either directly or indirectly. Even when he succeeds in destroying what he protests against, he does not replace it with anything but reflections of his own distortions. He is motivated by a spirit of negation.

Because of superego defects, he either rebels against social authority and cultural norms without having an integrated set of personal standards to replace them, or he exhibits a confused vacillation between sets of values. Because of his weak, distorted, and ambivalent wishes for relationships with an authority figure, he interprets limitations or restrictions as rejection. Although he exhibits an irrational, destructive, rejecting, and blind hatred of all authority, he also reflects a latent readiness to capitulate and identify with an authority figure. Basically, he masochistically seeks punishment and self-destruction by hostile provocations. His conflicts between isolation and intimacy and his unusual difficulties in heterosexual relationships represent dependency anxiety which is unconsciously bound by mechanisms of denial, projection, and reaction formation.

Although he may exhibit superior psychometric intelligence, he clearly functions below his capacity level in his adaptation to academic and social situations. His narcissism and egocentricity preclude involvement with any problem situations other than his own. Because of his acute needs for status, prestige, power, and recognition, he demands special consideration but does not provide demonstrable grounds upon which he can be regarded as an acceptable exception.

He does not rebel out of a sense of helplessness or an occasional or unusual intensity of impulse, but because his resistance to temptation is weak. Because of his defective superego, his needs for immediate gratifications, and his lack of foresight, he has a propensity to act out his frustrations, conflicts, and problems without due regard for or ability to cope with the consequences. Instead of achieving a synthesis between instinctual and reality demands, he attempts to gratify his impulses despite the reactions of others or of his superego.

His defensive weaknesses and strengths are intertwined in a baffling but effective way. Occasionally, he becomes confused because he cannot manage his impulsivity and compulsiveness in complex situations and relationships. Usually, he shrewdly assesses that part of reality which might be antithetical to his exploits and thereby efficiently manipulates his environment. He frequently manages to get away with deviant behavior and to defend against the threat of punishment by duping others and his own superego so that his acting out can be enjoyed tax free. His lack of personal identity and integrity enables him to adapt in a chameleon fashion. Thus, his defensive system is so efficiently organized that it constitutes a formidable block to both education and reeducation.

He actively battles on four fronts. First, he contends with his own superego in order to freely obtain impulse gratification without guilt, embarrassment, or shame. Second, he avoids those situations which directly imply control or change. Third, he resists intervention by change agents and cleverly appraises change agents to learn how far to act out or provoke before it becomes too dangerous for him. Fourth, he continuously searches for allies and external support for his rebellion.

The pathological rebel exhibits the following typical traits: low frustration tolerance, inability to postpone gratifications, intolerance of authority, antisocial conduct, defective insight and judgment, lack of foresight, shallow emotionality, egocentricity, magical omnipotent thinking, need for status striving, inability to empathize, failure to respect the rights of others, lack of capacity for emotional rapport, lack of genuine guilt, failure to learn from experience, paranoid attitudes, inability to use and understand words in their conventional meaning, pathological immaturity, and diffusion of the instincts.

The classical acting-out dynamisms of pathological rebellion are: defiance, overactivity, negativism, withdrawal, lying, stealing, playing both ends against the middle, self-aggrandizement, grandiosity, exploitation, extraction, hypercompetitiveness, terrorizing, extortion, trickery, deception, crookedness, impulsivity and compulsiveness, a penchant for excesses of all kinds, distrust, deviant sexual behavior, manipulation of others as objects, and redesigning situations to suit his whims.

Pathological rebellion varies in time of onset, reversibility, intensity, and specific traits and dynamisms. It is more conspicuous in some adolescents than in others. In some adolescents, negative-destructive rebellion is clearly the root of their adaptive mode and persists throughout their lives. In others, rebelliousness dominates only in intermittent episodes of acute stress. Otherwise, their typical behavior patterns fall mainly into another diagnostic category.

The pathological rebel is not only antiauthority and antisocial but also antihuman. Social relations are perverted from the purpose of love to hostility and destruction, that is, they are shunted from affection to power for its own sake, for cruelty, and for the experiencing of human beings as objects, agents, and tools rather than as distinct individuals. Basically, this type of behavior reflects an arrest in the processes of socialization, a deformation in the patterns of identification and internalization, and a fixation at an immature, egocentric, omnipotent, manipulative level of adaptation.

Pathological rebellion is a projection of the distorted relations of personal identity, a corresponding disruption in the family ethos, and a lack of communal integration. The intrapsychic and interpersonal aspects are interrelated and interdependent. There is a typical history of conflict and communication difficulties. There is a failure of social and cultural integration. The rebellion expresses itself in warped behavior. The "I" aspect of the personality is continually asserted whereas the "me" aspect is continually denied. In short, the motives, means, and ends of pathological rebellion are negative and destructive.

## Compromised Insurrection

Some authorities contend that the adolescent in contemporary society is confronted by developmental factors and environmental conditions which stimulate him to either adjustment or rebellion. Essentially, the adolescent is required to choose between individuality-autonomy and conformity-adjustment to cultural norms and social sanctions as mediated by superego dictates, ego ideals, and other significant factors.

Because some adolescents do not sufficiently appreciate these alternatives and cannot tolerate the anxiety associated with the conflicts involved, they resort to short-lived unsuccessful insurrections which degenerate into a compromise or magical solution somewhere on the neurotic-psychotic continuum. These compromise formations between rebellion and the imperatives of adjustment are miscarriages of rebellion and miscalculations of adjustment. Under certain conditions of situational stress and ego development, compromised insurrection is the only adaptation of which some adolescents are capable.

Dynamically, compromised insurrection represents ambivalent attempts to serve two masters simultaneously. On the one hand, there is a capacity for positive, affirmative, creative, and rectifying rebellion, and on the other hand, there is a compulsive worship of the graven image of conformity and false gods of adjustment. There is also a lack of understanding and skill in the strategy and tactics of rebellion. Because of a fifth column of ignorance, fear, and ambivalence, and because of the punitive and restrictive reactions of others to rebellious behavior, the half-hearted rebellion typically miscarries and neurotic or psychotic compromise solutions to the conflict between rebellious urges and the imperatives of adjustment are established and reenforced.

Compromised insurrection is typically regressive, unproductive, destructive, and expensive. Some adolescents whose rebellions have miscarried do not make an abject, total surrender of sacrificing their individuality, but many of them, for a variety of reasons, eventually yield their struggles, relinquish their symptoms, or withdraw into isolation. In general, they suffer out by inverting their rebellion upon themselves rather than by acting out upon the environment.

In short, some adolescents in contemporary society are limited in their capacities and opportunities to rebel successfully. Consequently, their rebellious urges are expressed in an insurrection which miscarries and yields to compromise solutions on the continuum of neurosis-psychosis. Although their rebellious potential may remain strong, it is limited by a lack of means and opportunities to extravert it positively, by a lack of competence and resoluteness to rebel successfully, and by the overwhelming counterreactions of both their superegos and significant others in their environment.

## Innovative Rebellion

The innovative rebel typically identifies with the culturally prescribed goals of material success and social status, but rejects the institutionalized means to these goals. The combination of the universal emphasis upon cultural goals and the lack of uniform distribution of practical, approved means to reach these goals in the various strata of society produces intense precipitating pressures for innovative rebellion. When the socioeconomic class structure is not fully open at each level to individuals of capacity who are ambitious for success, achievement of the cultural success goal by legitimate means is relatively rare and notably difficult. The dominant pressure leads the predisposed individual, that is, the insufficiently socialized but capable and ambitious individual, toward the gradual abandonment of legitimate but ineffectual avenues and toward an increasing use of illegitimate but more effective expedients.

Thus, the frequency of innovative rebellion is not only generated by cultural emphasis upon material success, and by a lack of social opportunities, but also by cultural systems that exaggeratedly extol common success goals for everyone while the social structure rigorously restricts or denies access to approved modes of reaching these goals for a considerable number of people. When an egalitarian ideology holds that the success symbols apply to all despite the fact that the actual social organization is such that there exist class differentials in accessibility of symbols, the predisposed adolescent resorts to innovative rebellion. When economic and educational deprivation, limited civil opportunity, and associated disadvantages in competing for the cultural values approved for all members of the society are linked with a universal cultural emphasis upon material success as the dominant assigned goal without differentiation according to class, innovative rebellion is the expected reaction in predisposed, capable, and ambitious adolescents.

Innovative rebels are not necessarily aware of the sociological sources of their thwarted aspirations, that is, the universal cultural emphasis upon material success and the class hindrances to full opportunity. They may be more inclined to attribute their difficulty to mystical sources, for example, the workings of fortune, chance, and luck. The "doctrine of luck" as expounded by the successful innovative rebel serves the dual function of explaining the discrepancy between his merits and rewards while condoning the social structure which allows the discrepancy to persist. If success is primarily a matter of luck, it is beyond human control and will occur in the same measure whatever the social structure. The "doctrine of luck" serves the psychological function of enabling the unsuccessful innovative rebel to preserve his self-esteem in the instance of failure by the process of rationalization. The "doctrine of luck" may also invite resignation, routinized activity, ritualism, and fatalistic passivity in less innovative rebels.

The innovative rebel typically eschews approved institutional means but retains his aspirations for the culturally prescribed goals of material success and social status. However, he not only resorts to illicit means to these goals but also simultaneously exhibits negativism and destructiveness which have little utilitarian character or calculated rationality. The latter are probably a function not only of acute stresses created by the discrepancy between culturally induced goals and socially structured opportunities, but also of previously experienced frustrations and failures. Thus, the rebel's destructiveness and negativism may represent a chronic state of frustration which is expressed in terms of a sustained repudiation of a society which exemplifies the paradox of legitimized cultural aspirations and restricted social opportunities.

Because of his disadvantaged position as well as his distinctive personality configuration, the innovative rebel is more vulnerable than other adolescents to the stresses and frustrations arising from the discrepancy between cultural ideals and effective access to their practical realization. In addition, if his innovative departures from institutional means are personally and socially rewarded by successful achievement of cultural goals, his deviant but successful behavior tends to attenuate the legitimacy of prescribed institutional means for both him and others in similar situations. As a result, anomie spreads, is reenforced, and, in turn, creates more acutely anomic situations for those adolescents who are less vulnerably disposed initially. Thus, anomie and innovative rebellion may be conceived as dynamic processes of personal, social, and cultural interaction with cumulatively disruptive consequences for the individual, for others, and for the normative structure unless effective remedial or control mechanisms are activated.

## Ritualistic Rebellion

Ritualistic rebellion, in contrast to innovative rebellion, is a frustration-response pattern in which culturally defined aspirations and expectations are perceived as threatening or frustrating, and are inhibited or abandoned while the adolescent continues to cling compulsively to established institutional norms and approved social practices. Ritualism, exemplified in some dancing and dating patterns, involves the devaluation of the cultural goals of material success and vertical social mobility which inherently involve the threat of frustration and failure in the intense and ceaseless competitive struggle. The culturally induced obligation to attempt to get ahead in the world is displaced onto a compulsive conformity to institutional rules which are literally interpreted.

It may be questioned whether ritualistic rebellion constitutes a genuine rebellion because the overt behavior is culturally permitted though not preferred. Whether or not ritualistic rebellion is considered to be true rebellion, it clearly represents a significant deviation from the cultural model toward which every adolescent is expected to strive actively, preferably through institutionalized means, in order to move onward and upward in the societal hierarchy.

In contemporary society where the adolescent's status is largely dependent upon his continued achievement of cultural goals, the competitive process produces status anxiety. Ritualistic rebellion is designed to allay status anxiety by lowering one's aspiration level and engaging in substitutive routinized activity. Acute status anxiety in situations which overemphasize the achievement motif may induce ritualistic overconformity and overcompliance to established rules and practices. The anxious and insecure adolescent responds to potentially threatening and distressing situations by clinging more tenaciously and rigidly to institutional norms and routines. He thereby becomes less consciously anxious and insecure and more self-satisfied and proud because he perceives himself as modest, prudent, unpretending, voluntarily self-restrained in his ambitions, and indifferent to competition which entails risk, exposure, and ambiguity. Thus, the ritualistic rebel has learned not to stick his neck out, but to play it safe, to be satisfied with what he has, to avoid involvement, and to keep his head low. The rationale is that ambitious striving only invites more frustration and disappointment, whereas literal rule keeping guarantees satisfaction, security, and approval.

The ritualistic rebel insures reliability and predictability of response by strict allegiance to regulations which he transforms into absolutes and which he no longer conceives as relative to situations or purposes. However, his literal adherence to rules interferes with a ready and easy adaptation to special or unforeseeable conditions. His ritualistic conformity to those rules which conduce toward adaptive efficiency in general produce maladaptive inefficiency in specific instances. Full realization of this consequence is seldom attained by the ritualistic rebel because he does not distinguish between the symbolic and utilitarian values of rule keeping.

Ritualistic rebellion is a function of lower middle-class family patterns of discipline and socialization which promote characterological predispositions toward scrupulosity. This rebellion is implicit in those adolescents who carefully regulate their initiative and productivity to a constant quota in situations where they have occasion to fear that some drastic reaction may occur if their behavior varies.

Ritualistic rebellion may also be a response to previous unsuccessful attempts at rebellious innovation. Some reactive ritualists conform meticulously to institutional rules because of unresolved guilt feelings engendered by previous acts of nonconformity. Infrequent, defiant outbreaks of illicit behavior may also result from prolonged periods of ritualistic overcompliance.

## Rebellious Retreatism

The rebellious retreatist is a true alien in society not only because he relinquishes culturally prescribed goals, but also because his behavior is inconsistent with institutional norms and practices.

Rebellious retreatism typically occurs in situations where the adolescent has assimilated both the cultural goals and institutional means, has imbued them with affect and value, but has not succeeded in using the legitimate institutional means available to him. He feels obligated to reach the goals by approved institutional means which are not sufficiently available or effective. If he cannot reach his goal by legitimate measures and is unable to use illegitimate means because of internalized prohibitions, he retreats from his frustrations and conflicts by abandoning both his quest for cultural goals and his utilization of institutional means. Because he feels inadequate, frustrated, or handicapped, he drops out of the competitive process. If his escape from the cultural prescriptions and social requirements is complete, his conflict is eliminated. However, he is considered asocialized and a nonproductive liability by society. He reacts to this additional conflict by resigning himself to his lack of any claim to virtue or distinction, negating any value in the goals of material success and social status which our culture prizes, and withdrawing from and ignoring the institutional practices. He becomes a quiet, resigned, passive "nobody" who eventually joins the ranks of ne'er-do-wells and misfits in society.

### Rebellious Resentment

Rebellious resentment in adolescence involves the continuous experiencing of diffused feelings of craving, envy, frustration, and hostility, together with a sense of impotence to actively direct these feelings against those persons or situations evoking them.

In comparison with other forms of adolescent rebellion, rebellious resentment is truncated and does not involve a genuine change in values but rather a sour-grapes attitude which merely asserts that prescribed and desired but unattainable cultural goals do not actually embody real satisfaction. The resentful rebel does not abandon his craving for sweet grapes but communicates only that certain grapes are sour. Active rebellion, on the other hand, leads to a more complete and genuine denunciation of previously prized values and/or the prevailing means to these values. Rebellion is a transvaluation because it renounces the taste for sweet grapes and/or the means to them. Although rebellion and resentment are distinct, adolescent rebellion draws upon the reservoir of sour-grapes resentment in contemporary society.

### Regressive Revolt

Some adolescents, by virtue of their fixated personality development, overtly revolt for the covert motive of satisfying their infantile dependency needs in the form of a submissive and compliant adjustment to authoritarianism.

Regressive revolt is actually a masking of rebellion, or a pretense. It is neither designed to realize absolute freedom, nor is it conducted in the service of hostility. It is not in the interest of ontogenetic development or phylogenetic evolution, but it is a personal regression to a more primitive level of development and functioning. It represents an adaptational failure in which the individual's needs for emotional security and succorance outweigh his needs for self-identity, freedom, and independence. It is actually a helpless response to frustration and conflict by which the individual attempts to manipulate a self-ordered relationship to an authoritarian leader who commands slavish submission in return for protection and nurturance.

To obtain the regressive security and satisfactions of infantile dependency in an authoritarian relationship without experiencing guilt or a loss of self-esteem, the adolescent *pretends* rebellion by revolting in an attention-getting, provocative manner to the point where an authoritarian leader restrictively intervenes.

In short, regressive revolt is unconsciously used as a means to the end of infantile adjustment, conflict-free satisfaction, and protection in a symbiotic relationship with an authoritarian leader.

### Adolescent Rebellion and the Concept of Freedom

Insofar as the adolescent is a member of a social and cultural order, he is not absolutely free but must surrender his individuality and spontaneity to a degree. His decisions and actions are relative to situations, relationships, and conditions. This relativity does not mean that his life is completely determined by outside forces but that his freedom is limited by necessity, circumscribed by reality, and bounded by his capabilities.

Freedom does not exist in the abstract because it is relative to time, place, and relationships. The adolescent is a particular, specific social being who is free to the limits of his freedom. His is a true freedom based upon the immediate recognition of necessity as a limiting factor and operating according to actuality rather than fantasy. Within the limits of reality, he can exercise his uniqueness, freedom, and responsibility in a relatively unencumbered manner.

Many middle- and upper-class adolescents in contemporary society are confronted with a condition of considerable freedom, that is, a multiplicity of choices and actions. However, this condition unavoidably involves the potential consequences of frustration and failure. A plethora of alternatives can be more anxiety-provoking and frustrating than a lack of socioeconomic opportunities. Thus, considerable freedom aggravates more than it alleviates the adolescent's insecurity, because freedom involves the necessity for individual responsibility for the consequences of decisions and actions.

Most adolescents define their limits of freedom by reality testing, that is, by making rational estimates based on the testimony of authority or the results of experiment. They also continuously validate their ideas and actions by analysis of feedback data. However, the adolescent rebel typically exhibits defective reality testing. He distorts reality according to his fantasy images and he confuses the coextension of himself with reality. He fears reality and systematically avoids testing it to the point that his misperception, and not objective reality, becomes the determinant of his attitudes and behavior.

Because the adolescent rebel typically deprecates the present (one form of reality) and rejects himself (another form of reality), he misperceives reality and typically reacts by rebelling against freedom. He wants exemption from freedom because its responsibility is an irksome and unrewarding burden. Of what avail is freedom to choose and to act if the present is not real and the self is ineffectual? What is worth doing compared to what has been left undone?

For the rational concept of relative freedom, the adolescent rebel substitutes the fantastic concept of absolute freedom, that is, the despotism of license. Basically, he seeks an escape from the burdens, responsibilities, anxieties, frustrations, and despair of his untenable individual existence. He considers rebellion as a means of deliverance and redemption. However, he really seeks equality and uniformity, not freedom. When he clamors for freedom, it is the freedom to establish the condition of equality or anonymity by which he cannot be designated, distinguished, measured against others or norms, or exposed for what he thinks he is.

Although he demands freedom he is likely to be most unhappy in a truly free situation. Actually, his unconscious wish is to eliminate the competition, testing, and measurement to which the individual is continually subjected in a free society. In short, he protests too much. He does not desire relative freedom but desires license, which consists in absolute freedom from those opportunities which involve the assumption of responsibility for uncertain consequences. He does not want freedom of opportunity but anonymity in the form of equality and uniformity. His concept of absolute freedom is a rebellious myth which is not only impossible but also undesirable. Even if he could escape into chaos and anarchism he would not be a happy savage but a compulsive, fearful, dependent person.

### Adolescent Rebellion and Some Concepts of Authority

Because adolescent rebellion connotes resistance to or defiance of authority, clear concepts of authority are essential to the development of a systematic understanding. Although authority is usually referred to in an indiscriminate manner, it can be analyzed and classified into two distinct categories, each of which contains several important aspects.

A. *Formal Authority,* which is derived from:
1. *Authority of Legitimacy,* which, unlike the related notions of power and influence, implies ethical sanctification. For example, a parent's formal authority is a function of the ethical legitimacy of the parental status role.
2. *Authority of Positions,* including the sanctions inherent in the position, is the power of influence and control which derives from the acknowledged status associated with the position and not from the particular occupant of the position. For example, a person in a position of authority has the delegated right to demand obedience and the delegated power to reward conformity and punish deviation. Those subject to the position have a duty to respect and obey.
B. *Functional Authority,* which is derived from:
1. *Authority of Competence,* which includes appropriate knowledge, ability, and experience.
2. *Authority of Person,* which includes leadership and human relations skills based upon reason or the potentiality of reasoned elaboration.

In general, functional authority enhances formal authority and a relative lack of functional authority will attenuate formal authority. Authority of legitimacy and position almost invariably must be supported by the demonstrable competence and human-relations skills of the person who occupies the position.

The exercise of authority in the family situation is related to the child's development of the capacity to reason and to assume responsibility. In the beginning, the infant is helplessly dependent upon the parents. Their authority is almost absolute in the early phases of the child's development but it is gradually replaced by reasonable communications as the child matures. As the child increasingly identifies with parental demands, expectations, opinions, and beliefs, he internalizes them and discipline is transformed into self-discipline.

Most parents contribute to insight development by seeking to develop in the child an understanding of and a participation in their reasons for requiring obedience. Authoritative communications of the parent, whether opinions or commands, are not transmitted through rational dialogue alone. Because they possess the potentiality of reasoned elaboration, however, they are worthy of acceptance.

Thus, functional authority indicates that the person in a position of formal authority possesses the capacity to issue authoritative communications that are based on implicit or explicit reasoning and are related to knowledge, opinions, beliefs, and values which are or can be shared by everyone in the communications network. For example, some parents attenuate their authority over their children because they issue authoritative communications which do not allow for reasoned elaboration or validation. The falseness of their authoritative communication is revealed when the pretended potentiality of reasoned elaboration has to be actualized. In short, parental authority is most secure when the communications can be potentially reasoned upon, defended, or supported by valid and reliable evidence.

One might erroneously assume that adolescent rebellion is characterized by a rejection of formal authority as illegitimate, irrational, or tyrannical, and its substitution by individual reliance upon reason and reasoning. One might also presume that authority and reason are somehow the bases of rival methods of reaching the truth. However, authority and reason are not antithetical. Formal authority has a basis in reason and also rests upon the capacity of functional authority to issue authoritative communications which are capable of reasoned elaboration.

There is no inherent contradiction between an adolescent's reliance on authority and his reliance on reason. Authoritative communications rest upon their correctness and consistency with other information as obtained by other means from other sources. Authoritarianism, on the other hand, does not rely upon its correctness or consistency but on its capacity to mete out arbitrary rewards for conformity and arbitrary punishments for deviation.

In the light of the foregoing, adolescent rebellion is not a necessary means of emancipation from authority, nor is it necessarily based upon reason and implicit or explicit reasoning. Adolescent rebellion may be viewed as a closed state of mind involving a certain kind of relation between the individual and authority, a relation wherein the rebel is psychologically unaware that he cannot distinguish, evaluate, and act independently on communications received from authority. He rationalizes his rebellious attitudes and behavior so that he will not expose to himself or to others his dependency on authority and so that he can maintain the illusion that he is an independent, reasonable, and reasoning person.

Thus, when one examines a rebellious adolescent, one should not take at face value the manifest content of the information the adolescent consciously provides about his rebellious attitudes and behavior but should carefully evaluate the functional, structural, and dynamic processes of his relationships with authority. Adolescent rebellion is a state of mind about persons in positions of authority which is arrived at through the complex processes of perception, identification, internalization, rationalization, and projection. This mentality enables the rebel to believe what he believes and to act as he acts, under the illusion that he does so of his own free reason and will without realizing that his attitudes and behavior are overdetermined. In other words, the rebel's attitudes and behavior are a function of his perception of the situation and his relationship with the person in position of authority. The meaning which he attributes to authority, not the authority itself, accounts for his rebellious attitudes and behavior.

Adolescent rebellion does not necessarily imply a completely negative perception of and an absolute rejection of authority. Identification or lack of identification with authority is not a dichotomous black-white or all-or-none phenomenon. The authority figures with which the rebel does or does not identify are arranged on a graduated continuum which is positive at one extreme and negative at the other. Consequently, his attitudes and behavior toward various authorities vary according to their position on the perceptual continuum. He accepts or rejects authority according to its degree of similarity or dissimilarity with his own attitudes and beliefs. Thus, the magnitude of his acceptance or rejection of any authority varies as a function of its congruence with his belief-disbelief system.

The rebellious adolescent who seeks to discredit the authority of an individual, group, institution, or creed may do so not because he believes that the formal authority is illegitimate and/or arbitrary, but because he regards the functional authority as incomplete and/or unreasonable. If he reacts negatively to functional authority, he will generalize his rebellion to authority as a whole. He will tend to detach his allegiance from authority, rise up against it, ridicule it, deride it as irrational and incompetent, denounce it as illegitimate and oppressive, and demand absolute freedom of self-expression and self-realization.

The doctrine and slogans of the adolescent's rebellious cause constitute the manifest content of his rebellion against authority. If this rebellious content is taken at face value, phenomenological and objective reality will be confused and the rebellious cause will be articulated largely in terms of authority. However, if the structural, functional, and dynamic attributes of the rebellious cause are defined and measured, it will be found that the adolescent rebel typically acts out less against the wickedness of formal authority than against the failures of functional authority. He is not entirely convinced of the vileness of formal authority, but is certain about the impotence and incompetence of functional authority. By attacking all aspects of authority the rebel seeks to avoid the fearful burden of freedom and arduous responsibility of trying to realize his ineffectual self under unfavorable conditions of authoritative judgment. He seeks to sweep away the established authority, not to create a new order of rationality, freedom, and independence, but to establish a new structure of perfect unity with another form of authority. He does not seek the freedom of conscience and intellect, but instead the security of faith in some kind of authority. Thus, the adolescent rebel lacks both authority and freedom because his rebellion against authority is not based upon reason or the potentiality of reasoned elaboration.

### Adolescent Rebellion and the Concept of Norms

The abstract concept of adolescent rebellion is also a normative problem. Whether or not the referent is made explicit, the adolescent rebel usually deviates from the prevailing, customary, prescribed, or expected values in his particular surroundings. Of itself, no attitude or behavior can be characterized as rebellious unless it is assessed relative to some promise, canon, standard, value, or norm.

A norm is an expected or ideal mode of behavior for the members of a group. It is a group quality, a sociological phenomenon, which the individual internalizes and expresses in terms of his social attitudes and behavior. The adolescent's attitudes toward persons, groups, and symbols; his self-identity, stability, and security; and his strivings toward practical and ideal goals consist largely of normative data derived from his group membership during his lifetime.

Norms are not devoid of motivational dynamics and emotional contents. In fact, norms arise and are stabilized relative to motivationally important relationships and activities. Significant issues of both conformity and deviation arise relative to norms which pertain to matters of consequence to the group's existence, perpetuation, cohesion, efficient functioning, and effective achievement of major interests and goals.

Another referent of adolescent rebellion is the individual's particular status, his position in his group relationships. This referent is the group dynamics basis of the problem of adolescent rebellion, which can be more effectively identified and understood relative to significant persons and groups who stand in specifiable relationships to the rebel. Rebellious behavior is much more understandable when it is analyzed within the social field of interpersonal relationships. When the problem of adolescent rebellion is formulated within the framework of group dynamics, it becomes an integral and continuous function of interpersonal relationships, and not just an incidental issue. Within the concreteness of group relations as expressed in the actualities of everyday life, the problem of adolescent rebellion acquires functional significance.

In our highly differentiated contemporary society, the adolescent belongs to and is influenced by a number of different groups. His multiple group affiliations often place contradictory and conflicting demands and expectations upon him for his attitudes and behavior in given dimensions. The adolescent rebel may be conceived of as one who seems to be out of step with the procession because he is keeping time to another tune. This behavior is termed "remote conformity." For example, rebellion against the norms of one group may represent conformity to the norms of another group. It has been concluded that there is, therefore, no definite line between conformity and nonconformity; there are simply more or less characteristic or unusual ways of selecting and combining accessible influences. Thus, rebellious behavior can be adequately described in terms of the individual's membership in reference groups, considered as frames of normative and evaluative reference.

Conformity usually denotes internalization of the norms and expectations current in the adolescent's membership groups. Thus, public conformity to out-group norms is equivalent to what is ordinarily called rebellion, that is, public nonconformity to in-group norms. Truly private nonconformity, wholly unconnected with past, present, or realistically prospective reference-group norms, is autism, that is, capricious thought and action divorced from external reality. Adolescent rebellion is not autism because it is public, not private nonconformity.

When adolescent rebellion represents conformity to the values, standards, and practices of a reference group which is still enduring but is not uniformly accepted, it is often described as "conservatism" and pejoratively as "reactionary," particularly when it constitutes an effort to reintroduce values and practices which have been superseded or have become obsolete. When adolescent rebellion represents conformity to values, standards, and practices which have not yet been institu-

tionalized, but are regarded as the normative system of a future reference group, it is often described as "radicalism" and pejoratively as
"utopianism," particularly when it is believed to be impossible to
attain.

The reference-group issue is confounded by the fact that sizable
power differentials exist among various groups to which the adolescent belongs. The average adolescent has overlapping membership in,
and simultaneously relates himself psychologically to, various groups.
If the norms of various groups conflict and if the attractiveness of one
group is greater than that of the others, he will identify more with his
reference-group norms. His goal is not a state of normlessness, but the
attainment of standards which are not conflicting, frustrating, or self-
degrading. Thus, the adolescent who establishes one group as his
reference group, while maintaining membership in various other groups,
will psychologically relate and transfer his allegiance to the reference-
group norms. This transfer of loyalties, interests, and sentiments from
one group to another is a major socialization process in adolescence
and may precipitate a developmental crisis. The adolescent is expected
to live simultaneously in different groups, at a time when he lacks
mature insight into the peculiarities of life, society, culture, adults, and
peers. If his membership groups have incompatible norms, he may
experience frustration, hostility, and resentment, and will express his
normative conflicts by deviating from some and conforming to other
group norms.

The adolescent rebel does not try to hide his departures from the
prevailing norms of his membership groups. Instead, he communicates
his dissent and challenges or denies the legitimacy of the norms, or at
least their applicability to certain situations. His aim is to change or
supplant what he considers to be inappropriate, illegitimate, or arbitrary norms with an alternative normative basis.

In terms of group dynamics, the adolescent rebel's normative behavior activates regulative responses of social influence and control on the
part of those involved with him in interlocking networks of social
status roles. His failures to live up to the expectations of those with
whom he is in direct relationship constitute a threatening experience
for them. Because he makes their lives miserable or difficult, they try
to get him to conform so that they can go about their business. Even
those who are not directly engaged in a system of social relations with
the rebel respond with hostility to his deviations because they have
internalized the norms being violated. His rebellious behavior, in effect,

repudiates these norms or threatens their continued efficacy. Thus, other people typically react with indignation even when the rebellious behavior does not interfere with their role performance and even when they are not directly socially related to the rebel. If this reservoir of indignation did not exist, application of social-control mechanisms would be limited only to those who are directly disadvantaged by rebellious behavior. However, general indignation and opposition to rebellious behavior is mobilized because the latter is not only a threat to those who are directly involved, but it is also a repudiation of the society which sponsors the culturally established norms.

On the other hand, the adolescent rebel, with his typical appeal to a "higher morality," can, in historically propitious circumstances, draw strength from this latent source of indignation. Because it appeals either to the values of a past or future reference group, his rebellious behavior has a prospect of gaining the support of the initially less venturesome but restless members of society. Rebelliousness is not then a private dereliction but an explicit thrust toward a novel, historical, or ideal morality. Thus, the rebel activates or reactivates a set of norms, values, goals, standards, and practices of a real or ideal reference group which he deems less attenuated by practical concessions or expedient compromises with current realities.

In terms of the cultural and social structure, the adolescent rebel is a known deviant who incurs the risk of punishment for his behavior. He may even see himself as a martyr who persists in sacrificing himself for a sentiment, principle, or romantic ideal. Adhering to the norms, values, and practices of some reference group and resisting the expectations of his membership groups, he may accept and even welcome the probable and painful consequences of provocative public dissent.

Adolescent rebellion may be dysfunctional, or it may be instrumental in leading to constructive individual, social, and cultural changes. In any event, it exerts pressure for change. When social mechanisms for controlling rebellion are operating effectively, the tensions are kept within bounds and change in the social structure is imperceptible. Rebellion is no more dysfunctional for society than conformity is necessarily functional.

The indignant and oppositional reactions of significant others to adolescent rebellious behavior are more ambivalent than the apparently unalloyed manifestations might suggest. The rebel may be regarded with mixed feelings of resentment, admiration, respect, envy, and love, even by those who uphold the norms being placed in jeopardy. Acting openly rather than secretively and evidently aware that he invites group sanctions, the rebel may elicit positive responses, even among those whose sentiments, interests, and security are threatened by his deviant and iconoclastic behavior. Because he is apparently honest, dedicated, courageous, and willing to "shoot the works," and because these traits are potentially virtuous and functional for individual and social preservation and development in accord with ultimate values, he elicits positive regard even when he effectively prevails against the established norms.

When a normative conflict develops in a group situation, a solution is sought which is acceptable to most of the members and which adequately reduces the tensions aroused by the conflict. However, if the rebel rejects or interferes with the group's solution, he is perceived as a deviant by the majority. When this discord occurs, the anxieties and tensions come to the fore as a common group problem that must be dealt with by the group. In order to deal with the rebellious threat to the group's integrity, the members reenforce the group solution to the problem or deviation by influencing the rebel to conform to the norms, by reinterpreting the rebel's behavior so that it no longer threatens the solution, by modifying the solution so that it encompasses the rebel's deviant behavior, or by changing the normative system of the group.

From the adolescent's point of view, the rebellious crisis occurs when the interpersonal conflicts develop in resonance with certain unresolved personal conflicts. When the group conflict and the personal conflict are fused, the individual is likely to attempt solutions which were previously efficacious in dealing with the primary conflict. He becomes more rebellious when he rigidly acts out his own solution to the detriment of the group solution.

It would be unrealistic to dwell upon adolescent rebellious behavior that is considered peripheral to the normative standards of the groups affected. It is also recognized that value judgments about deviant behavior in a particular group or situation may or may not be significant and relevant to societal, cultural, and moral laws. Although normative deviations in noncritical areas of behavior may signify deviations in critical areas, rebellious behavior in adolescence is not necessarily important or worthy of serious consideration unless it forms a pattern which significantly threatens the integrity of the person, group, society, or culture.

# 8. Two Case Studies in Discipline and Rebellion

ALEXANDER A. SCHNEIDERS

JOSEPH D. McGOVERN

## The Rebel in the Family
(ALEXANDER A. SCHNEIDERS)

### The Causes of Rebellion

The preceding paper on the dynamics of adolescent rebellion has explored with unusual clarity and thoroughness the factors that underlie and promote rebellion. It indicates in particular the specific gains that the rebel hopes to derive from his behavior in the home or in society. What we would like to do here, primarily through the medium of the case-study technique, is to explore those relationships within the family that set the stage for rebellious behavior.

Let us begin with the case of a boy whom we shall call Henry. He was a good-looking, seventeen-year-old junior in an exclusive private school for boys, located in one of the many suburbs of New York City. Henry's family was prominent and wealthy, and he was the oldest of five children which included three boys and two girls. Henry's father was an eminently successful lawyer and his mother a professional school teacher.

Henry first came to the attention of the guidance counselor at the school because of excessive absences, conflict with other students, and rebellious attitudes toward teachers. This behavior was a reflection of the home situation, wherein the relationship between Henry and his father was always at a point of complete rupture. Henry's mother was an unusually gentle and somewhat passive person who was disposed toward protecting her oldest son from the demands of the father. Henry's father, on the other hand, was just the opposite. In his opinion, the more children are disciplined, restricted, deprived, and punished, the better they will turn out to be. He repeatedly imposed curfews on the rebellious Henry, denied him the use of the family car for one or two weeks at a time, and insisted on intruding into every one of the boy's personal relationships, whether with other boys or with girls, in order to make sure that Henry would not be victimized by "bad company." There were also times when the father, a man of considerable size and strength, would strike the young man with his fist in order to "teach him a lesson."

For his part, there is no question that Henry was a very angry young man whose continuous conflict with his father had spilled over into other situations and relationships. His rebellious behavior at school clearly reflected the frustration and the anger caused by the father's totally inept discipline. It also reflected conflict in attitudes between Henry's mother and father, so that the behavior was also in part an expression of Henry's confusion regarding his relationships with the significant persons in his life. An intelligent young man, Henry indicated in his counseling sessions that he was aware of the inappropriateness and the danger of the course that he was following, both at home and at school, but took the position that there was no alternative for him to follow. He stated clearly that if he did not resist the inordinate and thoughtless demands of his father, he would lose all identity and individuality of his own and thus become a mere puppet to his father's wishes. As Henry evaluated the situation, rebellion was his only hope for independence and individuality.

### The Logic of Rebellion

Henry's case is a fairly typical one that would find its analog in the files of every counselor working with young people. In some cases it is the girl in the family who is the acting-out rebel; in other instances, the background is somewhat different from Henry's, but the dynamics remain pretty much the same. In many of these cases rebellion appears to the adolescent as the only means of rescuing, protecting, or defining his own individuality. Just as conflict is to an important extent necessary for sharpening the boundaries of the ego, so also rebellion is often necessary for ego identity and for functional independence. At this point of rebellion it is crucial that parents learn how to guide the adolescent to strike a balance between a stultifying conformity and an extreme independence that can lead him to serious consequences. When rebellion against parental demands and restrictions spills over—as it often does in the case of teenage girls—into sexual misbehavior and other socially disapproved conduct, the price for independence is much too high. I have seen many instances of young girls whose rebellion against the parents and their all too rigid codes has ended in the tragedy of pregnancy, venereal disease, or wholesale promiscuity. It is this sort of outcome that parents must guard against most carefully

Returning to the case of Henry, it is abundantly clear that he was striking out in every direction against an authoritarian, rigid disciplinarian whose love for his son was overshadowed by his love for the law. It is not uncommon to see lawyers and judges and others devoted to upholding and enforcing civil laws treating their children much the same way that they would treat legal offenders. The professional lawyer and judge has obviously committed himself to the side of the law and tends to regard offenses more harshly than do others for whom the law has a less personal meaning. In fact, it is not at all unlikely that their dim view of any wrongdoing is part of the motivation for their choice of a career in the legal profession. Certainly, this motivation was strong in Henry's father, who regarded himself as the guardian of public morals.

But there is more to Henry's story than the father's motivations. It has been observed clinically in countless instances that rebellion is often related to the child's position in the family. The chances of the firstborn son or the firstborn daughter becoming the rebel in the home are considerably greater than for children who occupy another position in the family. Time does not permit a thorough exploration of the dynamics of this factor, but certainly it is known that younger, overanxious parents are much more prone to overdiscipline and overcontrol the firstborn children than those who are born later on. With experience there is greater wisdom in the handling of children's development, and just as often a mellowing of the disciplinary attitudes. With the firstborn children, the damage to relationships is often done long before the parent has profited from his own experiences and growth. Henry was undoubtedly the victim of this type of inadequate relationship, as he was a victim of the inconsistency in disciplinary approach between the mother and the father. As he saw the situation, therefore, Henry had no alternative but to exploit rebellion in the service of individuality and ego identity. After several months of fairly intensive counseling the young

man developed a more realistic attitude toward the family situation, at the same time that the parents were encouraged to modify their own disciplinary attitudes so as to make rebellion less necessary for their maturing adolescent. But rebellion runs deep, and counseling is not always successful in modifying behavior patterns that have become embedded in the human personality.

## A Case of Adolescent Rebellion
(JOSEPH D. McGOVERN)

During the Christmas season several years ago a middle-aged wife of a professional man and mother of eleven children voluntarily visited me for counseling. Approximately one year earlier, her first child, a twenty-year-old daughter, had physically withdrawn from the home to marry as a result of a premarital pregnancy. Recently, her second child, a nineteen-year-old daughter, followed suit by dramatically, abruptly, and violently establishing herself independently of the family on the grounds that her parents were "crazy" and had used her as a "slave" in the home. The mother expressed concern about:

1. The scandalous effects of the withdrawal of her two oldest daughters on her reputation as a devout Catholic and Christian mother.

2. The continuing influence of the two oldest daughters on her adolescent children through bad example and covert communications.

3. The moral and spiritual welfare of her nineteen-year-old daughter and how she could get her daughter to return to parental control.

4. Her own mental, emotional, and physical health. She had low blood pressure; weighed only one hundred pounds; had a thyroid deficiency; was dangerously dehydrated; was emotionally exhausted and depressed; was obsessively preoccupied with the problematic behavior of her older daughters, the care of her younger children, the burdens of an invalid parent and an alcoholic relative who lived with the family, financial insecurity, and apprehension about the rebellious behavior of her two mid-adolescent daughters.

After the mother visited several times she decided to discontinue counseling for financial reasons. She was definitively informed that the family situation was disruptive and it was predicted that other rebellious acts of defection would follow the established family pattern unless both she and her husband entered marital or family counseling to resolve or control their destructive contributions to the problem situations. She passively resisted these interpretations of parental involvement in the family disruption and claimed that continued counseling would constitute an additional financial stress. Consequently, she was referred to a public facility and was firmly advised to encourage her husband to participate in the counseling process if it were recommended.

Several weeks later a priest telephoned the counselor and stated that the nineteen-year-old daughter whom he was seeing in pastoral counseling had claimed that her mother had informed her that she had been professionally advised that she (the mother) had no problems as the daughter alleged, that the daughter was at fault in her ungrateful attitudes and behavior, and that the daughter should return to her family. The priest volunteered his opinion that it was the parents rather than the daughter who contributed most to the family difficulties and it was the parents who needed to change.

Shortly thereafter, the father telephoned to inquire whether the counselor had notified the priest about the family situation and was informed that he had not. The father volunteered that his nineteen-year-old daughter had told the priest falsehoods about his wife because she was a "pathological liar" and a "troublemaker." The father also warned the counselor that if he were to divulge any confidential information to an unauthorized person he would be subject to legal prosecution. The father was directly advised that both he and his wife should pursue the counselor's previous recommendation because it was now even more necessary than previously.

Three months later the father telephoned that his fifteen- and fourteen-year-old daughters had run away from home and inquired about what he should do. He was again advised to enter counseling when the daughters were returned home by whatever prudent means he chose to exercise as a professional man and as a father.

Several months later both parents visited the counselor and revealed that they had attended a community agency which had diagnosed their problem as due to parental factors and family conditions. Thereupon they had initiated family counseling together with their fifteen- and fourteen-year-old daughters, but the fifteen-year-old was so overtly hostile and destructive in her communications about her parents in the initial counseling sessions that the mother had attempted suicide. Because of this attempt and the mother's subsequent refusal to participate, the father decided that group counseling was not appropriate and consequently discontinued visiting the family-service agency. The father then decided to refer the two daughters to the counselor because of his familiarity with the family situation. This decision was acceptable to the counselor on the condition that the mother independently enter therapy with a psychiatrist of her own choice. They agreed to abide by these terms.

The two daughters were subsequently interviewed and examined individually on a diagnostic basis. It was revealed that both were in an acute stage of adolescent rebellion and were in immediate need of parental understanding, acceptance, and support if counseling were to be successful. Upon the completion of the diagnostic evaluation and before counseling was initiated, the parents were conferred with in an attempt to foster a more positive and constructive relationship with their two disturbed daughters in the interest of all concerned. This they agreed to do.

When the two girls were again seen individually to begin the counseling process, the fourteen-year-old girl immediately declared that the counselor was an agent of her parents because he had informed on them and that she would never say another word to the counselor. She remained completely silent and uncooperative for the next several sessions. When her father learned from her of her defensive behavior with the counselor he withdrew her from the counseling relationship against professional advice, on the grounds that counseling could not be effective if she were not cooperative.

The fifteen-year-old, who exhibited a black eye, explained to the counselor that after her parents had conferred with the counselor they had returned directly home, had dragged both girls out of bed, had physically assaulted them with the accusations that the counselor had told them the whole story about their plans to run away from home again, that they had again scandalized their parents by their revelations to the counselor, and that they were responsible for all the difficulties in the current family situation.

In contrast to the fourteen-year-old girl, the fifteen-year-old daughter realized that the counselor had to confer with the parents because the daughters were minor children, that he had not divulged any confidences, that he was not an agent of the parents, and that he was truly interested in helping the family. She agreed to continue to cooperate in counseling despite the fact that her younger sister could not trust the counselor and had vowed never to talk to him again.

Thereafter, the counseling relationship was continued and deepened with the fifteen-year-old daughter, who revealed marked problems in adjusting to home, school, vocational, and social life. She suffered severe feelings of personal inferiority and inadequacy. She made no bones about her hatred of her mother, and she despised her father as a passive, submissive, inadequate man, an "agent" who was completely dominated and controlled by the unstable mother. She also complained continuously of being used as a housemaid and substitute mother for her younger siblings because her mother, who chronically complained of poor health, lay in bed all day long. (It was not learned until much later that the mother had problems with alcohol).

The parents visited the counselor shortly after the counseling relationship was established with the daughter and inquired about the feasibility of institutionalizing her. Although she was noticeably progressing in the counseling relationship, they were markedly concerned about the cost of continued counseling, even though they had not yet made payment and could even defer payment. It became obvious to the counselor that the parental pattern was one of rejecting the children as soon as they were old enough to leave home to make room for the younger children and to reduce the parents' burdens. The parents were informed that the daughter would interpret such an arbitrary action as a reinforcement of her feelings of rejection, and that she would probably react by acting out destructively or regressing. Thereupon the parents arbitrarily withdrew their daughter from counseling and threatened her with institutionalization if she caused them any more trouble.

Several months later the parents returned to the counselor and related that the fifteen-year-old daughter had run away with a nineteen-year-old boy with the intention of becoming pregnant and being married, but the couple was unable to obtain a license. Upon apprehension by the police the fifteen-year-old daughter was remanded to the juvenile authorities, who placed her in an institution where she was diagnosed as an adolescent rebel who was out of the control of her parents. The parents dwelled upon their plans to prosecute the nineteen-year-old boy for contributing to the delinquency of a minor. They also requested the counselor to advise the Juvenile Court to return the daughter to their custody. However, the counselor refused to comply on the grounds that the daughter should be committed for her own protection, and for the opportunities the institution afforded for responding to a therapeutic environment without parental interference and without the strain of her own conflicts which forced her to act out by running away from her difficulties.

Thereafter, the Court returned the daughter to the temporary custody of the parents on the basis that a psychiatrist whom the parents had privately engaged for a consultation had advised that the best place for an adolescent was in the home rather than in an institution, and that the daughter be returned home on the condition that the mother enter psychotherapy. The daughter also expressed her desire to return home rather than remain in the institution. However, it was suspected that she was motivated to leave the institution so that she could reestablish contact with the young man. The parents requested the counselor to resume a working relationship with the daughter to restrain her from seeking out the young man. They were advised that the daughter was now completely out of control, that utilization of counseling for control purposes was not recommended, and that she was still under the jurisdiction of the Juvenile Court, which represented the legal authority in her case. Although the counselor indicated a willingness to comply with any Court request for professional assistance, he could not make an independent arrangement with the parents because of the issue of legal responsibility.

Several weeks later, the Juvenile Court informed the counselor that the daughter and her boy friend had recently eloped and married in a nearby state by falsifying their ages. The daughter, who now claimed to be pregnant, was unwilling to return home or to an institution and simply wanted to live with her husband, who was also being held for Court action because he had broken and entered a property to obtain funds to finance the marriage and to purchase tools so he could learn a trade. However, her parents were seeking to annul the marriage and to institutionalize the daughter.

The Court requested that the counselor conduct a reexamination of the girl and advise the Court about a disposition of the matter. During the evaluation procedure, the counselor was visited by the parents, who indicated their primary interest in annulling the marriage, determining if their daughter was pregnant, and prosecuting the young man. The counselor was also visited by the young man, a typical adolescent rebel who had dropped out of high school, was working part-time as a flunky in a body-building emporium, was living at home, and was dependent upon his parents for support. His chief problems, according to him, were that he would like to heroically rescue his wife from the control of her father, whom he also hated; but he could not support her and was trying to enlist in the military service to avoid prosecution for felony. On the basis of the examination of the daughter, the counselor advised the Court that she be retained under jurisdiction of the Court and remanded to an institution where she would receive proper care, control, and direction to prepare her for adulthood and protection from well-intentioned rescuers.

Thereafter, the Court informed the counselor that the District Attorney had considered the couple to be legally adults by virtue of their marriage, which could not be contested under state law. Consequently, the wife was released to her husband who was still awaiting trial for a felony.

Since then, the mother had occasionally called the counselor—while intoxicated—to express her distress about her daughter's sinful marriage, her own martyrdom, and her concern about her fourteen-year-old daughter who was acting out in general. It was also learned that she had discontinued psychotherapy after a few visits to the psychiatrist.

This case exemplifies a pattern of adolescent rebellion in four daughters whose unconscious motives were to cooperate with their parents' repressed wishes to reduce the size of the family. By provoking their daughters to hostile-destructive behavior eventuating in their tumultuous withdrawal from the home, the parents felt self-righteously relieved of guilt for their own inability to completely discharge their parental duties and responsibilities.

From the evidence available, it appears that the fifteen-year-old daughter had not experienced cohesive familial influences nor continuous, consistent developmental conditions favorable to proper socialization, identification, internalization, conscience-development, conformity, self-definition, and self-esteem. Because of disruptions in the family relationships and the punitive methods of parental discipline such as rejection, physical abuse, and deprivation, her social behavior was marked by dependency-anxiety, insecurity, and a lack of integrated controls. She overtly expressed her resentment and envy of her mother and was covertly critical, disparaging, and resistant to her father's ineffectual influences. Her generalized rebellious reactions were self-defeating and fixating because they further alienated her from the affectionate rewards she already felt deprived of and also brought her under additional and more impersonal controls of other authority figures whom she generally distrusted and resented.

Because her parents were inconsistent in their professed standards and actual behavior, and because they disciplined in the spirit of manipulation, intimidation, and retaliation, they were ineffective with the daughter. They were also increasingly faced with the dilemma that although the rebellious daughter required more surveillance and control to keep her out of trouble in adolescence, she also expressed more resentment and withdrawal when such methods were attempted. Moreover, because of her physical and mental growth, she progressively ignored and defied her parents so that they lost their effectiveness as disciplinarians in her adolescent development. They also failed to act as mature patrons and sponsors of her independence because they failed to accurately and consistently provide appropriate models for identification and objective norms for internalization and failed to competently discharge their parental responsibilities under conditions of mutual freedom, trust, respect, support, encouragement, and protection.

The daughter experienced significant inconsistencies, acute discontinuities, and chronic frustrations in the nurturing and rearing process. As a result of repression and partial fixation of her development, certain aspects of her personality did not with time and experience participate in further maturation. Some of her motives remained unconscious, unchanged, frustrated, and constantly demanding immature satisfactions. She was also predisposed to certain defensive attitudes and maladaptive behavior during the critical period of adolescent development.

Her parents not only constituted immature and conflicting models for identification and provided inappropriate norms and inconsistent values for internalization, but they also reversed the family role structure by requiring her to assume a parental role with her younger siblings to compensate for her parents' inadequacies. Because she could not realistically meet her parents' narcissistic, regressive demands and expectations, she was perceived as incorrigible and was subjected to various manipulative, punitive, and threatening tactics to get her to comply. The result was a chronic power struggle between the daughter and her parents which included acute conflicts over giving and receiving and extreme mechanisms of withholding and coercing.

This form of parental incompetence and family role reversal was manifest more clearly in adolescence, when her regressive symbiotic relationship with her mother was more acutely intensified and reinforced by the cultural expectations that she begin to emancipate herself from her family and cope with reality independently of her parents. Although she vigorously demanded her rights to freedom and independence, both she and her mother were terrified at the mere thought of their separation. She did little to prepare herself for self-sufficiency.

Even when she acted out by physically leaving home for night wanderings and periodic flights from home, she typically resisted all opportunities for genuine emancipation from her mother. Under conditions
of her craving for continued contact to satisfy her frustrated needs and
drives, her rebellious crisis was complicated and exacerbated.

Her full-fledged rebellion represented a destructive acting out in
conformity to the unconscious and poorly integrated impulses, wishes,
and fantasies of both her parents and older siblings with whom she
identified. Her rebellion did not occur as a result of a defective conscience but as the result of an identification and compliance with those
exemplars who unconsciously suggested, encouraged, fostered, and even
seductively elicited the rebellion to experience vicarious gratification
for their own impulses. Her exemplars not only achieved vicarious
gratification for their forbidden urges but also concomitantly satisfied
their hostile-destructive wishes because her rebellious behavior was objectively destructive and regressive to all concerned. Because she was
conditioned to react anxiously to the recurrence of threatening situations from which she had previously regressed or which had arrested
her development at an immature level, and because she obtained sanctions and gratifications from her exemplars who stimulated her to
continue to achieve gratification by regressive means, she was unconsciously saddled with her exemplars' conflicts and was actually scapegoat
for acting out—in the form of adolescent rebellion—her exemplars'
repressed impulses.

For the exemplars, the vicarious gratifications obtained from her rebellious behavior were preferable to the satisfactions that would have
been derived from her development of a more mature personality or
alternate form of behavior. The regressive symbiotic relationships assumed such complicated interdependency that neither the daughter
nor her exemplars could release one another from the task of providing
gratifications until the situation was completely disrupted and the next
younger daughter was eligible to participate.

As a result of parental rejection, the daughter subjectively experienced tension, hostility, anxiety, helplessness, and resentment. Her emotional security was undermined and her self-esteem and self-respect
were impaired. Her self-definition and self-expression were handicapped
because her development was fixated on an immature level. Apparently
she had been accepted as an infant and young child but felt progressively rejected as she grew into womanhood. The key to her adolescent
rebellion is the severity of parental rejection, her dependency frustration,

and the age at which she experienced these feelings most acutely. It is likely that she received enough affectionate rewards from her mother in infancy and early childhood to establish the dependency motive, but her continued attempts to secure dependency gratifications and positive regard from both parents were increasingly frustrated and even actively punished. Increasingly throughout her later childhood and early adolescence, her feelings of parental rejection, frustration, and punitiveness became consciously realized. As a result of having been progressively blocked by parental rejection from behaving dependently, she exhibited relatively little transfer of dependence to other parent surrogates and even peers. Thus, she was almost completely without opportunities to mature.

In adolescence, the increases in her instinctual drives, accompanied by an increase in her anxiety, were projected onto her social environment and were subjectively experienced as fear. She behaved unconsciously toward her parents as she did during the oedipal period and responded to her anxiety by rejection of them and psychological withdrawal from them. Thus, her perceptual distortions and communication problems were reinforced. One fantasy which motivated her rebellious strategy involved the tactic of driving her mother crazy or to suicide so that she could fully assume her mother's primary role in the family. Although she exhibited no insight into this expressed wish, she was compulsively motivated in this regard. She accepted the hostile-destructive components of her fantasy because she could easily rationalize her grievances as justified.

Basically, she was involved in what is considered a double approach-avoidance conflict. In her adolescent approach to adult status, she was fearfully ambivalent because adulthood involved both the exercise of relative freedom and the correlative assumption of responsibility for both the positive and negative consequences of her decisions and actions. Simultaneously, she was also attracted to the securities and satisfactions of a remembered infancy and early childhood, but was also repelled by the lack of primary status and freedom of these relatively restrictive states. In essence, she was simultaneously attracted to and repelled from the incompatible states of adulthood and childhood. This feeling constituted a double approach-avoidance conflict which involved her in an attempt to approach the perceived positive values of both childhood and adulthood while trying to avoid their negative aspects. The closer she drew to the time of emancipation, the more desperate and reckless she became.

As a rebelliously predisposed person, this young woman reacted to the double approach-avoidance conflict situation of adolescence with excessive frustration and a displacement of intense aggression upon those persons and situations which she perceived as inducing or exacerbating her conflicts. Because her notions of both her personal past and future were more fantastic than realistic, she reacted to this double approach-avoidance conflict situation by feeling unjustly dispossessed and handicapped by an arbitrary order. The more she perceived her frustrating agents and situations as arbitrary and unreasonable, the more freely and openly she expressed her hostile and destructive reactions. Because she already felt insecure, inadequate, and inferior, she reacted to the stress of the double approach-avoidance conflict situation by not only attacking others and her situation, but also rejecting herself in a destructive manner. In the process she was highly reactive and capable of intense emotional arousal. She finally escaped from the conflict situation by aligning herself with a rebellious partner who represented recklessness, nihilism, sympathetic support, and a means to her rebellious ends. In short, her acting out response to the double approach-avoidance conflict situation of adolescence was a maximal, maladaptive, deviant, hostile-destructive, and generally unacceptable one.

Whereas the differentiated adolescent is relatively free of boredom and is engaged in a creative endeavor, in an absorbing pursuit, or in a competitive struggle for advancement, this young woman was "bored stiff" and repelled by a consciousness of her isolated, barren, meaningless self and existence. She was consumed with anomic boredom and ennui and was restless for innovation or escape. She was inclined to desperate and fantastic rebellious extremes to provide meaning and purpose to her life. She considered herself a failure not only in terms of various objective criteria but also in terms of her parental and subjective standards. Consequently, she focused her nihilism and hostility upon herself and her environment, in an attempt to destroy whatever frustrated her.

Also, because of her inability to assume and enact practical roles of creative, constructive action, she zealously, recklessly, and self-righteously sacrificed herself, others, relationships, and situations in the interest of her rebellious cause. In the hostile-destructive process, her tension, passion, and ruthlessness constricted her consciousness and her acting out dissipated her creative potential and negated whatever constructive opportunities she may have had. Her rebellious fervor and actions drained her vital energies and interfered with her executive capacities to contemplate, analyze, and constructively resolve her problem situation. Under these antecedent and consequent conditions she became increasingly less interested in creating to express and satisfy herself, to modify her situation, to construct new relationships, or to discover her true identity. She became more narcissistic, egocentric, rigid, barren, and repetitive. She became more imitative than original in her attitudes and behavior. Her rebellious propaganda and behavior were finally corrupted to an unabashed application and exploitation of the ideas and methods of her exemplars.

Apparently, this young woman's chief burden was her consciousness of a blemished, ineffectual self and her preoccupation with her unhappy situation. Her main compulsion was to shed her unwanted self and situation. She tried to do it by provoking and manipulating others and her situation. Because she lacked the inclination, ability, and patience to independently evolve or adopt a creative solution to her problems, she readily adopted the negative ones available. The examples of her older sisters, her pact with her younger sisters, and her alliance with her rebellious companion, converted her self-contempt into an active hostility which not only stifled her creativity but also crystallized her mimicry of the persons around her.

Another basic motive which determined her attitudes to the prevailing order was her excessive craving for status, attention, and recognition, motivated by a reactive sense of conceit, vanity, and false pride. Her compulsive need for special status was a function of her personal and social insecurity, which resulted from her self-rejection which, in turn, was consequent to parental rejection. She continually tried to prove her worth to herself and others by seeking exalted recognition and status. Even her sympathetic identification with her rebellious partners whom she considered to be underdogs was a function of her hostility toward whatever and whoever frustrated her compensatory needs for status and recognition. Of note is the fact that she did not seek status by means of ordinary achievement because she felt she shouldn't have to work for what was due her and from which she had been disinherited.

An important dynamic of her advanced stage of rebellion was her need for a partner-in-crime who exhibited sufficient willfulness, audacity, vision, and skill to articulate her resentment and frustration; to justify her rejection of her present situation; to dramatize her vision of a breathtaking personal adventure; to realize her self-sacrifice in combined action; to provide a make-believe situation to liberate her from her meaningless autonomy; and to mobilize her rebellious attitudes and behavior into a more effective effort.

The partner whom she selected was not particularly intelligent, mature, noble, or creative, but was passionate, superficially self-confident, manipulative, willing to cater to her basic craving for union, and personally familiar with the visionary and hostile-destructive notions of her rebellious cause. Each made and extolled a love pact with the other. To attain a form of unity with him, she surrendered her distinct self by the process of identification and impressively solemnized the union under the supreme virtue of obedience which she equated with faith and equality. She was especially obedient and believing in his leadership because it was compatible with her rebellious needs.

Because her need for freedom from responsibility was greater than her need for freedom from restraint, she exchanged her isolated autonomy for relief from the responsibilities of independently willing, deciding, acting, and assuming the consequences. She relinquished her self-direction to a person who promised to command and assume responsibility for the outcome. Her obedience to her partner was the touchstone in her chaotic existence and anarchic situation.

She was a clever initiator and steadfast follower of this rebellious union and was not discouraged by the obstacles involved. She cast her lot with her rebellious partner not because she truly believed that she would be led to a promised land but because she would be led away from her unwanted self and despised situation. Her surrender to the rebellious partnership was not only a means to these ends but also a fulfillment in itself.

This young woman not only rejected the status quo by perceiving her existence as mean and miserable but also fulfilled her perception by acting out her attitudes in a hostile-destructive manner. She evaluated ordinary adolescent pursuits as trivial and discreditable because to engage in them was to recognize and accept a reality which she needed to despise. Her prime objective was to breed contempt for and negate the value of the present so that she could reject it and fix her consciousness on the images of her fantasied past and future. She did not perceive the present as legitimate but loathed it as an aberration and a deformity. For her, time was unhinged. She had no affectionate familiarity with things as they are because she did not experience them as tangible, satisfying, or secure.

As a result of deprecating her current reality, she felt free to proceed impractically, ruthlessly, and recklessly in her rebellious acting out. By ventilating her grievance and expatiating on the apparent baseness and vileness of her problem situation, she allayed her poignant sense of inadequacy and isolation. By rationalizing that not only her own life was worthless and wasted but also the lives of her contemporaries— even the most satisfied and successful—were to no avail, she achieved a sense of social equality and communality.

She further belittled objective reality by glorifying her fantastic images of her personal past and future while discrediting the historical past and present of her parents. Her attitudes and behavior were motivated by specious images of her infancy and early childhood, during which she felt secure, powerful, loved, and free of responsibility. Her preoccupation with her fantastic images stemmed not only from a need to realize the power and legitimacy of her rebellion but also from the impotency and illegitimacy of the prevailing order. For her, the present was only an exile and a vale of tears, whereas her personal past was an ideal state from which she had been disinherited and her personal future held a glorious promise of redemption. Thus, the reality of her present life was naught compared to the idealized version of her personal past and future.

In short, her image of her personal future was neither an extension of the real present nor of the historic past, but a glorious continuation of her infantile past. By fusing her visionary future with her infantile past, she revived her glorified past in anticipation of a Utopian future. Thereupon, she not only championed her image of her personal past and future against observations of the actual present and past which encroached upon her narcissism, but also destructively attacked the actual present and historical past to liberate her projected future to reexperience her selectively remembered past.

This young woman fantastically manipulated real time because she needed to escape reality demands, camouflage her felt shortcomings, rationalize her rebellious recklessness, and excuse her unsuccessful adaptation to her problem situation. Because she essentially perceived herself as almost a complete failure, she felt she could not afford to fail any more. By glorifying her notion of her personal future, she located it outside the realm of possibility. Thus, if she were to fail in attempting to reach the impossible, she could later justifiably attribute this failure to the magnitude of the task. In short, her extravagant audacity in fantastically manipulating the reality of time and experience permitted her to rationalize and deny her overwhelming sense of inadequacy and to purchase insurance against future failures and their consequences. Because she did not live a full, worthwhile, creative, productive, and satisfying life, she willingly sacrificed it for an illusion.

Since she tended to locate the directing forces of her existence outside herself and because she unavoidably attributed the reasons for success and failure to environmental conditions, she conspicuously selected rebellion as an instrument of manipulating others and situations. However, her frustration and discontent with her environment would not have necessarily resulted in disaffection and rebellion if she had not also harbored an irresistible sense of power derived from a narcissistic investment in her fantasies of infantile omnipotence. When she combined her sense of power with her motivation for radical situational change, reckless daring, extravagant hope and faith in her personal future, exorbitant concepts of her prospects for destructive acting out, ignorance of the practical consequences involved, fantastic elaboration of her rebellious doctrine, and utilization of the negative means available to her, the rebellious climax was consummated.

Following her dependency anxiety, which was related to her fear of rejection, she was emotionally guarded, indifferent, and resistive in overt dependency relationships with authority figures. She aggressively manipulated them to covertly satisfy her frustrated needs for dependency and attention so as not to experience intolerable anxiety. She had a developed capacity and desire for succorance but was blocked by her fear and distrust of authority from exhibiting her succorance openly and directly. She was unable to delegate any of her fantastic power to anyone in authority because she reasoned that shared power is dangerous and partial power rendered her vulnerable to frustration and rejection. She did not perceive authority as predictable, powerful, consistent, protective, and providing of dependency gratifications. Because she had not learned to trust and depend upon authority; because she had not resolved her anxiety and hostility about authority; and because she defended against her insecurity with compensatory fantasies of infantile omnipotence, she inverted her legitimate needs for an overt dependency upon authority into an aggressive manipulation of authority.

It is not that her aggression was intense but that it was fused with hostility and was not adequately controlled by internalized standards. She persisted in her aggressive-hostile, manipulative-provocative behavior toward authority not because she was primarily motivated by an unconscious sense of compulsive guilt or masochism but because she needed to experience dependency gratifications without experiencing intolerable anxiety. If she were primarily motivated by a need for punishment to relieve guilt feelings, she would have masochistically sought to incur severe penalties under circumstances where the outcome was certain. Because she did not typically behave this way, her dependency anxiety rather than her compulsive guilt was more basic to her rebellious aggressiveness. She solved her dependency conflicts by inhibiting an overt dependency on authority and seeking dependency satisfactions by the indirect and disguised means of adolescent rebellion.

Another accessible and comprehensive unifying force in her rebellion was her irrational hostility, destructiveness, and self-contempt, which detached her from herself and moved her to ally with rebellious causes and allies to retaliate against those persons and situations that she felt had wronged her. By aligning herself with other rebellious allies, by worsening her situation and relationships, and by projecting her hostile-destructive motives onto those persons in authority whom she considered adversaries, she attenuated her sense of personal responsibility and increasingly evolved a license to hate and destroy without incurring culpability and the associated anxiety, guilt, shame, or remorse. Because she was also ambivalent in all her significant relationships, that is, she simultaneously loved those whom she hated, she could hate more fervently. By doing others injustices, she incurred legitimate grievances against herself. For her, this was much more potent a reason for hating others than only having a just grievance against them.

Also, her unreasonable and unreasoned hostility and destructive intentions impelled her to identify with sympathetic exemplars and associate with another rebel who similarly hated and was willing to destroy. Her most effective and safest way to express her unreasonable hostility was to consort with another rebel whom she had selected and cultivated as a partner-in-crime. She concluded that to pity, forgive, or be indifferent toward those who had wronged her and whom she had wronged would only have caused her to experience more self-contempt. Thus, she not only nursed a fanatic grievance but also dedicated herself to a hostile-destructive mission and alliance which would relieve her guilt anxiety and give dramatic expression, spectacular meaning, and unifying purpose to her contemptuous self-concept, her perception of her despicable behavior, and her evaluation of her mean and miserable existence.

She progressively exhibited the dynamics of anarchic acting out, through which she unconsciously relieved tensions and frustrations by taking rebellious action rather than by considering the antecedents and consequences and resolving her problem by rational, constructive means. Thus, her acting out brought temporary emotional relief and provided a sense of purpose and worth, but it was chiefly a means of evading rather than coping with reality. Although she was prone to acting out, she was not particularly active but was inclined to be passive, lethargic, withdrawn, introverted, isolated, autonomous, and disinclined to strive for adolescent achievements. Her energy was channeled into her fantastic strivings for a state of anarchy and chaos which, when achieved, would provide her an unhampered sense of status, importance, deliverance, and identity. She was not interested in reform because she had concluded that her situation and relationships were irredeemable. She justified her anarchic acting out with the blatant assertion that there could be no new beginnings so long as she was "a prisoner with no hope of escape."

She became more resolute and ruthless in her acting out when she proved that her fanatic belief in her rebellious cause was shared by significant others. Because she felt her rebellious cause possessed the truth, she did not doubt its righteousness. Because she felt supported by her efficacious skill, fantastic power, and intimate knowledge of her adversaries, she proceeded with abandonment. Because she was convinced that her opponents were evil incarnations and must be dealt with accordingly, she was not encumbered by second thoughts. Because she exalted in her self-estrangement and her rebellious fervor, she felt organized and equipped to handle any contingency. Her proneness to sacrifice herself readily and manipulate the real order in her commitment to a rebellious cause was a function of her imperviousness to the realities of life. In fanatically pursuing her rebellious cause, she was not dissuaded by authority, slowed by danger, disheartened by obstacles, nor baffled by apparent contradictions, because she unconsciously denied that they had any power to deter her. For her, the efficacy of her rebellious cause did not derive from the essential meaning of its doctrine but from her fanatical certitude about it. She was able to be absolutely certain about the validity of her rebellious doctrine because she did not really understand it. If she had explored it sufficiently, she would have discovered that it originated in herself and her relationships with those whom she despised. Because she had renounced herself and was ready to destroy her relationships, she could not possibly be so certain of a doctrine which derived from such sources.

Although her fanatical investment in her rebellious creed actually represented a clinging dependency of a desperately insecure person, her obsessive and compulsive fanaticism appeared to her to be evidence that her rebellious doctrine was worthy of being championed. To demonstrate her conviction to both herself and others, she was disposed to sacrifice anyone and everything for it. Nevertheless, her emotional security and certainty were derived more from her passionate attachment to the rebellious cause than from its excellence, justice, or truth.

Her passionate investment transformed her rebellious cause into a holy crusade. She could not detach herself from it because she had publicly committed herself to it and burned her bridges behind her. Moreover, if she were left without such a consuming cause, she would have to adjust to her own self and existence, which she regarded as despicable, trivial, futile, and evil. Without her rebellious cause, she would have felt completely adrift and abandoned. She obsessively clung to her mythical cause and compulsively acted it out because she could not afford to do otherwise.

The dynamic determinant here was not the quality of her rebellious cause but her need for an intense and total dedication to an ideal. She would have willingly joined in a crusade against her own rebellious cause if it had had a passionate, uncompromising, intolerant leader, a mission which proclaimed the one and only truth, a requirement that she completely disidentify with her despised self, and a promise of finding herself thereby. It would have been easier to convert her to another cause than to partially or wholly detach her from the one she espoused.

This adolescent rebel did not basically seek freedom, independence, or self-reliance because she associated them with the frustrations of isolation and autonomy. Basically, she sought to escape her ineffectual self by identification with someone or with a symbol. She wanted refuge from the barrenness, meaninglessness, and despair of her frustrating existence. Her chief motive was to belong, and she could not belong enough to satisfy her needs. However, the social attachments she had were unreal, unreliable, impermanent, and inadequate. As an autonomous individual she felt she had to determine her own life style and be responsible for the outcome.

Because of her ambivalent identifications with others and her lack of status in a cohesive group, she perceived her difficulties as evidence of her own inadequacy and inferiority. She felt like a member of a discriminated minority but was less bent upon assimilating into a majority group than upon joining a group of her own creation. She stood alone, pitted herself against the majority, objected to the status quo, and burdened herself with the misery of a renegade. However, when she affiliated with her rebellious cause, she was no longer frustrated because she had found a new purpose, identity, and role in life. She felt like one of the elite who was supported and encouraged by both the symbolic leadership of her rebellious doctrine and by her comrades-in-arms. Because she felt like she had escaped from freedom and herself, she felt powerful and immune from counterattack. As long as she felt attached to her rebellious cause and nothing else, she felt inde-structible and immortal. Thus, she clustered all her fervor and fanati-cism around this attachment. Nevertheless, her striving for union with another human being became more intense in her rebellious escape from her frustrated, untenable existence.

This case delineation of the social and personal dynamic processes of an adolescent rebel leads to the conclusion that one cannot really help the committed rebel by rationally confronting him with absolute truths or by restructuring the environment which made him feel mean and miserable to begin with. The preferred course of therapeutic action is to help liberate him from his ineffectual self and from his rejected situation. This liberation cannot be accomplished by contesting his unification with the rebellious cause which he has chosen or accepted, but by converting him to a better rebellious cause and helping him assimilate into a cohesive, exultant, and corporate whole.

Because the adolescent rebel's psychodynamics are intertwined with group dynamics, it is necessary to manage and control the group dy-namics, or any attempt to help the individual will be sabotaged. Where parents, siblings, and others are materially involved in the rebellious acting-out behavior because of their poorly integrated impulses and defenses, this regressive symbiotic relationship may become so compli-cated and interdependent that neither partner can release the other from the destructive task of providing regressive gratifications. Fur-thermore, if the rebel or partner is removed from this relationship, it is likely that he will transfer to a surrogate whom he will manipulate or scapegoat in a similar fashion. For the benefit of all concerned, it is necessary to resolve this symbiotic adaptation in the process of man-aging the rebellion.

It should also be kept in mind that when the adolescent rebel is en-couraged to identify with and internalize other values, more self-es-trangement is required. Although conversion consists of the inculcation and cultivation of dynamic proclivities and responses which are already indigenous to the rebel's frustrated psychology, it also demands more self-sacrifice and self-diminution. Fostering and encouraging the adolescent rebel's assimilation into a true and just cause essentially means not allowing the rebel to be himself. This self-denial can be accomplished only in a structured or controlled situation by reinforcing the rebel's deprecating attitude toward undesirable conditions; directing his interest and attention to practical ideals; inculcating a motivational doctrine; preventing the reestablishment of the previous psychological equilibrium; stimulating fervor; providing the means necessary to achieve status; and proving by experiment that his joys, sorrows, pride, and confidence derive from the fortunes and capacities of genuine brotherhood rather than from autonomous prospects, isolated endeavors, and illicit liaisons. Above all, the rebel must never feel abandoned or limited to his own individual resources. His only source of strength is in not being himself but in being part of something or someone that connects him to the universal and eternal order. Thus, by the complex, difficult, and hazardous process of conversion, identification, and communal cohesion, those adolescent rebels who have not yet reached the point of no return can be helped to heroically sacrifice their despised selves and relinquish their transitory situations for a more perfect self and a more universal reality.

# PART III

## *Critical Choices and Goals in Adolescence*

▲▲▲▲▲▲▲▲▲▲▲▲▲▲▲▲▲▲▲▲▲▲▲▲▲▲▲▲▲▲▲▲▲▲

# 9. Adolescent Development and the Decision-Making Process

JOHN R. McCALL, S.J.

## The Problem

Adolescence is that period in development which begins with pre-puberty and continues until the person becomes capable of successfully handling the decision-making process on his own. If the task of adolescence is self-definition or the achievement of self-identity, the best indicator of the success of this task is an increasing competence in handling the decision-making process.

Today adolescence is stretching itself out farther and farther on both ends. Both physically and socially this period is beginning earlier than it did in the past. A boy is an adolescent when he begins to notice that girls notice boys who notice. On the other end of the scale, adolescence is stretching increasingly farther into adult life. This stretching of the adolescent period is illustrated by the fact that we have formal dances and coke-tail parties for seventh graders and remedial English in the graduate school.

In contrast, I think back to a time just before the turn of the century when my father lived his adolescence. I don't know when puberty came to him; but I do know that at thirteen years of age he was working full time, ten hours a day and six days a week, in a factory. I marvel at the shortness of his adolescence. Life was thrust upon him, and he had little time to get ready for it. How quickly he had to learn how to handle the decision-making process and how to achieve self-definition.

In no sense am I advocating the abolition of the Child Labor Laws; but I would like to point out the fact that in just sixty years the adolescent period has changed drastically in length and importance, if not in purpose. If my father learned to be a good decision maker under such adverse circumstances and in such a short time—and believe me, he did—then the task of adolescence is not accomplished solely by extending the adolescent period.

Our duty as adults should be to hasten this process of decision making in youth rather than to prolong it unnecessarily. Granting the need for long education and training in our complex society, I wonder if the specialized education and training might not be much more profitable if it were given to young people who had already reached a high level of skill in decision making and in self-definition. The success of the Harvard freshman dropouts who work for a year and come back to school and graduate successfully seems to indicate that there may be some validity to this contention.

I would like to talk about this decision making process in adolescence, ask why it is that so many of our young people are ineffective in decision making, and point out a way in which this situation might be improved.

### Today's Adolescent as a Decision Maker

This problem is two-edged. We know that good decision making promotes maturity. In fact, a person is considered mature when he is capable of making good decisions regularly. In our society people are praised, recognized, and rewarded on the basis of their decision-making ability. A professional man is honored because he is a decision maker in important matters. An executive is a decision maker by definition. The higher the occupation level, the more decisions are required; the lower the level, the less decisions there are.

Without experience in this ability of decision making, one never becomes competent at it. You remember the mother who told her son not to go ice skating until he learned how. The problem is two-edged. How can an adolescent mature except by making decisions, and yet how can he make good decisions unless he has some self-definition and maturity? It is said that adolescents shirk decisions today, and because they do, they go on being immature. Actually, adolescents don't shirk decisions today; in fact, today's adolescent makes more decisions in a week than we did in a month or a year. As the variety of activities and products increases, the youngster is faced with more and more situations that demand a decision.

Thirty years ago when we went to the store for an ice-cream cone, there was chocolate, strawberry, and vanilla to choose from. When the store was out of chocolate and we didn't like strawberry, the decision was easy—vanilla or no ice cream at all. And even this decision we did not have to face too often. Now the teenager faces a choice of 28 flavors daily! Adolescents are certainly making many decisions these days—perhaps too many; but they are seldom making the type of decision for which they have to take responsibility and pay the price if the choice turns out to be wrong. The youngster who chooses pistachio ice cream against his mother's advice—"It's green; you won't like it"— and finds that she was right knows he can throw it away and try something else. This type of decision or choice is not maturing. For, implicit in this behavior, there is a principle which is calculated to keep a person always immature. The principle is this: "I need not worry too much about what I decide, for I can always change my decision, and in any case I will not really suffer for my poor choice." This principle is the source of the lack of commitment which we find in so many young people today.

So we see the adolescent of today making more decisions than ever, but they are not the type that lead to maturity and self-definition. The French have a saying, "Every choice involves a thousand renunciations." If the adolescent can make choice after choice and never suffer for his poor ones, he certainly is making decisions but not the kind built on maturity or leading to it.

Is it fair to say that the adolescent of today is a poor decision maker? He is certainly sophisticated. He knows what he wants and he seems to get pretty much what he wants. Macy's Department Store carries a stock of over 400,000 items, and the adolescent seems not at all threatened by this plethora of alternatives. The real trouble comes when we ask the adolescent to make a critical decision—his vocation in life, choice of a marriage partner, and so on. When the decision has far-reaching consequences the adolescent goes into an agony of indecisiveness. High-school teachers and counselors, I am sure, have seen how difficult it is for the youngsters to decide on a vocation in life or even on their choice for a college.

My experience in a college guidance office confirms this adolescent indecisiveness. Many college seniors opt for graduate school mainly to give themselves more time to decide on their vocation in life. The number of adolescents who have long-range, clearcut goals to which they are deeply committed is getting smaller and smaller.

## The Decision-Making Process

A decision is part of a larger process which we call *voluntary choice*. There are four phases in the voluntary-choice process: motivation (alternatives), deliberation, decision, and execution (Zavalloni, 1962, p. 75). Motivation includes the alternatives from which the individual may choose, that is, the reasons or factors which influence the process of choice—28 flavors of ice cream or the vocations of doctor, lawyer, merchant, and Indian chief.

Deliberation consists of an internal discussion on the part of the person, sometimes verbalized, sometimes not, in which he evaluates the possibility of choice. Here there is often doubt, hesitation, a state of expectancy, and indecision: "What flavor shall I choose?" or "What shall my vocation be?" In clinical studies muscular tension and respiratory disturbances are noted.

Decision is real choice in its fullest sense. It is an act by which a person decides in favor of one of the possible alternatives. With this act the person commits himself with a definite solution to the problem of choice: "I'll take butter pecan" or "I'll be a lawyer."

Execution means the actual carrying out of the decision already taken. "I'll tell the man, pay my money, take the cone" or "I will apply for law school."

The adolescent has a great variety of alternatives to choose from, whether we are talking about ice cream, clothes, cars, vocations, or marriage. In his deliberation, however, as he discusses with himself and evaluates the possibilities of choice, he often suffers from these feelings of doubt, hesitation, or tension and decides that any quick choice is better than this painful state. "I'll do what the others are doing." This decision is poor, for it is based on group conformity, relief of tension, and a compromise. It is not satisfying, for it involves only a minimum of commitment and responsibility. It is revocable, facile, and really unprincipled in any positive sense.

This type of decision is not founded on maturity nor does it lead to it. It does not prepare one for a decision which is known to be irrevocable and demanding deep commitment, postponement of pleasure, tolerance of pain and anxiety, and a real and permanent renunciation of the other attractive alternatives.

## Adolescent Development and Decision Making

In their excellent book, *Teen-age tyranny* (1963), the Hechingers blame this state of affairs at least partly on the overly permissive child-centered schools. Such schools overlook the fact that schools are established by adults to give young people the advantage of systematic teaching and learning which should help them in their deliberative and decision-making tasks.

The Hechingers point out that our youth have not been kept from making decisions; on the contrary, they have been given excessive responsibility for making choices without the benefit of experience. They say (Hechinger and Hechinger, 1963, p. 17):

> Making decisions is the toughest task that faces human beings regardless of age. The mark of the successful executive is exactly that ability and the problem never becomes an easy one. It is an impossible one without the prerequisite of experience and knowledge, plus the prior mapping out of goals of conduct and targets of achievement. To make decisions we must know the alternatives and where they lead, in addition to knowing where we want to go, and where others have gone before us.
>
> To ignore this basic relationship between knowledge and action or between experience and decision making is to launch young people on ships without sails or rudders. It condemns them to indirection and drift. In the adult world, we readily acknowledge that the pressure to make decisions or take part without the proper intellectual or moral preparation is one of the major causes of failure and mental breakdowns. While the immediate effects on children are not as drastic (only because the child is not held equally responsible for the consequences of his actions for him and for those around him!), the long range results are insecurity and a lack of purpose.

The adolescent today is making poor decisions because he lacks the proper intellectual and moral preparation; and this need can be filled only by adults. Likewise, the decisions an adolescent makes will never mature him until and unless he is held responsible for the consequences of them to himself and to others. In Montana the juvenile-delinquency rate was cut in half recently when the magistrate decided to forget about the age of the offender and mete out the same punishment to youths that they would mete out to adults committing the same crime. I am not advocating this practice, but it does highlight the principles stated above.

As I said before, this problem is two-edged. If a good decision is one for which the person is willing and able to take responsibility for the consequences, and if it is unfair to ask youths who are morally and intellectually unprepared to make decisions for which they will have to take the responsibility, then we find ourselves in an impasse.

Where does one step into this moving stream? Youth needs moral and intellectual preparation so that they will be able to make the kind of decisions for which they can take responsibility. Without this preparation and without experience in making this type of decision, they will not mature and achieve self-definition and self-identity.

The only point of the stream where they can step in is in the field of voluntary choice and precisely in those phases of motivation that involve alternatives and deliberation. Perhaps we have been stressing the decision too much and not stressing enough the perception and evaluation of the alternatives and the importance of the execution of a choice with its consequences. Before an adolescent can make a good decision, he must know the alternatives and where they lead, in addition to knowing where he wants to go and where others have gone before him. Only an adult can supply these answers.

Unfortunately, adolescents spend most of their time dealing with alternatives which Lindworsky (1931, p. 304) characterizes as inferior or elementary—that is, alternatives whose value depends on the pleasant feeling evoked by them. When the adolescent is faced with a critical decision in which the only alternatives presented are of a superior type, that is, alternatives whose value is known only by understanding a relationship—scholarship vs. service, religious vocation vs. lay apostolate, Peace Corps vs. graduate school—neither his experience with elementary decisions nor his level of intellectual and moral preparation prepares him for this crisis.

### Problems in Adolescent Development Today

Usually, we point to the parents and blame them for their adolescents' problems. I find it hard at times not to be short-tempered with some parents. They bring in an adolescent with a problem and you know that they are ten years late in coming. The youngster has never been able to make a real choice, and now his indecisiveness is beginning to pinch the parents. But it is too easy to blame the parents alone. For a fuller picture we have to look at the culture in which both parents and adolescents live.

Permissiveness, self-expression, and the absence of competition—this is the ideology of our culture. We have allowed the development of an adolescent society which is more or less isolated from the adult stream of life. The adolescent borrows for his society the glamorous and sophisticated part of adult society—smoking, drinking, driving, night-clubbing—while the high goals and worthwhile activities of adults are looked down upon precisely because they involve responsibility (Coleman, 1961).

Many adults, especially those whose pictures get into the papers too often, give very poor examples to the adolescent, for these adults seem unwilling to take on real responsibility. Yet, despite the handicaps, many of our adolescents are making good decisions and growing in maturity and responsibility. But the damaging point is that these fine young people must resist the teenage society in which they live to accomplish this task.

Cut off from adult society, the adolescent turns to his peers, who tell him that popularity (an inferior alternative) is the only worthwhile outlet for his energies. To be really popular with the opposite sex, the girl needs clothes and the boy a car, and this is only the beginning. I believe that it is often the insecure mothers of teenage girls who are responsible for pushing their offspring into a whirl of date-happy popularity seeking. In any case, the peer group presents attractive alternatives that are definitely of an inferior type; their value lies in giving a pleasant feeling. To reject these experiences is hard for the adolescent for he must then differentiate himself from his culture, not on his terms but on the terms of the peer group.

Faced with the necessity for decision, the adolescent turns to his parents and other adults. Basically he still wants to please his parents and he does need adult approval, even when he denies this need most vociferously. He does not go to his parents and other adults to receive tailor-made decisions. He knows he must make these decisions himself, but he is looking to adults for a value system, some traditions and guidelines, and the moral and intellectual preparation without which he cannot make these critical decisions. Too often the adolescent asks for bread and we hand him a stone, or he asks for a fish and we hand him a serpent. "Do what the others are doing."

The adolescent of today feels that he should be given anything he wants. He certainly feels he should be able to have whatever adults can have. A teacher from New Britain says, "Children must learn as children that one cannot have everything one wants." Smoking, drinking, driving, dating are signs of adulthood only if they have been earned by responsible decisions; otherwise they are silly marks of immaturity. The teenager who clings to these symbols and thinks they make him mature is like an Indian in war paint; he looks war-like whether he is or not.

Here is an interesting quote from a teenager in a Gallup survey: "I don't want to be above normal, I want to be average. I have everything I want. I have security, clothes, love, a pet, a boy friend. I wanted a typewriter. I got a typewriter." This situation is not really very satisfying. A spoiled child is one who has been given everything his parents ever wanted. Or as a youngster told me recently, "A sweater? Why, that is what you put on when your mother is cold." The poor adolescent never feels the wonderful sense of accomplishment that comes from working hard for something and finally getting it. Some of the teenagers admit that they are really being punished by being pampered. The poor parents are caught without values in a vise between the teenage society and their own culture.

## Training Adolescents for Decision Making

Adolescents are making plenty of decisions, but they need training in making better decisions. With the passing of the years, a person's alternatives and goals should become more and more of a superior type. The Hindus say that a man should move up from a desire for pleasure to a desire for success; and from success to a desire for duty; and finally to a desire for service, charity and love. The adolescent has to climb this same ladder, but it is hard for him if he does not see adults doing it.

The aim of the training he needs is precisely what counselors have been trying to do—to give youngsters the moral and intellectual training to increase their control over their conduct. One of the end products of good decision making is adequate self-control. Without self-control, deeply felt relationships with other individuals are impossible. Without such relationships, there can be no self-definition or maturity.

The training has to be aimed at the integral formation of the whole personality. It is not just a question of training the will. It is rather the inculcating of a series of attitudes and values which will be a function of the entire personality. Hadley Cantril says, "A crucial question for education is to devise a method for teaching people how to improve value judgments which in turn will better guarantee a higher quality of experience" (1950, p. 54).

The attitudes we should try to teach should be just the opposite of the one I referred to earlier: "I need never worry too much about what I decide, for I can always change my decision, and in any case I will not really suffer for my poor choice." It is sad to see adolescents continually saved from their poor decisions; it is even sadder to see them deprived of making good decisions on superior alternatives and enjoying their wonderful consequences.

In order to deliberate wisely on alternatives *the adolescent needs a scale of values* whereby he can judge the relative worth of the various possible choices. For example, to have one's car as a sophomore in high school must be an appealing alternative for any youngster. Yet, some youngsters given this choice will decide to do without the car, because it might interfere with their school work and because the money can be set aside for further education. The alternative of further education has greater value than the car with its here-and-now popularity and convenience value. Usually, the youngster who makes such a choice has parents or other adults who have given him both a set of values and an example of denying present pleasure for future and superior goals. He has seen adults tolerate frustration, anxiety, and pain in order to aim for something of greater value at a future time. This type of decision making is based on *some* maturity and leads to *more* maturity.

As I see it, our duty as adults is to create conditions in which the adolescent—through intellectual and moral preparation—will be more apt to be moved by those alternatives which have longer lasting value. The adult who has no such set of values, or if he does, is afraid to teach and live by them, is really unable to help the adolescent.

If we are correct in assuming that there are ethical principles that are proper to man and that a well-integrated personality can act in conformity with the laws of its rational nature and thereby respect the moral laws of society, then there must be some objective norms of right and wrong which can be given to the adolescent to help him in his deliberation on the alternatives that must go into every decision. For this reason alone I would not suggest discontinuing Catholic education, although I admit there is much room for improvement.

The training of the adolescent, if it is to be truly human, must be essentially moral. In forming the moral conscience of the young, we must clarify in the light of moral norms all the sectors of human activity in which the young exercise themselves and offer them examples of adults who consistently subordinate other interests to the moral or superior good (Zavalloni, 1962, p. 300).

The adolescents who dump empty beer cans along the highways may be very much influenced by their peer group or by adult society; but their decision to do it in no way takes into account their responsibility to society. Social training should aim at increased internal freedom, not at the acquisition of external freedom. With improved decision-making ability, the adolescent should be more free within himself but in even greater control of his conduct so that he does not run rough shod over the rights of others in doing whatever he wants to do.

In the spiritual training of the adolescent the aim is also for internal freedom characterized by spontaneity of a spiritual nature. It is a freedom based on wisdom, and when it is perfected it coincides with sanctity. The saint is master of his own life because his personality is completely united with God, who is Wisdom. When youth turns to us and asks for bread and fish, they are looking for moral training.

This training, I think, is what the Hechingers (1963, p. 17) mean by the moral and intellectual preparation which youth need before they can make decisions and before we can hold them responsible for these decisions. The adult has the duty to train the adolescent to make rational use of his freedom of choice and to help him grow in the capacity of actualizing a constant preferential choice of the good. For this reason, it is indispensable to develop in youth the capacity to form judgments (deliberation), the spirit of initiative (decisions), and the sense of responsibility (execution), which comes from taking the responsibility for the consequences of their decisions.

Zavalloni put it well when he said, "It is absolutely necessary to instil the habit of making with serene deliberation the small decisions that orient the daily life, if we wish to train youth to make with full freedom and responsibility the critical decisions of life. To abandon one's self to one's impulses and to indulge in the unbridled conquest of pleasure is the surest road to maladjustment and unhappiness" (1962, p. 301). Our aim in training the adolescent is to develop in him an enlightened self-control; but this aim can be accomplished only if he receives the intellectual and moral training and the example of mature adults, adults who in their own lives have a set of values which lead them to subordinate other interests to the moral or superior good.

It is because I am sure that many youth counselors and teachers are this type of adult that I have great hope that many if not most of our young people will receive the proper training, both moral and intellectual, to help them in their decision making. For with responsible teaching, good example, and love they will have the light and strength to rise above the limitations of their culture and to deliberate about superior alternatives. They will be willing to choose long-range goals and suffer the minor frustrations and anxieties or the postponement of pleasure which is a necessary part of the constant preferential choice of the good. They will know where they want to go and where good mature adults have gone before them. They will be ready to forgo instant pleasures in favor of values that are eternal.

They will grow up, achieve independence (inner freedom), and self-identity, for as they mature they will come to realize as we did that a clear sense of self can only crystalize around something transcendental, around The Other Who Is God. Then they will be capable of a deeply felt relationship with God and man in time and in eternity.

# 10. Vocational Goals for the Adolescent

## LAWRENCE R. MALNIG

### History of Vocational Guidance

Vocational guidance came into being soon after the turn of the century and acquired the tools with which to operate from a number of movements already in existence. It originated as a professional service rather than as a scientific discipline and its object was to meet the pressing need to find proper employment for the large segments of population moving to urban areas. Many of these people were untrained and unskilled and could not be readily absorbed into an industrialized society. Appropriately, the National Vocational Guidance Association in 1913 stated that it was concerned with the selection of, the preparation of, and the placement of individuals in life vocations.

The spark for this movement was provided by Frank Parsons (1909), in whose conception vocational guidance was a rational process which involved the assessment of the individual's abilities, interests, and background and the careful study of occupational information. By means of "true reasoning" this information would then be used to help the individual enter a suitable occupation. Such was essentially the orientation of the vocational-guidance movement for many years to come, and all efforts were bent on finding existing instruments and in developing new materials to implement its objectives.

At the time of World War I the assessment of individual differences by means of psychological tests became a popular method. Many refinements were made in the evaluation of specialized aptitudes acquired in skilled occupations. This development continued after the war. In 1927 the Strong Vocational Interest Blank appeared; and in 1942 the Kuder Preference Record. These tests were followed by projective tests based on the personality theory of psychoanalysis. All these new instruments were eagerly employed by the vocational counselor.

During this same period, support from various quarters provided the research and funds for the publication of suitable occupational literature. The National Occupational Conference, financed by the Carnegie Corporation from 1933–1939, together with the NVGA published the periodical *Occupations,* which was the precursor of the current *Personnel and Guidance Journal.* With federal support the research division of the United States Employment Service published in 1939 the *Dictionary of Occupational Titles* in which precise definitions were provided for more than 20,000 jobs. As the market for these materials expanded, many private publishing companies entered the field.

This method of matching employee and job, with adjustment as the measure of success, became known as the trait-and-factor theory of vocational guidance and continued, virtually unquestioned and with few changes, for some thirty years. Vocational counselors were so absorbed with the refinement and promulgation of their services that they paid little attention to research being conducted in related fields, which was to have deep implications for the theoretical structure of vocational guidance.

In Austria, Buehler (1933) analyzed the case histories and autobiographies of old people and established a theory regarding psychological development throughout a life span. She saw the developmental process as passing through five stages—growth, exploration, establishment, maintenance, and decline—and provided a flexible estimate for the age span within each stage. Although this theory was a theory of life, it also had implications for vocational development.

The concepts of pattern and development in a person's work history received attention in the investigations of Friend and Haggard (1948), who were social workers, and Miller and Form (1951), who were sociologists. In the research of the former many variables found in case histories were related to vocational choice and adjustment in an attempt to develop a pattern which would distinguish the successful from the unsuccessful. These investigators found that satisfactory identification with at least one parent was essential for occupational success, and that patterns of childhood family adjustment were repeated in the adult work situation. In the Miller and Form study a classification of work periods in an individual's life span was made through an analysis of case histories. These investigators established a sequence of work periods which closely paralleled the psychological stages of Buehler.

This progression consisted of a preparatory work period, initial work period, trial work period, stable work period, and, finally, a retirement period.

Although the germs of a dynamic theory of vocational development were present in these works, they remained dormant until Ginzberg, an economist, proposed his theory. He proposed a tentative theory of occupational choice which consisted of a fantasy period, a period of tentative choices, and a realistic period. Most noteworthy, however, was the criticism he levelled at those who had concerned themselves with the problem of occupational choice. He stated that the environmentalists, who saw choice as dependent on the nature of jobs available in the community, explained too little, too patently. The psychoanalysts, who attributed choice to early unconscious needs, explained too much, too simply. Of vocational counselors, he wrote, "After a comprehensive study of the literature of vocational guidance, my colleagues and I came to the conclusion that the movement was severely handicapped because both investigators and practitioners were working without the help of any theory at all or with severely limited theories" (Ginzberg, 1952, p. 492).

When the many stormy reactions to this criticism finally abated, the realists who assessed the situation came to the conclusion that indeed there was no definite theory of vocational development. The trait-and-factor approach was based on the psychological theory of individual differences, but counselors did little to advance beyond this point. They were so occupied with their own methodology that they largely ignored the probings of investigators in other fields.

Under the impetus of such criticism, vocational counselors turned in large numbers to theory building. In fact it would be safe to say that the last decade has produced more contributions towards a theory of vocational development than were seen in the previous forty years of the existence of the vocational-guidance movement. The most noteworthy perhaps is the Career Pattern Study of Donald Super (1957). In the plan for this research he attempted to synthesize the contributions of various disciplines, and by means of a longitudinal study he hoped to establish the basis for a functional theory of vocational development. The investigation was concerned with the concept that vocational development is a continuous and generally irreversible process which is also orderly and patterned.

This research also considered new developments in counseling theory, so that personal values, attitudes, and the individual's self-concept were seen as an integral part of vocational guidance. This confluence of new ideas led Super to propose a new definition of vocational guidance in which he indicated that it is "a process of helping a person to develop and accept an integrated and adequate picture of himself and of his role in the world of work, to test his concept against reality, and to convert it into a reality, with satisfaction to himself and benefit to society" (Super, 1957, p. 197).

## Problems in Vocational Counseling

As a result of this ongoing, energetic research in career patterns and vocational development, the future holds much promise for a workable theory which we can use in daily practice. However, to date we have only some tentative findings; the counselor still has no definitive theory with which to work.

The vocational counselor is further bedeviled by the fact that even with regard to occupational information and vocational training in the schools there is considerable confusion and conflict, in great part caused by the lack of a sound theory. For example, Hutson, who examined the vocational choices of high-school students in 1930 and again in 1961, found that while a little more than twelve per cent of the nation's workers could be classified as professional, 38 to 64 per cent of these high-school pupils were planning to enter professional occupations. From this he concluded that "guidance for vocational choice has not become more effective in the three decades that have elapsed between the surveys" (1962, p. 219). On the other hand, at the 1963 convention of the Personnel and Guidance Association, research was cited showing that the aspirations of our youth were not adequate to meet future shortages at the top of the occupational ladder.

The place of vocational training for adolescents within the school curriculum is also a subject for controversy. In answer to those educators who believe that high school should develop skills which will enable our young people to enter the labor market, Robert Hutchins has this to say (1963, p. 11):

The object of American education is to get everybody into school and keep them there as long as possible. Since they are there and must stay there, they have to do something. What they do is to learn what Dr. James B. Conant calls "marketable skills," to the acquisition of which he thinks 85 per cent of our school children are destined. This in spite of the fact that Dr. Conant knows perfectly well that by the time they graduate the skills will be unmarketable. Either the skill will not be in demand at all, or it will be in demand at an entirely different level. This means that the pupil who spends his time acquiring a marketable skill will have nothing to market.

The counselor who must work with these youngsters every day cannot wait for these conflicts to be resolved or for an all-inclusive theory to be developed. He must utilize what is available and be guided to a large extent by the needs and behavior of the students themselves. The psychology of the adolescent has been so well documented in the literature that we need not dwell upon it here at great length. But I would like to discuss one basic conflict which, it appears, all adolescents must resolve before an adequate career choice can be made. I would like also to suggest ways in which we might reconstruct some of our current practices to facilitate the solution of this conflict.

Since work, or entry into a career, is essentially an adult activity, the adolescent who is called upon to make a choice is faced with the problem of asserting his independence. In so doing he must come to grips with the fear of competition with his father, the most important adult in his life. The deep implications and consequences of this conflict are too frequently overlooked. The self-concept with which the adolescent emerges from this struggle will pave the vocational path he will follow.

In discussing a young man's inability to choose a vocation, Pearson noted:

The patient had an unconscious fear that if he grew up, he would die. This really was a fear of punishment for his desire—which he also kept unconscious —to surpass his father when he became a man. In order to keep himself alive, he had to refuse as much as possible to grow up; if he did have to grow up chronologically, he had to follow closely in his father's footsteps but never do as well as the father did, lest he die (1958, p. 99).

This fear, as Menninger indicates, may be an important factor even when the individual does make a decision. He states that "many a son who disappoints his father by what appears to be an aggressive rejection of the parental hopes is unconsciously deterred by the fear of entering into competition with him" (1942, p. 162). When upward mobility in vocations was less prevalent some generations ago, and following in one's father's footsteps was taken for granted, this problem was not as intense. Today, however, social pressures have made this problem more pronounced. As Gobetz (1961) has noted, a child in our present society is expected to exceed his father rather than merely follow in his footsteps. It is exactly when the child attempts to do this that his fears and feelings of guilt bring the conflict to a head.

A few case histories might be useful in illustrating this process. The first case involves a senior in college who had a very good academic record and was preparing to enter the teaching profession. He suddenly found it almost impossible to study and to complete his required thesis. There were no recent changes in his situation nor any pressing problem to which his difficulty might have been attributed. At a later interview, however, as he was discussing his father, he expressed a very deep sense of gratitude for the sacrifice his father had made so that his son might be better off than he was. He had always found comfort in looking up to his father and he had begun to feel this would no longer be possible when he would have surpassed him at graduation. He also generated intense feelings of guilt because he felt the attainment of a superior status upon graduation would automatically constitute rejection of his father. The almost complete immobilization which followed was a way of coping with an unbearable conflict. Only after this student was able to see the irrational aspects of this conflict was he able to carry his studies to successful completion.

In another situation we find that the fear of competition constituted a threat to the student's independence and prevented him from following in his father's profession. The test scores and grades of this student indicated a distinct superiority in the verbal area. His activities included membership in the Literary Club, the Debating Society, and the Glee Club. In spite of this background John chose physics as a major and came to our attention because he was on probation.

In counseling, John described his father, a lawyer, as a truculent, domineering person who took every opportunity to belittle and control anyone within reach. So afraid was he of a rebuff that John would not even ask for use of the family car to go on a date. It is interesting to note that on one of these few occasions when he tried to influence his father's behavior, he chose the issue of attending Mass on Sunday so that he would have the support of the church behind him. When even this attempt did not succeed he felt he could never stand up to his father, as he felt he would have to if he wanted to be a lawyer. The prospect of such competition was so unnerving that in spite of the advice he received from teachers and the poor grades which stared him in the face, John could not bring himself to make a choice that would involve the utilization of his verbal skills.

The counselor's frustration mounts in such a situation because time cannot be stayed until the threads of the problem are unraveled. In this particular case John was well into his junior year so that to an extent his educational direction could not be changed. In time, John decided he did not want a research career in physics. His own investigations made him aware that he enjoyed interpersonal relations, particularly in a helping situation. He felt that he could best implement his new orientation by entering the teaching profession, and eventually he did.

This case illustrates not only the effects of parental conflict, but also the flexibility which exists in vocational planning. It emphasizes current thinking that in vocational development certain compromises must be made and that there are careers rather than a single occupation by means of which an individual can implement his self-concept.

There is also the case of the individual who is not ready to accept the responsibility for independent choice or to face the fear of parental competition and temporarily seems to solve his dilemma by escaping into his father's profession. The student in question seemed to be well qualified for the curriculum he had chosen, but he was puzzled by his growing inability to grasp the work. His high-school record and test scores gave every indication that he could be expected to do well in the pre-med program in which he was enrolled.

Both of Greg's parents were college trained and his father practiced dentistry. On the surface there seemed to be a strong bond between father and son, judging from the fact that they very frequently attended sports events and college functions together. After a short while, however, as Greg began to feel more comfortable in the counseling relationship, he revealed that he was not really interested in medicine but could not make a change for fear of bitterly disappointing his father. Forestry and animal husbandry were the courses that interested him. He eagerly accepted the suggestion that he at least satisfy his curiosity by reading about these occupations. Still, as he was about to leave, he asked that the counselor never make any mention of this interest to his father.

We had other indications of the nature of this father-son relationship when Greg said with some hesitancy, "I sometimes feel that if my father were not alive I would really settle down and accomplish things!" and when he later asked with some vehemence, "Why does my father have to be a buddy? Why can't I treat him as a father instead?" This kind of close relationship was too threatening to Greg because equality also invited competition, and this fact made him

more painfully aware that if he became a physician he would have surpassed his father. On the other hand, Greg did not feel sufficiently
independent to repudiate his father's wishes in choosing a career. Academic success in the face of this conflict presented a double-barreled
problem: he would have to abandon his own career interests, and he
would also surpass his father professionally. The apparent solution to
this problem was failure.

As this intricate pattern of relationships began to unfold, Greg began
to see that he could no longer pursue this course of action. He made
real efforts to muster enough strength to change his course in spite
of the mounting anxiety he experienced. While in the throes of this
struggle one day he suddenly came to the decision that he too would
become a dentist. Once this decision was made all his problems seemed
to vanish and he discontinued his counseling. On the surface all
seemed to go well because his grades rose dramatically and he gained
admission to a first-class dental school—the one his father had attended!

Unfortunately, this peace of mind, achieved through appeasement,
had a short duration. In his very first year in dental school it became
agonizingly clear that he could not continue to betray himself. His
first step towards independence was to get married, and at the end of
the academic year he withdrew from school. He later came to the counselor to report that his parents had taken the news with surprising
calm and understanding. He then proceeded to work out a plan by
which he could continue his training in biology while in the employ
of the Government in the Fish and Wildlife Service.

## Some Suggestions for Improved Vocational Counseling

In these case histories we see the toll that is taken by the irrational
and generally unconscious fear of competition with one's father. It is
also apparent that if a student succeeds in establishing his own identity
and feels sufficiently independent to explore and implement his plans,
this conflict could be greatly mitigated, if not entirely avoided.

We cannot expect to develop this kind of freedom and independence
with a single program or even a number of sporadic activities. Our
efforts must be consistent and continuous, and we must seize every
opportunity to put students in situations which will help to transform
their attitudes. In other words, it is not sufficient to tell them; we must
provide the experience which will develop an inner conviction.

We have found, for instance, that we could obtain beneficial results by having upperclassmen administer the Freshman Testing Program and conduct individual interviews and group meetings with freshmen during Orientation Week. The old adage that we learn through teaching was never more true. The upperclassmen had to examine their own objectives before they attempted to orient freshmen, and they had to familiarize themselves with the services of the college before they could explain them. In this process they began to feel they were partners in the educational venture, not just reluctant followers. As a result many more of these participants in orientation utilized our guidance services to make plans for the future than did the general college population.

We also directed our attention to the task of effecting a transition which would make career planning a student-centered activity. We approached the activity presidents and showed them how their clubs could provide a useful service to members by conducting career conferences. A student committee would investigate careers related to a particular major and then invite representatives from these occupations to the college for a conference. The student leaders expressed some hesitancy about extending personal invitations to guests and moderating the conferences, but with a little assistance they soon overcame their fear of dealing with authority figures. What's more, they communicated their confidence to the other students, who began to show new and imaginative ways of assuming adult responsibilities.

This kind of behavior, however, does not affect all students, nor can we expect it to continue without providing occupational reinforcement. We must be ever vigilant to seize every opportunity to help students face and surmount the anxieties that assail them as they try to enter the adult world. These anxieties, unlike what some may suspect, are not solely characteristic of the maladjusted students. They are normal stresses which provide the adolescent with an opportunity to shape and mold an adult image of himself.

The problem of establishing an adequate self-concept is clearly demonstrated in a program which, for want of a better name, was called "Industrial Testing Program for Seniors." Repeatedly, we had noted that when students came to our office to discuss their plans to become teachers or counselors, they became uneasy and flustered when asked if they had considered work at the college level. It was apparent that students would not openly admit that they could imagine themselves occupying the position of the counselor for fear of being considered presumptuous and, perhaps, of inviting a hostile reaction. We began to wonder how seniors would react to an interviewer on campus who would ask them what position they hoped to occupy in five or ten years.

To determine how they would react, we decided to invite seniors in small groups to undertake a thorough self-evaluation, starting with testing and ending with a simulated employment interview. We obtained measurements of intelligence, values, and personality, the meanings of which were discussed in group meetings. Individual test results were interpreted in a personal interview. We then discussed with the students the purpose of various questions which appear on personal-data sheets, work histories, and other standard forms which are used in industry to screen applicants. The main purpose of these discussions was to alert students to the implications of the questions asked so that they would be prepared to explain any unusual information about themselves at the time of the interview.

For the interview itself, we used a four-part guide which covered personal background and educational, social, and financial history. Each student was interviewed for approximately five minutes on one of the four sections of the schedule, after which we discussed the meanings and implications of the questions. We then evaluated each student's responses and rated his performance. This program made one fact compellingly clear: The students felt they were being put through the "third degree"; few of them felt that they in turn could and should evaluate the company which was being represented by the interviewer. These students were concerned only with the impression they were making; they failed to seek information which would be indispensable in considering the acceptance of an offer of employment.

We can see from this brief account that up until the time students obtain a job they view the adult world of employment with apprehension and with a fear of being rejected unless they are subservient. The counselor's task once again is to help the adolescent overcome his fear of adult competition and to assert his positive values.

Many recent studies of college populations have indicated that attitudes and values are more likely to be transmitted to the individual if they are an integral part of the student culture itself. As Freedman put it, "Critical thinking ability and changes in attitudes and values are usually caught rather than taught. Student culture and teacher personality play more important roles than specific attempts to teach critical thinking techniques" (1960, p. 1). To achieve our goal, therefore, it would seem desirable to modify our approach to vocational planning in such a way that students would be able to incorporate critical thinking into their own value system. If they are able to do this, students will be able to plan a career without fear of competition and with the support and encouragement of their peers. Independent investigation would then become a socially acceptable activity which would be less likely to generate conflict and anxiety.

If we understand why adolescents are threatened by the idea of competition with parents, and if educators in the school environment recognize the importance of serving as a willing bridge to the adult world, many more methods can be devised for guiding young people into meaningful vocational activities.

# 11. Adolescents and Marriage

HENRY V. SATTLER

Art and prudence are not proper subjects for instruction. Both can be learned only by doing, by in-service training. Art is correct reason in making; prudence is correct reason in acting. Though knowledge about art (science) may be helpful to the budding artist, and ethical science may be helpful to the prudent man, neither will, by itself, make a good artist or a prudent lover—else the most eminent critic would be the greatest artist, and the most complete moralist would be the greatest saint.

In our modern scientific and technological age, many professions demand a great deal of knowledge and technical skill. But, even here, it is true that the existential insights of art or prudence are necessary for success. Though a man cannot become a good doctor or surgeon without medical knowledge and endless hours in the dissecting laboratory, the best medical student or the best dissector does not necessarily become the best diagnostician or surgeon.

I believe that it is impossible to adjust to a state of life or a kind of work ahead of time. One must be *in* the state or performing the professional function in order to develop the prudence and art of living. Possibly adjustment skills and role perceptions can be indicated immediately before entering a new state of life or profession; however, these indications remain but warnings and suggestions which may or may not be of value. I do not believe that anyone can show me "how" to hear confessions beforehand. It is for this reason that most pastoral theology courses are so boring.

Marriage and family life, in their functional reality, are concerned with the virtues of art and prudence. The interpersonal relationships in the family are a matter of the prudent choice of means towards the love of self, partner, children, and God. A successful working out of

143

home roles is a process involving the art of making a family, a home, and a family living. Though knowledge (science) and technique may, respectively, enlighten and carry out the prudence and art of family life, there is no guarantee that a family sociologist or a family counselor will live a happy and successful family life.

Of all possible ways of living a human life, life in the family is the most natural. I do not mean instinctual. The inherent basic intelligence of a human being which we call common sense must be applied to the natural relationships of husband to wife, parents to children. Though science and the technique of role adjustment may be helpful, particularly where maladjustment is present, the actual interpersonal relations within the walls of the home cannot be learned beforehand.

To my mind, the best marriage preparation for an adolescent would be to come from a happy family. Since he cannot control his origin, the next best preparation is the best possible adjustment to his own adolescence. Perhaps a story will illustrate: A sociological surveyor once rang a doorbell and a harried mother, with a crying child in her arms, another clinging to her skirt, and surrounded with battle noises from within, answered. The interviewer asked: "May I inquire which, in your opinion, is the most difficult year of marriage?" She paused distractedly and answered: "The most difficult year? . . . the one you're in!"

I believe that the year which is at once the most difficult and most enjoyable is the one you are in. If we can help adolescents to adjust to the various roles of adolescence, to suffer and to enjoy the experiences of the moment, they will make the best possible marriage partners. If we are going to present to them functional roles, we must focus upon their present situation. We must help them to love being adolescents; to learn what it is to be a man or a woman (by comparing and contrasting their own growth and development with the maturing of others); to accept and develop their progressive freedom while growing in responsible contributions at home; to look towards the future and to face the horrendous choice of vocation, whether the single state in church or cloister, the single state in the world, or the married state; to love learning the science and technique which will eventually be of service to them in their work and in their social, political, and recreational world.

Though adolescents cannot help posturing as they imagine future possible roles, we must help them to reduce this imaginative role playing to realistic proportions. They should dream dreams, but we must help them not to project fairy tales! If it is true that every adolescent tries on successive false faces until he finds one that fits, he must also avoid grotesque or unrealistic caricatures.

It is for this reason that I am opposed to functional (that is, practical) courses on marriage and family in the high school. It will be argued that "this is our last crack at them." I agree, but if we can help them to function effectively within their own adolescence and to develop their intelligence to the highest possible level by the standard scientific and technical courses, we will have served them as fully as possible.

I am also opposed to such functional courses for other reasons:

1. Functional courses tend to focus attention to a great extent on marital roles. This focus leads youth to conceive of marriage in the immediate future, when we should be distracting them from such a possibility. I wonder whether this rushing into marriage is not the reason why we have monogamy before marriage and polygamy afterwards!

2. Functional courses distract them from effective intellectual growth and the development of possible professional or technical competence.

3. Functional courses may unconsciously encourage steady dating with a corresponding dissipation of emotional energy.

4. Functional courses tend to encourage youth to live out imaginatively future roles which they cannot possibly understand. I do not believe that parents, counselors, or teachers can help them to cross bridges before they reach them; and, I suspect, such imaginative projections into the future will too frequently prepare them to cross bridges which they will never meet.

5. Functional courses make an immediate preparation for marriage seem "old hat."

Aside from the consideration of choice of vocation, should there be courses on marriage and the family? Certainly. But they should be scientific rather than practical. Marriage and family life are areas in which we have a great deal of scientific and technical knowledge, and this knowledge must be imparted on the same level as knowledge in other courses. I am not an educational philosopher, so I leave to others how such courses on marriage and family are to be set up. Some believe that marriage and family should be taught as a separate subject, from an interdisciplinary approach. In this approach, the disciplines of religion, philosophy, sociology, economics, psychology, law, and physiology will all have something to say. Others insist that each of the sciences should be taught within its own context, in which case proper place should be made within each science for material which affects marriage and family. For example, a course in sociology must give ample space to family relationships within the culture. Human physiology should include the physiology of human reproduction. Religion must include the Sacrament of Matrimony, the Canon Law of impediments, the morality of the marital embrace, the principles for rhythm, and the like.

No matter under what philosophical predisposition a course on marriage and family is taught, it should include the following areas:

1. The nature of love—its growth and development.

2. The qualities of self or of potential partner necessary to make an effective marriage (whether from a physical, emotional, intellectual, moral, religious, social, or vocational viewpoint).

3. The nature of marriage as a social institution with all its social involvements: (a) ecclesiastical involvements of impediments, requirements for ceremony, validity, place within the Mystical Body; (b) the civil involvements of marriage license, blood tests, legal contracts, and the like; (c) the social involvements of finances, in-laws, and the like; and (d) community involvements of neighborhood, race, and place of the family within the community.

4. The nature of marriage as a Sacrament, including: (a) the sacramental graces of matrimony; (b) the ends of marriage as instituted by God; (c) the morality of the marital embrace, of contraception, and of the rhythm method; and (d) the educational and religious functions of the home.

5. The sociopsychological differences between the sexes as worked out in our culture.

6. The physiology of reproduction, including insemination, ovulation, conception, birth, lactation.

In conclusion, I hope that this paper will provoke vehement discussion. Though there are many high-school and college texts which claim to be adequate on marriage and the family, I know of no single text or curriculum that seems universally satisfactory. I suggest that we have not clearly, or even confusedly, roughed out a philosophy of marriage instruction, guidance, or counseling which could form an adequate background for our prudential choice of materials or for the artistic insights which would enable us to teach such a course or do adequate counseling.

# 12. Special Aspects of Adolescent Choices

PAUL J. CENTI

MOTHER M. STELLA MARIS

ABRAHAM SHUSTERMAN

## The Educational-Vocational Problem Child
(PAUL J. CENTI)

The counselor working in an educational setting often deals with problems which are primarily educational. The major problem of many students who come to him center on their inability to succeed with their studies. In working with such a student, the counselor is first concerned with identifying the factors which are determining the student's level of achievement. Among such factors are the level of intelligence of the student; his proficiency in reading, writing, and studying; the appropriateness of his educational program; and the personal-emotional factors which affect his general adjustment, his power of concentration and attention, and his motivation. When these factors have been identified, the course of counseling can be more clearly determined.

Other students come to the counselor with problems of educational choice, questions concerning what programs to follow and what courses to take. Here the counselor is concerned with assessing the potentialities, interests, and other characteristics of the student in the light of the opportunities available as well as the vocational goals of the student.

Some problems brought to the school counselor may be primarily educational or vocational, but they are seldom just educational or vocational. The problem of poor achievement, for example, involves also

147

the consideration of vocational orientation. The choice of courses and programs should be made in the light of appropriate vocational goals. The choice of vocational goals leads ultimately to a consideration of the academic programs leading to these goals and to a consideration of the student's chances of success within these programs. The differences between educational and vocational problems are, therefore, more evident in theoretical considerations than in actual practice.

The following case describes a student whose educational and vocational problems are clearly interrelated.

### The Case of John B.

John first came to the Counseling Center with the problem of whether or not he should change his courses. He was a college sophomore enrolled in the B.S. accounting program in the School of Business at a large university. He lived at home in a nearby city and commuted daily to school. He indicated that he was thinking seriously of not only changing his program but also of transferring to another college. He wanted to know how many of his credits would be accepted in an engineering program in a nearby engineering school. He indicated that he was very much interested in automobiles and felt that he would eventually like to design and build his own cars. He was looking for an engineering program which would prepare him for designing automobiles. He objected to the current models of automobiles coming out of Detroit. Their engines and bodies were too large and they were not economical. He felt he could build better ones. When I asked him where he would get the money for his venture, he replied that if he designed a good product, he was sure that he would get the financial backing.

John's academic average after three semesters in college was slightly better than C; in the last semester, however, he had received a D in his accounting course. His College Board scores indicated that he had considerable scholastic ability. Both his Verbal and Mathematics scores were above 650. His freshman test scores indicated that he was considerably above average in vocabulary, reading ability, and English expression. He realized that his college grades were lower than one would expect from a person with his potential.

John had graduated from a nearby high school with a C-plus average. He was the oldest son of a successful businessman. Both mother and father were college graduates active in many civic and social organizations and well known in the community. His father had started his own business about twenty years before and the business had grown and prospered rapidly.

In looking back, John felt that his choice of accounting as a career was more his father's decision than his own. His father had often spoken in glowing terms of the opportunities available in business and of the advantages provided by an accounting background.

John spoke of his feelings about the school. He disliked it; he felt that many courses were impractical and the disciplinary regulations too severe. He was not happy. As a day student in a school that was primarily a boarding school, he felt somehow that he did not belong. He would come to school each morning, attend his classes, and return home each day. He did not participate in campus activities except as a spectator at the university football and basketball games. He had no close friends on campus.

At home, he did have two close friends who had been his friends since high-school days. One of them was married; the other was engaged. John was in the company of the two couples a great deal. They would often stop by his house to pick him up and he would tag along with them to a dance or to the movies.

John had had only two dates in the last five months. He did not attend any of the college mixers or dances. His dates were girls he had known since high school. In the recent past he had dated a girl for about ten months and had thought that their relationship was a serious one. The girl, however, had told him that she liked him only as a friend. He had tried to date other girls recently but was refused a number of times.

He indicated that he was discouraged because he was not studying as much as he felt he should. At home, he was spending almost all his time, with the exception of the limited socializing that he was doing, repairing the cars of his friends. He did this repair work in the driveway and garage. His parents objected to his cluttering up the driveway with cars. His father, John said, also objected to his dirtying his hands with grease. Despite his parents' objections, John was preparing to work during the summer-vacation period as an automobile mechanic.

In the process of counseling, a number of tests were administered. On the Kuder Preference Record, Vocational, John indicated high interest only on the Mechanical and Artistic scales. His lowest interest scores were on the Computational and Social Service scales. These scores would seem to have indicated that John was enrolled in the wrong program and perhaps in the wrong school. His stated preference for engineering would seem to have been confirmed as a good choice.

On the Edwards Personal Preference Schedule he indicated high manifest needs for self-abasement (tendency to self-criticism with feelings of inadequacy and inferiority), affiliation (need for friends and friendships), aggression (tendency to be critical of others), autonomy (need to be independent of others in making decisions), and heterosexuality (need to socialize with the opposite sex). Test scores also indicated that he had low needs to achieve something of significance and to defer to other people for help in making decisions.

A sentence-completion test was also administered. Responses on this test, the scores on the other tests, and the data of the counseling sessions seemed to indicate that John's three major areas of difficulty were the following:

1. John was reacting to rather deep feelings of inadequacy and inferiority, having to do primarily with intellectual ability. He did not see himself as a successful college student nor as a college graduate.

2. As a consequence, he did not participate fully in the life on the campus, nor was he motivated to do well with his studies. Socially, he was also having difficulties. He had been rejected recently by a girl he liked and had dated for ten months, and he had also been refused dates by other girls. These refusals made him depressed. His feelings were aggravated by the fact that his two closest friends, with whom he often socialized, were married and engaged. Being constantly in their company increased the pressure on him to date girls. His need to socialize became more impelling than his need to achieve.

3. There was also a conflict with his parents. The parents were both college graduates. The father was a successful business executive. John felt that his father in particular dominated him. He felt that he had majored in accounting under his father's pressure. He felt that his parents were critical of his interest in automobiles because they considered such work beneath the dignity of the family. On the sentence-completion test John wrote, "My father never considers me capable of making a decision unless my decision agrees with his." John said he objected to any order or suggestion given him because he felt that they implied that he could not make a correct decision himself.

This conflict generated several problems. John realized that he tended to act contrary to his parents' wishes in everything. He objected to everything they suggested and favored everything to which they objected. These feelings were also displaced to other authority figures. He readily acknowledged that perhaps one reason why he was insisting on continuing to repair cars on his driveway was because his parents objected to it. Also, there was some indication on the sentence-completion test that perhaps he was doing poorly academically because his parents were pressuring him to succeed in a course which he felt he had not freely chosen. He wrote, "Whenever I do below-average work, I feel a certain triumph in having done it."

A number of counseling sessions were devoted to a discussion of John's relationship with his parents and with others. The counselor also had a long talk with the parents. Eventually, John's relationship with his parents began to improve. He said that they were beginning to listen to him. He also began to develop new friendships on campus and to attend college mixers and dances. Slowly he began to apply himself to his studies and to earn higher grades.

The question of whether or not to transfer to an engineering school was discussed at great length in the early counseling sessions. Gradually, however, the discussions turned to other matters, primarily John's relationship with his parents, and his social problems. As counseling progressed, he came to see more and more that he may have been pursuing the role of an automobile mechanic and may have chosen the vocational goal of designing and building cars as compensation for his inability to succeed with his studies. As often happens with students who do poorly in college, John was involving himself in what he considered to be his only area of competence—repairing cars. He also came to realize that he was perhaps persisting in these endeavors to spite his father, to have his own way regardless of his parents' objections. He began to feel that his objections to college, and especially to the accounting program, may actually have been reactions to his parents' pressure.

Finally, he began to feel that his dissatisfaction with school may really have been the reflection of his personal unhappiness at home and of his social inadequacy. It may also have resulted from his inability to do well academically and from his hesitancy to participate actively in campus life.

In the final counseling session in late May, John indicated that he had given up the idea of working as an auto mechanic during the summer months. He had found a job working at a nearby summer resort, which he said would provide him with a good salary and the opportunity to socialize with boys and girls his own age. He indicated, too, that he had decided not to transfer to an engineering school. He now felt that his problems were within himself and not caused by the school or by the accounting program. He said he was pretty certain that if he did transfer he would only take his problems with him.

The counselor had no contact with John during his last two years in college. But if his academic performance is any indication of his general adjustment, it can be surmised that John continued to improve until his graduation from college.

## A Case Study in Religious Commitment
(MOTHER M. STELLA MARIS)

### History and Development

Rosemary was a college freshman who came to a rather sudden decision to embrace the religious life. During Thanksgiving holidays, 1947, she made an appointment with the Mother Provincial and having heard what would be expected of her, felt the price was too great to pay. Mother encouraged her to give herself to her studies and to pray that she might make the best choice when the issue had to be faced.

In February, 1948, Rosemary returned to the Provincial House with the request for entrance papers, as she had decided to come to the novitiate in September, 1948. The community had decided differently: a girl who had shown instability in her decision could not be accepted until she had first proved herself over a period of time. Upon learning this news, Rosemary was truly crestfallen. It was suggested that she read certain books, find herself, and analyze her motives. Incidentally, she was advised to stop smoking.

She was totally unprepared for the refusal and seemed dejected for about a week. However, being an intelligent girl she decided to get help with her problem. On her own admission, she thought the Sisters would be so happy to have her in their community that she had given no thought to the development of her own spiritual, intellectual, or social life. Now her inflated ego had been shattered. If she were to choose the religious life, she had to begin from scratch and build the character Christ would want her to have. It was a rude awakening. Later she confessed, "I mused: 'Apply yourself to your studies.' Yes, I'll show them I can work. And there was something about being able to work with others. I never could stand Mary Jane, but I'll begin with her. First I must find something of interest to us both . . ."

Rosemary is now in her sophomore year. She has followed advice and grown some. Rather timidly one day she picks up the telephone and asks if the Mother Provincial would be willing to see her. She receives an affirmative answer and soon trips lightly but still fearfully down the hill. What if she receives a negative reply to her request? Well, she has prayed, worked, read the suggested books. If it's her vocation God will show her a way. Faith, and trust, and love—this was what Sister X kept repeating; and Father Y had not been easy on her, constantly pointing out her foibles.

A smiling Sister admits her to the parlor. Mother Provincial does not even allude to the previous visit but inquires casually about her academic progress, if she likes her college, and so forth. Then, to Rosemary's relief, asks, "Do you have some problem you wish to discuss?" "Oh, yes, Mother, I came to beg you to give me a chance. I really know now that God wants me to be a Sister. I have no doubts. They are all resolved. I was just selfish. I love nice clothes, my car, my own way of doing things, but I've thought it all over and made a decision. In fact, I have already informed my boyfriend that I have other plans for my future and he has a right to know this. Please let me come in September." Without hesitation Mother takes a set of papers from the file and together they peruse them. The usual questions are asked and answered. As soon as both are satisfied that there is mutual understanding, the interview is brought to a close and Rosemary rushes up the hill and into the chapel. She is so grateful. Next she must get in touch with her favorite teacher and also let Father know that the first hurdle has been overcome. For a few brief moments she is literally walking on air. But ere long fear settles over her again. What if she doesn't pass the physical? She must make an appointment soon. Mercy Hospital! She never did like doctors and nurses. But why complain about another sacrifice if it would help her get that postulant's cap!

On May 1 she has her physical and survives the ordeal. Within the next two weeks she has seen her dentist and oculist. By the end of the month she has accumulated all the required data and delivered the papers to the Provincial House. She leaves school for home and rather impatiently waits for *that* letter. Finally it comes. The answer is what she desires—or is it? She reads: "You will be welcomed at Mother of Mercy Novitiate at 4 p.m., September 8, 1948 . . ." Two whole months and longer to wait. Suppose this is a mistake. Does she really have a vocation for the religious life? Many thoughts rush through her mind. What will she miss most? Why did she ever make such a decision? But she did, and of her own free will. No one encouraged her too much. No one pushed her into it. Mother and Father were not too happy when she told them, but they would not oppose her. They loved her and wanted her to be happy. Right now she wishes they had said "No" because it would give her an excuse. She must pray. An idea strikes her: Why not write to Sister Mary and ask if one has to be sure all the time? Does God really tell you in some way? Meanwhile she must see about a job for the summer. She will need some money to buy necessary items. Having found the job, she concentrates upon it; doubts about convent life vanish and she is at peace. September is here and the farewell parties are in full swing. She is very tired, but she will have plenty of time to rest when she gets to the convent. Don't the Sisters go to bed at nine?

The first few days of the postulancy are exciting: new friends, new surroundings, new schedules. College classes begin again, but now in a different setting. She has been too preoccupied to think of home. Soon she must learn routine. Silence is a must at certain times, in certain places. She loves to talk. Just think of trying to be recollected while you climb in and out of a postulant's outfit trying desperately to reach the chapel before the second bell rings! She begins to feel repressed. She has set her heart on an ideal. Overnight, so to speak, she expects to be a woman of prayer. She wills to be detached from home, family, friends. She makes a desperate effort to be someone she is not. The road ahead is going to be very difficult. She will need much counseling. Her mistress recognizes the signs. She must help her know herself. To her mistress she admits she felt pretty virtuous when she decided to enter. Now she is beginning to see a lot of flaws she doesn't like. Actually, she has begun to grow spiritually, but she is not conscious of the fact. She has to battle two extremes: willfulness and will-lessness. It has been something of a jolt to find that just because she wills to cast aside all past emotions, memories, experiences, they don't just go away. She wills to detach herself from her family, but she has very close ties to them. Memories at times overwhelm her and she secretly weeps because she misses her home so much. She recalls only the pleasant and attractive things. She never remembers the corrections, the quarrels, the minor or major difficulties that are a part of family life. It will take years for her to realize that nature abhors a vacuum, and for every diminishment there must be a fulfillment and vice versa. Detachment from family can only be complete when attachment to the Lord is perfect. Growth is painful.

Because Rosemary has shown signs of growth and good will, her request for the habit is granted. She is now Sister Rose Agnes. Dangers still beset her path. The novice must act as becomes a novice. She wants to grow too fast and in the effort ceases to be herself. By repressing her true feelings, she has become artificial, rigid, tense, strained. She complains of headaches. She is exhausted. (Any wonder?) Aversions for silence and for certain types of work come to the fore. She is developing some hostility toward persons and reaching a stage where she feels she might just as well give up. In this disturbed state, at the end of her canonical year, she arrives at the blessed decision to let her mistress in on all that has been transpiring within her soul. After an hour or so, she is led to see that she has been quite unfair to herself. She has dealt with herself not as a person, but as if she were a piece of stone. She has misunderstood the nature and task of the will in religious growth. She is encouraged to take some extra rest, to relax a little, and not to take herself too seriously because the Lord doesn't. Since she really loves Him, all will be well.

Her second year of novitiate passes comparatively smoothly. She is back at secular studies. Her theology and philosophy classes help her understand herself and others a little better. She seeks guidance and profits by it. She still makes mistakes. She encounters a few personality clashes. She works on these and succeeds fairly well. She is more tolerant of her own shortcomings and those of others. She knows now she is not perfect and that it will take a long time for her to reach her ideal. At times she shows signs of immaturity, looking for attention from her friends; but her heart is centered on the Lord.

She is admitted to profession of temporary vows and leaves the novitiate with the satisfaction of having come a long way in three years. Two more years of intense training in the juniorate lie ahead, at the end of which she will be expected to take her place in the apostolate. Her religious formation continues under a mistress, and she is to finish her collegiate studies and get some enrichment. She is more on her own. She is given opportunities for decision making, for taking responsibility on a somewhat larger scale, for making mistakes from which she is expected to learn but which she is expected not to repeat. She has to adjust to the house of studies. This adjustment she does not find too easy. Some conflicts arise within her, and a certain superficiality comes to the surface again. Her life is religious and regular externally. She

never misses a religious exercise. However, there is pious self-deceit
underneath. This willful self of hers is closed, cumbersome, compulsive.
Signs of stubbornness and obstinacy appear. Her companions look upon
her as a "wet blanket." All joy seems to have left her life. Her self-
image of religious perfection is distorted. Instead of listening for the
voice of God, she is addicted to her own blueprint of perfection. She
assumes a holier-than-thou attitude which is obnoxious to her companions. They can't understand the sudden change that has come over
her. She used to be so thoughtful of others and the life of the novitiate;
but now in her willfulness she has developed a code of tangential perceptions of God, herself, and everybody else. While in this stage, she
does not admit weakness or limitations. In fact, she fails to understand
the deepest meanings of the Christian life as expressed in Scripture,
dogma, and liturgy. She has lost sight of the dictum: Grace builds on
nature. She must learn to work as if everything depended on her, to
pray as if all depended on God. In her confused state she doesn't realize the need for balance.

  When she had been convinced she had put too much reliance on her
will power, she veered toward the opposite extreme. Now she searches
for things in her past and present life to blame for failure and imper-
fections. She becomes rather will-less and unfree and claims her life
is defined by public opinion, social approval, her own impulses and
passions. There are now reactions instead of responses. Impulsiveness
is evident. Her face shows a little more joy. Her mistress helps her
begin a dialogue between her freedom and her mood. This free discussion leads to growth in holiness, a glorious commitment to God, a new
beginning in the spiritual life. This growth from within is genuine,
honest, and radical because it is unseen by others.

  Behavior is conditioned, but conditioning can be influenced by meaning—something that the young Sister has to learn very often. Her attitude toward authority may be a carryover from parental attitudes.
Sister Rose Agnes had a healthy attitude toward her father and mother,
and this attitude has proved to be a real asset to her as she strives to
grow in religious maturity. She accepts her superior not only as a
person having authority over her, but also as a human being capable
of understanding her at least insofar as she can make herself understood. She can therefore be open, relaxed, trustful, and spontaneous
with those in positions of authority. Her spirit of obedience is unques-
tionable. She gives due attention to the practice of the three vows of

poverty, chastity, and obedience. Her attitudes are positive rather than negative.

Having finished a year at her first mission, Sister Rose Agnes returned to the Motherhouse for the summer of preparation for her perpetual vows. By giving herself to others, she found her true self.

Today, fifteen years after she entered the postulancy, Sister Rose Agnes is a well-integrated personality capable of directing her own life and of guiding others, thanks to her own efforts to grow in virtue and to the painstaking efforts of those in whose charge she was placed. The difficulties she encountered and overcame were stepping-stones to real religious commitment. The road was long and hard. It will never be easy, because she has dedicated herself by vow to follow a thorn-crowned Spouse. Love will make it possible. She persevered in her good resolves despite obstacles. She went from one extreme to another in her search for balance and succeeded in finding the middle path and in holding fast to it. Long ago she learned not to negate spontaneous inclinations but to give them direction. Her spontaneity radiates warmth. Her interest in people grows out of gratitude for what people have done for her. Faith illuminates her mind and enables her to see God in those about her and in those with whom she works. Her desires for a family of her own have been sublimated. Her thirty-five girls for whom she acts as home-room teacher are her children in the real sense of the word.

Wholesome growth in her religious existence calls for the integration of will, spontaneity, and decision in the light of Grace and Revelation. The virtue of prudence regulates the practice of other virtues. There is no longer a tendency to deny either the mean or the exalted drives within her as she searches her soul at daily examination of conscience. In real humility she begs pardon for her faults and thanks God for the increase in virtue which He has allowed her to achieve. She has come to realize that the only soil in which personality can grow is freedom. She is more free now than she ever was before because she knows what love means and has the constant awareness that God is Love. As a result her love for her family has increased, her attachment to all things of earth has decreased. Her heart is attached to God, and in loving Him she loves all else as well. She no longer worries about reaching the ideal she built for herself. Instead, she lets Christ model her by submitting to His will as it is made known through rules and regulations, through commands of superiors, through the teaching Church.

She sees her role as witness to the world of the 1960's that Christ still walks this earth, that His Gospel brings peace, that in suffering here below with Him and for Him we are preparing ourselves and others for the Beatific Vision. Only when she beholds Him face to face will she have fully achieved her ideal.

### Analysis and Conclusions

Sister Rose Agnes as a college freshman was a typical teenager. She showed initiative, enthusiasm, insecurity, fear. She was indecisive when it came to big issues. She was selfish and expected things to go her way. As her story unfolded, you watched her grow. At times her zeal was too great. She attempted too much in too short a space of time. By trying to be something of the Spanish mystic, she bordered on becoming a neurotic personality. She did not take temperament into account. In fact, she seemed to forget that its roots lay deep in her biological make-up. Temperament has much to say about the swiftness or slowness of our movements, how our thought processes operate most efficiently, how intense are our feelings, affections, and passions. Sister Rose Agnes attempted to change her temperament in an absolute way and found she could not succeed. Temperament is a limitation set by nature, and when one tries to bypass it, nature rebels. A temporary change in her personality was noted. Instead of the happy, carefree Sister, we saw the awkward, tense, unhappy, ineffectual person.

Fortunately, this Sister had a mistress of experience and motherly understanding who perceived her true character, had insight into her temperament, and had the ability to lead her to a necessary understanding of herself as a person. No two people, religious or otherwise, can be cast into the same mold. God makes each soul uniquely one's own. This individual difference has to be considered in all phases of human growth and development. Growth in religious experience and commitment is no exception. It is easier to look good than to be good, to sound learned than to be learned. Confusion of temperament with religious personality could be fatal to one's development. Each one must go to God in his own way, not by blindly aping someone else. To reach holiness or sanctity is to be wholly oneself in and for God. Saint differs from saint as night from day. The goal is identical, the means as varied as human nature permits.

The conclusion is evident: much patience, sympathetic understanding, interested charity, and encouragement are the ingredients necessary for the healthy growth of youth. The wise counselor will exhibit these traits and thus enable the young to develop God-given potentialities to the fullest. Where these traits are lacking, growth is dwarfed.

External faults are life-long companions. They are not barriers to sanctity. God searches the heart. A person with a fortunate life history may reach personal maturity but love God less than the neighbor who, bogged down by past history, is slow to mature but has already acquired tremendous love for the Lord. Good insight into the characteristics of a real personality helps superiors and administrators appoint the right persons to the right places. The guides of youth have a grave responsibility to encourage and not kill initiative, to instill reverence and respect for lawfully constituted authority, to give opportunity for constructive criticism, and to establish a climate of trust and openness.

The vision of the ideal keeps us all humble. We know what we would like to be and what we are not yet and perhaps never will be. It makes us tolerant of others, appreciative of their efforts, slow to find fault with outcomes, and keenly conscious of what we might have become were it not for the Grace of God.

## Early Marriage Problems
(ABRAHAM SHUSTERMAN)

There are both advantages and disadvantages to the position in which I now find myself. I am neither an authority on marriage nor an experienced marriage counselor. Therefore, the following are words of an amateur in this important field of endeavor. But as the rabbi of a congregation, I hold a position similar to that of the parish priest in that my experience is varied and my door always open to troubled people, not only to members of my own synagogue but also to nonmembers, Jews, Christians, and the unaffiliated. Those of you who are fellow Baltimoreans may be acquainted with our weekly television program. The fact that we are now completing our eighth year on the air has helped cause a path to be beaten to my study and, I am sure, to those of Dr. Helfer and the late Msgr. Dunn. People come to us to discuss their problems. What experience I share with you today and whatever insights I may offer grow out of my status as a religious general practitioner.

There is another important limitation to my experience: the character of my congregation, which is largely suburban and middle-class. Most of my members are neither rich nor poor. Many of them are reasonably comfortable and a few are rather affluent. Their problems are those of northwest Baltimoreans, of family-conscious, well-to-do Jews. There are certainly difficulties which grow out of great wealth or abject poverty that have not been brought to me.

Today there is to some extent a changing pattern in Jewish family life. A generation ago we could boast of families whose solidarity resulted from a complete dedication to their religion and whose response to a non-Jewish environment was largely that of people who were acutely aware of their minority status. I can remember how often my parents remarked that a Jewish boy must be more studious or that a Jewish citizen must be more careful in his behavior because he was a clearly distinguishable member of a minority. He bore the disabilities of both the individual and of the group. In my boyhood days in Dayton, Ohio, a Jew ran afoul of the law and my father commented that, if he were the judge, he would throw the book at him. In other words, a Jew had to behave because his misbehavior was a reflection on his family and his faith.

We have come into a different period of history and these minority fears are no longer typical. Also our homes have begun to be influenced by the centrifugal forces that lead our young people away from the family hearth. This is the result of the automobile and the other advances in transportation. Home is often a place where a person takes his meals and sleeps. It is no longer the center of his religion and culture, the locale of his recreation and the place of his greatest satisfactions. If the Jewish home is still stronger than the homes of other Americans and if there are less divorce and delinquency among Jewish people, we can only be grateful for small blessings. We are part of the world, and the impact of this secularized society can already be felt.

As regards teenagers who marry, I find that there are problems of at least two kinds. The first is the problem of the boy or girl who, as the years pass, outgrows his spouse. At eighteen or nineteen the couple seems to be so compatible. They are both young, attractive, alert, charming, eager to love and be loved. They may even come from the same kind of families, and their romance may have flowered within the same synagogue. In almost every case of early teenage marriage, children are soon brought into the world. Usually financial difficulty is not the main reason for discord. On the contrary, I can think only of reasonably successful couples who have faced financial problems. The woman of thirty is different from the girl of eighteen. She has taken advantage of cultural opportunities: she has studied poetry, literature, art, drama, even classical dancing. The years have made her somewhat of an accomplished and even sophisticated young matron. She is conversant with ideas, historic trends, and schools of art. Her taste has been refined. But her husband has remained a teenager in every respect except physically. His tastes are those of a teenager and seem anachronous. After all, he is a man in the early thirties whose response to life should be that of a grown man. His major concerns, in addition to making a living, are poker, drinking, athletic contests and, of course, golf. He falls sound asleep at the ballet or opera. In fact, he finds it difficult to become interested in what transpires on the theater stage.

Please understand that I am not evaluating this couple or placing the blame on either of them. The husband has been hard at work, providing the necessities of life for his family and some of the luxuries. The wife has had cultural opportunities offered by her synagogue, the neighboring community center, and the women's club to which she belongs. Each has begun to go his own way. In my counseling I can only urge her to show patience and understanding. She cannot be asked to forfeit her right to intellectual and aesthetic growth. He must be shown the light and urged to begin to share some of her interests, if not all of them. I have often urged them, and with some real results, to begin to do things together within the confines of their temple. They have been urged to attend a few classes together and to work with a few of the groups that combine sociability with the study of wiser parenthood and the literary monuments of religion. A truly patient couple that wants to restore their family to its original unity can get results if they are earnest and give their hearts to the venture.

A second type of problem grows out of the status of the husband. Frequently his wife comes from an affluent family. She is accustomed to many luxuries which her father can provide. Her husband is really only a boy and his earning capacity is limited. In her immaturity she wants the luxuries her mother enjoys and that she enjoyed in her years in her parents' home. It is so easy to accept gifts from her father. Does she need a car of her own? Surely her father can provide one for her. Does she want a full-time maid? Her father is always generous and indulgent.

The great danger in this arrangement is that the husband begins to feel that he is no longer—indeed, never has been—the head of the household. His wife takes her problems to her father, not to her husband. In my experience this has been the source of discord and disharmony within the family. Often I have had to convince fathers to adopt a less generous, certainly a less lavish, policy with their married daughters. Usually it is easier to convince the father to show wisdom and restraint than it is to convince his daughter that her husband is first in her life and the provider for his household. Again, patience, understanding, and a genuine desire to save the family are needed.

I cannot give you statistics about the success or failure of these ventures. There have been divorces. There have been failures. There have been successes. But, as a rabbi and a spokesman for an old religious tradition, I try to reason with young husbands and wives. At times it is hard to convince them to postpone marriage until they are spiritually, educationally, and emotionally ready for it. Biology has a way of winning out over the other disciplines. I try earnestly to help them grow in understanding and patience, so that they will see how important it is to make their marriage work. Marriages are truly successful only when both parties are grown up, and it is a task of religion, as it is the task of education, to help people grow. Were this a sermon instead of a case history I would use the text from Exodus II:11, "And it came to pass in those days, when Moses was grown . . ." Only when Moses was grown was he ready for religious leadership and marriage.

# PART IV

## Adolescent Feelings and Emotions

▲▲▲▲▲▲▲▲▲▲▲▲▲▲▲▲▲▲▲▲▲▲▲▲▲▲▲▲▲▲▲▲

# 13. Emotional Development in Adolescence

## LEO H. BARTEMEIER

For many young persons the onset of adolescence is a sudden and un-expected emotional storm of such intensity that it shakes the founda-tions of their previous moral and spiritual training and their education. There is no other period in life during which previously healthy per-sons experience the profound emotional upheaval that characterizes adolescence. Our discussion of these difficult years between being a child and becoming an adult will, we hope, add to your understanding of the emotional development of young persons after the onset of puberty.

The preparation for emotional development in adolescence is deter-mined by the inherited predispositions, by the maternal environment prior to birth, and by the life experiences from that time until the onset of puberty. Unfortunately, the emotional development of many children has been so severely arrested that they remain emotionally retarded or, as we say, emotionally immature. These youngsters are not our concern here.

In our discussion of the emotional changes that take place in young persons who are relatively healthy, I first shall consider the biological concept of inborn behavior patterns. These patterns appear in succes-sion at specific stages of development in all human beings. They are characteristic of the wholesome development of each person. They are latent and appear and develop with the assistance of those in charge of the training and education of the young. They develop in a rela-tively orderly sequence, and as we shall see, they begin to appear early in life and exert a marked influence on human behavior. We are here speaking of nature and nurture, and we may compare these behavior patterns in human beings to the potentialities for growth and development in plant life. A seed has the potential of becoming a specific kind of plant, but it needs the proper soil, light, and moisture to go through various stages of its growth and development. Without this assistance from the environment the seed cannot develop.

Now let us consider a behavior pattern which appears during babyhood and which has relevance for our discussion of emotional development during adolescence. Throughout the first year of life, the infant is continuously in a passive relation to its mother. It can do nothing for itself. It is completely helpless and dependent upon its mother for survival. Beginning with the second year, or soon thereafter, when the first teeth have come out, when locomotion has begun to develop, and when language is being acquired, a remarkable emotional change first appears in the baby's relation to its mother. This change consists in a persistent opposition to the complete dependency on the mother and manifests itself in repeated attempts on the part of the baby to feed himself instead of being fed by his mother. He is still too young to manage eating by himself and his attempts to do so, as we all know, are very clumsy and awkward. He spills his food over himself and his mother. But he keeps trying and he is very determined to succeed. Between his efforts he also lets his mother feed him. He also plays at feeding his mother and combing her hair.

The second year of his life is the so-called negative year—the year of refusing to comply with many of his mother's requests. This change, which invariably appears during the second year of life in all healthy babies, is characteristic of an inborn pattern of behavior. The previously helpless infant now manifests his first struggle towards autonomy and his first efforts to master the outside world. It is important for our discussion to reemphasize that this marked change in behavior during the second year of life appears with unswerving regularity in all healthy babies and can always be predicted with certainty. This pattern is the same as the striking behavior pattern which appears after the onset of puberty. This pattern consists of an intensive striving by young persons to sever their dependency upon their parents and to develop new identifications in their struggle toward becoming adults.

The biological changes that mark the onset of puberty have a profound influence on emotional development, with the result that adolescence is a period of terrific turmoil. The remarkable physical changes which take place from the onset of puberty are caused by the release of specific hormones by the pituitary gland at the base of the brain.

We have been informed by Doctor Eamonn F. O'Doherty, Professor of Psychology at the University College, Dublin, that

. . . a radical change in the development processes of the young people with whom we are concerned is becoming clearer throughout the world. We now know, for example, that every ten years, for the last one hundred and twenty years, adolescence has been progressively occurring earlier, about four months earlier every ten years in the case of girls. It is easy to measure it in the case of girls, awfully difficult in the case of boys, and so we are not quite so certain about the rate of change in boys. But we do know that girls are entering adolescence earlier than their great grandparents, than their grandparents, and than their parents. If we summate the changes we could say that our girls are now entering adolescence four years earlier than their ancestors a hundred and twenty years ago. We also know that boys are a little later than girls, but the relative difference means that they are about a year later. But still they will be about four years earlier than their forebears of over a century ago.

At the other end of the scale we know that society is prolonging adolescence into what would have been adulthood for our forebears. Two processes are occurring therefore. Biologically, we are getting into this period earlier, and socially we remain in it longer. This should have had the effect of stabilizing our young people, because one would have expected that this longer formative period would have produced more stable, more mature adults. We must ask, "Is that, in fact, the case?" The answer appears to be "No."

There are many reasons for this. Perhaps the primary reason is that we have ceased in many respects to attempt a positive formation of young people, perhaps largely because we are not clear ourselves as to what the end product ought to be. Moreover, it may very well be that this prolonged period of adolescence instead of stabilizing the developing personality, may be, itself, the source of many problems and conflicts which appear in the context of mental health, both during and after college years. The prolonging of adolescence means, in effect, that we are not calling forth, from the young persons, at an early enough point, the controls of adulthood, and we are permitting the prolonging of the adolescent type of thinking and the adolescent type of feeling.

It is important that we should remember that the developing intellect reaches its maximum expansion at the age of sixteen, or thereabouts. The emotional development, however, goes on much longer, and one cannot expect now to find emotional maturity much before the age of twenty-four or twenty-five. I would go further and say much before thirty or thirty-five, or even forty-five. The physical development, however, has reached maturity much earlier even than the intellect. So we are concerned with three curves of development which are rarely in phase. If we try to plot the physiological curve on the one hand, the emotional curve on the other, and the intellectual curve on the third, we will find on the whole that when one of these is undergoing a rapid development, the other two have slowed down. For example, at puberty, when the organism is undergoing tremendous and rapid and sudden changes, the developing intelligence slows down considerably, and the emotional development has been, in fact, slowed down for several years before that, during the latency period. Once the organism has made its adjustment to the puberty situation, the intellect goes through an enormous burst of development, and when the intellect has reached its maximum expansion, the emotions start to catch up, and they go through their development to maturation also.[1]

Some of the young persons with whom we are concerned undergo a psychological regression in early adolescence. As their emotional attachments to their parents are withdrawn, they are unable to reinvest them in other persons of their own age or older persons outside the family. In such situations their love feelings become invested in themselves. When this occurs, they tend to regard themselves as they regarded their parents when they were very young. In those early years they believed their mothers and fathers were omniscient and omnipotent, and they now come to feel this way about themselves. They become inflated about their knowledge, their beauty, and their power, and remind us of persons afflicted with delusions of grandeur. It is characteristic of these young people that they tolerate no disagreement with their opinions. Their knowledge of history, of politics, or whatever subject they may have studied is absolute and final and "the last word." They become almost belligerent whenever their parents disagree with their ideas.

Unfortunately, these adolescents who were predisposed by their previous life experiences to undergo a psychological regression remain emotionally immature. They are incapable of caring as much for others as they care for themselves, and their social maladjustment is intensified by marriage and parenthood.

It is characteristic of all adolescents to manifest *some* of the changes which I have been describing. But for the majority of young persons, exaggerated notions about themselves are less intense and more transient. The changes are the natural consequence of their struggles for emotional independence from their parents and of their need to displace their affectionate and hostile feelings toward them onto persons

---

[1] Unpublished lecture.

outside the family. It is through such displacements that healthy young persons develop additional identifications and become more capable of controlling their impulses.

It appears that these changes take place primarily under the influence of an innate behavior pattern which is similar to the pattern which characterizes the second year of life when the baby makes his initial effort to overcome his complete dependency on his mother. Both patterns are efforts on the part of the organism to overcome dependency and to become self-reliant. Both the baby and the adolescent are developing and progressing emotionally.

I have previously stated that endogenous behavior patterns need environmental influences to evoke them. The observed pattern in early adolescence is nurtured by the attitudes, the behavior, the manner of personal attire, and the like, of classmates and others whom the young adolescent imitates and with whom he identifies. This pattern is also nurtured by store clerks, bus drivers, police, and other public figures who behave toward the adolescent as though he were already of their own age.

Dr. C. Knight Aldrich provides the following pertinent information for our discussion:

In the period just before puberty, the average child experiences relative emotional comfort. His ego has developed enough to master most of the usual internal and external pressures. He pushes ahead boldly to establish new relationships with friends and to develop new skills. He is reasonably independent and responsible. Confident of his ability to accomplish his goals and to make his decisions, he begins to seek a life more separate from his parents. Until now, his identification has been primarily with his parents; in the process of beginning separation, he reaches out for new objects of identification beyond his parents. By the end of adolescence, in order to be ready for the tasks of adulthood, he must have achieved his own identity, or a firm sense of self, by means of a successful synthesis of his early identifications or part identifications with the unique elements that he alone has contributed.

The new objects of identification cover a wide range. For the boy, an older brother, the father of a friend, or the high school athletic hero are possible transitional substitutes for the parents. Sometimes he may choose a more remote object—a television star, perhaps, or a professional athlete, but in any case he begins to draw comparisons between the new and the old objects, with emphasis on the deficiencies of the old. He becomes more critical of his father, and although he by no means discards his earlier identification, he uses criticism as a testing ground for his independence. The success of his tests depends to some extent on his father's tolerance; if the father rigidly clamps down on any sign of rebellion, his son may give up his attempts, at least for a while. If, on the other hand, the father takes criticism so seriously that his feelings are hurt by the unfavorable comparisons, the boy may inhibit his independent strivings, feeling that he may be jeopardizing his own basic security by threatening his father. The father who is secure in his role has helped his son feel secure enough to make the challenge and is prepared to welcome the challenge when it comes.

The girl goes through an analogous period of challenge. Hers is both more intense and less intense than the boy's—more intense because she is in closer contact with her mother, less intense because of the girl's greater subtlety in expressing aggression.

So begins, at a reasonably modulated pace, the child's effort to break away from family protection and to establish his own identity. Just as the process is getting under way, however, the balance between ego and drives is upset. Until puberty the ego (in a child who is relatively secure) has increased in strength faster than the drives, thus exciting an ever-increasing degree of control. Now, within a short time, the strength of the drives increases tremendously, leaving the ego in a relatively much weaker position.

The relative ego weakness generally becomes evident as the familiar phenomena of adolescence. In adolescence, smooth and predictable behavior is ordinarily replaced by clumsy and unpredictable behavior, relative responsibility by relative irresponsibility, and smooth development of maturity and independence by a spasmodic oscillation between demands for equal rights and regression into helpless dependency. The phases of the oscillation are often so irregular that no parent, however astute, can keep up with them.

The average adolescent, halfway between boy and man, wants desperately to be grown up but is appalled at adult responsibilities. Typically, when he looks at what is ahead of him, he retreats into the safety of his home; once safely ensconced under the protective wings of his parents, he feels more secure, his adult strivings take over, he becomes enraged at the failure of his parents to give him the recognition he believes he deserves, and once again he returns to try to master simultaneously both his drives and his environment. Eventually, as he accumulates some successes and particularly if he is able to fall back on the security of parental understanding without too much loss of self-esteem when he fails, his ego begins to catch up with the adolescent surge of instinctual drive. As he discovers that he can identify with his father and still be an individual, he reduces the intensity of his rebellion and moves on into maturity (Aldrich, 1966, pp. 171–173).

Doctor George Engel discusses the adolescent who does not succeed in displacing his attachments from his parents onto other persons:

He may defend himself by reversing his feelings and turn his love into hate, his dependence upon them into revolt, his respect and admiration for them into contempt and derision. This may occur from time to time in any adolescent but some adolescents utilize such devices in a sweeping manner. They imagine themselves to be free but actually they remain as securely tied as ever to their parents and to their great distress and suffering, and that of their parents, continue the same struggle. They do not actually move away from their parents but instead linger as hostile, belligerent, and irritating youngsters, rationalizing their behavior and projecting their hostility by claiming that they feel and act as they do because of the controlling and hostile behavior of their parents. In some cases this aggression may be turned against themselves, resulting in depression, self-destructive behavior and even suicidal consequences (Engel, 1962, pp. 147–148).

These and many other severe emotional reactions, precipitated by the physiological changes occurring after the onset of puberty, necessitate the mental-hospital treatment of adolescents. During their psychiatric treatment in these institutions, it becomes evident that some of them are more severely ill than was apparent at the time of their admission. It is not uncommon to discover that they manifest schizophrenic reactions, and that these grave mental disorders were developing at earlier periods of their development. In some instances their school teachers had recommended that these children be referred to mental-health clinics but in other instances the incipient mental disorders were not recognized because they occurred in the so-called "model children" who never gave their teachers any trouble.

We now know that it is useless to undertake the psychotherapy of seriously ill adolescents unless their fathers and mothers are also willing to engage in psychotherapy during the hospitalization of their sons and daughters. When this is not possible, it is often necessary to recommend that these young persons be relocated in more healthy social environments after they have improved sufficiently to warrant their discharge from the mental hospital. The hospital treatment of these young persons serves the purpose of relieving them of the acute manifestations of their mental disorders, and when they have regained enough control over their thinking and their behavior, they are returned to the community for the continuation of their psychotherapy with psychiatrists in private practice or on the staffs of mental-health clinics.

Many other adolescents who are overwhelmed by the intensity of their instinctual impulses, and who are unable to defend themselves in the various ways which we have been describing, discharge their feelings in destructive actions against their parents or other members of their families or engage in other forms of juvenile delinquency. The late Doctor Adelaide Johnson and her associates at the Mayo Clinic conducted intensive clinical investigations of the delinquent behavior of adolescents. They discovered that in many instances one of the parents had unintentionally encouraged or otherwise stimulated their sons and daughters to participate in various kinds of delinquent behavior that had been denied them during their own adolescent years. Much of this behavior was sexual in nature, was known to the parent involved, and provided the parent with vicarious pleasure.

The actions of other adolescents are devices for defending themselves against powerful heterosexual and homosexual impulses. These actions include murder without apparent motivation, addiction to narcotic drugs and alcohol, and intentional and accidental suicides. These, and many other tragic developments, occur in young persons of good intelligence and physical health who have suffered severe emotional damage in their earliest years, and whose subsequent relations with their parents also crippled their potentialities for renouncing their infantile dependency on their parents and on parental surrogates.

In describing the emotional aspects of adolescence, Doctor Sol Ginsberg, who had many years of clinical experience with young persons and who possessed a fine talent for expressing his views, said:

To understand adolescents it is important to remember that they are bewildered, frightened and confused. An adolescent patient of mine did a series of beautiful and expressive surrealistic paintings to express her feelings; woven in the design of one of them is the phrase, "I'm a stranger here myself." I could think of no expression truer or more revealing. The adolescent finds his newly approaching adulthood strange indeed; he finds the departure from childhood frightening, and the attitude and the demands of the adult world little short of terrifying. To help them, adults must understand them. Young people welcome the expressed recognition by adults, especially parents, that they too were once adolescents and behaved in pretty much the same way. Although suspicious and distrustful of the grownups' motives, boys and girls will profit by good-humored explanations especially when an adult is not aloof. What makes the situation difficult for the parent, though, is the fact that love, generosity, kindness, or permissiveness are often not enough to deal with the adolescent's problems. After all my years of experience, in fact, I know of nothing that so completely defied any generalized prescription as adolescence. I believe this is so because its conditioning begins in the cradle. I often feel that in the end the only solace for adolescent and adult alike is the recognition that this too passes (Ginsburg, 1963, pp. 67–68).

# 14. Emotional Disturbances in Adolescence

## LEO KANNER

Every day of man's life constitutes a transition between yesterday and tomorrow, converging in the intrinsic values of the moment. The past and present continue to shape and modify directions and goals, mostly through quiet evolution, sometimes in lively spurts. One of the liveliest spurts occurs during adolescence, at a time when a person is no longer a child and not yet an adult.

Many incisive changes take place in that period. Body growth, in a remarkably rapid surge, attains its maximum. The physique assumes its characteristic configuration. Sexual development reaches procreative capacity. There is striving for emancipation from sheltered existence, a trend toward increasing self-dependence in thought and action. The sphere of interest and participation expands from the confines of home, neighborhood, and school to the community at large. The choice of vocation, until then a playfully considered matter, becomes a real issue. Current standards and precepts are submitted to criticisms not as yet leavened by the tests of experience. The established order is challenged boldly and then, after some struggle, appropriated gradually with more or less reservation.

Adolescence, in our culture, is a great translator. It translates the language of parental direction, attitudes, and behavior into an individualized idiom. This process is much less evident in primitive cultures. One might go so far as to say that in primitive societies there is no conceptual equivalent for that which we call adolescence. Childhood ceases abruptly when, through a set of elaborate rites, the young person is transported into full-fledged adulthood. Tribal ritualism, rather than personal spontaneity, determines status and function. In our social structure, a child is given several years in which to find his way from a more or less manipulated and regimented existence to the acquisition of initiative in a loosely competitive environment in which the taboos are blurred, the semantics are equivocal, and the variety of occupational, political, and theologic choices offer opportunities for perplexities. The adolescent translator's dictionary is full of confusing synonyms and antonyms.

A combination of inner soundness, wholesome parent-child relationships, and guidance from understanding adults helps most adolescents to emerge safely from the groping and floundering which precede maturing stabilization. Overreaching or falling short of the target can be attenuated by bringing aimer, aim, and target into reasonably comfortable harmony. However, the great variety of backgrounds and personalities is fraught with possibilities of troubling conflicts and clashes. Developmental shortcomings, early exposure to pathogenic parental attitudes, and burdensome life situations may work singly or together to intensify perplexities and twist emotions and performances. Hurdles taken by others with sufficient skill and economy of effort may come to loom as conspicuous barriers and are circumvented inefficiently, avoided shrinkingly, or allowed to inflict serious damage during clumsy and incongruous attempts to surmount them.

The normal adolescent has his puzzlements and preoccupations; trouble starts when the puzzlements and preoccupations threaten to "have" the adolescent. It is then that the tasks of accepting one's identity, fitting oneself to things and people as they are, and establishing and maintaining give-and-take relationships come to a crucial test. Sensitiveness about physical appearance and functioning may become a predominant feature, with excessive self-observation and logically as well as empirically inadmissible causal associations. Prevailing superstitions and pamphlet lore, sometimes echoed even by physicians, make masturbation a focus of worry and dread. The search for social and cosmic orientation confronts the fledgling with ill-defined generalizations which he can brush aside without much ado, explore in pseudophilosophic ruminations and debates, eventually sift for practical usage, or confuse to a degree that is out of proportion with utility and reality. Ambitions may fall in line with expectations and serve as guides for consistent planning, lag behind expectations through want of ability, purpose, initiative, or self-confidence, shoot far beyond the attainable mark in fantasies but little related to actualities, or miss the mark through jerky, misdirected, prematurely spent thrusts.

Many young people, well prepared biologically and educationally, go through the second decade of life without essential disturbance. Some get entangled temporarily, but emerge steadily, pulling themselves up by their own bootstraps or, if need be, holding on to a guiding hand. Others may become thoroughly engulfed in all-embracing moods, ensnared in abstractions, trapped in blind alleys or mystic preoccupations, drawn away from or rudely tossed into realities—and thus come into serious danger of getting lost in their efforts to find themselves and their place in the scheme of things. These persons are the ones whose road to adult socialization often leads over bumpy detours from which the main highway may or may not be regained. The detours, more or less profound deviations of feeling, thinking, and acting, may take the shape of overpowering anxieties, obsessions and compulsions, hysterical reactions, delinquent behavior, alcohol and drug addiction, depressions and elations, and disorders of the schizophrenic variety.

## Diagnosing Emotional Disturbance

There was a time in the not too distant past when the inception of a psychiatric problem was regarded as coincident with the appearance of observable symptoms. This practice is fully justified from the point of view of descriptive clinical pathology. It is a practice common to all branches of medicine; the onset of an illness is dated from the time of the first subjective complaint, objective manifestation, or both. Medicine, nevertheless, has come to appreciate the significance of incubation periods, insidious bacterial invasions which take some time before they announce themselves symptomatically and tumor formations which betray their presence only after a period of hidden expansion.

These realizations are a help in the understanding of analogous developments in the field of psychology. The onset of behavior symptoms is not the onset of the problem; it is the point at which the problem has broken through to the surface, has become manifest through its externalization, through the annoying and frightening form which it assumes, through the nuisance value which it represents. The appearance of the clinical picture is, in effect, an outcome, at least a temporary outcome, rather than something which comes as a bolt from an untroubled sky. It arouses curiosity about the nature of the pathogenic agent which, instead of being a toxin or an encroaching tumor, is a combination of psychodynamic forces closing in on the person. It is, when it occurs in adolescence, a set of harrowing experiences that interfere with mental composure and functions at an age when parental cushioning or parental intimidation can no longer be tolerated as a substitute for a desperately needed opportunity for self-expression.

It may be said without exaggeration that there is no major psychiatric problem in adolescence which does not have its origins in earlier life experiences. The character of these experiences not only forebodes the probability of the occurrence of personality difficulties, but also predetermines the patterns in which the difficulties will express themselves if the pathogenic constellations persist.

What are these pathogenic constellations?

Every human being, starting out in life as a biologically helpless creature, grows into maturity to the extent to which he can attain a fully differentiated identity. Emotional growth is essentially a successful struggle for identity. It results in a progressive development of self-dependence and self-reliance, a gradual emancipation from an initially receptive and submissive subordination to direction by adults. The degree and form of the emancipation are governed by cultural pressures for an irreducible minimum of conformity, identification with the parents and other persons important in the child's life, and parental attitudes expressed in behavior which may encourage or suppress spontaneity.

Some people find it difficult to see how experiences in infancy and early childhood can so affect an individual's emotional equilibrium that they could burst out in delinquent, neurotic, or psychotic flames in adolescence when no noticeable smoldering seems to have preceded the catastrophe. The connection would be more easily comprehended if two things could be demonstrated convincingly: first, that noxious attitudes can play as much havoc with personality formation as organic infringement on brain structure; and second, that an interval of apparent conformity does not always signify emotional health in a child subjected to noxious attitudes.

The first demonstration, which is one of the major contributions to psychiatry in the 1940's, was offered by Goldfarb and verified by others (Goldfarb, 1943a, 1943b). Goldfarb studied two groups of adolescents. The one consisted of persons who in their first three years of life had been cared for in orphanages, where they had all the prescribed nutritional and hygienic attention but were deprived of personal stimulation and affection. The control group was made up of boys and girls from the same social strata but who from the beginning were reared in foster homes. The majority of the orphanage group, even though they were later transferred to foster homes, were so seriously injured by the early emotional deprivation that their adolescent behavior, their psychometric and Rorschach responses showed marked resemblance to the essential features of postencephalitic reactions. These responses were not at all present in the members of the control group.

The second phenomenon, that of apparent normalcy prior to the clinical onset of disturbing symptoms in adolescence, also has an analogy in organic pathology. Juvenile paresis, a consequence of congenital syphilis, may not come to the fore until the patient is well along in the second decade of life. He may have done reasonably well up to that time and presented no problem, even though the spirochetes had been active from the beginning and worked busily toward disaster.

The apparent normalcy of an adolescent headed for psychiatric upheaval is largely a matter of evaluation, as is the scenically beautiful calm of a seemingly quiescent volcano a short time before its eruption. E. K. Wickham's pioneering book, published almost twenty years ago, has pointed out flaws in the evaluation of children's behavior, flaws which are still prevalent. Wickham asked teachers and psychiatrists to rate children's behavior from the point of view of their seriousness. Teachers stressed the pathologic importance of self-assertive behavior which offended their sense of decency, dignity, or authority. They were not impressed by meekness, submissiveness, obsessive meticulousness, or indications of withdrawal, which were regarded by the mental hygienists as far more ominous than aggressive conduct. Laymen generally tend to judge children's behavior on the basis of its nuisance value. Hence, the deceptive impression often persists that breakdowns in adolescence may arise without warning; the warnings expressed through a child's anxious bid for acceptance and approval, through his striving for perfection, through his timidly unquestioning obedience, which, far from being recognized as storm signals, are mistaken for wholesome conformity by autocratic adults. It is often pathetic to listen to the puzzled account of parents of adolescents of all the evidences of a seemingly sudden schizophrenic catastrophe. How, they ask uncomprehendingly, could this have happened to their child who had always been so excessively good, polite, obliging, industrious, a prodigious reader, the pride of the teachers who have always given him "excellent" ratings in conduct—in short, a model child?

**Conditions Leading to Emotional Disturbance**

There may be a degree of truth in the saying that the tree will incline as the twig is bent. However, many adolescent problems arise from an overbending of the twig to the point of breaking.

Quite a bit, of course, will depend on the elasticity of the twig itself, something that has been referred to variously as constitution, inherent personality structure, ancestrally predetermined tendencies, basic ego strength, and the like. The cortical cells, the basal ganglia, the glands of internal secretion, the types of body configuration, and other factors have been dragged in for an explanation of the differences of individual responses to situational perplexities. It has been customary to fall back on the word "puberty" as a sort of bugaboo supposed in some diffuse and mysterious way to set off emotional fireworks. There is an analogous trend in the lay public to ascribe neurotic problems of middle aged women indiscriminately to menopause or, as the vernacular has it, to "change of life."

There are different kinds of twigs, to be sure. Nevertheless, all of them have a chance to become sturdy trees provided that they grow in good soil, are not afflicted with crippling diseases, and have the nutrition and sunshine they need. Let someone keep pulling constantly at a twig, flood the soil incessantly, try to insist that a young forsythia become an oak or an oak become a forsythia, wrap it in protective layers of cotton, overheat or overfreeze it, try to change the direction of the sprouting leaves—and the result may not be a very healthy tree or bush. The human twig needs a good home, physical care, and adequate nutrition. He also needs an opportunity to unfold his potentialities, the potentialities which are uniquely his, with a minimum of the kind of agitation which frustrates naturalness and spontaneity.

Close observaton of parent-child relationships in our culture leads to the conclusion that parents, in serving their own complex emotional needs, much too often take immoderate measures in raising their children.

Children can be comfortably warm or may swelter or freeze in the emotional climate maintained by parental attitudes. The homes in which they grow up can be pleasantly air-conditioned places or be ovens or refrigerators. Children can be objects of enjoyment, recipients of anxious overprotection, organs of parental hypochondriases, screens on which hostilities are projected in a cold war or in the form of unmitigated atrocities, and often the fields of battle on which the fathers and mothers, sometimes with varying strategies, test the tactics of their campaigns.

The statement may be premature because it is not as yet backed by statistical material, but it is nevertheless justified on empirical grounds that children reared in a comfortable emotional climate have the best chances to become well-balanced adolescents and adults. Many of those who are reared amid emotional turmoil may begin to show the effects in the years of childhood, carrying them over into adolescence unless something happens to improve the climate. However, there are many who do not externalize their conflicts until circumstances permit them to translate the established domestic relationship patterns into terms of relationships with the world at large. If you wish to translate, you can do so only when you have had some experience with the language used in the translation. These adolescents have been kept from learning the language spoken by the majority of free people. They are familiar only with one limited type of communication, that which has been impressed on them and pressed into them for years. It is a language which says in effect: "You had better remain under the protection of parental regimentation because you have never been taught how to rely on your own initiative." Or it says: "You know exactly what we expect of you, and you owe it to us to live up to these expectations regardless of how you feel about them; in fact, you have no right to have any feelings of which we do not approve." Or it says: "Your recent departures from one-hundred-per-cent compliance are signs of treason. Your arrival last night half an hour past the allotted time, your failure to hang up the sweater, the opinion you expressed the other day about grandfather or the political candidate, the teacher's report about your saucy remark in the classroom, all these are signs of depravity about which you should feel guilty and duly apologetic."

There are some adolescents, as there are nations, who, having experienced autocracy, develop sufficient maturity to strain at the shackles and to throw them off with the aid of relatives, teachers, friends, or physicians.

Again, there are adolescents, as there are nations, who never achieve the equivalent of a Fourth of July. Revolt, nurtured by the accumulation of unbounded and unredeemable hostility, has led one nation to the mass use of the guillotine; it has started some adolescents on the road to delinquency and crime, with a transfer of vindictive resentment against the parental oppressors to everyone in the path of their retaliatory aggression. Submission, held up for centuries as a virtue, has made of another nation, famed for its poets and philosophers, the complying tool of one of history's most hideous despots. Some adolescents have become so inured to unconditional surrender that they are unable to cope with the inescapable need for meeting the challenge of communal adjustment. The entrenched habit of seeking approval through excessive meticulousness and the search for perfection in an imperfect world may drive the frustrated seeker to preoccupation with obsessive symbols which place perpetual obstacles between him and ordinary routine functioning. On rare occasions, the overwhelming impact of demands on the adolescent's emotional resourcefulness may result in the conversion of the conflicts into paralyzing, blinding, or deafening hysterical phenomena.

Adolescence is the age par excellence in which the temptation to give up, to get away from it all, to substitute unchecked fantasy for frightening reality, to regress to the sheltering comforts of infantile passivity can become so alluringly irresistible as to make schizophrenic capitulation attractive. The textbooks of psychiatry state that schizophrenia often begins in adolescence. This statement is correct only in the sense in which it would be correct to say that a war begins on the day when the shooting starts. Actually, the shooting has been preceded by rivalries and hostilities of long standing. The schizophrenic manifestations are a culmination, a radical withdrawal from realities which have for a long time played havoc with the patient's emotional equilibrium. Schizophrenia is a drastic retreat to isolationism. It is a case of cold feet, resorted to when there are no other resources left, when goodness, dependence, or quickly crushed abortive attempts at rebellion are no longer serviceable. It is a refusal to make further emotional investments after so many previous investments have yielded no returns. It is an escape from the unpleasantness of further rebuffs.

### Treatment and Prevention of Emotional Disturbance

Once the storm has broken and a problem has become manifest, the psychiatrist is the only person prepared to struggle with it. The struggle is easy or difficult, depending on the patient's and the parents' felt need for help, the virulence of noxious attitudes, the degree to which the adolescent's emotional distress has entrenched itself, and last but not least, the therapist's own personality and therapeutic skill. In psychiatry, as in all other fields of medicine, there are benign and malignant conditions. Progress in medicine is often rightly measured by the extent to which potential malignancies can be recognized at the earliest possible time and so treated that ominous developments are nipped in the bud.

While the treatment of psychiatric problems which have arisen should be left in the hands of the psychiatrist, pediatricians, school teachers, and school social workers are in the best strategic position to recognize and alleviate those pathogenic situations which, if unrecognized and not alleviated, work toward discomfort, maladjustment, and possible malignancy. Their role as mental hygienists can do much to prevent or nip in the bud behavior problems of children, and at the same time to prepare conditions best suited to guarantee a reasonably wholesome adolescence and adulthood. Their principal function may be compared loosely to that of a thermostat, a regulator of emotional climate in which the child is brought up. However, while a thermostat functions automatically, the counselors' function requires a great deal of personal sensitiveness, orientation, and experience. If they have these qualities, they will sense the excessive heat of overprotection, the type of mothering which smothers, the chill of parental rejection peering through a thick coat of coercive perfectionism.

The modern pediatrician and educator have put these concepts and practices to a test. They have found them empirically sound. They are learning to appreciate the etiologic and personality-shaping significance of parental attitudes. They know that noxious attitudes cannot be modified merely by telling a mother that she should not overprotect, be overanxious, coerce, and hold on to an umbilical cord which has not been severed psychologically. The parental carriers of noxious attitudes are not villains who wish to drive their children into confusion, dependence, and emotional agony. They are troubled people with perplexities and anxieties of their own. Their emotional condition cannot be altered by admonitions and it may be aggravated by condemnation. However, the toxicity can be reduced by understanding, by giving the parents a chance to come out with their feelings, by rendering them the kind of support which reassures, mitigates anxieties, and removes the emotional basis from factually unwarranted solicitudes and agitations.

Thus, the thermostat can help, whenever necessary, to maintain or create a comfortable emotional climate for the child, who can then find his identity without struggling unsuccessfully to throw off the blankets of smothering overprotection and without shivering in the chill of parental rejection. There is no better and no alternative prophylaxis against psychiatric problems of childhood or adolescence. It is common experience that a person who comes out of a comfortably warm house can stand the vicissitudes of outside weather much better than the one who comes out of an overheated or a chilled house.

# 15. Emotions and Interpersonal Relationships

GHISLAINE GODENNE

## Emotional Development

The adolescent's emotional development involves several major tasks which he has to face and deal with before attaining maturity. For the sake of brevity I shall confine them to three groups: (1) his conflict between dependence and independence; (2) his search for identity; and (3) his search for sexual identification. In each one of these areas, his relationships to his parents, siblings, educators, and peers are of utmost importance. My task here is to consider the implications of his emotional development for these interpersonal relationships.

Let us first study the problem of the adolescent facing the struggle for independence while he is still basically a child. In this task, his conflicts are mainly in his relationships with his parents or parent substitutes. Ideally, the adolescent wishes to be recognized as a responsible and valued member of the family group; he wants to be accepted, and he wants his friends to be accepted. He longs for parent companionship and needs their encouragement, but at the same time he strives for independence. He lives at home, and is financially dependent on his parents, particularly because he is under social pressure to go to college and thus may marry only as an adult. The adolescent is caught between this forced dependence and his striving for independence.

How does the adolescent deal with this contradictory situation? Some regress, and we then see adolescents who are noisy and untidy, who tease their siblings and act silly. Some, on the other hand, become rebellious in order to achieve their independence; they create disturbances in the home so as to leave it with less difficulty.

182

The adolescent relives with considerable anxiety the oedipal situation. The parent, almost overnight, becomes a dangerous object, and the adolescent becomes unreasonable, sarcastic, and alternates, with no apparent provocation, from hostile behavior to affection. Some utilize flight as a means of decreasing their anxiety; they turn away from their parents, form gangs (in the broad sense of the term), develop intense friendships, become secretive about their coming and going. At the same time, the parent, who up to then was his model, is pushed aside as he strives to incorporate new parental images. He develops strong ties with teachers, or with older boys, and passes through the period of "crushes."

In his eyes the parents have changed; they no longer give love and protection unconditionally. The adolescent's narcissism is threatened. He comes face to face with reality. He is eager to receive but rebels against the need to give. During this adolescent turmoil, the parents are alienated, and their reaction often accentuates the difficulties. Some resent their child's desire for independence; some are not able to tolerate his continuous need for dependence. The parents, at times, relive their own adolescence when their child enters this phase; some are threatened by the reality of physical maturation; and some see their children as objects of competition for social and sexual success. All these reactions create anxiety in the parents and increase the existing tension between them and their offspring.

I have briefly discussed what can happen in a normal home. I wish now to call to your attention two abnormal situations: the rejected child and the child who has never known any constant parental figure. The rejected child is eager to leave home but will have trouble in his future relationships; he will be prone to be suspicious and cautious. The child who has had many foster homes and has never been able to form a stable object relationship with a parent or parent surrogate will, in adolescence, have great difficulty in establishing any kind of meaningful relationship with an adult.

Siblings at times accentuate the problem; the rivalry with a sibling is not a direct envy of what the other possesses but an envy based on relationships with the parents. It is increased in homes where parents do not find satisfaction in each other because of decreased availability of their instinctual drives.

The first task of gaining independence is closely linked to the second goal of attaining identity. The adolescent is constantly in search of knowing who he is and who he wants to be. He will acquire his identity by identifying with the symptoms, character traits, and attitudes of the people around him. Global identification is rare. In this task, the adolescent turns away from his parents and turns toward other adults, but mainly toward his peer group.

The girl faces this problem with greater facility; she has a main role in life to be a wife and a mother. She is dependent on the responses of other people toward her. The boy, on the other hand, has to make a career choice; he has to prove his masculinity, and his self-esteem will be based on his evaluation of how capable he is in dealing with environmental threats or problems. For a girl in high school, group identity is based on what she is; for a boy it is based on what he does, and in this respect his participation in athletics is the principal measuring rod of his popularity.

The adolescent wants to be recognized by his peers; he values their reactions to him; together they form a subculture. He feels at ease with them because of an underlying identification. At times, he is part of a clique, a group, or a gang; he shares with the other members a common emotional factor. He feels that his group provides him with a social life of which he is a part, and it protects him against the pressures of the adult world.

An adolescent who has lost his main identity figure at an early age or whose parents are overly intrusive or overly dependent, may have trouble reaching his identity and one can then see in him what Erikson calls role diffusion or negative identity. In the former case, he has trouble making any career choice, oscillating between many possibilities; in the latter, he becomes the opposite of what his parents intended him to be.

Finally, I wish to discuss the adolescent's search for sexual identification. This, also, is strongly influenced by earlier family experiences. The attitudes which the adolescent develops in relation to his parents are likely to be generalized in relation to his contemporaries during adolescence. The young adolescent relates mainly to peers of his own sex and does so with no open sexual desires. The girls whisper and giggle together, excluding boys from their chatter. The boys engage in rough play and stay away from the girls whom they view as sissies or weaklings. If boys and girls date at an early age, this is more a game than a means of satisfying sexual needs. When sexual urges come into awareness, they often cause the adolescent to seek as a first love object someone of the same sex. Kinsey reports that 27 per cent of male adolescents between the ages of 17 and 25 have had homosexual experiences.

While this homosexual phase is transient and fleeting, its suddenness and the intensity of the crush relationship can frighten the adolescent who experiences it. A few years back a sixteen-year-old girl was admitted to the Phipps Clinic after a suicidal attempt prompted by her experiencing sexual feelings for another girl, which convinced her that she was turning out to be a homosexual to the disgrace of her socially prominent family.

The first heterosexual love experience is often as fleeting and transient as the homosexual experience, and it is only when adolescence is completed that an individual can succeed in a fully mature sexual relationship. The sexual mores of adolescent males and females differ. Kinsey reports that by the age of 20, 71 per cent of boys have engaged in intercourse compared with 40 per cent of girls. Full sexual activity often is undertaken for extrasexual reasons; this is especially true for girls. Sexuality is often used not as an experience of love, but as a means of living up to peer expectations or of proving that one is grown up. Girls generally are interested only in petting with affection; boys are more apt to engage in petting with or without affection. Boys often want to date girls who will allow sexual gratification, but on the other hand wish to marry a girl who has not been sexually promiscuous.

## Interpersonal Relationships

Now let us examine in more detail how the adolescent relates to the different people around him. He moves away from his parents but still needs their support; he has trouble confiding to them any kind of troublesome experience for fear of making them ashamed of him. His search for independence often gives rise to guilt feelings, especially if the parents have trouble accepting it. He has thus to make many new and varied social adjustments which cause him to feel anxious and insecure and to be secretive and suspicious of others. He has to cope with feelings of dependence, independence, and interdependence. The adolescent turns toward other adults and toward his peer group. In a certain way, he is more comfortable with adults, since he is less concerned about their reactions to him and probably more experienced in a close relationship with them. However, he often confuses the image of the adult with that of his parents, and in psychotherapy with adolescents, this is an important issue to keep constantly in mind. He also sees the adult who is unduly kind to him as someone false or patronizing. He is aware of his brattish behavior and wonders what's behind the adult's unlimited patience. He wants the adult to set limits so that he will not have to test how far he can go and in so doing become more anxious.

The adolescent seeks approval of his peers; but the closeness he experiences with his peers when he goes to college is a new experience for him and creates anxiety. During this period of his life he will probably create the most friendships and the most intense relationships. He spends hours with his peers discussing problems, religion, philosophy, and political issues, but he rarely talks about his inner feelings. He adopts a front; he acts and talks like the person he wants to be and plays his role throughout his relationships. Recently, I saw a young college boy in treatment who wanted to terminate psychotherapy because, among other reasons, his peers and his peers' parents told him he did not need it. I questioned this statement and he said, "They all know I am an optimist at heart." I commented that to me he seemed depressed and pessimistic about the future, and I sensed in him more of a "What's the use" attitude than the feeling "I will do all right without it." He seemed somewhat surprised at my remark and after a brief silence he said, "Yes, but they don't know that." The peer influence is strong and identification with the peer group is of major importance. I treated a sixteen-year-old girl who came to see me because she didn't know if she wanted to be white or colored. She was brought up in a white family, had an olive-colored skin, and after being placed in an institution with colored girls, she was questioning her racial identity.

In the adolescent's new environment, outside of the home, he finds his peers judging him by factors which may never have occurred to him; up to then he felt sheltered by his parents or by older people. The adolescent feels self-conscious about his first experience with the opposite sex. He and his date are aware of their physical clumsiness and their conversational ineptitude in social situations.

The adolescent needs props to find himself at ease in his social group; cliques, gangs, and fraternities bolster his self-assurance. The security of belonging to a group helps to neutralize the panic resulting from his unresolved conflicts. He suffers deeply if he is considered different and is seriously rocked in his self-esteem if he find himself rejected by his peers.

How does the adolescent express his inner turmoil, his feelings of despair, his inadequacy? Mainly by talking to himself. He spends hour after hour thinking; he writes a diary, becomes a poet, or has vivid daydreams which he rarely shares. As he grows up and finds security in his friendships, he expresses more openly the feelings and thoughts with which he is struggling. He comes to realize that he is not alone on the hard road to maturity, and this sense of sharing a common turmoil allows him to be freer in the expression of it.

I have tried to summarize my views on the interpersonal relationships of adolescents. I have probably omitted some aspects of it. I am sure that I could be challenged in many of my statements. I work with adolescents, and every day I learn through them and about them. My views today may be different from the ones I will have tomorrow. However, I firmly believe that for more than any other period of a person's life, the interpersonal relationships during adolescence are what make or break the man or woman to be.

# 16. Emotions and the Educative Process

## ARTHUR G. MADDEN

▲▲▲▲▲▲▲▲▲▲▲▲▲▲▲▲▲▲▲▲▲▲▲▲▲▲▲▲▲▲▲

In the brief time allotted to me [during the sessions of this work-shop] I would like to indicate some ways in which emotions and atti-tudes affect and are closely woven into our thinking and learning processes. I shall point out these effects, first of all, by analyzing our-selves on this occasion which is, I hope, a thinking and learning situa-tion. I shall leave it to you to make the application to the adolescent as you meet him or her in a learning situation. Second, on the negative side, I wish to point out some emotional factors which inhibit learning. And finally, I shall indicate some implications of these facts for the personality and functions of the teacher.

### The Effect of Emotions on the Intellect

By way of preface I would like to refer briefly to two extreme views of the goals of education—the view of education for intellectual excel-lence alone versus education for life adjustment. Like all extreme views these ideas are guilty of oversimplification and of abstraction from concrete realities. Education at all levels aims at intellectual develop-ment but also shows concern for emotional, social, moral, and spiritual development which involves the satisfaction of basic needs as well as other motivational tendencies. Intellectual development cannot properly take place without good adjustment, and adequate adjustment does not take place without adequate intellectual development in accord with the abilities of the person. Intellectual development and the ac-quisition of necessary skills are important aims of elementary educa-tion, and these aims become more dominant as we move up the academic ladder. But we are not dealing with pure intellects. We are dealing with persons who are conscious beings, who have physical and psychological needs, who are happy or sad, angry or fearful, who have many different attitudes and goals. Thinking and learning take place within this complex of psychological states.

Let us apply this knowledge to ourselves. We are here and now engaged in an intellectual enterprise. Yet, the mere fact of our presence stimulates the college to provide for our physical needs—food, drink, lodging, and as much circulating fresh air in this room as is possible on a warm day. The administration also tries to make us socially comfortable by giving us a sense of belonging, by making us feel at home, by getting us acquainted with others by means of introductions and name cards. Members of the faculty mix with the participants. The speakers try to develop in us favorable attitudes by their clarity of presentation, the worth of their material, their wit, and their courtesy in answering queries. In this way we will more readily learn about the adolescent, satisfy our need for achievement, and attain the goals for which we are striving in this workshop.

As I speak to you, I present my thoughts, but not in a purely intellectual way. I am emotionally involved in the ideas which I am trying to express because I experience the joy of having grasped what I think is some small corner of reality. I am emotionally involved with you because I *want* you to consider my ideas. I have that pleasant feeling of mild fear mixed with some confidence which I usually have when I begin to address an audience. I myself am expressing the need to achieve and to be accepted. Your adolescent student operates in the same way in or out of your classroom when he tries to express his ideas.

In the learning process you respond intellectually, but also from needs, feelings, past experiences, attitudes, and goals. The differences in the notes which each individual writes down or in what each of you will remember—in other words, the selectivity of your responses to my comments—will depend upon your own particular frame of reference. It will depend also on the amount of ego involvement that develops. This frame of reference and ego involvement are the result of your past experiences, your needs, desires, attitudes, goals, and emotional dispositions. Your adolescent student responds to you in a similar manner inside or outside the classroom.

In other words, thinking is not a purely intellectual process divorced from other psychological factors, although many of us who were trained in the rationalistic, scholastic tradition were led to conceive of it as such. All kinds of emotional and motivational factors subtly penetrate our thinking. Not only do the objective factors within a total situation condition thinking, but oftentimes a wish or a fear or a prejudice is father of the thought. As David Russell has stated: "Emotions and attitudes not only help determine what reaches consciousness but act as directive forces in most thinking processes" (1956, p. 165). Russell tells of a cartoon in the *Saturday Review* which in its way illustrates how the stage of motivational and emotional development of children affects their perception and thinking. The cartoon shows two young boys standing in front of a movie theater in which a Western is showing, and one is saying to the other: "In the love scenes I always close my eyes and imagine he's choking her." Russell points out that although the child may delight in the fast action in the movie and spurn the love-making scenes, the adolescent may feel too sophisticated to be interested in the Western adventure but may be strongly affected by the love scenes. Here again we have selectivity in perception, and thinking arises out of the level of social and emotional maturity at a particular stage of development.

This tendency of individuals to do their thinking in terms of their needs or wants is called autistic thinking. Often the emotional element in the process will be unconscious. When a student remarks that the science class is more interesting than the history class, it may be that he is not giving an objective appraisal of the actual value of the instruction but rather is remembering with emotional satisfaction the day he was able to shine in the science class by giving an answer no one else could give.

Attitudes can also influence the thinking of students. They have been defined as "systems of ideas with an emotional content" which produce a learned readiness for response. Allport has said: "Attitudes determine for each individual what he will see and hear, what he will think and what he will do." Attitudes are learned, many of them socially, and they are transmitted by the family, teachers, peer groups, and others. We are familiar with the varied responses on the part of students when the teacher says: "Let us turn to the poem on page so and so," or "Today we shall take up quadratic equations." What sort of thinking will go on in the different students in accordance with their positive or negative attitudes?

In dealing with emotional factors which inhibit learning, I would like to refer to the studies of Irving D. Harris. Harris deals primarily with factors in the home which tend to inhibit learning. These factors create conditions in the student which he brings with him to the school, and it is the student thus conditioned whom the teacher must face. The teacher can either reinforce the inhibiting factors or help to alleviate them. As inhibiting factors to learning, Harris mentions socioeconomic status, family disorganization, parental ambitiousness, birth order and expectation of maturity, and aggression or submission.

Under socioeconomic status as an inhibiting factor, Harris points out that many of the nonlearners came from families of low income in which there was a lack of motivation to learn for the sake of learning, lack of stimulation of the student's mind, and lack of care about the student's repeating a grade.

Parental incompatibility and employment of the mother outside the home were included under the factor of family disorganization. The students from such homes showed difficulty in concentration and in reading problems. In many cases they repeated grades. These difficulties were ascribed to a "chronic feeling of anxious insecurity in the boy as to whether his home would stay intact or come apart. This feeling, in turn, was traced to the personality of the mother who was unable to function as a homemaker or rejected that role" (Harris, 1961, p. 140).

Parental ambitiousness, particularly as visited upon students of low-average intelligence, resulted in resistance to the teacher by all kinds of delaying tactics. Harris explains this resistance as a way of punishing the pressuring parent by thwarting him (in order to preserve his own independence) or as a fear of being tested and of failing to meet the expectations of the parent.

Under the heading of birth order and expectations of maturity, Harris tells us that the first-born child tends to be more serious because of the greater expectations of maturity by the parents, whereas the last-born tends to be less serious and diligent because less is expected of him, and he is allowed to remain a child longer.

Among other students whom Harris studied, the nonlearner often showed extremes of aggression or submission, both of which were associated with difficulties in reading. Harris' explanation is that the extremes of rage or of anxiety in repressing rage interfered with learning in general, and with reading in particular, because of the complexity of the reading process.

Although, as I have indicated, emotions sometimes act as a block to thinking, it does not follow that emotions should be eliminated from thinking. Emotions can also have positive effects. It is often thought that strong emotions such as fear and anger impede thought processes, and that the milder emotions of joy and affection stimulate thought. This is not necessarily the case. Vital thinking can take place under the goad of fear or of anger, provided these emotions are kept under control. Much of creative thinking, poetry, oratory, and other imaginative productions would never have been realized if the creative artists had not been deeply moved emotionally.

### Functions of the Teacher

What do these conclusions have to do with teacher personality and the teaching process? The teacher is an essential part of the educative process. One cannot adequately study the pupil except in relationship to his teacher. The aim of the school, which means primarily the aim of the administrators and teachers, is the growth of the student toward maturity—intellectually, emotionally, socially, morally, and physically. This growth cannot be accomplished with any degree of ease unless the teachers are themselves mature adults. If the teacher is immature, and if this emotional, intellectual, social, or moral immaturity blocks the satisfaction of the adolescent's needs and drive to maturity, the teacher will either create or increase emotional problems in the student. Similarly, an emotionally unbalanced administrator can create tensions in the teachers which will ultimately affect the students.

I am sure we can remember from our own school experiences sitting through many class days with taut nerves. The teacher may have had the reputation of being a fine teacher who kept students on their toes every minute. Yet the methods used by this teacher may have actually impaired learning efficiency because of the nervous tension which they caused. Expecting immediate answers from everyone without regard to personal differences, lack of respect for the shy or awkward student, silencing students who think independently or who differ from the teacher, sarcasm for those who do not know the answer or are too slow in answering, dire warnings about the results of failure—all such tactics make a class something to be despised. The mature teacher would not want to endure such treatment from a principal or supervisor. Oftentimes too, a teacher unwittingly cooperates with an overambitious parent in what seems like good school-home cooperation and as a result aggravates the student's emotional difficulty. Caught between two fires, the student has the choice of either submission or aggression. In either case he probably goes into his shell, hates school, and whatever talents he has are blocked in their development.

On the positive side, we also know the great joy that can come from a class which the teacher approaches in a happy mood, with enthusiasm for his subject, and an eagerness to communicate. Such a teacher recognizes differences, is willing to accept students as they are, and gives them a sense of belonging and of importance. This teacher will win over the student and make him docile, that is, teachable. For some children, the school rather than the home becomes the place where they can find emotional security, achievement, even affection. In depressed areas, the school, and especially the teachers, are often the one hope for lifting the student to a higher level of attitudes, of values, and of achievement.

The teacher can also do a great deal to alleviate some of the poor emotional tendencies which the students bring to the learning process. In heading off aggressive tendencies he can be firm and consistent in imposing standards of work and conduct, but with enough flexibility to conform to changing circumstances. Praise at the appropriate time can make a just censure more bearable; help and instruction on diffi- cult problems can stimulate competence which dissolves anger and aggression. A teacher who permits verbal expression of "gripes" helps students get a lot of aggressiveness out of their systems.

Teachers can also help to dispel fear and stimulate security. A help- ful measure is to accept students as they are, and then encourage them to face up to the reality of their problems. An explanation of why a problem is difficult can be followed by an explanation as to how it can be met and by practice in meeting it. Praise and encouragement always help; and if the student talks the problem over with other stu- dents who may be experiencing the same difficulty, considerable insight may be gained.

Teachers cannot be expected to do everything in the handling of emotional problems, but they can do a great deal. The more difficult cases have to be referred to the guidance counselor, or psychiatric treat- ment may be necessary. It is important for teachers to remember that they do not possess the knowledge and skill of trained counselors or therapists, and therefore referral is at times unavoidable. Referring the troubled student to the right person for help is also good teaching.

# PART V

## Mass Media and
## the Adolescent Mind

▲▲▲▲▲▲▲▲▲▲▲▲▲▲▲▲▲▲▲▲▲▲▲▲▲▲▲▲▲▲▲▲

# 17. Forms and Content of Mass Media

## MRS. EDMUND D. CAMPBELL

In presenting this topic I wish to acknowledge my indebtedness to Mr. Robert C. O'Hara for the treatment which he has given to the process of mass communications in his most provocative book *Media for the millions*. I have made use of it for both topical analysis and illustrative material.

The general topic, "Mass Media and the Adolescent Mind," might have indicated a concentration of interest in mass media's message, but the topic which I am discussing, "Forms and Content of Mass Media," acknowledges that we cannot ignore its mechanics. As we look briefly at each form—and see some of the problems which its built-in specifications and requirements pose for the originator of the ideas to be communicated—we may reach a better understanding of the interdependence of content and form and the implications of this interdependence for the mind of the receiver.

For the purposes of this discussion I am including only those forms of mass media which are developed and distributed with commercial backing and are not oriented directly toward formal education. The forms to which the general public, at all age levels, is more or less exposed in this twentieth century are: the printed form, the only one which predates this century; the filmed form (movies); and the electronic form (recordings, radio, and television).

We shall also confine our thinking to the United States, although mass media cross all national lines. One of the most recent examples of this international exposure is the "Beatle" phenomenon. We not only have these British teenagers visiting our shores, but we have books and articles about them and by them, recordings, radio programs, and television shows. Who has escaped them?

We shall see each of these media in relation to contemporary American society as we seek to understand what each one communicates. They do not operate in a vacuum; they are shaped by the society they serve and they, in turn, help to shape that society by interpreting life in terms meaningful to it.

The printed form, the oldest of the communications media, has undergone great changes in the twentieth century, many of these directly related to other media forms. Magazines have changed their size and shape and content; the news weekly has developed a streamlined style; the paperback is truly a pocketbook, its length related to the speed of air travel. Covers of magazines tell their own picture story.

The printed form is characterized by its permanence and by the demands it makes of its reader; reading requires skill and interpretation —skills which may develop with education and age. In a very real sense the appeal is to an individual first and then, hopefully, to all individuals in a class, or category, or age group. The reader must project himself into the reading or there is no meaning.

The filmed form is limited by time both in its presentation—one hour or two—and in the fact that it is intended for one exposure. It involves group viewing and hence a social and socializing situation.

Time is a significant consideration in presenting ideas—"the message"—via radio and television recordings. All programs must fit into time slots, and must be organized, produced, and manufactured to meet the specifications of the industry. Who is responsible for these arrangements? Is there a mass communicator?

In a very real sense, the originator, the source of the ideas to be communicated, must have the assistance of the editor, the arranger, and the producer, who knows the limitations and the possibilities of the medium, the cost, and the market (readers, viewers, or hearers). In all instances material must be simplified to meet mechanical specifications, and in many instances to meet the limitations of time and space and public demand.

Who are the public—the "mass"—the individuals whose individual tastes cannot be considered except as they become a composite? This is the question which the owners of mass-communications businesses are forever trying to answer. For the answer they rely on polls, ratings, questionnaires, sales, admissions, receipts, magazine and newspaper circulations and subscriptions, and advertising market reports. These are the people of America, of all ages, of many economic, social and educational backgrounds. They are one and yet they are not one. On newstands and in libraries we can see some evidence of the different groups and individuals who make up our society. It is often more difficult to find this evidence in the television audience.

We may not be typical in our taste, but for us, too, the medium requires simplification of content material. Our interest is in the methods of selection used for simplification. The view of life which the mass communicator has selected for communication includes items selected for exclusion as well as inclusion. What we don't see or hear may also influence our attitudes and actions. The media communicators must frame their messages in terms that are meaningful to us as members of American society. These terms may be stated thus:

1. Those things of which we approve are presented in an approving manner;
2. Those things of which we disapprove are presented unfavorably.

This simplified view is often distorted, but it is uniquely American. Thematic material can be vastly different in treatment between countries. For this reason we encounter foreign criticism of American films and television programs. The British are concerned about American television in their country, not so much because of the quality of the offerings, but because the view of life depicted on these programs is in many instances antithetical to English customs and values. They feel that, in time, such programs cannot help but have a rather sweeping effect on their society.

The Koreans are concerned about American television and films because of the lack of seriousness shown about family problems and the lack of respect of children for their parents. However, the view of life the receiver gets reflects values, codes of behavior, and the selection of alternate courses of action that have either been modified or are in the process of modification in the existing American social situation. Often this view of life is not only anachronistic, but it is also in conflict with life as it really is.

But perhaps the greatest determinant in the final outcome of the interaction between form and content in mass communication lies in economic pressures. It is financially safer for mass media to preserve the status quo—that is, the economic and social attitudes upon which the past economic success of the media was built. Hence there are variations of theme rather than the appearance of new ones; we have Westerns (adult and juvenile), Western Westerns, private-eye Westerns, gangster Westerns, and even a Russian Western. So producers arrive at a formula: "Certain actions are always performed in a certain way; certain attitudes are always evoked. These actions and attitudes are offered to the receiver, usually implicitly, as desirable patterns to imitate should he ever find himself in roughly analogous situations."

What is the danger of formula thinking? Its superficiality will preclude an intelligent and perceptive view of life; it will lead to hasty action on the basis of imperfectly formed or imperfectly understood attitudes; it will lead to bandwagon thinking rather than seeing the problem. Some of the formulas which are manifestations of our culture are:

"Love conquers all."
"Work hard and you will succeed."
"Virtue is rewarded and evil punished."
"Any problem can be solved by faith in oneself, someone else, or God."

An awareness of the relationship between the form and content of mass media can make reading, listening, and viewing more meaningful, and can result in a more critical involvement on the part of the receiver. Parents should create opportunities to share the offerings of mass media with their children, and teachers should do the same with their pupils. I suggest: (1) frank and friendly discussions of appropriate television programs, with questions such as, "What would have been the outcome of this situation if it had forty minutes for its development instead of thirty?"; (2) the reading aloud of stories and poems; (3) the comparing of the original novel or play with a movie or television version; and (4) the keeping of a television viewing diary in which are recorded the programs watched, the length of each, and a brief personal reaction.

Through mass media the world has been opened to all who can see and hear. It is our responsibility as adults to develop within ourselves the critical measures by which we can evaluate the sights and sounds which come to us and also to help the younger generation develop criteria for making their own judgments of the true and the false, the beautiful and the ugly, and the good and the bad, so that mass media may be used for the enrichment of American life.

# 18. The Impact of Literature on the Adolescent Mind

SARA L. SIEBERT

Librarians speak for books which make an impact on young adults who read. They speak for the simple, usually slick, often maligned junior novel. They speak for Cather, Hemingway, Koestler, and Dostoevsky. They speak for Walter Lord's *A Night to Remember,* the story of the sinking of the Titanic, which is enjoyed by the most reluctant reader; and for Carl Sandburg's massive Lincoln biography, which requires a special interest and background. They speak for "West Side Story" and for its source, *Romeo and Juliet* by William Shakespeare. And they speak for an ocean of books which fall between these poles—books which have something positive to say to the high-school student and which promote the habit of reading and a taste for literature.

The above-mentioned books by necessity run a wide gamut, for it is a fact that the average reading level among public-school students in Baltimore City is two grades below their actual grade level. Reading does not come naturally to the majority of Americans. David Dempsey in an article in the *New York Times Book Review* for May, 1964, cites a 1961 Gallup poll which points out that Americans of high-school age read only an average of three books a year outside of class assignment. The Pratt Library-sponsored Deiches study on the student use of public libraries notes the heavy use of Pratt by youngsters of high-school age. Why? Because "they want to make good records in school" (Martin, 1963, p. 14). This sentiment is admirable, one which should be fostered, and not only at a time when the threat of Communist political and scientific supremacy jogs a complacent America. But it is not a final answer if books and reading are to leave an impact after school years are over.

Many teachers, as well as librarians, recognize this fact. Dr. Val Clear, Chairman of the Department of Sociology and Social Work at Anderson College, wrote in the *Saturday Review* of February 15, 1964 (p. 73) : "After fifteen years of teaching social problems, I had come to the conclusion that the only permanent value of a course in social problems was in the attitude the student carried away with him. Knowing the biological effects and the statistics related to alcoholism is of little lasting worth; feeling the crushing hopeless isolation of the alcoholic with Don Birnam in *Lost Week-end* can never be forgotten . . ."

What the professor did was to pick twenty-six books, such as *Black Like Me, Hiroshima, All Quiet on the Western Front, The Status Seekers,* and *To Kill a Mockingbird,* and assign these popular titles, which packed a social wallop to one of his classes. "The objective," he continued, "was to affect attitudes rather than produce stereotyped academic knowledge." He concurrently assigned another class to study what he considered the best text book on social problems. Attitude tests were given to both classes at the beginning and close of the courses. "Both sections became more tolerant of those involved in the problem, the paperback (popular) group showing a higher rate of tolerance than the text book section. Each class also showed a gratifying decrease in ethnic isolationism, the fiction section having an average drop in prejudice more than twice that of the text book group" (Clear, 1964, p. 73).

Professor Clear's article hits home to librarians—and, it is hoped, to this audience. I do not wish to imply that twentieth-century students can complete their education with only a packet of interesting and popular paperbacks in hand. But if Professor Clear's findings are valid, we know that creative and popular literature can leave a desirable impact.

Closer to home is an experiment in creative reading at St. Paul's School for Boys in Brooklandville conducted by William Ticknor of the Pratt Library staff. On his own time, he chose ten boys with an unusual proficiency in English. A psychologist gave them the Wechsler Intelligence Test and the Children's Personality Questionnaire at the beginning of the year. It was hoped that by retesting when the project was over, results would show an advance in the boys' maturity "beyond that which would normally be expected."

The project used adult books, which included Ralph Moody's *Little Britches,* an account of the author's childhood on a run-down ranch in Colorado; *Life with Father* in play form; Lansing's *Endurance;* Sir Ernest Shackleton's *Voyage to the Arctic; Men Against the Sea,* one of the "Bounty" trilogy; *Cheaper by the Dozen,* which stars a disciplinarian father; and *The Miracle Worker,* the moving play about Anne Sullivan Macy's relationship to the deaf, dumb, and blind little Keller girl. Discussions were led by two faculty members. The boys gave their own time to the activity and received no credit.

The summary of the psychologist's report is interesting. "There was an average gain in I.Q. of four points. The boys became more relaxed, more tolerant, more ready to see the other person's point of view. Those who had been most aggressive at the beginning lost some of their dominance, while others became more vigorous in self-expression . . . Mr. White (the psychologist) finds a marked advance in the boys' maturity as a result of the program" (Ticknor, 1964, p. 272).

Formal programs are not the only clue to the impact of literature on the teenager. One unknown counselor at a fashionable New England camp for girls deserves special mention for quick action with a popular paperback. She overheard a fifteen-year-old Southern girl being verbally clobbered by her more liberal Northern campmates during some nightly arguments over civil rights, especially the treatment of the Negro in the South. Elizabeth could only counter with that tired Southern cliche: "But would you want your brother to marry a Negro?" As far as I know, the counselor stayed clear of the discussion, but she saw fit to give Elizabeth a copy of *Black Like Me,* which the girl was still reading when she returned home. As you know, it is novelist John Howard Griffin's account of how he darkened his body with a chemical and then traveled through the deep South in order to experience living as a Negro. Her mother found the book amid the covers of an unmade bed and on quick perusal was shocked and disturbed by what she read. She questioned her daughter about the book and heard that the camp counselor had suggested that Elizabeth read it. Elizabeth was not only fascinated by the idea of the book, but also was obviously not ready to toss the book off as liberal propaganda.

"But Elizabeth," said her mother, "that book is an exaggeration and only describes what sometimes happens in the deep South" (a usual rationalization by the so-called educated and basically human Southerner).

But the indignities dealt to one human being as described by Griffin had had their effect.

"Well, maybe so, Mother, but that book makes me *think*."

This is a true story, very close to me. If only more Southern teenagers could be made to think!

Enlightened social goals are close to us at this moment of our nation's history, but they are only a portion of that toward which librarians shoot with books. And although no foundation has seen fit to spend a fortune to prove scientifically what librarians at least sense or feel through constant contacts with young people and books, it is with conviction and some proof that we say that books "help young people to live with themselves as citizens of a democracy and to be at home in the world." The Pratt Library sets its goal for young-adult work as a "progression from self-realization to responsible American citizenship to a belief in the brotherhood of all men. Books in the Young Adult Collections are purchased in the light of these goals" (Siebert, 1964, p. 1).

How does the young adult discover what love is all about? Of course, we have excellent titles dealing with dating and families and marriage. But a good reader will find richer material on the relationship between man and woman in *Anna Karenina,* Tolstoy's novel on the consuming passion of a beautiful woman for a younger man which leads to tragedy and despair. But not every young girl who avidly reads sentimental teenage stories will learn that true love is wanting someone else to be happy. Dolores Warwick's *Promised Spring* says just that in a junior novel which she wrote as an honor project while a student at Notre Dame of Maryland.

Local politics and what citizens, including young people, can do to help sway the political course is the theme of *One Small Voice* by Bob and Jan Young. Such a book has a place in library collections. A year of political campaigns may again give a special push to a masterpiece of political reporting which many teenagers have read, *The Making of the President, 1960.* Who can forget the description of the TV debates with Vice President Nixon, almost a recluse in his hotel suite with his wife as he prepared for his public battle? And Senator Kennedy parrying with his bevy of young advisors with a footlocker library of facts and figures always close at hand? Theodore White wrote impartially of the two candidates, but the book stands out as a vibrant portrait of the late President in all his youth and vigor, and it affected this speaker's feelings to such a degree that her brief introduction to the book at a high-school book fair brought forth a comment from a teacher at hand: "The librarian must be a Democrat!" Yes, books can leave an impact on librarians.

Anne Frank's touching *Diary*—though it leaves one with a message of hope—has more to say about man's inhumanity to man than some stronger library meat. But *Lord of the Flies,* the current most asked-for book in the Young Adult Collections at Pratt, questions the depth of man's goodness and, as does *Black Like Me,* makes one think.

Many readable books have impact. But to exert their impact fully, the books must be read and understood by teachers, social workers, and parents as well as by the library staff. There must be thoughtful talk and discussion; there must be an understanding of the books and the author's intent.

For thirty-one years there has been an ongoing program to promote books and to develop the reading habit among Baltimore youth. Book talks, book fairs, trained librarians who understand and like teenagers, popular booklists, supplementary school lists, attractive collections of books, special programs—all these have been the ammunition of the Pratt Library as it shoots toward its goals. It is an exciting program and has been successful.

One of the best-known projects of the program is the student book-reviewing periodical, *You're the Critic.* This booklet, published eight times a year when school is in session, provides a source for examination of high-school reading tastes and is the best book promoter we have because library recommendations by peers carry more weight than those from librarians. All types of adult books are reviewed, but the over-all effect is quality backed by understanding. Last year marked the fifteenth anniversary of *You're the Critic,* and in an article in *Top of the News,* a publication of the American Library Association, Mrs. Linda Lapides, the Assistant Coordinator of Work with Young Adults, decided to see what had happened to some of the earlier reviewers. Mrs. Lapides writes:

Witness Volume 1, Number 1. In that debut issue, the lead article was written by Arthur Waskow, then a member of the Critic editorial board, now a staff member of the Peace Research Institute, author of magazine articles . . . and a book. In this early Critic review of October 1948, Mr. Waskow begins by saying, "In *Peace or Anarchy,* Cord Meyer, Jr., sets forth his views on how to bring peace to the world." It is interesting that this is exactly what Mr. Waskow sets forth in his own book, *The Limits of Defense* (Doubleday, 1962). Also in that historic issue is a review by Anna Anthony, now Mrs. Anna Curry, [then] Head of the Central Young Adult Department at the Pratt Library. In succeeding issues appear the names of student reviewers now teaching in high schools and colleges all over the country, many currently or previously affiliated with Pratt or other libraries, and one who is assistant conductor of the San Francisco Opera Company (Fishman, 1963, p. 61).

This impromptu survey may not be very scientific, but from it one can assume not only that books influence one's life in a special direction, but also that readers are achievers.

In 1960, to help celebrate National Library Week, a Pratt Library committee decided to take a look into the reading tastes of some teen-agers of the past—Baltimoreans of various ages now prominent in business or in professions. It was assumed that they were readers when they were young. And the assumption proved correct. When they were asked to list books they remembered reading when they were 14 to 18 years old—not necessarily the classics but books that were meaningful or exciting, especially those read for enjoyment—they came forth with some telling comments as well as with impressive authors and titles.

After noting that he had read Cooper's *Leatherstocking Tales*, Scott's *Ivanhoe*, and Henty's *The Bravest of the Brave*, Dr. Philip Edwards, former Principal of City College explained:

> I was in the first year class of Professor Edward Lucas White at City College. Mr. White assigned each member of the class a different English author . . . I drew Shelley. Imagine what a boy of fourteen would do to that assignment . . . Fortunately, I was plucked like a brand from the burning. Before my time came my parents moved to Annapolis. Years afterwards, I read "To a Skylark" to my father . . . He told me how as a boy in England on his way to work in the early morning his foot would stir a skylark so that he knew first-hand his "And singing still dost soar, and soaring ever singest."

A very frank correspondent, Mr. Ralph Reppert of the *Sunday Sun*, listed his favorites: Henry A. Shute, Horatio Alger, Tom Swift series, and Ernest Seton's *Wild Animals I Have Known* (20 to 30 volumes; ol' faker, but interesting). He was the only contributor to Teen-Age Testimony who admitted that influences other than books helped guide his life. "At 16 I became aware of girls, and after that Tom Swift just didn't seem to have the old zing."

But, more to the point of this talk, one prominent Baltimore lady listed Tarkington's *Seventeen*, Christopher Morley's *Pipefuls*, Chesterton's *Essays*, and Lowell Thomas's *With Lawrence in Arabia*. Christopher Morley's *Pipefuls* was one of my favorites. I read as many of his essays as I could find. He introduced me to the seventeenth century. I did not understand Chesterton, but his paradoxes appealed to me. Today, *With Lawrence in Arabia* is called a semihoax, but to the lady educator it "opened the door to many interests; later to Lawrence's translation of the Odyssey." And she concluded: "It gives me great pleasure to remember all the joy this reading has given me through the years. To Morley, for instance, I can never be sufficiently grateful: he made the 'classics' palatable and inviting . . ." These comments are those of Sister Cleophas, President of Mount Saint Agnes College. For the impact of literature, I need say no more.

# 19. The Impact of Movies and TV on the Adolescent

HAROLD E. HILL

At the outset let me say that most of my comments will be directed toward television—for two reasons: first and most obviously, television is my field, whereas movies are not; secondly, there is evidence that since the advent of television teenagers do not spend as much time at movies as they used to, and even more important, that the general impact of each is about the same. Therefore, much of what I have to say about the impact of television will be also applicable to movies.

Due to the naturally great interest in the newer medium of television, there has been little research into the impact of movies in recent years. However, there is little reason to doubt the continuing validity of movie research done several years ago before television became so all-pervading. However, even before the advent of television, there was not as much attention paid to the movies by media researchers as there was to radio, magazines, and comics. Nevertheless, a few findings have some significance for us here.

Holaday and Stoddard (1933) discovered that most young people—and many adults, I might add—tend to accept unquestioningly all presumably factual information in films. Inaccurate statements of pictures are apparently accepted as truth. Obviously, many pitfalls are offered for the young mind when movies glamorize the lives of gangsters, those dishonest in business, and those with rather loose moral standards. The teenager is apt to accept, without question or deep thought, the fact that people who engage in such activities are going to have more fun in life than the rather humdrum people around them are having. The real danger here is found in the format of most movies of this sort where the "bad guys" spend ninety per cent of the movie "living it up," and only the last few minutes are spent on the fact that the police finally catch up with them, resulting in arrest. Along this line, too often the movie implies that the wrongdoer is caught only because he made a mistake, rather than through good police work; in fact, the police are often made to appear like fools throughout most of the film.

The end result of this latter fact was emphasized by a study made several years ago on the effects of movies on delinquency. Careful analysis of the backgrounds of teenage inmates of the Chicago jail showed that many of them had been impressed by the fact that movie criminals seemingly were caught because of their own mistakes rather than good police work, and the teenagers reported that they felt that they would not make the same mistakes, that they were smarter and could get away with the criminal act.

This same study also showed that some of the teenagers followed the specific plans for crimes as shown in the movies in attempting their own robberies or other illegal acts. In other words, the movies gave them a blueprint to follow. Many of these young people reported that they realized that they might get caught, although, as I've indicated, they thought they were smarter than the screen criminals, but they felt that it was worth it. The glamorized life of the criminal as depicted on the screen was so appealing that these teenagers felt crime was worthwhile even if they got caught, because they would have so much money, so many girls, and great prestige among their peers up until the time they were arrested. These findings seem to underline those of Holaday and Stoddard mentioned earlier.

I submit that we might expect many of these same findings if a similar study were made of television's effect on teenage delinquents, but none so specific has been made to my knowledge. Other studies of television do reveal certain adverse results, and I shall get to those in a minute. First, however, I want to emphasize what to me is the most important finding in that Chicago study. In nearly all cases, depth studies indicated that movies had the adverse effects I have enumerated only on those teenagers who were already inclined toward delinquency as the result of the combined effects of other stimuli. The movies reinforced this predisposition toward criminal activity but did not create the drive unless the other stimuli were also present.

This latter point, as it applies to television now, was reinforced by two widely respected and informed social psychologists a few years ago when they were part of a program on mass media conducted by the Child Study Association of America. At that time, Joseph T. Klapper said, "I think it is pretty well demonstrated that mass media do not serve as the primary determinant or even as a very important determinant of any of the basic attitudes or the basic behavior patterns of either young people or adults."

At the same conference, Otto Klineberg (1960) pointed out that certain major questions present themselves when we try to understand the nature of the influence of mass media. Several of these questions are particularly pertinent here. "Do mass media really change prevailing attitudes? Do mass media create values in our society, or are they merely the mirror of values in our society? Does what happens to a child when he looks at mass media depend on what kind of child he is—or on what is in the media?"

I believe this quotation might well serve as a text for my talk today, because I am firmly convinced, on the basis of research findings available and of personal experience and observation, that the media do not mold the teenager, but that the teenager's reaction to media stimuli depend upon what kind of a person he is to start with. And I think this premise, if we accept it, puts a much greater burden on parents, because we then must face up to the fact that we cannot blame the media—and particularly movies and television—for the unsatisfactory and even delinquent behavior of our young people. No, we must realize the unpleasant fact that it is the basic environment provided by the home, the church, and the school which molds the teenager. It is only following the influences of the environment that exposure to the media may act as a reinforcing agent and cause the child who is leaning toward illegal or immoral acts to actually take the final leap.

Therefore, it seems to me that our responsibility regarding television and movies and the teenager is two-fold. First, we have the basic, long-range task of supplying the sort of environment, love, and understanding which will make the young person strong and secure, with few doubts about what is right and wrong. And second—and the importance of this point will become more evident, I believe, as I continue—we must exert influence in the matter of what sort of television and movies young people are exposed to. And this influence takes two forms, especially so far as television is concerned: first, doing everything we can to assure better programming—and this is worth a long talk in itself, so we won't get bogged down here; and second, exercising some control over the types of programs our young people watch.

I believe this latter point is important because, while we've seen that programs of crime and violence tend to reinforce delinquency characteristics rather than create them, we cannot ignore the other potential influences that television brings to bear on our young people.

It seems to me that too many of our television programs tend to contribute to the general weakening of the moral fibre of impressionable teenagers. Their general attitude about values is very apt to be influenced because, unfortunately, the most exciting and popular TV shows of the dramatic variety show people with a very amoral, if not truly immoral, outlook on life. We see marital unhappiness treated as a natural and unsolvable problem of today's life; divorce is made to appear not only acceptable but actually desirable in many cases; people with very normal concerns, like those we all have, are depicted as suddenly beginning to suffer from some growing mental illness, traceable more than likely to an unhappy childhood; drinking is accepted not as an occasional but as an everyday, even an around-the-clock occurrence (the majority of scenes show people with either a drink or a cigarette, or both); and promiscuity is apparently condoned. It is this sort of morality with which we must concern ourselves, more than with shows of crime and violence.

A study done for the Nuffield Foundation in England by Himmelweit, Oppenheim, and Vince (1958) indicates that television brings about changes in children's outlook and values, gradually and almost imperceptibly. The similarity of views and values conveyed time after time in different television programs makes a cumulative impact on the mind of the young person. This study found that the impact is especially great if the values are presented in dramatic form so that they evoke primarily emotional reactions.

I have said that I believe it is up to the home, school, and church to create cooperatively an atmosphere and environment which will establish values so firmly in the young mind that media will have minor if any effects. The study I have just mentioned has this to say: "Values shown on television will have the greatest impact on the youngster if through his friends, parents or immediate environment the viewer is not already supplied with a set of values which would provide a standard against which to assess the views offered on television."

I wish we had more time for this aspect of the problem because I feel very strongly that we must work constantly to establish the proper moral values in the minds of our young people so that they will not be overly influenced by any of the media; and I feel sound judgment must be exercised by those in authority to regulate what young people see in movies and on television. Freedom and the development of initiative and self-confidence are certainly desirable, but we cannot turn these young people completely loose to set up their own values. We must first lay a better than adequate groundwork, and then they will be able to proceed more readily on their own without the great danger of falling prey to outside influences of an amoral or immoral character.

Let us turn to another related problem, and that is the loss of interest in other things that often results from too much television viewing. In fact, a sort of ennui seems to set in for many teenagers if they are exposed to television too many hours a week and make no real attempt to develop or promote other interests. Too often we find these young people glued to the television set, especially during vacation periods, seemingly having lost all interest in swimming, tennis, hobbies, and books. Here again I believe we all have a responsibility to help mold the young person's interests so that he will devote time to sports, hobbies, and general outdoor activities. It seems to me that parents, for example, have a definite responsibility to guide the television viewing of their youngsters: if necessary, to limit the hours of viewing; to suggest viewing of documentaries, news, and educational programs; and to encourage the development of outside interests.

The problem of excessive television viewing by adolescents ties in with the general lack of family conversation and mutual interests present in the family addicted to TV; no one wants to be interrupted by conversation, and no one wants to get outdoors and do other things. Our young people too often are made to feel that they are encroaching on their parents' TV time if they try to discuss their problems; thus, the teenager, too, becomes addicted, and the whole family becomes a family of zombies.

Eleanor Maccoby, in a paper on the impact of TV on children which appeared in the *Public Opinion Quarterly* a few years ago (1951), reported that television brings families into close proximity but restricts social interaction; that children in television homes tend to spend less time with their peers; that they substitute television for radio, movies, and reading; that watching TV prevents family members from reading, conversing, or engaging in other activities; and, most discouragingly, I think, that parents very commonly use TV as a pacifier.

Paul Witty, in one of a continuing series of reports on the effect of television, printed in *Elementary English*, reported that excessive television viewing often resulted in neglect of homework, increased nervousness, fatigue, impoverishment of outside activities, disinterest in school, and reduction in reading.

The importance of parental and other adult influence—both in the adult attitude toward television and in the extent to which the adult tends to assist the youngster to become more interested in other activities—is pointed up in the report on "Television and the Child," completed for the Nuffield Foundation. This report states that viewing seems to become a habit on which the young person falls back when nothing more interesting is available. Consequently, the one with many interests, the active youngster, and the outdoor type tend to view less than others. It is up to all of us to help develop these other interests in all adolescents.

The report also states that the social level of the home has little effect on how much viewing takes place. Much more important is parental example and to a lesser extent, parental control. In homes where parents themselves are selective and moderate viewers, the researchers found that the youngsters also tend to view relatively little. Also, the study found that how much television is wanted depends on the relative emptiness of the child's life and on his emotional needs. Here again we find strong evidence that those of us who shape the child's general environment can certainly play a definite role in this area.

I mentioned a few moments ago the effect of television on general family relations. The Nuffield report also has some pertinent findings in this regard. This study indicates that television does keep members of the family at home more, but it is doubtful that it binds the family together in more than this physical sense. As the children grow older, their viewing becomes more silent and personal. Also, as children grow into adolescents, the increased time spent with the family may set up strains, since it runs counter to their need to make contacts outside; they may therefore do less in the way of other joint activities with their parents than they did formerly.

I don't have any really rousing note to close on except to reiterate some of the things I have already said. One of the biggest worries of the uninformed seems to be that crime and violence on television will lead teenagers into delinquency. This worry, I believe, we can dismiss on the basis of the evidence available, remembering, however, that the viewing of such programs by teenagers with a predisposition to delinquency may help push them over the brink. We have found that too much television viewing tends to lessen the young person's interest in other, perhaps more worthwhile and certainly more diverse activities. We find that the youngster follows somewhat the pattern set for him by the adults with whom he associates. We know that television affects the values which the young mind establishes unless stronger outside influences counteract any bad effect television might have.

My most important point—the one I hope you will remember—is that we have a tremendous responsibility to prepare properly the field in which the seed left by television will be planted. If we are to help the medium to serve the best social purposes of which it is capable, we must direct our attention to the molding of the young audience at least as intensely as we direct our attention to the content of the medium. If we, as responsible adults, in helping to mold the teenagers we work and live with, bring to bear the proper influences, the proper lessons, and the proper examples, we will establish a moral ethic for these teenagers which will be the real foundation of their growth, and they will be able to absorb the good things television brings them, and not be adversely affected by the bad.

# 20. The Impact of Pornography on the Adolescent

JOHN F. O'GRADY

The word "pornography" comes from the Greek *pornein,* meaning to prostitute, and *graphein,* meaning to write. In its strict sense, pornography means to write about prostitution. Today, however, this word has taken on a broader meaning; it means obscene, licentious, lascivious, and lewd writing, drawing, photographs, and films. Another adjective, "prurient," has recently been added by the courts.[1] The purpose of this paper will be to describe the impact of pornography on the teenager and to define the scope of pornography.

## The Impact of Pornography

The adolescent period of life is a most difficult period both for the adolescent and for those trying to help him—parents as well as professional people. The adolescent is bewildering and the parents are bewildered. The youngster in this period of life is growing so fast and in so many different ways that the child and his parents easily become confused. Confusion in the adolescent seems normal because the body, mind, and emotions are undergoing such great changes. Weight, height, and voice changes, muscular coordination and awkwardness are all signs of this transformation. In adolescence the youngster is afraid of

---

[1] The Supreme Court has had a very difficult problem in defining obscenity. In 1957, the U. S. Supreme Court held that obscenity is not the kind of speech protected by the First Amendment to the Constitution, and used the following test as a guide in determining what is obscene: "Whether to the average person, applying contemporary community standards, the dominant theme of the material taken as a whole appealed to prurient interest." "Prurient," according to Webster's Dictionary has the meanings: uneasy with desire or longing; morbid or lascivious in language, curiosity, or propensity; lewd.

being different from his gang. At the same time, he wants to be by him-self and to work out his own problems. He is secretive about himself and his feelings and finds difficulty in expressing his feelings; yet, at other times, he will bare his soul. There is quite a contradiction between his words and his behavior. He likes to participate in games that involve skill and team cooperation. He is noisy, runs around disorganizedly, laughs loudly, sings too often, forgets his manners. At three o'clock he sees his parents as sinners, but at three-thirty they are saints. At four o'clock he wants nothing to do with his parents, but at four-thirty he cannot do without them. At times, he thinks his parents know too much, while at other times he thinks they know nothing. He does not want to be told what clothes to wear, what hours to keep, what food to eat; yet, at times, he will ask advice about these things. He is unpredictable, self-conscious, irritable, fatigued, depressed, easily hurt, quarrelsome. The adolescent girl is distressed because she is growing too tall while the boy shows anxiety because he is not tall enough.

Josselyn (1952, p. 25) describes the period of adolescence as follows:

> During the entire period of adolescence, the individual is more responsive to all stimuli. The sunset, which in pre-adolescence was meaningful only as a signal to return home for dinner, now at adolescence becomes an esthetic experience. It becomes beautiful, depressing, or stimulating. Trees, which previously were of value for climbing, now take on symbolic meaning. Music, which was a matter of rhythm or melody, is now associated with all the emo-tional turmoil of the individual. Thoughts that were previously accepted or discarded on the basis of their reality functioning now take on poetic coloring. The individual may be compared to a violin. Previously, the instrument may have seemed to be a cigar box strung with catgut; at adolescence it may seem suddenly to have become a Stradivarius. Played on by varying forces, it some-times responds as if played by a concert-master, at other times, as if by an untalented amateur. At times, it refuses to produce music at all.

Of all of the characteristics of adolescents, however, there are three which stand out, namely, their desire to imitate adults, their susceptibil-ity to ideas, and their curiosity about and interest in sex. Because of this curiosity and interest, the adolescent is prone to pornography in whatever form it may take. The impact on the teenager, especially if he has emotional problems, can be dangerous both for the youngster and the community. The effect is to portray abnormal sexual behavior as normal and thus wreck the chance of impressionable youth to achieve a normal healthy relationship upon reaching adulthood. Once initiated into a knowledge of the unnatural, the young mind hunts for something more daring, something with a greater thrill, and this hunger can cause damage to another person. If pornography comes into the hands of a fairly well-adjusted adolescent with a good home, backed up by a good attitude toward sex, it will probably have little effect. But the child who is emotionally upset may be triggered into sex crimes and will experience other personality problems.

The New York Academy of Medicine vividly describes this impact in its statement on pornography:

. . . such reading encourages a morbid preoccupation with sex and interferes with the development of a healthy attitude and respect for the opposite sex. It is said to contribute to perversion . . . it is undeniable that there has been a resurgence of venereal disease, particularly for teenage youth, and that the rate of illegitimacy is climbing. It is postulated that there is a correlation between these phenomena and the apparent use and sale of salacious literature, and perhaps it is causal, but the latter observation cannot be definitely demonstrated. It can be asserted, however, that the perusal of erotic literature has the potentiality of inciting sane young persons to enter into illicit sex relations and thus leading them into promiscuity, illegitimacy, and venereal disease (*Christopher News Notes,* April 1964, p. 2).

It is interesting to note that our legislators must think that pornography has a bad effect on our youth because every state in the United States makes the sale and distribution of obscene publications a crime. A conclusion of the Senate Committee headed by the late Senator Estes Kefauver was that "the impulses that spur young people to sex crimes are unquestionably intensified by reading obscene publications." And J. Edgar Hoover, referring to pornography, had stated:

We know that an overwhelmingly large number of sex crimes is associated with pornography. We know that sex criminals read it, are clearly influenced by it . . . I believe that if we can eliminate the distribution of such items among impressible school-age children we shall greatly reduce our frightening sex crime rate . . . The peddlers of obscene pictures and writings have so flooded the market with toxic trash within the last few years, that to find news racks without samples of it is a rare exception. There is today a vicious movement to undermine the traditional spiritual and moral principles of our nation (*The Granahan report*).[2]

---

[2] Reports to Congressional committees by Kathryn Granahan, hereinafter referred to as *The Granahan report;* no single publication with the title *The Granahan report* exists. Refer to the Congressional Record, Vol. 105, Part 8, and Vol. 108, Parts 3 and 9, for reports by Kathryn Granahan relating to obscene literature through the mails.

Rabbi Joseph Klein of Worcester, Massachusetts, states his concern when he writes:

I am also concerned about the widespread dissemination of obscene literature throughout the country. I believe much of it is corrupting the minds of our young people, giving them false understandings concerning the nature of sex and marriage. I believe that much of the literature that is made easily available to our youth can have no other but disastrous effects upon their thinking and upon their emotions. Young people normally are curious about sex and because of this the purveyors of this literature find it quite profitable to publish and disseminate it (*The Granahan report*).

Dr. Benjamin Karpman, Chief Psychotherapist at St. Elizabeth's Hospital in Washington, D.C., states flatly that he believes there is a direct relationship between juvenile delinquency, sex crimes, and pornographic literature.[3]

Dr. Nicholas G. Frigrito, Medical Director and Chief Neuropsychiatrist of the County Court of Philadelphia, has ventured the opinion that

. . . in too many instances the increase in sexual offenses was traced to the persistent and constant exposure to obscenity in all media of communication. Delinquent boys and girls coming to the attention of the Court for robbery, larceny, burglary, carrying concealed and deadly weapons were avid readers of crime stories, obscene comic books and lewd stories . . . The most singular factor inducing the adolescent to sexual activities is pornography, the lewd pictures, the smutty story book, the obscene playing cards . . . Though little physical damage results from sexual misconduct, it does have a devastating effect on the intellectual, emotional and moral development of the children. Demoralization leads to or enhances anti-social or delinquent behavior. Pornography fosters impure habits and desires, as a result of which sexually aggressive acts may follow. These indecent attacks often terminate in physical injury if not the slaying of the victim. This is particularly true when aggressive delinquents have been stimulated by smut devoted to flagellations, sadism, and masochistic retreats . . . It is absurd to say eradication of pornography is suppression of sex knowledge or that smut reading is a practical and safe outlet for the sexually aggressive who would otherwise act out these inclinations. The reading of erotica is not a harmless psychological aphrodisiac; it is a serious danger and threat to morality. Pornography is a scheme of avaricious and depraved psychopathic persons to enrich themselves (*The Granahan report*).

Throughout the hearing before the Subcommittee on Postal Operations—better known as the Granahan Committee—there have been

---

[3] *The Granahan report.*

statements from police officials to the effect that police investigations of serious crime reveal that the persons convicted of said crimes were early collectors of pornography.

Walter Lippmann, one of our most respected and admired commentators, has stated:

There can be no real doubt, it seems to me, that the movies and comic books are purveying violence and lust to a vicious and intolerable degree. There can be no doubt that public exhibitions of sadism tend to excite sadistic desires and to teach the audience how to gratify sadistic desires . . . For my own part, believing as I do in freedom of speech and thought, I see no objection in principle to censorship of the mass entertainment of the young (*The Granahan report*).

Judge Michael A. Musmanno of the Pennsylvania Supreme Court, who also presided at the Nuremberg trials, has stated:

What is this doing to the moral health of youth? Love, in its pure sense, is being commonized, cheapened, and vulgarized to an extent that is simply appalling to contemplate. Sex, perhaps the most potent force in life, since it involves the creation of life itself, is being hammered into the minds of the young with such shattering force and incessant repetition that it is displacing from the minds of millions of children the concentration due other vital facets of life. Devotion to country, ambition for wholesome careers, desire for approval in the eyes of the community are being violently shoved aside for this artificially stimulated craving until that craving reaches practically irresistible demands for gratification—gratification which expresses itself, wholly or partially, through the viewing of lewd pictures, the reading of dirty novels and eventually illicit behavior (*The Granahan report*).

## The Scope of Pornography

It is not possible to state in exact terms that pornography is having a bad effect on 10 per cent, 50 per cent, or 60 per cent of our adolescents. The facts simply cannot be determined. What evidence there is, however, is frightening.

Mr. Arthur E. Summerfield, former Postmaster General of the United States, estimated that the business of pornography is a $500,000,000-a-year enterprise. It is no small business adventure but a racket of major proportions. Mr. Summerfield also estimated that about one million children a year receive pornographic filth in their family's mail box. Other estimates vary from 30 million dollars a year to 5 billion dollars a year.

Part of the problem in estimating the scope of pornography is that the money spent is not the only guide. Adolescents pass on indecent magazines to others so that a fifty-cent magazine can find its way into the hands of several children. Recently, a boy appeared before me in Juvenile Court, and his mother told me she felt part of her son's problem was the reading of pornography. She later brought me three magazines, and the total cost of the magazines came to $15.00. Referring to the extent of pornography, Dr. Frigrito of the Philadelphia Court says:

It respects no family, no cultural group. It is true that much of the smut is carried by adolescent boys, particularly delinquents. Pornography is available to all groups and, in our experience, the smut handlers are boys in the 8th and 9th grades, the high school student, the perverted young adult, the homosexual adult. Many of the boys we examine admit carrying smut to show others. We don't often catch them with it but they tell us they have access to it, that they read it, and a majority of them do. Only 5 per cent say, "No, I didn't see anything like that" (*The Granahan report*).

## Conclusion

How much money is involved in pornography and how many adolescents are affected are matters extremely difficult to estimate. All of us are certainly aware of the magazines for sale in our drug stores and how easy it is for children to purchase such trash. One cannot help but think of the well-worn analogy of the pebble being tossed into the pond and the ripples spreading in all directions. The pornography pebble is thrown into many ponds and, I am afraid, that the ripples are spreading to far too many adolescents.

All professional people dealing with adolescents—doctors, judges, lawyers, legislators, police officers, teachers—agree that during this most formative period, the adolescent needs good examples on the part of his parents, good habit training, and wise supervision. The reading of pornographic material is not good habit training, and no one having any supervision over adolescents would encourage such reading. Sorokin has aptly expressed this view (Sorokin, 1956, p. 56):

Overindulgence of the sex urge tends to undermine the physical and mental health and vitality of the individual, destroys his sense of morality, brings misery and shame upon himself and his family and his friends, diminishes his creative energy, and ruins his prospects for happiness.

No one will ever prove in a test-tube experiment that obscene literature has an impact on the adolescent and that it causes sexual misbehavior. However, common sense and experience are sound guides for
the prudent man in trying to keep such trash away from the adolescent
because of its potential danger to him.

The problem of pornography is very difficult not only because of
too much unadorned flesh but also because many magazines attack
morality by ridiculing virtue, chastity, fidelity, or control of the emotions. The person who lives by a code of morality is pictured as living
in the Middle Ages. The Judaeo-Christian concept of love and marriage is pictured as being outmoded, and a pagan, immoral life is
advocated. These magazines are not able to picture the kind of con-
tentment that shines in a woman who knows she belongs to one man
and that one man belongs to her.

One word of caution. The continued use of pornography is really a
symptom, and should not be considered as the cause of juvenile delinquency or the cause of sexual crimes. The adolescent or the adult
addicted to pornography is probably suffering from an emotional problem. Through the use of pornography, the adolescent steps into a
fantasy world and in effect tries to avoid a sexual reality which he fears.

Also it is well known that a child learns his basic philosophy or
attitude toward sex in the home. Even if it were possible to rule out
pornography, we would not cure delinquency or sexual problems. It
is not enough to stop pornography; we must also obtain help for the
person who craves for it. In our great anxiety to stamp out pornography,
we often forget the great need for research and the need for mental-
hygiene clinics to help those who are addicted to pornography.

Our own society's attitude toward sex needs to be reevaluated.
Cardinal Newman once said that you cannot expect a sinless literature
about sinful people. Sex is and should be considered a dignified relationship. The pleasure attached to the act must be coupled with
responsibility. There is a need for censorship that is not controlled by
fanatical puritans or by the sexually inhibited. Both extremes are really
alike because each looks upon sex as something evil.

Most of us here have passed beyond the adolescent stage and pornography means little or nothing to us personally. We pay little or no
attention to it unless we have children, and our attitude is that we
do not want our children to look at such filth. The following poem
is worth consideration:

An old man, going a lone highway
Came in the evening, cold and gray,
To a chasm vast, both deep and wide.
The old man crossed in the twilight dim,
The swollen stream was but naught to him,
But he stopped, when safe on the farthest side,
And built a bridge to span the tide.

"Old man," said a fellow pilgrim near,
"Your journey will end with the closing day.
You never again will pass this way,
You have crossed the chasm deep and wide,
Why build you this bridge at even tide?"

The laborer lifted his old gray head.
"Good friend: In the way I have come," he said
"There followeth after me this day
A youth whose feet must pass this way.
This chasm which has been naught to me
To that fair-haired youth may a pitfall be.
He, too, must cross in the twilight dim,
Good Friend: I am building this bridge for him."

What responsibility do we as adults—having crossed the bridge of adolescence—have toward those following us to help them bridge the chasm of adolescence and avoid the pitfall of pornography?

# PART VI

## *The Counseling Process*

▲▲▲▲▲▲▲▲▲▲▲▲▲▲▲▲▲▲▲▲▲▲▲▲▲▲▲▲▲▲▲

# 21. Development and Administration of a Guidance and Counseling Program

## LAWRENCE R. MALNIG

A shot heard around the world was fired by Russia on October 4, 1957. Sputnik I created many shock waves in the educational world, and its reverberations were felt very strongly in guidance and counseling. Renewed attention was given to the role of the counselor, government funds were poured into training programs, and the goals and objectives of counseling were seriously examined.

The origins of guidance were documented; its philosophy, or lack of philosophy, was brought to light; and the nature and theoretical foundations of this movement were thoroughly examined. As a result of all this activity, we find a renewed vigor in guidance and counseling; but it is also in a state of flux and on the brink of many changes.

### Development of the Counseling Movement

This state of change makes it very difficult to discuss the development and administration of guidance in very specific terms and formulations. If we were to start with the many theories now in vogue, it would be impossible to devise a structure that could incorporate them. On the other hand, were we to set up a precise outline for a program based on a single theory, we would probably find it to be totally inadequate in meeting the needs of our local situation. Therefore, we shall examine some of the essential issues in guidance and counseling that can help us arrive at an approach that will be useful in getting started. We can then consider what type of administrative structure is flexible enough to meet new and emerging student needs.

Our area of interest, which is concerned primarily with student services, is difficult to describe with a single term. "Pupil personnel" or "student personnel" is too broad a term because it includes food, housing, and social services; and "counseling" seems too narrow a term to include occupational information, testing, and educational and vocational guidance. For this reason we shall use the term "guidance and counseling" to refer to those professional services rendered outside the classroom which are usually provided to a student on an individual basis.

You will note that most definitions of guidance and counseling assume that all individuals at critical times in their lives require professional, individual assistance in understanding themselves and the world in which they live, and in making decisions about the vast array of choices they continually must face.

Patterson states that "counseling and guidance services are provided mainly for the more or less normal individual—to assist him in functioning optimally, in developing his potentialities, and in achieving to his capacity. The goal is to increase the individual's achievement and his contribution to society through the use of all his abilities and capacity. The terms self-realization and self-actualization have been used by some to designate this goal" (1962, p. 18).

In quite similar terms Feder et al. say that "counseling is concerned with assisting the student (1) in understanding and evaluating his potentialities and limitations, and (2) in discovering and developing ways and means of working out his problems and taking full advantage of his opportunities" (1958, p. 7).

Finally, Dugan, in a review of guidance practices, maintains that "guidance during the last two decades has been interpreted as encouragement of youth's development in terms of a basic concern about individual differences and an active assistance to youth in making appropriate adjustments to personal, educational and vocational needs and problems. In short, guidance services have aimed primarily at self-realization of the individual" (1960, p. 105).

In the light of current values in our society, these definitions seem quite commonplace, but we must remember that they were almost fifty years in developing. The guidance movement did not start as a discipline, nor did it have any philosophical roots when it began. As a matter of fact, guidance and counseling had somewhat different origins in college and secondary schools, a fact which has affected its development up to the present time. The one thing in common was that at both levels new services were added from time to time to meet new needs.

At the college level, developments were relatively uniform, because the problems different colleges faced were the same. After the turn of the century there were major curriculum changes with the introduction of the psychological sciences, business education, and electives. Coeducation, rising enrollments, and efforts by pragmatists to justify education brought both deans of men and women to the American campus. Supervision of women students, maintenance of academic standards, and even vocational guidance were some of the problems handled, but programs were generally shaped by the individual preferences of the deans.

After World War I, college staffs took on specialists recruited from new fields such as psychological measurement and mental hygiene. These specialists tended to work independently, and as late as the 1930's there was still no plan for the integration of services.

The depression brought more students to the campus and reemphasized the need for student services. In 1937 at a conference held by the American Council on Education, a statement entitled "The Student Personnel Point of View" was issued, which emphasized concern for the whole person—not intellectual training alone—as the goal of education. Since that time, college programs have been organized in terms of services; and except for attempts to find better ways of integrating these services, there have been few essential changes. At the present time there is still a great deal of fragmentation, overlapping, and even rivalry.

The beginnings of guidance and counseling were quite different on the high-school scene. The movement had a vocational orientation with practical and specific goals which helped it to gain quick recognition and support from the schools and the community. As early as 1913 the National Vocational Guidance Association stated its goal as the selection of, the preparation for, and the placement of individuals in a life work. Frank Parsons (1909), the originator of the movement saw vocational guidance as a rational process which involved the assessment of the individual's abilities, interests, and background and the careful study of occupational information. Rapid industrial changes and the movement to urban areas of people who could not be absorbed in the city for lack of skills and training created many problems which the vocational-guidance movement promised to solve.

After World War I, the assessment of individual differences and psychological tests were introduced to evaluate specialized aptitudes required for skilled occupations. For almost thirty years, the field was basically dominated by the trait-and-factor theory—the method of matching employee and job, with adjustment as the criterion of success.

In the 1950's a great deal of research was centered on the expansion of this narrow concept of vocational guidance, and much more attention was given to the role of personality factors and individual needs in vocational development. Super expressed this broader view of guidance as "a process of helping a person to develop and accept an integrated and adequate picture of himself and of his ideas in the world of work, to test his concept against reality, and to convert it into a reality, with satisfaction to himself and benefit to society" (1957, p. 197).

In recent years, with so many more high-school students going on to college, counselors have become much more concerned with social and intellectual development. In addition, they have had to deal with problems concerning delinquents, dropouts, the retarded, the gifted, and the like, but the movement is still strongly influenced by vocational guidance, and we still do not have a fully organized and integrated program for dealing effectively with this broad range of problem areas.

## Counseling Goals and Techniques

In the light of this background, let us look at some of the current issues that are exerting an influence on guidance and counseling today and that are likely to shape future developments. Since the purpose of any guidance program is to implement the basic educational objectives of an institution, the philosophy of the educational system will have a profound influence on the nature of the program. Let us look at some of these broader philosophical issues that are likely to influence any program.

The first is what we might call the controversy between the "Essentialist" and the "Life Adjustment" view of education. Advocates of the Essentialist view, such as Hutchins (1953), maintain that the basic responsibility of education is the training and development of the intellect and that spiritual, moral, and social training should be the responsibility of the church and the family or any other agency in the community that may be available to provide it. This is a view that seems to gain favor whenever education is under attack for having failed to meet an immediate crisis, such as Sputnik I or an economic recession.

The proponents of this view consider responsible citizenship as a goal of education but somehow fail to recognize that the attainment of this goal entails more than intellectual training. The most significant criticism of this view is that it considers the student as a disembodied intellect and ignores the fact that learning can be greatly impaired if physical, social, or emotional disturbances are present.

On the other hand, the Life Adjustment position declares a concern for the whole individual and his preparation for participation in a democratic society. The need for this approach has much more validity today, since the training functions of the home and the parish have been considerably weakened as large urban centers have developed. Today more than one-third of mothers work, commuting fathers often see their children only on weekends, and the automobile has greatly reduced dependency on the parish for social activities.

The further disruption of family life produced by World War II and the greater acceptance of the insights developed by psychology and sociology started, in the early 1940's, a trend away from the Essentialist view. The individual was no longer looked upon as being composed of many parts, each of which could be trained separately. The interrelationship of all experiences was recognized, as well as the need to center our attention on the individual and his present universe rather than his specific course requirements. One result of this new orientation was the emergence of the core curriculum and a greater tendency to integrate the different disciplines. Even more recently we have seen the development of team teaching at the secondary level, where a history and an English teacher, for example, combine their courses and teach them together as a unified experience.

The need for unified experience was equally present in the nonacademic areas. Whether or not we like it, the school environment has a profound influence on the social, moral, and ethical behavior of the individual and influences not only his academic development but also his self-concept and his future aspirations. This relationship has been the object of much research in recent years, and as Freedman has explained, "Critical thinking ability and change in attitudes and values are usually caught rather than taught. Student culture and teacher personality play more important roles than specific attempts to teach critical thinking techniques" (1960, p. 1). Consequently, in order to have the student derive maximum benefit from his education, all these forces which influence behavior and development have to be unified and coordinated. Let me cite just one example to illustrate this point. A survey of our alumni some ten years ago showed that close to half went on to graduates school but that only an average of three seniors per year received graduate awards. We felt the situation could be remedied by publicizing available awards and by having applications readily available. When all attempts failed to stimulate interest, we conducted individual interviews and found that because we were a small college many students felt they would not stand a chance in competition. Through counseling and encouragement by the faculty, students began to apply and met with surprising success. This change in self-concept soon communicated to the entire student body, and since then the average number of graduate awards has risen sharply. Thus we find that although all the necessary elements for success were present, cooperation and understanding were needed for the behavioral change that resulted in achievement of potential.

Of course, there is always the danger of putting too much emphasis on adjustment and considering it an end in itself. Should this occur, there would be no difference between an educational institution and any other social agency. For this reason we must constantly bear in mind the goals and purposes of our institution and remember that our fundamental role is to promote its educational objectives.

This issue of concern for the whole person is not likely to be put to rest in the near future and is certain to arise whenever educational practices are questioned or when there is pressure for change. However, on the basis of past experience, it seems that when a crisis subsides, the services we offer are usually strengthened and there is greater acceptance of the fact that we cannot simply expose students to educational experiences and just hope for the best.

A second issue that waxes and wanes and is sure to continue to attract much attention is concerned with methods and techniques in the counseling process. I shall not dwell too long on this problem but would merely like to trace the development of this issue in order to provide a background for understanding present-day trends.

When the vocational-guidance movement got underway, counseling was looked upon as a rational process of collecting information about the individual and relating it to the world of work. On the basis of this synthesis, the courses of action likely to produce success were then given to the counselee. This method—which continued to be used with little change until the 1940's—has had various labels such as "trait and factor," "prescriptive," and "directive." The main emphasis was on helping the individual find his place in society. With the emergence of psychological tests to measure intelligence, interests, and aptitudes, the directive or advice-giving method gained even greater acceptance, for now it appeared to have a statistical and scientific objectivity.

Gradually the emphasis shifted away from the individual's place-ment in society and greater attention was placed on the relationship between counselor and counselee and on the client's perception of himself. Carl Rogers, the exponent of the movement that was first called "nondirective" and later "client-centered," maintained that the individual possessed the resources to resolve his own problems and that the function of the counselor was to enable the client to utilize his resources. Advice, direction, threat and prescription, all terms which placed control in the hands of the counselor, were considered inap-propriate, and the emphasis shifted on what was happening within the individual. Testing, information gathering, and analysis were no longer of central importance; instead, as Patterson states, "The major techniques of the client-centered counselor are listening, acceptance, and the communication of understanding through reflection and clari-fication of feelings" (1962, p. 121).

The view of the counselor as an objective, catalytic agent dominated the 1940's to such an extent that self-respecting counselors were almost reluctant to talk of testing, diagnosis, or the dissemination of occupa-tional information. Soon, however, it became apparent that these tests and techniques had their place, and that all counseling situations could not be handled in the same manner. It is at this time that the term "eclectic" began to enter guidance literature. Counselors felt that technique should be determined by the nature of the client and his problems, and that there were circumstances in which one approach could be much more effective than another. In other words, if the counselor could arrive at a differential diagnosis or evaluation of a student's problem, he would then select the procedure or technique that would be most effective in coping with the problem.

In recent years we also find that the behaviorists, led by B. F. Skinner, have been applying their findings in conditioning experiments to guidance practices. In their view, manipulation of the environment could serve to reinforce desirable behavior and to extinguish undesir-able or self-defeating behavior patterns. As conditioning techniques become more effective, and if society can agree on a set of objectives, it is the contention of the behaviorists that any type of society can be formed.

This view inevitably led to the question of goals and values in coun-seling. The client-centered theorists who supported the idea of self-actualization felt that through counseling the client would be free to set his own goals in terms of his clarified self-concept, and that the counselor was not to impose either his values or those of society on the individual. However, not only the behaviorists but other theorists as well questioned the possibility that a counselor could function in any given setting without reflecting the values of his institution and society at least implicitly if not openly. This inherent conflict is pointed out by Shoben, who said, "To the extent that a guidance worker accepts as referrals those children who are perceived by teachers as disruptive, disorderly, or discordant with the classroom group, he accepts in some degree the definition of his job as that of fitting children to the dominant pattern of the school. This task may be an essential one, and on occasion, it may be quite harmonious with that of aiding an individual child to actualize his distinctive potentialities. The fact remains that there are other times when the two enterprises are certainly different and may be in opposition to each other" (1962, p. 435).

We can also see the immediate reality of this issue of values in our day-to-day work as it relates to manpower needs. As the space race gained international importance, many felt that our schools had failed society by not providing enough scientists to meet our country's need. But those who do not have short memories will also recall the cutback in defense contracts after the Korean War that literally left thousands of engineers without jobs.

Are we to guide students into careers to meet society's current and future needs, or should we be concerned with the development of individuals according to their own unique pattern and allow them to change society?

The view that we should guide students in terms of social needs was expressed by Hutson, who examined the vocational choices of high-school students in 1930 and again in 1961 and found that while a little more than 12 per cent of the nation's workers could be classified as professionals, 38 to 64 per cent of high-school pupils were planning to enter professional occupations. He concluded that "guidance for vocational choice has not become more effective in the three decades that have elapsed between the two surveys" (1962, p. 219).

Those who accept this position will argue that we are doing youth a disservice if we permit them to plan for positions that may not be available when they are ready to take their place in society. The dilemma counseling and guidance faces is highlighted by Mathewson, who stated, "The crucial consideration for guidance seems to be whether we shall regard the student as a statistical unit—a piece of socio-economic mass to be planned, directed, and otherwise manipulated—or whether he is to be perceived as a potentially free and responsible individual and citizen who, every day in his adult life, will be personally engaged in his own pursuit of meaning and in determining, with his fellows, the essential nature and direction of our culture and economy" (1964, p. 338).

As you can see, there are still many issues to be resolved with regard to educational objectives, counseling goals and techniques, and the needs of the individual as opposed to those of society. The problems facing us are great and so is the challenge for the future.

## Current Trends and Future Needs

But what about present-day needs of the student? One very basic reason for establishing guidance services was to personalize instruction so that in the expanding world of mass education the individual would not be lost. Have we succeeded in this basic function? There are many indications that we have not.

Speaking of students at the University of California at Berkeley, Cass stated, "They refer to the university as 'the factory' and claim that the administration views them as the raw material for the university's educational production line. Intelligent, informed, and sensitive to the world around them, they seek a place in which they can achieve a sense of identity that the university denies them" (1965, p. 68).

In a similar vein Rappaport and Goldman speak of the lonely student and point out that "There is an increasing deterioration in the relationship between the freshman and the experienced professor, the master teacher, the established scholar, the practical classroom educator. The graduate assistant or teaching fellow handles the quiz and laboratory sections; the professor is relegated to the giant lecture section where he talks once a week to two or three hundred anonymous students" (1963, p. 225).

This criticism is being echoed throughout the land and both the large universities and rapidly expanding colleges are wondering if size is the answer to the population explosion in higher education. It could easily be shown that guidance and counseling services seldom expand in proportion to the physical growth of an institution, and at least part of the students' problems must be attributed to this fact.

Have we been more successful in career and vocational guidance, which has such deep roots in the historical development of our profession? In this age of the computer and automation many new problems have arisen with which the counselor must still learn to cope. Samler has indicated that, "We are becoming aware of the need to identify the psycho-social aspects of work—for instance, the particular culture of the shop, the status characteristics of a given position, the way in which personality needs can be met in an identified work setting. It is important that these understandings be sought for the new range of occupations and work settings" (1964, p. 65). While the need is becoming clearer, the means for meeting it, however, are still lagging behind. At all levels, an educational decision is also a career decision. As stated by Kauffman, "It is inevitably bound up with vocational counseling and career guidance. Yet in very few colleges and universities is significant effort given to career choice or eventual entry into the world of work" (1964, p. 357).

It would almost seem from all these comments that we have been thrashing about for more than fifty years without very much to show for all our effort. This conclusion, of course, is not true. What we can conclude from this state of affairs is that we must constantly be alert to new developments in society, in the student culture, and in our own institution. To make this alertness possible, it is necessary to have organizational arrangements in which there are good communication and administrative flexibility.

While the difficulties in outlining an ideal program should be more apparent at this point, it might be useful to look at current trends and some of the needs for the future. The terms most frequently used in speaking of organization are centralization and decentralization, especially with reference to colleges. The high schools as yet are not too concerned with this problem because individual institutions are small and the relatively few specialists are usually consultants rather than staff members.

In colleges, when deans first appeared, they usually taught and had considerable contact with students. After World War I, as many specialists in psychology, mental hygiene, vocational guidance, and placement were added, deans became increasingly concerned with administration and the maintenance of cooperation among the various services. At this time, the director of student personnel services appeared on the college scene and began to replace the deans, who were relegated to positions of lesser authority. The purpose of this move was to centralize the services by the many offices—23 in one institution —that were available to him for assistance.

While the trend, especially in large universities, has continued in the direction of centralization, it has not necessarily solved the problems of our bewildered student. The grouping of services led to refinements which produced jurisdictional disputes and even rivalry. Whittington (1963) has pointed out how the counseling office in one university allegedly failed to refer seriously disturbed students to the psychiatric staff in order to prove that they too were competent in doing psychotherapy. The difficulty on the college level seems to be that guidance and counseling services were introduced rather recently and had to find their way into an already existing administrative structure. These services are described as being located somewhere between faculty and administration, but their relationship to the entire institution is still to be explored and defined. For that matter, there is still very little agreement as to which services are essential and should be provided for the college student.

With respect to organization, the high school again presents a difficult set of problems because on this level the function of guidance and counseling is quite amorphous. For this reason it might be useful to touch briefly on the organizational pattern of counseling programs and some of the problems that interfere with their development.

The educational philosophy of the school system is particularly important at this level, for in order to start a program one must have support of the school administration and faculty, as well as the school board and parents. The formation of a guidance committee is generally recommended for this purpose in order to study the needs of the students and the resources available in the community and to obtain assistance from faculty and parents. Planned services should be coordinated with those already in existence such as nursing or remedial reading, and they should be carefully explained to faculty and students if they are to be used properly and are to serve their purpose.

Specialists can be brought in gradually as specific needs are established. Bringing them in does not usually present any particular problem since specialized personnel are used on a consulting basis, or, in larger school systems containing several high schools, they operate from a centralized bureau located outside the school itself.

When possible, it is better to offer only those services that can be reasonably performed with success than to attempt too much without staff or facilities. Dissatisfied clients and parents find little comfort in the fact that you may have done the best possible with your limited resources. It is therefore better to start with freshmen or seniors and gradually provide counseling for other groups as counselors are added to the staff.

Evaluation and feedback are also important in order to maintain communication and to keep the faculty alert regarding the need for referrals. Since much of the work the counselor does is on an individual basis and frequently confidential, it is easy for others to take it for granted and to forget that it is carried on. Reports and follow-up studies can therefore help to point up the value of the program and to keep faculty and administration informed about the activities that are being conducted.

Even when a program is fairly well established, counselors will find many problems which can hinder its continued development. Some of these problems may be inherent in the system we have inherited, while others can be attributed to the counselor's failure to assume leadership.

One problem concerns recruitment of staff members. Counselors in 45 states must have teaching certificates in spite of the fact that two out of three states have reported counselor shortages (Weitz, 1958). This requirement has led to a system of released time for teachers to serve as counselors. As part-time counselors acquire training and eventually certification, they often move into full-time positions. Many feel that by having teachers become counselors, rapport with the faculty would remain at a high level. Frequently, this rapport has not been the result, for many teachers see counseling as an opportunity to flee from the classroom, and those who fail become resentful and hostile. Furthermore, because these counselors do not have a full teaching schedule, they are saddled with many extra duties such as record keeping and proctoring, which could be performed much more economically by clerical assistants.

Another serious problem concerns confidentiality both in the counseling situation and in the handling of records. In many schools I have visited I found counselors in very cramped quarters and one, for example, had a five-foot glass partition separating his office from another. The counselor in this school told me that he saw his function as one of processing, not counseling, and that when a confidential matter came up he had to see the student after hours in order to have some privacy. This situation can only mean that the school is simply paying lip service to guidance and has no real understanding or concern for this professional service.

What I have found to be even more disturbing in many schools is the utter disregard for the maintenance of confidential records and information. In practice counselors fail to realize, and make known to others, that they are involved in a professional relationship which requires them to maintain confidentiality. In many schools administrators and teachers have free access to all counseling files and in many instances such information is readily given over the phone to prospective employers without checking their credentials! Such blatant disregard of ethical principles makes it difficult to believe that any kind of effective counseling can be carried on.

Counselors working with us at the state level in developing a code of ethics have told us that these conditions are imposed by the school and that they are powerless to do anything about it. The fault here lies not with the administrators who are uninformed, but with counselors and their professional organizations who have the responsibility of developing a code of ethics and seeing to it that it is accepted by school boards and administrators. Only in this manner can counseling rightfully establish itself as a profession and earn for its members the freedom and autonomy that they need to function effectively on a professional level. To be sure, it will take considerable time to bring about this rather fundamental change, but considering the alternatives, it seems imperative for counselors to move in this direction.

Both on the high-school and college levels there are many problems to be resolved. As usual, we also have many more questions than we do answers. But it is only by asking the right questions and by deepening our professional commitment and competence that we can move forward.

# 22. Education, Guidance, and Counseling

## ROSE MARIE DICKSON

Guidance is a popular word these days and is vaguely felt by most people to stand for a Good Thing. We are not quite sure what this Good Thing is, but we will buy it; we'll go to summer school and study about it and we'll appoint people as directors of it and we'll have PTA meetings in which there will be a lot of support for it. But it's a wooly word, and tricky. The only strong connotations that it has are not particularly acceptable to people who have tried to understand what guidance is; mature guidance workers don't want to guide, they want to help people learn to guide themselves. So guidance is not guidance, you see, and if we hunt for a meaning with too literal an eye, we may get into trouble (Hobbs, 1952, p. 229).

Just what does this "wooly word" mean? What is guidance? Is it the same thing as education? Is it synonymous with counseling? Much disagreement exists concerning the distinctions among these three terms. Turning to the experts fails to clarify the issue. In fact, the better acquainted we are with the literature, the more the clouds of confusion gather. We find such terms as educational guidance, educational counseling, guidance therapy, counseling therapy, vocational education, and vocational guidance. Some authors use the terms guidance and counseling interchangeably. Others use counseling and therapy synonymously. Among those who attempt to make distinctions, we find some who contend that the title of guidance counselor is a misnomer. To guide is one thing, to counsel another; and it is complete heresy to express both in the same breath. Though the term guidance program is commonly used, many think this term has too narrow a connotation. They recommend, instead, the use of the term personnel program.

238

To illustrate the disagreement and confusion even more vividly, let us cite some of the views of the experts on guidance. Although many people not connected with the program have expressed the following sentiment, it was a little surprising to find one of its pioneers (Reed) saying, "Guidance has become a meaningless term—a commercialized racket" (Farwell and Peters, 1960, p. 84). Dissatisfaction with the term is expressed by Wrenn, who claims, "it has lost its usefulness through excessive use" (Farwell and Peters, 1960, p. 84). Kitson says it is an abstraction, and Williamson and Darley dislike the term because it is polyannaistic. Parsons sees guidance as self-analysis and self-direction. The National Vocational Guidance Association views guidance as facilitating vocational and occupational adjustment. Some see guidance as education. Hawkes states unequivocally, "education is guidance, and guidance is education." Keller reiterates this idea with the statement, "I have a notion that guidance . . . in all its implications is education" (p. 86). Hand emphasizes the distribution of students as affecting both the educational and vocational adjustment. Myers and Jones believe that guidance is necessary only when a choice must be made. Patterson and Williamson are advocates of guidance as a clinical process. And some take the approach of combining theories from different sources, which gives their interpretation an eclectic flavor. Prominent in this group are Traxler, Erickson, Warters, Strong, and many others (Farwell and Peters, 1960).

Some of this confusion, no doubt, stems from the vocational beginnings of guidance. The guidance movement, if it can be termed such, began as an effort to help boys and girls adjust to the world of work by providing occupational information and orientation. At the same time that Frank Parsons began his vocational-guidance program in Boston, Binet was publishing his intelligence scale in Paris. World War I assisted in converging these two streams. Growth or expansion of the movement was initiated by Brewer's focus on exploratory experiences in guidance and by Hull's emphasis on psychometric tests as a basis of vocational guidance. Interest in psychotherapy in the 1930's added its impetus. Guidance has experienced such phenomenal growth in such a short time that it has been difficult to keep up with its expansion.

A further complication in making distinctions is the impossible task of precisely pinpointing lines of demarcation. To appreciate this impossibility, picture, if you will, education, guidance, counseling, and psychotherapy as existing along a continuum in the order named. Just at what point does education cease and guidance begin? Or where does guidance stop and counseling start? A teacher can and often does give guidance in her classroom. A counselor may engage in guidance and counseling during the same interview. Obviously, it is not easy to see hard-and-fast distinctions.

Of the authors with whom I am acquainted, Father Charles Curran, a highly regarded figure in the field of client-centered therapy, makes the clearest distinction. He would have us imagine an inverted triangle divided horizontally into three sections. At the top, which is the widest area, he places education, utilizing the largest space to indicate that this section represents a program required by all students. In the second area, he places guidance, which encompasses a smaller space because it is not required by so many students. In the final area he places counseling, which is necessary for even fewer students (1952). With this picture in mind, let us see how education, guidance, and counseling are similar and then try to draw some distinctions.

The three are united by their underlying philosophy, by the nature of the process involved in each, and by their over-all aims or goals. It is natural that a philosophy reflect the cultural setting in which it occurs. Since ours is a democratic society, our philosophy of education, guidance, and counseling reflects democratic principles. Hand sees these principles encompassing the following:

1. The belief that human life, happiness, and well-being are to be valued;
2. The assertion that man is master of his own destiny, with the right to control it in his own interests in his own way;
3. The determination that the dignity and worth of each person shall be respected at all times and under all conditions;
4. The assumption of the right of individual freedom; the recognition of the right of each person to think his own thoughts and speak his own mind (Hand, 1942).

The process involved in each area is learning. In order for education to occur or guidance and counseling to be effective, the individual must learn something he didn't know. We are all familiar with the learning that takes place in education. Guidance provides the opportunity for the individual to learn many facts about his abilities, performance, potential, and interests and to acquire educational and occupational information to help him achieve goals consonant with his potentialities. Learning in counseling involves gaining insight as well as understanding the needs, emotions, and behavior. The learning process is incomplete, however, unless it effects changes necessary to help the individual develop his abilities to the fullest. The aims of guidance, education, and counseling include the adequate development, adjustment, and mental health of the individual to enable him to achieve self-realization.

These are their links and similarities. How do the three areas differ? Referring once more to the triangle, Curran says:

> On the wide end of the triangle opening out into universal principles which are permanent and certain is the area of General Education. Founded on theology and philosophy, this broad area also includes the field of particular sciences as they are related to laws and principles and the various arts which form the cultural, social, and material world in which we live. Without the foundation of a valid general education, a person's life will not be oriented to ultimate reality. Particular choices based on special sciences or expediency may appear to work for a time. But, if life is looked at as a whole and a man's purpose is seen in its entirety then, without an adequate basis in ultimate principles of living, particular choices must eventually prove short sighted and ephemeral (1952, pp. 19–20).

Education, then, is the basis for successful living. And the more complex life becomes, the more necessary education is. Primarily, it entails learning those skills which enable an individual to communicate with his fellow man, develop his native potential to achieve self-actualization, and acquire the proficiency in an occupation which will permit him to care for himself and his family and to make a contribution to the society in which he lives.

Guidance is more specific in focus than education. It is predominantly concerned with giving a particular individual or group of individuals certain information needed at a specific time. It would be foolish, for example, to provide information about courtship and marriage to first graders. Although at the rate children are maturing in some areas, it may well come to this. Curran explains the more specific quality of guidance:

> Since we live in the contingent world we must be able, in a limited way, to find some security and achievement in the framework of a particular state of life which the aptitudes, skills, and vocation which God has given us. Consequently, we need also a detailed kind of knowledge and understanding of our own abilities and capacities, as well as of the responsibilities, privi-

leges, and obligations of the different temporary and permanent situations in which we find ourselves. This kind of knowledge is more personal . . . and is more applicable to immediate life problems than the knowledge acquired from general religious, scientific, and cultural education and training. Consequently, we might call this the field of spiritual, moral, psychological, or sociological Guidance to distinguish it from the more general area of education in theology, philosophy, and the sciences and arts (1952, p. 20).

A general trend in guidance has been to acquire increased knowledge of all factors of personality growth and formation and to search for improved ways of communicating this information to individuals to help them understand themselves and the problematic situations they may encounter. This trend, then, is directly aimed toward an ever-growing understanding of personality development and the giving of information of a personal nature. This information may be given in various ways. Perhaps, the interview is most frequently used, but the round-table discussion and classroom or public lectures are also suitable. The number of persons dispensing information may vary from one to eight or ten. And the information may be presented to one person in an individual interview or to several hundred people at the same time. The information may vary from the interpretation of particular test results to one student to a discussion by a group of experts on various aspects of a problem such as family relationships. Curran states:

. . . giving people greater knowledge of various factors that enter into personality growth and development should be classified under the heading of guidance to emphasize its primary function of supplying pertinent information (1952, p. 43).

Curran's emphasis on the supplying of information aids in distinguishing guidance from counseling, which focuses upon "personal reorientation, by which a person is aided in acquiring new self-understanding and integration and better modes of action" (Curran, 1952, p. 43).

Two developmental factors are important to a better understanding of counseling. The first was a shift from simply presenting information and advising people to an emphasis on the individual's solving his own problems. This emphasis concerns itself with providing a relationship which aids the person to think his problem through, abetted by the skill, understanding, and acceptance of a counselor. The second factor that has increased understanding of counseling has been research, particularly that of Carl Rogers. More than anyone else, he has attempted to study objectively what occurs in interviews and has devised ways of analyzing the data.

Counseling seems to have been born of a need. It soon became apparent that education and guidance were not enough. In spite of both, some people persisted in having problems. Simply supplying information and giving advice did not always clear up difficulties. The advice was often not heeded. The information at times appeared to provoke the problem and make it worse. Questions were raised about the adequacy of increased knowledge as the solution to all problems. The deterministic view that environmental handicaps were not amenable to being conquered began to slip from favor. Otto Rank was among the first to break with the determinists: "A person was fixed on the past, not because he was absolutely determined that way, but because he feared the present and was unable to cope with it" (Curran, 1952, pp. 45–46). Counseling owes much to Rank for his distinction between knowledge and experience. "The person was helped," said Rank, "not by the psychological theory or interpretation of the counselor, but by the actual experience he underwent, in terms of feeling and willing . . . The counselor had to become a tool, the material which the person could use according to his needs" (Curran, 1952, pg. 46). An additional contribution made by Rank to counseling was his realization that resistance to taking advice was not conscious lack of cooperation but rather a result of a negativistic will. This resistance, he proposed, could be overcome only in time and only if the counselor allowed the individual to make his own decisions. Rank's greatest contribution, however, was in renewing the belief that individuals could change if given help. Once this view of human nature is accepted and belief in the person's ability to overcome his genetic and environmental inheritance is restored, the counselor's role becomes more complex. His skill must include the ability to help the individual to grow in self-responsibility and self-direction.

Counseling, then, directs its attention to those persons who need help in choosing among the various means of using the skills and knowledge education and guidance provide. It focuses on those who have deeper problems than the learning of their capabilities; it concerns itself with individuals who need to understand and accept additional aspects of their personality—their needs, fears, and anxieties, their frustrations, anger, and hostility. Counseling offers help in understanding these feelings in others. Some persons require "individual integration both in [their] ability to cope with the disorder within [themselves], the unreasonable impulses of [their] emotions and instincts, and the disorder in the world, in other personalities and in reality itself" (Curran, 1952, p. 21).

We can aptly conclude with Arbuckle's definition of counseling as

. . . a process which takes place because of the relationship between two people. It is in the uniqueness of this relationship that the individual called the client begins to see things that he never saw before, begins to realize strengths that he never knew he had, so that he can see and accept the unpleasant, and begins gradually to see a new and brighter world. The magic that causes this is indeed magic, but it is not supernatural. It is not to be found in a set of secret formulae and techniques, but rather in the rare experience the client has in finding someone secure and capable enough to accept him completely and without question as he is, and thus to help him to learn, because now he has reason to learn new and better things (1961, p. 139).

# 23. Aims of Guidance, Counseling, and Psychotherapy

LAWRENCE R. MALNIG

Although there is considerable overlapping in the functions of guidance, counseling, and psychotherapy, we use special labels for each and treat them as separate entities for convenience in distinguishing one from the other. These labels are in a sense similar to those used in the academic area to refer to disciplines such as history, economics, and sociology. Each of these disciplines is concerned with behavior from a different point of view. These disciplines, as we all know, are not mutually exclusive, but they emphasize a specific viewpoint and a specific approach in order to bring new meaning and understanding to a collection of facts. The ultimate goals of guidance, counseling, and psychotherapy are also basically similar in that each service is interested in helping the individual function effectively so that he can make maximum use of his potentialities and abilities.

In many discussions of these services we seem to dwell a great deal on their similarity and then try to make very fine distinctions which ultimately seem to disappear into thin air. In this discussion I will assume that we know that there is a great deal of overlapping, and I will concentrate on the essential differences among these services and on the unique contribution that each can make. In order to clarify these differences I shall consider each of these services in terms of (a) the setting in which the services are carried on; (b) the point of intervention, or the manner in which the service reaches students; and (c) the activities and immediate objectives of each service.

Of all the services, guidance is perhaps the broadest and varies considerably from one institution to another, depending on the viewpoint of the individual running the program. However, guidance is performed almost exclusively in an educational institution, and its basic aim is to help students achieve the objectives of the educational program.

With regards to intervention, guidance has the widest possible range of contacts with students. Students may come to the guidance office by means of referral, or they may come in on their own. But, in addition, the guidance staff may contact students directly or reach them through group activities, career conferences, and clubs. The guidance person also has a wide range of contacts with the faculty and administration and will often serve on faculty and administrative committees and seek every opportunity to maintain communication with all professional staff members in the institution.

The activities of a guidance office are quite varied; and, for purposes of convenience, I shall divide them into three categories: preventive, developmental, and remedial. Perhaps the best description of the preventive function was made by the counselor who stated that he was tired of fishing students out of the stream and wanted to go and find out who was throwing them in. The idea of instituting programs to eliminate the causes of difficulty is not a new one, but too often a guidance office is so burdened with immediate problems that there is no time to take preventive measures. Orientation, the proper selection of courses, and early faculty referrals are some of the activities that can be called preventive. The last one is particularly important because the faculty member, so to speak, is on the firing line and sees students more frequently than anyone else and is, therefore, in a position to detect sudden changes, loss of interest, or other symptoms that may indicate a need for referral. For this reason it is important for guidance people to get out of the office and to meet faculty members wherever they can—in the lunch room, the faculty room, lounges, and the like. The use of referral forms does not seem to work because faculty members are reluctant to fill them out. At one time we used some elaborate referral pads only to find that they were used for doodling and that all the referrals came by personal contact in the most unlikely places on campus.

Under the developmental function of guidance we can include orientation to studies, career planning, social relations, and activities. In this area guidance has a unique function in that it is concerned with the welfare of all students, not only those with problems. For this reason every attempt should be made to have these services extended to the entire student body. You will find, for instance, that inefficient reading and study skills are characteristic not only of the poor student or the student in difficulty, but that also honor students have similar deficiencies, except that through added effort they seem to compensate for them.

Routine interviews with all freshmen can also serve to provide motivation for studies. Quite often we have found that relatively good students will be satisfied with average performance since they feel that their life is made of one little hurdle after another, and they fail to see the long-range implications of their behavior. When one points out to them that what they are doing now could mean the difference between obtaining or not obtaining a graduate scholarship or gaining admission to or being refused by a select graduate school, they often change their attitude and become much more highly motivated to perform at the peak of their ability.

The remedial function is probably more closely related to the other services in that it is concerned with students who have problems and are in difficulty. Personal counseling, tutoring, or the realignment of goals with demonstrated abilities are all part of the remedial function; and the counselor here is interested in getting the individual to utilize his resources in overcoming his immediate difficulties. The major focus, however, is on the normal problems of development, and all the resources of the institution as well as the guidance office can be legitimately used to meet these problems. Essentially, the guidance view is that adolescence is a phase of normal growth and development, not a disease, and can, therefore, be dealt with by using all available environmental influences.

Counseling, as distinguished from guidance, is carried on almost exclusively in the private office of the counselor, who deals with individual clients in a confidential relationship. Students are referred to this office, or come in voluntarily, for the most part to seek assistance at the time they feel that they have a problem.

Intervention, therefore, is determined by the presence of a problem. This problem may take the form of a conflict or a crisis, which we can define as a situation that the client cannot resolve with his usual patterns of behavior and must change in some manner in order to cope with it. The assumption in counseling is that the individual has the information he needs about the environment and about himself, but requires some kind of corrective change in order to interpret, understand, and develop insight which will permit him to resolve his problem.

The basic activity of the counselor is to help the client reorganize his thinking and behavior so that he can solve his problem. The goal is not to bring about a general change in personality but rather to marshal the person's resources so that he can cope with a specific problem. Therefore, counseling should result in action or in a decision about choices to be made. We can expect that choices regarding the selection of an academic major or a career might be resolved in the counseling relationship.

However, this function does not mean that we simply give a student information or make other resources available to him to resolve the specific problem, because there may be underlying difficulties which must be dealt with first. Let us take, for example, the situation of a student who is in conflict about selecting a major. We may find that after helping him organize all the information about himself and a career, there is still a great deal of indecision which can be traced to a fear of making a commitment to a specific field of study. This underlying fear must then be treated before the client can move forward toward a decision.

If we are to consider the counseling process as one primarily concerned with the crises and conflicts that occur in normal personality development, we must then make a distinction between the counseling psychologist and the clinical psychologist. Currently we think of the counseling psychologist as helping either the normal or disturbed client to utilize the healthy and positive resources within his personality so as to cope more effectively with his immediate situation. On the other hand, the clinical psychologist is mainly concerned with the pathological elements in both healthy and nonhealthy individuals and utilizes his skills to remove them. While this distinction may give some added focus to the work of these two professionals, I am sure that there are many who will object to this distinction. To be sure, in actual counseling practice we can never adhere to such strict dichotomies, but this distinction will serve to put the counseling psychologist in the counselor category and the clinical psychologist in the psychotherapy group. If we make this distinction, we can then say that the fundamental aim of both guidance and counseling is the utilization of the potentialities and resources of the individual for normal growth and development.

One of the criticisms of counseling today is that we have become too problem-centered and clinical in our approach and have tended to neglect the growth needs of students. If we look upon counseling as an adjunct or a supplement to education, then it should be made available to all students at all levels. Naturally, the problem of staffing enters here, and, as we know, very few schools have the recommended ratio of 250 students to one counselor. Nevertheless, we should try to reach a greater number of students even if it can only be done by group work. I have noted that in more than 90 per cent of freshmen interviews, students have indicated that it was the first time they had ever sat down with anyone to discuss themselves, their plans, and their thinking about the future. In most cases the only counseling students received was from friends and relatives who gave them advice and tried to influence them to enter a field which they thought was lucrative. For it to be more effective, we should consider counseling as an educational tool to assist students to mature socially and emotionally as well as intellectually.

Finally, there is the area of psychotherapy. We all have a fairly good idea of what it is, but it always seems to escape us when we try to get a definition down on paper. The setting for psychotherapy is usually a private office where the client is seen on an individual basis. With regard to secondary schools and colleges, the office of the psychotherapist is usually not on the premises of the institution. Of late, however, there has been a trend to incorporate psychiatrists into student personnel services, and in certain universities they occupy offices within the institution. The psychiatrist acquires his clients almost exclusively by referrals which are screened through guidance and counseling officers. On some campuses the psychiatrists are located in accessible areas so that students may come in directly, but this practice seems to be more the exception than the general rule.

Referrals are made to the psychiatrist when a student manifests a disturbance in the functioning of his personality and a general inability to cope with life's problems. The aim of psychotherapy is mainly reeducative and involves basic personality change. Although the methods and the procedures will vary, psychiatrists usually work with unconscious processes and strive toward the removal of anxiety and the defenses used to cope with anxiety. As the defenses are replaced by more spontaneous forms of behavior, we can then expect a change in the personality structure. The relationship in psychotherapy is very intensive and often extends over a considerably long period of time. For this reason the psychiatrist is much more limited than are counselors, with respect to the number of students he can see within a specified period of time.

Today there is a growing trend for many colleges to retain the services of a consultant in psychiatry, and there are many others who have psychiatrists in residence at the university itself. In spite of this trend, educators have been questioning the inclusion of psychotherapy as an educational service. The argument is that guidance and counseling are an integral part of the educational program because their goal is the implementation of educational objectives, whereas psychotherapy is mainly concerned with personality change. The counterargument is that if education is concerned with the total development of the individual, then psychotherapy does indeed have its contribution to make, indirect though it may be.

If the past is any indication of what we might expect in the future, then certainly there will be a number of changes, realignments and adjustments in guidance, counseling, and psychotherapy services, but it appears certain that these services will remain even though their general functions may be somewhat altered. Although these services do overlap, each one is separate and distinct in its major emphasis, and each one has a unique contribution to make to the growth and adjustment of the individual. To summarize, then, I would state that the aims of guidance, counseling, and psychotherapy are as follows:

*Guidance:* To utilize all those elements within the educational environment which can promote development of the individual and realization of the objectives of the institution of a personal life goal.

*Counseling:* To help the individual cope with specific crises and conflicts which are characteristic of normal personality development.

*Psychotherapy:* To assist the malfunctioning individual in changing his basic personality structure in order to cope more adequately with life situations.

I would like to emphasize that each of these services has a specific justification for its existence, and all must work cooperatively if they are to provide maximum assistance to the individual, to the school, and to the community.

# 24. The Necessary Conditions of Effective Problem Solving: Some Interpersonal Factors

ARTHUR G. MADDEN

The centrality of interpersonal factors in effective problem solving can be understood if we keep in mind that a guidance or counseling situation, whether in a classroom or in the office of the counselor, is an encounter between two unique persons, a response of one person to another with expectations of what the counterresponse will be. To be effective the encounter must be, in the terminology of Martin Buber, an I-Thou rather than an I-It relationship. That is, we must meet the student as a unique person and not merely as an object—a thing, like a piece of furniture. My consciousness of myself as a unique person is a function of my consciousness of other persons. I am not aware of myself unless I am aware of other things; I am not aware of myself as a unique person unless I am aware of other unique persons in interaction with me. Many writers have emphasized the importance of the concept which others have of a person in shaping the concept which that person has of himself.

What are some of the interpersonal factors we must look for if the counselor is to enter into an effective relationship with the counselee and enable the counselee to make the decisions needed for continued growth in psychological effectiveness? We have all heard most of these factors mentioned in connection with various aspects of the counseling process. Let us gather them together and see what is involved in each, realizing that they are not mutually exclusive but that they interpenetrate one another. Just as white light is the mixture of all wave lengths

251

of light reflected diffiusely, so all of the qualities of the counselor blend to produce a unified, integrated impression on the counselee.

The first quality is *acceptance*—an unconditional acceptance with no "ifs" attached. Acceptance means to be open to the student as the unique person he is, to respect him as a complete person and not just because of certain features we might select, and to manifest an awareness of his intrinsic worth and dignity. It involves respect for his questions, his attitudes and feelings, his silences, the decisions he makes—including his mistakes. It involves taking him and his problems seriously, not making light of them. An outcome of whole-hearted acceptance is a sense of support which the counselee feels, a sort of base on which he can make a stand and begin his attempts to unwind and solve his problems. Acceptance can also bring about a necessary release of emotions and a reduction of tension.

The second quality is that of *understanding*. It is the ability to enter sympathetically into the student's thoughts, feelings, and attitudes so as to experience them from his point of view. It is the grasp of the meaning of what the student is trying to convey, of the problem he faces, and especially of his capacities for coping with the situation in the direction of growth. Important to this understanding is the uncovering of the student's concept of himself. Under this heading we may also include the counselor's understanding of himself in relation to the student. He must try to be aware of whether he is judging the student on the basis of his total personality or out of some bias or narrow frame of reference. He must ask himself whether or not he is properly qualified to give information or to counsel a particular counselee in a specialized field.

The third quality is the *ability to communicate*. As we have seen, communication can be verbal or nonverbal, and where there is acceptance and understanding, it is to a great extent nonverbal. There can be little or no effective communication without acceptance, nor acceptance without some communication. Likewise, understanding cannot take place without acceptance and communication. To communicate with a child or adolescent we must understand and speak the peculiar and current language of the child or adolescent, recognize his fads in music, art, and entertainment, all of which are his means of communication. Communication involves what has been called "active listening" to what the student is trying to express both verbally and nonverbally.

The fourth quality is *confidentiality*. This quality is absolutely necessary if there is to be a sound relationship between counselee and counselor. The counselee must be assured that what he says in an interview or the results of tests he takes will be held in strictest confidence unless he agrees that some of the information be given to others. It is sometimes necessary that this assurance be repeated if communication is to continue. Also, the ethical and legal factors involved in such a confidential situation cannot be ignored.

The fifth quality is *insight* into the nature of people and into the world in which we live, the ability to see persons and things as they are and as they can be. It is the distinctive feature of a human being that he is not simply determined to adjust to the forces of his environment, but that he can change himself *and* his environment. Man is free and he is creative. There is an element of both realism and idealism in him. He is a realist in seeing things as they are and an idealist in transcending the present situation to strive for something fresher and better. The good counselor can by his example and by his techniques open the eyes of his client to these realities and ideals.

This recognition of the real and the ideal will be the basis of the counselor's own set of values to which he should be committed with a total commitment. The greatest and most basic need of the young student is the need for a firm set of values and a sound philosophy of life, for it is out of his set of values that his attitudes, his interests, his aspirations, and his decisions will come. He looks to his parents, his teachers, his counselors for help in forming this set of values. What greater assistance can we give him than to show the example of our own sound set of values and to live by them? Through everything we are and do, we subtly transmit our values to him. Young people will reject those who merely pay lip service. I believe that much of the unrest on the campuses comes from a search for values after the rejection of the supposed value system of the adult society. We pay lip service to certain values and then leave them standing in the cold. As the Roman satirist Juvenal said in commenting on the decadence of Rome, *Probitas laudatur et alget:* Honorableness is praised and left out in the cold. If the student can realize that the teacher or counselor *lives* by a set of values, and that out of his values spring his acceptance and understanding of the student and his desire to communicate with the student, we have taken a long step forward in guidance and in counseling.

I would like to close this brief summary of interpersonal factors on a negative note that may help by contrast to point up the positive characteristics I have been discussing. In her book *The adolescent views himself*, Ruth Strang (1957, p. 536), by way of summarizing an article by George Speer entitled "Negative Reactions to College Counseling," gives a list of complaints made by college students about the counseling they have received. Her list is as follows:

Wasted their time in irrelevant chitchat, without apparent goal or
  purpose
Talked too much
Were "vague, indefinite, unclear, or uncertain"
Treated them as "cases" and showed little real interest in them
Explained all difficulties in accordance with a "pet theory"
Broke appointments, were late
Permitted interruptions, seemed to have their minds on other things

Implicit in these complaints is a negation of the I-Thou relationship; a lack of real acceptance, understanding, or insight; and evidently a lack of communication. They are excellent examples of noncounseling.

# 25. Evaluation and Diagnosis in Counseling

## JEANNE G. GILBERT

An evaluation is an assessment; a diagnosis is a label. Viewed in this manner, evaluation is readily seen as a much broader concept than diagnosis; it may encompass any part or all facets of an individual's personality or of a situation with which he is confronted.

Evaluation provides the information which is basic to diagnosis and essential to the solving of a problem. Diagnosis, on the other hand, involves the clinical procedure by which any disorder is identified, classified, and differentiated from other disorders (Schneiders, 1965). Diagnosis will be the result of an evaluation or analysis of the patient's behavior, his symptoms, his test results, and other data concerning him. Thus we may find a diagnosis of mental deficiency; of a major mental disorder or psychosis, such as manic-depressive psychosis or schizophrenia; of a psychoneurosis, which might include chronic anxiety, hysteria, obsessive-compulsive states, and phobias; of organic brain damage; of grand-mal or petit-mal epilepsy; or of psychopathic or sociopathic conditions. If we encounter a disorder in a patient, we must know what that disorder is before we can treat it. For example, to treat a basically depressed patient with the same medication that might ordinarily be used for an agitated patient just because both are "disturbed" might result in worsening of his condition instead of relief from his symptoms.

We must differentiate between a disorder which is primarily organic in nature, that is, due to a disease or damage to the organism; that which is functional or due to malfunctioning of a physical system in the absence of disease or injury; and that which is psychogenic in origin or caused by psychological factors (Schneiders, 1955). This differentiation is possible only by an evaluation of all the data available. The diagnosis then rendered gives us some idea of the condition we have to treat, and this diagnosis, in turn, constitutes the germ of prognosis, since it tells us what we might reasonably expect the outcome of therapy to be.

We have been speaking of diagnosis with reference to a disorder, since this is the way in which the term is usually used. However, strictly speaking, I suppose we could have a diagnosis of "normal—no pathology—no personality disorder." In this case, of course, the diagnosis would have little meaning. A diagnosis of paranoid schizophrenia tells us that a patient has a major mental illness—a psychosis characterized by odd behavior, withdrawal, and probably delusions of a persecutory type, along with other symptoms; but a diagnosis of a "normal" condition would have little definite meaning except for the recognition that the individual had no clinically manifest neurosis or psychosis and was neither mentally deficient nor psychopathic. He might be average, bright, or dull in intelligence; he might be popular and well liked by his peers, or he might be disagreeable and not liked by others; he might be an excellent student or he might be poorly motivated and barely manage to secure passing grades.

For both the normal and the abnormal individual, then, we would have a label—a diagnosis—but this would not be enough. We would also need an evaluation of his abilities, his intellectual strengths and weaknesses, his motivation, his interests, his maturity, his personality assets and liabilities, and his usual mode of reacting to normal life situations. With the abnormal individual we would need to evaluate the depth of his abnormality or illness and what treatment might be indicated; we would need to evaluate his ability to get along in his home and school environments; and we would need to evaluate the possibility that he might harm himself or other people.

We might consider a few cases of these abnormalities which may be encountered in school or college. For example, a young person has been diagnosed as schizophrenic. Is his condition so severe that he requires hospitalization, or can he be maintained on medication in an outpatient environment? As far as his education is concerned, is it in any way possible for him to adjust to a school environment? We may know that it would not be advisable for us to do anything which might further his withdrawal, but, on the other hand, would a school environment be too disturbing to him and thus worsen his condition? Also, what about the school, his instructors, and the other students?

Can they tolerate his odd behavior? Can they make the adjustments to routine which may be necessary in order to maintain him in school? While we want to do everything possible for the patient, we must also consider the welfare of others in the environment. We cannot disrupt a school or a classroom for one student, even though he may be ill, and it is not fair to permit the disturbed behavior of one individual to cause emotional distress to countless others. Also, if the patient is paranoid and feels that others are plotting against him, we should not take the chance that he may retaliate violently to imagined persecutions or take what he considers to be defensive measures to protect himself against impending injury.

On the other hand, some schizophrenics are able to adjust at home or in school without causing any disturbance or being bothersome to anyone else. One 14-year-old schizophrenic, for example, was a very quiet, very good boy who never gave anyone any trouble. He kept to himself so that his classmates were scarcely aware of his existence. The only odd thing noticed by those around him was that he would often stop what he was doing, look straight ahead, and then solemnly and politely say, "Good evening, sir." He lived in a boarding home and his diagnosis of schizophrenia was known, but it was not until conferring with his foster mother that the reason for his strange behavior was understood. He regularly had a frightening visual hallucination in which a strange, sinister-looking man in a long black cape appeared to him and seemed to be threatening him. When he confided in his foster mother, that worthy woman told him to say, "Good evening, sir" to the apparition so that the man would not harm him and would probably go quietly away. Since this was his only bit of odd behavior and since it was apparently not too disturbing to his teachers when they understood the situation and did not particularly unsettle his classmates, there seemed to be no reason why he should not remain in his school and continue with his studies while he was being treated on an outpatient basis. Another young woman for years heard voices of saints which alternately praised her and abused and condemned her. Nevertheless, she was able to complete high school without having her condition detected, and she successfully held down a position with the telephone company for more than a year before she herself sought aid.

In most instances, the neurotic individual should remain in the school or college environment if this is at all possible, since to remove him may be to intensify his neurosis and to encourage the secondary gains he derives from it. However, not only the patient's condition and his strengths and weaknesses must be carefully evaluated, but also the school set-up and his home situation, since adverse conditions in either one or both of these places could militate against successful treatment of the patient. Examples of this adverse effect can be seen in the case of two high-school students, both phobic. The first, a girl, was fearful of going to school and of traveling anywhere alone. Her mother's reaction was, "I can't force her to go. If I tell her she has to go to school she has a tantrum, and I'm afraid she'll get sick. I can't do anything. I'd rather have her home than sick."

After a few interviews the girl was induced to try to return to school. She did, and upon going to her classroom, was greeted by her teacher with, "Well, you're back! I never expected to see you again," whereupon the class tittered. The teacher then added, "You know you can't come in here without a note from the principal, so you'd better go to the office and get one." Trying to wink back the tears, the girl walked slowly toward the principal's office. School had started by that time, and when the principal, who was coming out of her office, saw the girl walking along the hall, she went up to her and said sharply, "What are you doing here? Why aren't you in your class where you belong?" The girl fled out of the school building to her home and refused to make another attempt to return to school. Perhaps a better evaluation of the school situation and better preparation of those in charge for the return of this disturbed girl—who had no support from home in her efforts—would have resulted in a more successful outcome.

By way of contrast, the other phobic youngster, a high-school boy of 15 with a history of trying unsuccessfully to attend three different high schools, had parents who were desperately anxious for him to return to school. They had nagged, beaten, and coaxed to no avail, but they still tended to attribute his failures to the schools. The boy himself seemed fearful, sullen, and stubborn, and at first refused to talk about his difficulties. Later, however, he became more friendly and confided that he shook all over and became sick at his stomach when he tried to go to school. After some discussion of possible reasons for his difficulties, he agreed that he would try to go if he would be permitted to go home if he became too upset to stay. The school agreed to this plan, and the guidance counselor, a warm and understanding young man, was on hand to greet him when he arrived the next morning. He introduced him to the principal of his new school and then took him to meet his new teachers and left him in his home

room with the understanding that he could come down to his office
or to the principal's office any time he felt the need to do so.

The first day he stayed for only part of his first class and then spent
the remainder of the day in the counselor's office where he talked,
read, and did a few chores. The parents, although their first attitudes
had been quite negative, cooperated to the fullest. Gradually the boy
began spending more time in classes and less time in the office until
he finally managed to attend his full quota of classes regularly. At no
time did he leave the school building although he had been told that
he could do so any time he felt he could no longer remain in the
school. Two years after termination of treatment his mother telephoned
to say that he had been at the top of his class for the last year and a
half and had just undertaken to "become therapist" to a younger boy
in school who was suffering from a school phobia. He was confident
that he could help the boy because he knew just what to do since he
had been through it all himself!

A careful evaluation of the depressed patient is especially important
because of the ever-present danger of suicide. We hear of too many
young people, even children, who commit suicide, so that it is advisable to assess carefully the strength of self-destructive drives when dealing with depressed young people. When problems seem overwhelming
and life too hard for a young person to face, just the feeling that the
counselor is interested and cares what happens to him is sometimes
enough to tide the youngster over a difficult period. However, when a
counselor is in this position, it is a grave problem to evaluate the depth
of his young patient's depression and to know when to seek outside
professional intervention.

In contrast to the depressed young person who is likely to harm himself, we have the psychopathic or sociopathic individual who makes
life difficult for teachers and all others in authority. I do not refer here
to schoolboy pranks or normal adolescent rebellion, but rather to that
state of repeated delinquency where there is a lack of moral sense or
of regard for right and wrong—a state where no punishment is effective, no remorse is present, and no feeling exists save for the self. Because the psychopath is often personable and appealing, it may be
difficult to evaluate the seriousness of his psychopathy and the extent
to which he may damage others, and yet this evaluation is necessary
in order to make a decision as to whether he should remain in or be
excluded from his school or college. We must evaluate the circumstances of his environment and the possibility that he may be able to

receive enough careful supervision to prevent overt and harmful acts of delinquency; we must evaluate the severity of his delinquent trends; and we must evaluate his influence on other young people. For example, is the sex delinquent deliberately seducing others? Is the user of marijuana cigarettes, "pep pills," or "goof balls" encouraging other young people to try them also? And to what extent of delinquency will he go to obtain money to satisfy his craving for the drug he is using? An adequate evaluation of all these factors can be made only when complete pertinent information, social as well as personal, is available.

Fortunately, the bulk of the work of school and college guidance counselors does not consist of these serious abnormalities and maladjustments. Since their work concerns itself primarily with the furtherance of normal growth and development (Malnig, 1963), they will encounter mostly those problems which occur in the normal processes of maturation and growing into adulthood and of acquiring education and training for the future. Usually there is no question of a diagnosis, for the young person presents no deviant behavior or personality disorder, but, in order to guide him toward normal growth and development, an evaluation is essential. This evaluation will generally consist of an assessment of his level of intelligence, his special abilities and disabilities, his school grades, his interests and motivation, his personality traits, his maturity, and his social background, plus an integration of all the information obtained from these different areas to form a composite picture of the individual. Only then will it be possible to guide him effectively in accordance with his needs.

For example, a student may be doing barely passing work in high school or college. Without a careful appraisal of all the factors involved, we cannot know whether he is a well-motivated student of limited abilities who is doing the very best he can; whether he is a bright, potentially good student who is too disturbed emotionally to study effectively; or whether he is a potentially able student who is poorly motivated because his interests lie elsewhere. Also, it could be that his level of intelligence is unsuited to that of the group with which he has been placed. Illustrative of this situation is the case of a junior-high-school boy who was recently referred to me because of poor school work. This boy had an intelligence quotient of 95 and, according to standardized tests, was up to grade placement in reading, arithmetic, and spelling. However, the average intelligence quotient in his school was 117, and his class scored more than two years above grade in all school subjects. Consequently, this boy appeared dull in this particular school setting although he might have done quite well in a group where the average ability and achievement were more nearly like his own.

In contrast to this case, another junior-high-school boy was avoiding school whenever possible, and even when he did get there he was not doing good work. This boy, however, had an intelligence quotient of 168. During his frequent absences from school he amused himself by studying German, Russian, and mathematics. A couple of years later he took a New York State Regents examination in Advanced Algebra and obtained a grade of 100 although he had never had a single day of classroom instruction in algebra. Obviously, this young man was bored because the school he was attending had little to offer him.

### Use of Tests in Evaluation

I have spoken much of evaluation and assessment. I might now speak more in detail about the making of an evaluation. Tests, about which I shall speak more in a moment, will be of great help to us in making an evaluation, but we must remember that all test data should be interpreted in the light of the background of the individual. Consequently, the first step in evaluation should involve securing a personal history of the client (Hadley, 1958). This history should include family background of the person—socioeconomic status, education of parents and siblings, presence of physical or mental disorders or defects, and relationships of family members. It will also include details of the individual's personal life—birth, development, health, illnesses, accidents, hospitalizations, school progress, reactions to parents, authority, and peers, special abilities, disabilities, and interests. School grades, attendance, adjustment, and activities will receive special attention.

Generally, in clients of high-school age or younger the history will be secured from the client's teachers and from one or both parents. In young people of college age parents and teachers may possibly supply the information, but usually most of the information must be secured from the client himself. Although, as has been indicated, certain definite information is sought from the history, this information should be secured, insofar as it is possible, by permitting the interviewee to tell the story in his or her own way with a minimum of direct questioning by the interviewer. This procedure will usually make the interview more natural, elicit more information, and give the interviewer more opportunity to gauge the importance of certain areas and reactions.

This technique of letting the client tell the story in his own words is perhaps even more important in the interview with the client himself than in the interview with his parents or teachers. With a warm, friendly, interested, accepting attitude, the interviewer can generally develop rapport with the client that will enable the latter to speak freely of his problem and determine what he is seeking from the counselor. In this atmosphere the counselor can guide the interview into areas he thinks should be explored further, at all times maintaining tact and respect for the client. Particularly important in a counseling interview that involves educational or vocational guidance is an investigation of attitudes, interests, ambitions, and motivations, the persistence in working toward a desired goal, and the ability to withstand frustrations.

The next step in evaluation will be the assessment of the client's mental ability, aptitudes, interests, and personality characteristics. This assessment will include first, tests of general intelligence with an analysis of intellectual strengths and weaknesses. Group intelligence tests are routinely given in most schools today, and for the classification of large groups these tests are the most practical measures to use. For individual diagnosis and evaluation, however, they may leave much to be desired. While it is generally true that the brightest students score the highest, average students fall in the middle range, and the dullest students in the lowest category, the intelligence of some students may be either grossly overestimated or underestimated on the strength of a group-intelligence test. Sad though it is, some limited students become quite adept at cheating and frequently copy from another's paper without being detected; consequently, they may be judged as brighter than they actually are. The same is true of the quick, superficial thinker who very speedily gives all the answers he knows and guesses at the rest without any waste of time.

In contrast to these situations, the slow reader or the precise, compulsive individual who must always carefully dot all the i's and cross all the t's may score much lower on a group test than his ability actually warrants. He may have all the answered questions correct but have too few questions answered to get a high score. For these reasons it is always desirable to give the client an individual intelligence test if there is any doubt about the group-test results, that is, if they are marginal or out of keeping with the school performance of the client. An individual test is also desirable if any serious problem is involved, since the subject's pattern of responses may offer some clues which will aid in making a diagnosis.

The battery of tests used in the evaluation of a client will necessarily depend upon the problem for which he is referred. For example, if he presents a personality or behavior problem, he will be given some tests of mental ability, but the emphasis will be more on tests of personality, particularly projective measures, in order to help us appraise the nature and depth of his disturbance so that we may know better how to treat him. Usually, tests of interest and special aptitude, if included, play a relatively minor role. On the other hand, when a young person has always given evidence of having a normal, well-integrated personality and presents no behavior problem, but is seeking counsel solely for educational and vocational planning, the use of projective personality measures may play a relatively minor role, and greater emphasis will be given to tests of intelligence, scholastic achievement, interest, and special aptitudes. Personality tests, when used, will be for the purpose of determining whether the subject has the characteristics which should help him to be successful in certain types of work rather than for the detection of abnormalities.

As the reader undoubtedly knows, there are many tests of all types on the market so that it is not easy to select the most suitable battery with which to make an evaluation. There are many things to consider in choosing a suitable battery. In the first place, we must consider the purpose for which each test is to be used. For example, if a battery of tests is to be given, the items included in the battery should be selected so that they will tap different areas of the personality rather than duplicate the same area.

The next thing to consider is the test itself. How well has it been standardized? To be of value, a test must be standardized on a sufficiently large and representative sample of the population on which it is to be used. If an intelligence test, for example, were constructed and tried out on a hundred adolescents and adults of different ages from a mountain town of Tennessee, we could not be at all sure that this test would be an adequate measure of the intelligence of New York City high-school children. To make sure that this test would be suitable for the measurement of the intelligence of American adolescents, it would be necessary to standardize it on sufficiently large and representative samples of the adolescent American population of both sexes from all parts of the country and from all socioeconomic groups, the numbers to be included in each group being determined by their percentages in the population according to the latest United States census.

After noting how carefully the test was standardized according to the samples used, we must then examine the validity and reliability of the test (Coleman, 1960). What evidence does the author offer to show that this test really measures what it purports to measure? To be of any value, we must be fairly certain that a particular test gives us a measure of what we are seeking; in other words, we must be certain that it is a valid test.

We must also know if a test is consistent in measuring what it is supposed to measure. We must know that when a test is administered by one qualified person, this same test can be repeated by another trained person under similar conditions and, barring accident or other unforeseen circumstances, similar results will be obtained. Obviously, a test of intelligence would be unreliable and of little use to us if one year the results indicated that a client was mentally deficient and the next year, that he was of superior intelligence.

Having selected a suitable test of intelligence, we must now consider the interpretation of the results obtained on this test. An IQ is not an evaluation. It is a single, rough estimate of an individual's intelligence as compared with that of others. This information is useful for us to have, but it is only the beginning; for guidance purposes we need also to know the composition of the individual's over-all ability, that is, his intellectual strengths and weaknesses. In order to guide him educationally and vocationally, we need to know, among other things, how well he is using his intellectual potentials, his linguistic powers, his ability to think abstractly, his facility in handling numbers and concrete material, and how well he can learn and remember new things.

The client's interests must be carefully considered when the matter of vocational choice is involved. Any of the good interest inventories will provide us with valuable clues as to his areas of interests; but test results should be supplemented with conference to narrow down the client's field of interest so it can be of practical use. It might also be desirable to know more about the subject's differential aptitudes which are in line with his vocational interests. There are tests which will give us this information, but it will be the job of the counselor to evaluate the importance of giving them and to determine which ones should be given. For example, there would be little point in giving clerical-aptitude tests to a client who scored low in arithmetic areas and indicated a strong dislike for all kinds of work of an arithmetical, detailed, or clerical nature. Scholastic-achievement tests, particularly in the areas of reading and arithmetic at the lower age levels and scholastic-aptitude tests at the higher levels might be desirable, but again it must be left to the judgment of the counselor to make the decision in the choice of tests.

One of the nonprojective personality tests might be used both as a screening device to uncover any unrecognized personality difficulty and as a guide in educational and vocational planning. For example, the shy, quiet young person who dislikes crowds and is slow to make new acquaintances would probably not be happy and comfortable in the type of academic environment or occupation that might be most appealing to the aggressive, outgoing extrovert. If the need for further personality evaluation is indicated, projective tests might then be used. Of course, if the referral indicated any personality or behavior problem, these tests should receive the major emphasis so that the counselor can render a diagnosis, evaluate the seriousness of the problem, give clues to treatment, and develop prognosis. The tests of interest and special aptitude should be given only if the need were indicated.

When the counselor has the test results at hand and has studied them carefully, he must consider them in the light of the history he has on the client, his academic record, and the reports of his teachers. Only then can he make an evaluation of his client. A diagnosis may or may not be necessary, but an evaluation is always necessary, whether it be of a client with a problem or of a situation which has arisen. If the data suggest the need for medical intervention or psychotherapy, the counselor should evaluate this need along with the availability of help and the client's (and perhaps his family's) willingness to accept the recommended treatment. If an evaluation of the total situation suggests that the client is not yet ready to accept the kind of therapy the tests indicate he needs, the counselor must then evaluate the possibility that he himself might work with the client for a while with the aim of leading him toward acceptance of his need of help.

If the problem is in the area of educational or vocational guidance, the counselor must first of all be realistic as he makes his evaluation of his client and his situation. Unfortunately, too many people have been sold a bill of goods, so that they have come to the conclusion that everyone must have a college education, and that no one can get a decent job without a college degree. This is not true. It is not true that everyone should have a college education, and it is not true that one cannot get a decent job without a college degree. Not everyone is intellectually suited to higher academic studies. A college education is geared to the intellectually superior student, and obviously not all students are intellectually superior. The same holds true of an academic high-school education, with the added disadvantage that this level of education prepares a young person solely for a college education and equips him with few useful skills that he can offer an employer as an inducement to give him a job. We hear so much of high-school drop-outs these days that the term has almost become one of opprobrium; and yet, when the available high school has nothing to offer but academic work with which the student cannot cope, one cannot help but wonder whether this student's discontinuance of high school may not have been one of the most intelligent steps he could have taken.

Evaluation of the limited student's abilities along other than academic lines and the information, wisdom, and tact necessary to guide him into different and more suitable types of education and training are problems and demands which tax the skill of the most able counselor, particularly when he must also deal with overly ambitious, driving parents. Nevertheless, many problems of adjustment may be directly traceable to intellectual unsuitability for the academic program required rather than to any personality abnormality, and this unsuitability is something which the guidance counselor must evaluate.

The selection of a suitable college or university for the high-school student who both wants and is intellectually suited to higher academic education is also important. This selection involves not only a careful evaluation of the student but also an evaluation of colleges and the programs they offer. Knowing his client's abilities, school record, interests, and temperament and knowing what colleges and universities have the particular courses of study in which he is interested, the counselor must then judge which college might best fit this particular student's needs. Evaluating all the factors involved, he must decide in which college or colleges this student would not only get what he wants in the way of studies but would have the best chance of success and would best fit both intellectually and socially.

Thus, we can see that we are constantly making evaluations of persons and of situations, both in our personal and in our professional lives. Sometimes our evaluations are made on the basis of the judgment and knowledge we have acquired through the years; but, as guidance counselors, we are fortunate in also having scientific tools to aid us in making our assessments. The assessments may be of behavior, competency, or fitness. In the case of aberrant behavior or personality, the evaluation will be basic to the diagnosis, descriptive of the depth of the disturbance and the dynamics involved, and indicative of the prognosis.

# 26. Problems vs. Syndromes

### JEANNE G. GILBERT

A problem, as defined in the dictionary, is "a difficult matter to be settled." Viewed in this sense, every human being is confronted with problems throughout his lifetime, problems which will necessarily vary in intensity and gravity, as well as in type. The period of youth, when the individual is developing and securing his education and training for the future, is especially replete with problems, but the fact that a problem exists does not necessarily connote abnormality or disease. A problem may be within the individual himself or in relationship to his environment. A problem may be the result of personality or character traits within him, or it may be the result of uncontrollable factors in his environment, but it is something which causes him concern and which he must resolve.

A problem, however, need not necessarily be a difficult matter which the individual himself must settle. It may be any difficult matter which confronts the community at large, the school, the teacher, the guidance counselor, or the parents. We know that we, as adults, may be greatly disturbed about many things concerning the young people of today, but these same things may not be considered problems at all by the young people themselves. In other words, a problem may be any difficult matter or situation which confronts an individual or society: it may concern one person or it may concern many persons.

A syndrome, on the other hand, is defined as "a series of symptoms associated with a disease and forming together a clinical picture of the disease." It is, then, essentially a medical term implying pathology and usually refers to an individual. It generally implies a physical involvement, although the term has also been used in connection with mental disease or disorder. For example, with brain-damaged children we may get a syndrome of perceptual difficulties, hyperactivity, blurring of reality, and difficult behavior. Or, with Down's syndrome (more popularly known as mongolism), we may find the typical characteristics of the short, odd-looking, retarded child with the Oriental-looking eyes, flattened nose bridge and occiput, large, fissured tongue, hyperextensible joints, and irregularities of the palmar creases. Again, with certain types of schizophrenia we may find delusions, hallucinations, inappropriate affect, and withdrawal from reality. Thus, a cluster of descriptive symptoms characterize the syndrome or the disease.

However, problems may arise from the interaction of the normal, developing individual with his environment as well as from a syndrome. The brain-damaged child may not learn as well as other children even though he may have good intelligence, because the damage syndrome may not permit him to concentrate long enough to learn or to see things in their proper perspective. This deficiency may result in frustrations which he cannot tolerate, with the result that he may lash out against his environment and thus create a problem to those around him as well as to himself. Decisions may have to be made regarding the best way to educate and manage this child so as to enable him to make the best possible adjustment to family and community life.

The mongoloid cannot make an adequate adjustment to society because his intellectual deficit does not permit him to comprehend, reason, think, learn, and perform as well as others, and his appearance is such that his condition is readily apparent to most lay persons. Adjustment then becomes a problem not only to the mongoloid himself but to his family and to society, who must decide what is the best way to take care of this individual who is incapable of taking care of himself. Should he be institutionalized or should an attempt be made to train him for self-help and domestic usefulness within a community setup?

The schizophrenic may create a problem in his environment because others cannot tolerate his withdrawal, inappropriate affect, and perceptual distortions which lead to bizarre behavior. He may have met his own problems by distorting reality, withdrawing completely from his environment, and living in his own world of fantasy. He may have become so detached from everything around him that problems no longer exist for him, but problems certainly exist for those with whom he has contact. There is the problem of medical treatment to be settled: should this individual have shock treatment, or medication, or both shock and medication? If medication is indicated, just which medication would be most effective with this particular patient? Then there is the problem of his care: would he be better cared for at home or in a hospital? Is he a potential danger to himself or to those around him? If he is to remain at home, what is the best way for his family to treat him? What attitude should they take? If his education has not been completed, should he return to school, should his program be modified, and if so, in what way? How should his teachers handle him, and how can his counselors and teachers best help him in his peer relationships? These are just a few of the problems which may occur as a result of a particular syndrome.

As guidance counselors we need to be aware of the various syndromes of mental illness in order to be able to recognize them when they occur in the high-school or college student. We must know when the problems we encounter are the result of a particular syndrome—in other words, when problems are attributable to pathology and when they are problems which can usually be expected to occur in the course of normal development. Important, too, along with the recognition of pathology, is the knowledge of when to refer and to whom to refer when a pathological condition is found. Ordinarily, when a mental-disease syndrome is recognized and medical intervention seems advisable, the guidance counselor should refer the student for psychiatric examination and possible treatment. Referral, however, should be exercised with caution and common sense, for there are times when a referral should not be made even though a syndrome is recognized.

For example, a nine-year-old child was recently referred to our clinic because of restlessness, hyperactivity, and very poor handwriting. The school guidance counselor suspected brain damage. Psychological-test results supported the counselor's suspicion of minimal brain damage. However, the child's restlessness and hyperactivity in no way impeded her school progress or prevented her conformity to classroom routine. She was found to be a bright child whose school marks, with the exception of handwriting, were excellent in both studies and conduct. She was effervescent, enthusiastic, and interested in everything. During the psychological examination she kneeled on the chair so she could lean over the desk and examine everything she could reach. She chattered spontaneously about everything, both relevant and irrelevant, but she cooperated well and was in no way difficult to manage. Her writing, however, was laborious and her letters were poorly formed. There was evidence of poor coordination and more than the usual difficulty in changing from manuscript to cursive writing.

There was no doubt about it: this little girl had very poor handwriting and probably a minimal amount of brain damage, but was she in need of outside help? I do not think so. No medical intervention was indicated. Her hyperactivity was not extreme and resulted in no disciplinary disturbance at home or in school. She adjusted well to her peers and presented no problem whatsoever aside from her poor handwriting, and even her poor handwriting did not prevent her from obtaining excellent grades in school. If every person with poor hand-writing were to be referred for professional help, I suspect that the offices of psychiatrists and psychologists would be overrun with medi-cal doctors and other professional people.

## Recognizing Syndromes in Adolescents

Since a syndrome implies pathology, this may be a good time to dis-cuss briefly a few of those syndromes which are most likely to be en-countered by the guidance counselor. There is no intent here to run the whole gamut of syndromes but merely to discuss some which might be seen in a school or college and which should be referred for pro-fessional help. The guidance counselor, of course, is not expected to make the diagnosis of these conditions, but should be sufficiently aware of such syndromes to recognize the possibility of the existence of a specific syndrome and the need for suitable referral for help.

The brain-damage syndrome of poor motor coordination, perceptual difficulties, hyperactivity, impulsive, driven behavior, and learning problems in spite of adequate intelligence has already been mentioned. In attempting to confirm the suspicion of brain damage, the guidance counselor will be best aided by any definite history of cerebral insult before, during, or after birth or of a prolonged high fever associated with one of the infectious diseases of childhood. Another group of organic conditions which should be recognized by the guidance coun-selor will include the convulsive disorders or epilepsies. Any one of three varieties may be encountered: grand mal, petit mal, or psycho-motor seizures. Due to improved medical procedures and more com-mon and frank recognition of the condition, grand-mal seizures are less commonly seen now than they were a few years ago. Nevertheless, it is not too unusual for a youngster to have a major convulsive seizure during school hours. Often he will experience some kind of warning beforehand and try to get to a place where he can lie down or be safe. Then he may go into spasms, become rigid, and fall unconscious, his eyes rolling backward. He may froth at the mouth and be incontinent;

if something is not placed between his teeth, he may bite his tongue severely. The convulsion generally lasts only a few minutes, after which the epileptic usually sleeps. Occasionally, however, instead of sleeping he may become highly emotional, act in a dazed manner, and perform many automatic or nonvoluntary acts.

Obviously, convulsive disorders require medical attention, although the guidance counselor can later help the student to face the problems arising from his convulsive seizures. Malingering and hysterical fainting are sometimes mistaken for grand-mal seizures which they may resemble to some extent, but the differentiating factors can be seen in the absence of the total syndrome in the former. The malingerer and the fainter are essentially egocentric, attention-seeking individuals who seldom hurt themselves in falling; rarely froth at the mouth, bite their tongues, or are incontinent; and are not likely to have a spell without an audience. While the counselor is not expected to make this differential diagnosis, it is important to be aware of the differences between the real and the simulated conditions.

Petit-mal seizures are often so mild that they may go unnoticed for years. Sometimes there is only a momentary loss of consciousness of which the patient himself is unaware—like a brief lapse of attention or absent-mindedness. At times, the child who has petit-mal seizures in school is unjustly accused of willful inattention and absent-mindedness. In these instances, the school counselor can do much to resolve the problem by helping teachers and others in school to understand the syndrome and be more tolerant of the child.

Psychomotor seizures are also often unrecognized for what they really are. The individual with this condition may have periods of extreme irritability and emotionality during which he is unaware of what he is doing and later has amnesia for his acts, many of which are meaningless and repetitive but which may at times be quite violent. These spells may last from minutes to days. Some believe that many unprovoked and unexplainable acts of violence committed by otherwise normally behaved youngsters may be carried out during an epileptic equivalent or psychomotor seizure. Obviously, both the diagnosis and treatment of all the epilepsies are matters for medical intervention, but the guidance counselor who is alert to these syndromes may save the child, the parents, and the school much time and unnecessary stress by prompt referral when the condition is suspected.

Unfortunately, psychotic syndromes are found among our high-school and college population all too often, although they are sometimes overlooked because the afflicted individuals may keep to themselves and not bother anyone else. Different syndromes are characteristic of different types of schizophrenia, but the total picture is usually one of oddness, withdrawal, and inappropriateness. An example of this syndrome can be seen in the young college junior who was referred by his priest, who described him as "a little scrupulous and upset." He had withdrawn almost completely from association with his family and peers; he had delusions about the decaying state of his internal organs which, he believed, was a punishment meted out by God because he had offended him by the sins of hiccoughing, swallowing his food too fast, blinking his eyes, and smiling at the wrong time.

He had never been out with girls and always considered them as animals and evil, and he became quite concerned over their sinfulness in wearing bikini bathing suits, which he had read about but never seen. Finally, curiosity overcame him, and he went into a small women's shop and asked the salesgirl to show him a bikini bathing suit. However, when the girl obligingly offered to model it for him, he fled in terror. This young man's mother confided to me that she had become aware that something was wrong with her son when he was a sophomore in high school because he was so very different from other boys and seemed "too good." She said that when she mentioned it to her husband he became very annoyed with her, and when she asked her priest about it he said she should be ashamed of herself and thank God that He had given her such a good and saintly son. Had this young man received help when his mother first noticed his need of it, perhaps he would have had a better chance of recovery from his illness.

Other schizophrenic conditions of even more obvious nature may also go undetected. For example, a boy of 14 was referred to me by his teacher because, to use her words, "he seems to have become very high-hat since returning to school this fall; his school work is poor, and he seems to think the other children are not good enough to associate with him." His parents said that he had become less sociable in the past few months, that he kept washing his hands all the time, that he was very afraid of germs, and that he refused to drink out of a freshly washed glass until he himself had thoroughly washed it with soap and water. On examination, the boy smiled inappropriately as he complained of the other children making fun of him because his organs were turning black. He grimaced and stared into space for minutes at a time, apparently oblivious to the examiner. Finally, when he went to the door to leave, he suddenly turned, leaned over the desk toward the examiner, and said earnestly, "Shall I kill him?" When asked "Who?" he replied, "My father," and proceeded to tell a long, involved tale of a plot he believed his father was concocting against him. He said a voice had told him all about it. Apparently, both his paranoid delusions and his hallucinations had gone undetected for a long time, and yet this boy was a potential danger to himself and to those around him. Obviously, the guidance counselor could not cope with the problem of a child as sick as this one, but an early recognition of the syndrome of schizophrenia could have resulted in earlier referral of the boy for help and preparation of the parents to understand and face his condition.

A depressive syndrome may also be found in high-school or college students, and it is especially important that the counselor be alert to this syndrome because of the ever-present danger of suicide. The usual picture presented is one of dejection and despondency, feelings of uselessness and hopelessness, a reluctance to do anything, frequent crying, and the feeling that life is not worth living. Anxiety is often present. Depression may come on gradually or suddenly, or it may be preceded by a period of gaiety and overactivity. Tom, a 16-year-old boy who was referred for treatment, had always been moody, but following his failure to win a part in the high-school play, he became quite depressed, stopped studying, and spent much time locked up alone in his room where his parents could often hear him crying. When teachers and parents tried to reason with him, he merely bowed his head, sighed, and said, "What's the use?" Fortunately, an alert counselor sensed the seriousness of his condition and when she found him alone in a secluded corner fingering a knife, was able to induce him to go for help.

Perhaps, though, it is not the psychotic syndromes, distressing though they may be, which are the most difficult to recognize and the most troublesome to a school or college. The psychopath or sociopath presents a syndrome which sounds easy to recognize but actually may prove very difficult to identify. He is often personable, breezy, and plausible; frequently he has the knack of charming people so that they are loathe to believe ill of him. However, the typical syndrome is one of a defective moral sense: the individual knows the difference between right and wrong but does not care and has no remorse for any wrongdoing. When apprehended for a misdemeanor he will glibly say, "I'm sorry," and then repeat the same offense at the first opportunity; punishment has no appreciable effect on him. The father of a 15-year-old boy who was referred because of stealing a car for joy riding put his finger neatly on the problem when he said to me, "You know, I'm not so concerned because he took the car and went for a joy ride. This I could understand because I know a kid his age might pull a prank like that. I'd punish him but I'd still be able to understand. What really worries me is that he has never in his life shown the slightest remorse for anything wrong he has ever done. I think his mother and I have good standards, and we have tried to bring him up right and see that he got good religious training, but he just does what he wants to do and doesn't care whether it is right or wrong, and he is never sorry." Young psychopaths are the people who can cause real difficulties in a school or college because they do not respond well to help or punishment.

Neurotic disorders, characterized by a variety of symptoms depending on the particular disorder, are even more prevalent among high-school and college students. The neurotic individual is often egocentric and socially maladjusted. His symptoms may include excessive fears or phobias, obsessions, compulsions, somnambulism, amnesia, functional paralysis, or numerous psychosomatic complaints. Generally, a symptom does not appear in isolation but as part of the syndrome which characterizes the neurotic disorder. The school phobia, a condition probably only too well known to most guidance counselors, is a good example. The phobia may be the most prominent presenting symptom, but it is extremely rare to find a child so afflicted who does not also have many other neurotic symptoms or signs of maladjustment.

The symptoms which make up the neurotic disorder and other syndromes are the unconscious means by which the individual attempts to adjust to stressful or frustrating situations. While it is not within the province of the guidance counselor to treat syndromes, it is within his province to be knowledgeable of them and to know how to find help for them when the need is indicated. It is, however, the special task of the counselor to recognize and understand problems. Understanding problems involves a knowledge not only of syndromes but also of other possible causative factors such as family conditions and relations, conditions within the school, and the student's relations with his teachers and peers.

Problems may be of many types and may occur in any area of living. They may be of a personal or a social nature; they may concern academic work, preparation for the future, or interpersonal relations. The guidance counselor who must deal with such a variety of problems must, then, be a very versatile person. In order to guide students effectively along educational and vocational lines, he must have an understanding of intelligence and personality in general; in particular, he must have an understanding of the abilities, the interests, and the personality of the student he is trying to guide. He must know something about the personal and educational requirements for specific occupations and where the required training can be obtained. Finally, he must understand something about the requirements and standing of different educational institutions so that he can guide the student to the one best suited to him.

For effective functioning within a school or college setup, a counselor must have a great amount of tact and understanding and must be able to establish quick rapport with people of all ages, for he will have to deal not only with young persons with problems but also with teachers who are having problems with particular youngsters and may feel too harassed to be as patient and understanding as they should, and finally, with parents who may not only be having a problem with their offspring but may indeed be part of that problem themselves.

Briefly, then, a syndrome implies pathology; a problem does not imply pathology, but pathology within an individual, a family, or a society may be a causative factor of the problem. A problem is something to be resolved, a syndrome something to be treated.

# 27. Communication in Guidance and Counseling

## ALEXANDER A. SCHNEIDERS

### The Centrality of Communication

To say that there is a great deal of emphasis on the centrality and importance of communication today would certainly belabor the obvious, especially for a group of teachers, guidance counselors, and psychologists. In the literature there are repeated references to the influence on values and attitudes, on thinking and behavior, and on personality development of the several mass media of communication, particularly radio and television, advertising and propaganda, and movies and periodical literature. In point of fact, in a workshop on teenage problems in the American culture, we had occasion to study the impact of these media of communication on both the mentality and the behavior of the contemporary adolescent. And the presenters left no doubt in the minds of participants that these methods of communication have a great deal to do with shaping the attitudes, the values, and the thinking of youth.

We also see repeated references in the literature to the importance of adequate communication in all kinds of interpersonal relationships, including marriage and family life, peer-group explorations in human encounter, teacher-pupil contacts, and just ordinary everyday give-and-take conversation. But those of us particularly interested in the arts of counseling and psychotherapy, including marriage counseling, are more especially impressed with the recurring emphasis on the importance of communication to counseling and psychotherapy. As Ruesch and Bateson say quite pointedly:

Regardless of the school of thought adhered to, or the technical terms used,

277

a therapist's operations always occur in a social context. Implicitly, therefore, all therapists use communication as a method of influencing the patient (Ruesch and Bateson, 1951, p. 19).

In a later book on therapeutic communication (1961), Ruesch develops this point to a considerably greater extent. Referring to the group-oriented cultural matrix of current thinking in the helping profession, Ruesch points out that

Psychotherapy has to be group-oriented and communication-minded. A psychotherapist, like his younger cousin, the psychoanalyst, and his nephew, the group therapist, relies upon communication to approach his patient. Scorning drugs and shying away from surgical procedures, he makes his living by observing and exchanging signals. The communication engineer, the semanthesist, the linguist, the propagandist, the anthropologist, and even the neurophysiologist come along and provide him with facts and theories about symbolic behavior. And having been exposed, in all likelihood, to psychoanalysis, the psychotherapist cannot help but discover that psychoanalytic theory is, and has been right along, nothing but another theory of communication in disguise. . . . All of a sudden it strikes home: notions of transference, counter-transference, transference neurosis, and working through represent nothing else but attempts to introduce notions of communication into a rather mechanical and linear theory of behavior. There is really no cogent reason why in therapy the patient's free associations, his coherent accounts, dreams, and non-verbal statements should be reduced to terms such as energy or instinct. We observe communication; we respond through communications; so let us stick to empirical generalizations of communication. The closer our theoretical thinking remains to our empirical operations, the better off we are; otherwise the relationship between theory and practice may become purely coincidental (Ruesch, 1961, pp. 22–23).

These statements of the relationship between communication and therapy can be applied with equal force and meaning to guidance and counseling relationships. Moreover, they can be made to serve several purposes. First of all, they serve to underscore the fact that the maintenance or the restoration of mental health or of personal organization or of academic productivity is often linked to an adequate system of communication. In the majority of counseling situations, communication is about the only technique that the counselor—whether guidance expert, teacher-advisor, psychological counselor, priest, minister, or psychiatrist—has at his disposal. Similarly, whoever attempts to reverse the process of marital breakdown must rely on communication, and the success of all these efforts will depend in large measure on the skill with which the counselor manipulates communication symbols.

There is a second point to note here also. When communication in the home or school—whether between parents themselves, between parents and children, or between teachers and students—breaks down, the most frequent remedy is to substitute for this lapsed relationship some process of communication within the framework of counseling or psychotherapy. In other words, as the noted psychiatrist Harry Stack Sullivan so often emphasized, the only real remedy for disrupted interpersonal relationships consists in opening up lines of communication so that these relationships can be reestablished on a healthier basis (Sullivan, 1954).

## The Nature, Forms, and Significance of Communication

The significance of communication processes to daily living, to academic adjustment, to mental health, and to adequate interpersonal relationships is emphasized by investigators from many different disciplines. As Leighton and his colleagues point out in their significant work on *Explorations in social psychology:*

Man is a communicating animal and . . . communication with other persons is not just a means, but is in itself one of its major goals. Man seems to take an active interest in joining in the pursuit of "agreed upon" goals as well as in the simple gratification of what are supposedly bodily instincts. Following Harry Stack Sullivan, we conceive of the oral, anal, and genital erogenous zones as serving an important function in communication (Leighton, Clausen, and Wilson, 1957, p. 181).

In this quotation the need to communicate is virtually identified with the nature of man, a position that reminds us of the basic Scholastic postulate that man is by nature a social being. The presence of so-called social needs, or what would be better termed self-other needs, clearly highlights man's dependence on other persons, and this interdependence is served to an important extent by channels of communication. Thus, according to Ruesch and Bateson (1951, p. 29), man's organism as a whole "can be conceived of as an instrument of communication, equipped with sense organs, the receivers; with effector organs, the senders; with internal transmitters, the humoral and nervous pathways; and with a center, the brain. However, the reader is warned not to think in anatomical terms when considering the internal network of communication; more appropriate is the comparison of the individual with the social organization."

This trenchant description of the nature of the communicative system in man can be easily related to a variety of social situations, since very often the receivers are bombarded incessantly with material or stimuli emanating from the senders. This is somewhat of an abstruse way of saying that quite often friends and neighbors, students and classmates, and teachers and administrators become involved in knock-down, drag-out arguments. In such instances, the communication system, as well as the aims of communication, are seriously impeded. This is exactly the sort of thing that the school counselor must confront in his or her efforts to solve human problems and to reduce conflicts, frustrations, or heartbreaks through the medium of interpersonal communication. One can think of scores of situations in and out of school wherein the essential difficulty is the breakdown of communication, and the essential remedy is the restoration of communication.

In order to understand more fully the implications of this philos-ophy of communication for counseling and psychotherapy and for problems in human adjustment and interpersonal relationships, we must consider both the different levels and the different forms of communication. For example, in order to understand why a lonely young adolescent encounters so much difficulty with communication, we have to realize that there is such a thing as talking to, talking with, and talking at people. We see the implications of these distinctions in the relationships between very young children and their parents, since the parents characteristically talk *to* children, not *with* them. Communication at this level is quite limited, mainly because of the child's natural limitations, but also because of the difficulty that parents have in developing an empathic relationship with their young children, so that this situation may provide little in the way of developing satisfactory interpersonal relationships.

We see this lack of satisfactory communication quite often in the faltering efforts of counselors to establish rapport with adolescent students. The counselor who has forever shut the door on his own adolescence and finds it impossible to retrace his steps into the past will find communication with adolescents extremely difficult. The adolescent, and the young adult as well, quickly senses this inability to establish rapport, and communication breaks down rapidly. To talk *to* adolescents is a common experience; to talk *at* them is an even more common experience; but to talk *with* them at the level of their own conceptual development and in their language, while a much rarer experience for the counselor, is also one of the most rewarding.

At higher levels of development this talking with another person is a more common occurrence. In the marital situation, to take a common example, this need to talk *with* someone is the basic reason why a wife needs to communicate with her husband after a long day's work, despite the fact that she has three or four children to talk *to* all day long. Talking *at* people, unfortunately, is a common occurrence in the marital situation, as for example when the wife incessantly harangues the husband about money, the misbehavior of the children, or his attitude toward his mother-in-law. This harranguing is not unlike that which takes place when the school disciplinarian pours out a torrent of meaningless advice and exhortations which literally drown the adolescent or the college student, but do very little to save him from his own folly.

Of equal importance to communication are its various forms. There is a general tendency to believe that because there is no verbal interchange there is no communication. Thus the student who lapses into silence when asked about his problem—because he can't find words to express what is troubling him or because latent hostility prevents verbal interchange—is communicating just as forcefully as if he were to break into a torrent of words. The silent treatment is devastating in its effects on interpersonal relationships since it speaks much louder than words ever do. Similarly, the husband, home from the day's work, calls out from the living room, "Let me know when dinner is ready," thereby telling his wife in no uncertain terms that he is a lot more interested in dinner than he is in her. Or he scowls at his breakfast and, without saying a word, pokes at it gingerly, takes one or two small bites, and then proceeds to ignore it completely. It would be a lot more forthright and honest and much better for interpersonal relationships if he were to say quite frankly, "What a hell of a cook you are."

These simple illustrations indicate clearly that communication takes a number of forms. In their definitive account of communication, Ruesch and Bateson (1951, pp. 21–22) distinguish written, pictorial, spoken, gestural, group, mass, self, action, and visual communication. All these forms are exemplified in the home and school situation at one time or another. For example, gestural communication occurs when a student waits respectfully for the counselor to sit down before he does so. By this socially significant behavior the student communicates; we could call it social communication. Gestural communication, one of the most common forms in the counseling situation, can also be observed when the counselee covers his eyes in order to limit visual communication, shrugs his shoulders in answer to a question, shifts nervously in his chair when the conversation turns toward touchy subjects, or uses his hands to convey the intensity of his feelings. Action communication occurs when a counselee moves his chair closer to or farther away from the interviewer, thus signifying by his behavior that he wishes to establish closer or less intimate relationships.

Verbal communication is of course the very essence of the counseling interview, although it is a form of communication that should never be taken for granted because of the many unspoken things that are implied in verbal communication. Written communication is exemplified in the self-descriptive essay, in letters received from the counselee, or in the sentence-completion test. One can easily supply examples of other forms of communication from his own experience. The most important fact to remember here is that communication assumes many different forms and it functions at many different levels; and if the counselor attends only to what the counselee is saying, he will miss about nine-tenths of the message which the counselee is trying to convey to him. Theodore Reik gave us the phrase "listening with the third ear"; and in counseling there is no more important lesson to learn than to listen with all of our senses and our intellect and our feelings and our past experiences. It is this kind of listening in the process of communication that promotes insight into the real problems, the personality characteristics, and the symptom complexes of the client with whom we are working.

The important point here is that persons in or out of the counseling situation communicate thoughts, attitudes, and feelings in almost everything they do, and therefore the counselor must be quite sensitive to subliminal as well as to more obvious behavioral cues. The counselor who is insensitive to these subliminal cues will quite often find himself at a loss to fathom the inner dynamics of the client's behavior difficulty. Nor will he be able to figure out exactly the nature of the relationship between him and his client. When, for example, a student expresses hostility toward a teacher, the principal, or the dean of the college, and this hostility is taken by the counselor at face value to mean that the teacher or administrative official actually offended the student in some way, he may be missing the more subtle implication of the boy's negative relationship to his father or the girl's equally poor relationship to her mother. When a student explodes verbally with the statement, "I hate this school," he may only be projecting to the school the anger he feels toward himself for having done so poorly.

In the interpersonal relationship which is the essence of counseling, there are a hundred little messages that are going back and forth between counselor and counselee which may easily escape the perception of both. The counselor must be keenly aware of the messages he is sending out subconsciously if he is to maximize the potentialities of the counseling relationship. The nod, the gesture, the shifting of position, the smile, or the look of boredom may make all the difference in the world between a successful and a completely unsuccessful interview. Look into your own experiences and compare them with others around you. Ask yourself how often you have alienated in some subtle way the client whom you most wanted to help because he or she suddenly aroused within you a countertransference with feelings that said in effect, "I don't know exactly why, but for some strange reason I don't like you. I want to, and I want to help you, but you make me feel uncomfortable, even perhaps annoyed or a little angry. I don't want you to take this seriously, but I have a feeling that you will."

The unverbalized language of the subconscious and of the unconscious works its way into the counseling relationship for good in some cases and for ill in others. But, however tenuous its form, it is a kind of language, a species of communication to which a counselee will most certainly react. Depending on the type of subliminal cues he picks up, he will want to terminate the relationship, prolong the interview, plead for acceptance, react with counterhostility, or lapse into muted silence. These facets of communication the counselor must learn to appreciate. He must discover that communication has many forms and that it functions at many levels, and he must develop a deep sensitivity to all of its characteristics. Only in this way can the counselor effectively exploit the values of communication for the higher aims of the counseling process.

## The Effects of Communication

From this interpretation, supported by numerous examples from clinical experience, one can see what tremendous effects communication of one kind or another can have on the human encounter as it is developed in the counseling relationship. Personal adjustment, academic performance, vocational orientation, stability of personality, mental health, and even creativity can be affected by communication processes. Ruesch and Bateson, whom we have already quoted on the role of communication in personal relationships, state succinctly, "Successful communication therefore becomes synonymous with adaptation and life" (Ruesch and Bateson, 1951, p. 18).

How readily these opinions can be applied to different adjustment situations is evident from the personal and social effects of successful communication. In peer-group relationships, in the classroom, on the athletic field, in the social group, in marriage, or in the counselor's office, the effects of successful communication can be readily observed. When, for example, husbands and wives learn to share their anxiety and their problems with each other on an objective and relatively non-emotional basis, interference with goal-directed behavior is quickly reduced, and each partner's chances of mastery of marital difficulties definitely increase. By the same rule, when teacher and student communicate effectively with each other, either in the classroom or in an advisory situation, anxiety is reduced and problems are more readily solved. These effects, and others like them, are more strikingly developed in the counseling and therapeutic relationship, because the whole intent of therapeutic communication is a change in value orientation, reduction of damage to feelings, improvement of the self-concept, better adjustment and mental health, and more effective interpersonal relationships. In the counseling interview, as Harry Stack Sullivan brings out so well (1954, pp. 122–128), the focal point of the interview is effective communication; and when communication breaks down, the interview begins to fall apart. Where there is poor communication or complete breakdown of communication—as happens in situations where there is endless conflict, criticism, or rejection, or where there are long lapses into intolerable silence—there is likely to be damage to the personalities involved and to interpersonal relationships. Communication is the life blood of interpersonal relationships; therefore, it is the life blood of effective and productive counseling. When this life blood drains away, counseling cannot continue.

# 28. Communication between Counseling Staff and Faculty

ROSE MARIE DICKSON

Is it possible that between two professions so actively engaged in human relations and so reliant upon the ability to communicate—counseling and teaching—there exists a dearth of communication? This lack of communication is a little baffling until we stop to realize that whenever a human-relations problem rears its head, more than likely a breakdown in communication has occurred. How often do we find the teenager and the adult unable to communicate? Too frequently we discover husband and wife talking *at* rather than *with* one another. If two persons in a union as close as marriage have problems penetrating the "sound barrier," we can well expect that two professions will also experience difficulty.

This lack of communication is not unique to the professions of counseling and teaching. Much too often there is little if any communication between faculty and administration, between doctors and nurses, between psychologists and psychiatrists, and even between teacher and teacher or counselor and counselor. A study by Russell and Willis, for example, disclosed that 31.9 per cent of the teachers in their sample did not believe that there were good channels of communication between teachers and guidance personnel (1964, p. 707).

Let us first explore some of the barriers to this much-needed communication and then attempt to find means of reducing these barriers. Some investigators believe that teachers feel threatened by guidance personnel. The older profession of teaching, they claim, looks upon the newcomer, guidance, as a fresh, impudent upstart. Shoben (1962, p. 579) expresses the effects of this attitude when he says:

285

Interprofessional frictions have something of the character of a vicious circle. The older professional group, like a father or an older sibling, may well be annoyed by the aggressive development of a brash youngster newly aware of its own potentialities. The historically prior group reacts punitively, the younger retaliates with self-assertion, and the struggle is progressively intensified. On the other hand, the senior professions have acquired a considerable wisdom about the services to society which justify their existence, and the challenging attitudes of the new group hardly facilitate a sharing of that stored experience.

If there is any truth to the threat hypothesis, perhaps it springs from a fear that the teacher's contact with the individual student in the personal, helping relationship is being usurped. For many teachers this relationship with the student is one of the most rewarding aspects of their work.

Ineffective communication may stem from the fact that some people attach a certain amount of status to counseling. Since teaching experience is so frequently required for certification in guidance, many teachers move from the classroom to the counselor's office and quite often from counseling into administration. This sequence gives guidance, in the eyes of some observers, a higher status than teaching. The fact that guidance personnel are often paid more than teachers adds to this illusion.

Experience in both guidance and teaching makes us aware of other impediments to the communication between these professions. In some elementary and high schools, guidance personnel are not requested to perform many of the irksome tasks required of other faculty members. Counselors escape duty in the halls, lunchroom, yard, and buses. Chaperoning athletic and social events is not required of them; nor am I advocating that it should be. But teachers naturally wonder why counselors are absolved from these assignments; and the wonder quickly turns into resentment.

Wrenn proposes other possible causes of friction which he explores in an enlightening article entitled "The fault, dear Brutus." As we know, the quotation continues with "is not in our stars, but in ourselves . . ." As the quote implies, Wrenn lays problems in communication at the doorstep of the counselor (1962, p. 562):

Our very lack of assurance, of course, is one of our greatest faults . . . When we are defensive against questions that we cannot answer, accusations about which we think there may be some truth, or in the presence of such ignorance of our work as to give us doubt that it is as important as we thought it was, we are apt to respond with either belligerent behavior, on the one hand, or apologetic behavior on the other. Both, as all psychologists know, are expressions of the same sense of inadequacy.

This belligerent behavior often results in overselling guidance services and claiming outcomes for which no proof can be shown. Guidance is sometimes offered as the panacea for all evils—a ludicrous assertion that is most often made by inexperienced members of the profession who have not yet learned the limitations of their abilities. "It is better to remain silent and appear a fool, then to speak and remove all doubt." Lack of assurance also produces an oversensitivity to criticism, no matter how just the criticism may be.

Of all the causes of noncommunication between these professions, the teacher's failure to understand the counselor's role is probably most basic. This failure is not always the teacher's fault. Rather, it would seem that counselors have not been too articulate in defining their role to other faculty members. Perhaps they themselves are not too sure of their role. An article by Knapp and Denny (1961) states that some counselors spend more time on tardiness, attendance, discipline, and academic failure than they do on vocational and educational guidance. A study by Hitchcock of 1282 counselors, cited by Knapp and Denny (1961), disclosed that 40 per cent did not believe that assisting students with occupational plans was their job. Of 986 counselors who worked with failing students, 41 per cent did not accept this task as a responsibility of counseling. Thirty-seven per cent of 893 counselors who interpreted test results to teachers did not think this interpreting should be a part of their task. And of 1101 counselors who assisted teachers with pupil's problems, 37 per cent did not feel that this task should be their job. One might well ask what some of these counselors believe their job is. Incidentally, a study of thirty-five counselors in San Francisco revealed that from 43 to 80 per cent of their time was spent on clerical work (Knapp and Denny, 1961, p. 49). In view of these data, it is quite understandable that teachers often experience confusion as to what the counselor's role really is.

One important difficulty that stems from this lack of understanding is the view of a counselor as a disciplinarian. Too many teachers and administrators see discipline as a function of guidance. Even more so than with guidance, counseling and discipline are by their very nature diametrically opposed. Discipline requires evaluation and judgment of behavior; counseling demands acceptance and a nonjudgmental attitude. Some parents can combine these roles, it is true; but equally true is the fact that the relationship between counselor and counselee is not the same as that between parent and child. There is not the same "flesh of my flesh" feeling in the professional relationship. And this is as it should be, because it allows for greater objectivity.

When counselors refuse to assume the role of disciplinarian, they are often accused of being too soft with students or only seeing things from the student's point of view. More than 56 per cent of the teachers in Russell and Willis' study believed that counselors tend to overprotect students (1964, p. 707).

These remarks are not meant to imply that counselors should be excluded from discipline problems completely. They can do much to aid teachers and administrators in finding the causes of problems; they can help students who create discipline problems to effect a change in behavior and attitude; they can furnish information about students (with permission, of course) that might help explain and make misbehavior more tolerable. An example of the counselor's disciplinary function is illustrated by a student who was failing gym and whose absolute defiance was exasperating his teacher. The student refused to wear a gym suit to class. After speaking with the student, the counselor found that an early childhood disease had left the student's legs deformed. He would rather take the wrath of the teacher and the failing grades than expose himself to the possible ridicule of his fellow students. When the cause of the behavior was disclosed, the teacher was most willing to make concessions. This type of participation a counselor can and should have in discipline problems. But if we expect guidance personnel to scold, to reprimand, or to mete out punishment, we are asking them to destroy the kind of relationship with students that is the very substance of their work.

These are some of the problems. Wherein lie the solutions? There is perhaps little credence in the idea that teachers feel threatened by guidance. However, if this condition exists, one way to alleviate it is to make teachers aware of the contributions they can make to the guidance program. It would be an unusual situation, indeed, for a counselor to have so few students to work with that he would not welcome some help. In fact, most counseling loads are overwhelming. The recommended number of students per counselor is between 250 and 300. But in actual practice a student load of 500 to 600 per counselor is more common. When these figures are multiplied by the minimum number of interviews per student per year, it is simple arithmetic to calculate the thousand or twelve hundred interviews involved. And interviewing is just one phase of the counselor's work. Any counselor would be wise indeed to accept any help a teacher might be willing to give. But it is up to the counselor to communicate this need to the faculty.

Faculty cooperation is almost always forthcoming if a counselor can communicate his need for teachers' help. One particular area in which a teacher can be indispensable is in supplying information about students. A teacher who sees a student daily, or even two or three times a week, knows aspects of his behavior that a counselor might never learn from an interview. The teacher has the opportunity to see a student interact with other class members; he sees the student's reaction to authority, to success, to frustration, and to failure. The teacher's more frequent contact gives him information about the student's health, his moods, his likes, and his dislikes. If the teacher has been in the school system for any length of time, he probably has had contact with the student's siblings. All of these bits and pieces of information fill in the gaps in a counselor's understanding and knowledge of a student. But even more important from the standpoint of communicating with faculty is the fact that when the counselor lets a teacher know that he needs him, the teacher is not so hesitant in making his need for the counselor known. With this mutual dependence will come the dissipation of the illusion that there is more status to one profession than to another. It is pretty difficult to lean on someone who is either far above you or far below you.

Displaying a sincere interest not only in the welfare of students but also in the well-being of the faculty is another means of unlocking the doors to communication. A counselor can do much to "sell" his program by his approach to and manner in dealing with teachers. If he is interested in them as individuals and shows this interest by taking the time to listen to their problems, his colleagues will quickly become aware that he is really part of the team.

When counselors are not required to take part in the many extra duties assigned to teachers, there should be good reasons. If a counselor must schedule late-afternoon and evening appointments with parents, or if he must work several hours each day beyond the school's closing time to keep up with clerical tasks, his release from chaperoning football games is understandable. Conveying this information to the faculty is an administrative task and should be directed toward developing more harmonious relationships between faculty and counseling staff. However, informal activities can be a tremendous source of information about students. The girl who in the counselor's office is quite meek and shy may turn out to be the life of the party at a school dance. Therefore, unless the situation does not warrant it, a wise principal will assign some informal duties to the guidance staff. And it is an even wiser counselor who accepts them graciously and realizes the contribution he can make toward promoting better relations with faculty members. As Knapp and Denny point out (1961, p. 49):

> If any real role definition is to evolve, the counselor must work to obtain it. The administrator may be expected to have a very general knowledge of the goals of guidance and of the reason for having a guidance office in the school, but the counselor himself must work out the numerous specifics and constantly strive for the refinement of responsibilities which will give meaning and direction to his activities.

The counselor can define his role for others only when he himself has a clear conception of it. This fact underscores the importance of good training. Adequate role definition will also aid teachers in their understanding of guidance services, of their goals and objectives. With increased understanding will come increased acceptance and in turn, better communication. It is worthwhile and beneficial for a newcomer to a guidance program to speak to teachers and to try to interpret the program to them. Students also need this interpretation, since so many of them are unaware of the real meaning of guidance and counseling. As Froehlich says (1960, p. 374), "Some [students] act as though they want their fortunes told. Others appear to want their problems removed without effort. A few frankly admit they seek employment or financial assistance." For these reasons, it is valuable to meet class-size groups of students and explain to them the nature, purpose, and type of services the guidance program offers.

In the university setting, guidance personnel often have neither faculty rank nor tenure. And because the counselor is thus divorced from the faculty, both students and teachers get the impression he has no understanding of classroom problems. In this setting he is looked upon as a specialist, and from this viewpoint springs the stereotype image of the counselor as a "head shrinker." One obvious solution to this difficulty is for counselors to assume some teaching responsibilities. At the college level, it is not too difficult to assume the two roles of counselor and teacher. At the high-school or grade-school level, however, students often find it difficult to relate to the same person in these two roles, especially when the teaching is done in the traditional manner, involving examinations and grades. When, however, courses are designed for group guidance as much as for information-giving purposes, the two roles do not appear to conflict (Warters, 1964).

Basic to fostering an understanding and acceptance of guidance and thereby opening channels of communication, is an honest appraisal of guidance services. Wrenn states (1962, pp. 562–563):

> There is no reason for us in personal conversations with colleagues or in professional meetings to be other than realistic about the work we are doing. The realism consists, in part, of admitting our weaknesses, but, also, in stating our strengths. We have many more strengths, as a matter of fact, than some academic disciplines that have prestige because of long life . . . For this reason I propose that we accept ourselves as a young profession with much to learn, but at the same time that we consider it unnecessary to be either belligerent or apologetic about the significance of our work.

> I think we have outgrown our swaddling clothes, that personnel work is a distinct personality in the family of professions. Personnel work never was an unwanted child for it was born of a need, a need well recognized by both students and administrators. It is true that some of our relatives, our academic aunts, uncles, cousins, and the like, have raised their eyebrows at us, but we are now a member of the family, whether always approved or not, and we are here to stay.

# 29. The Technique of Interpretation

JEANNE G. GILBERT

The purpose of interpretation is to promote insight. Interpretation in the work of the school or college guidance counselor emcompasses a wide diversity of areas for the promotion of insight, for it may involve not only the interpretation of the client to himself but also an interpretation of his test data, behavior, or feelings to his parents or teachers.

Interpretations by a guidance counselor to teachers or parents of a client must generally be accomplished in one or more interviews; interpretations to a client himself may be brief and given in one interview if they concern his aptitudes, or they may be frequent if he is under therapy. Because of this variation and the different degrees of emotional involvement, these interpretations must necessarily be handled differently. Unless a teacher has a strong emotional involvement with a situation—in which case the matter must be handled more delicately— the counselor can usually discuss the client with him quite frankly and objectively, although he must always remember the confidentiality of the client's revelations to him. Perhaps, though, a word of caution should be entered here regarding the counselor's appraisal of the discretion and tact of the teacher, for no interpretation should be given the teacher without these qualities in mind. Most teachers, we can be sure, have much understanding and tact, but there are some who do not use much of either. For example, when a guidance counselor brought to one teacher's class a difficult junior-high-school girl who was just being reinstated in school, the teacher said in the girl's presence, "Don't bring *her* here. I don't want any low IQ girls in *my* class." The fact that the girl was of average intelligence made the teacher no less resentful. Another time, a bright, disturbed, highly scrupulous high-school girl told her teacher that she had to leave her class early for a clinical appointment, whereupon her teacher said sympathetically in front of all the girl's classmates, "What's the trouble, dear? Is it mental?" Of course, the question arises here as to whether teachers of this sort should be given no interpretation whatever about their students or whether extra time should be spent with them in helping them understand and interpret young people's feelings.

Interpretations to teachers are primarily for the purpose of helping them understand the student better so that the teacher, in turn, can help the student to learn and to adjust more effectively. Generally, interpretations carry more weight when made in a personal interview than in a written report because in a personal interview the teacher has an opportunity to express his opinion and his feelings about the client, and this expression may be necessary before he is ready to accept any-one else's interpretation. Then, too, in a personal interview the astute counselor can gauge when and how much to interpret to the teacher. This limited interpretation is particularly important when there is a personality clash between teacher and student or when the teacher's feelings are involved. In a personal interview the counselor will be able to reflect back the teacher's feelings to him so that the teacher can begin to understand a little of his feelings and reactions to his student and thus arrive at a better acceptance of him. Usually, too, the teacher will then be ready to accept the counselor's evaluation of his client and of the total situation.

In discussing tests of intelligence with teachers, it is often advisable to avoid labels and IQ's and to interpret abilities, strengths, and weak-nesses as indicated by the results of the tests. Abilities and weaknesses should be related to practical points of learning and, insofar as it is possible, to the education of the student. The same holds true of behav-ior and personality: only those characteristics and dynamics which will be of practical help to the teacher in dealing with a particular student should be revealed, and they should be discussed in meaningful terms. For example, it may be of interest to the curious teacher to hear that a boy is difficult because he has castration fear or has never resolved the oedipal situation, but it will mean far more to most teachers if they are told that this boy is difficult in class because he has a poor rela-tionship with his father and tends to carry his resistance to him to all situations where authority is involved. For the most part, a teacher is concerned with teaching his class and seeing that each student learns to the best of his ability and without being troublesome to himself or to fellow students. When these ends are not being attained, the teacher wants to know why and wants to learn what he can do about it. He is generally not interested in esoteric terms and labels, but rather in receiving practical suggestions regarding ways to deal with a problem.

In interpreting to parents, the counselor must exercise greater caution and tact than in interpreting to teachers. Parents have an emotional investment in their offspring and therefore are inclined to be defensive and to project blame when a problem arises concerning them. Also, for many parents, the offspring are so much an extension of themselves that anything construed as a criticism of their offspring is a criticism of themselves. Other, more rejecting parents may use interpretations about their offspring against him and to his detriment. Thus we can see that it is particularly important to avoid the use of labels in interpreting intelligence or behavior to a young person's parents.

Often, in an interpretive interview with parents, the parents can be led, under the skillful guidance of the counselor, to reveal many of the things about the offspring that the counselor needs to know. Even with a retarded child, I have often found that parents can approximate the mental age of the child fairly well even while they are insisting that the child is normal. An offspring's abilities and disabilities must be interpreted honestly and directly to the parents, particularly for the purpose of educational and vocational planning, but if the appraisal is going to be a blow to the cherished hopes of the parents, the interpretation must be given cautiously and with kindness. Honesty need not mean bluntness and unkindness, and strengths as well as weaknesses can be stressed. It frequently falls to the lot of the counselor to inform parents that their high-school offspring is not college material, and if this college goal has been very important to the parents the news will, of course, be difficult for them to accept. However, if the counselor can stress the youngster's good points and try to steer the parents' thinking along other academic lines, the results can be happier. In this respect the counselor can do much to dispel the anxiety occasioned by the unfortunate current propaganda that *everyone* should go to college and that it is impossible to get a job unless one has a college degree. Obviously, this propaganda is not realistic, and perhaps parents need to have the situation interpreted to them by someone knowledgeable in the educational field.

When a young person presents personality or behavior problems and it is necessary to enlist the aid and cooperation of the parents to resolve them, the situation is more difficult because then the parents must face themselves and gain insight into the part they play in the difficulties of their offspring. Interpretations in these instances cannot be given in one interview but must come about naturally as a result of continued parent counseling. The same general principles apply to interpretations in these continuous parent counselings as in counseling the young person who is attending school or college, save that there may be a little more of a reeducative process involved in the counseling of parents. The high-school or college student is the primary client, and the parents are there only as adjuncts to his counseling. Ostensibly at least, the parents are not coming to the sessions because they feel the need of help for themselves but because they want to cooperate, or have been told that they must cooperate in efforts to effect an improvement in the adjustment of their offspring. This function may mean not only that they must gain insight into themselves but also into the school's point of view and into their offspring's feelings and reasons for behaving as he does. It involves developing a greater understanding of the problems and tensions between the school, their offspring, and themselves, and learning how to modify their own reactions and how to deal more effectively with difficult situations which arise.

There are many systems of psychotherapy, both individual and group, ranging from traditional Freudian psychoanalysis and its many deviations to directive therapy, nondirective thearapy, learning therapy, conditioned-reflex therapy, rational psychotherapy, and numerous others. Although each has its own special techniques, there are many similarities as well as differences between the various systems. Since this variation is particularly true in regard to interpretation, it might be advisable at this time to borrow a little from each system and present a few general principles of interpretation rather than to try to give the viewpoint of each.

There are circumstances under which it is not only desirable but necessary for a school or college guidance counselor to be quite direct in his interpretations and in his counseling of a particular student. The counselor should be direct when a student seeks his aid in educational or vocational planning; otherwise the student might be left in a state of complete confusion. To one he might say, "The tests you have taken indicate that you have the potential ability for higher academic education, but you are handicapped at present because of a weakness in reading. You say you have been unable to get any work done this year and that you feel discouraged and hopeless. This is basically because your reading is very slow, and it takes you a long time to comprehend what you read so that your homework assignments are difficult for you, and you are seldom able to complete an examination.

Fortunately, this is something which can be remedied, but it will take a great deal of effort on your part, so that the decision must be yours. There are other bright students who have the same difficulty in reading that you have, and we have a special class in this school for these students. If you are interested, arrangements can be made for you to attend this class. When your reading improves you will find that your school work is much easier for you and more enjoyable. Think it over and let me know your decision tomorrow." Or, to another student, "You tell me you are considering studying engineering because your father says that engineers make the most money, and yet you show little interest in anything of a mechanical nature. You also indicate a dislike of science and mathematics, and your marks in these subjects have always been your lowest. On the other hand, you seem to have strong literary interests, particularly in the classics, and you have done exceptionally well in English and foreign languages. These things suggest that you might be happier and more successful in a field other than engineering. Perhaps you would like to think it over and we could discuss other possible vocational choices for you at the time of our next interview."

Sometimes, direct interpretations must be made both to the client and to his parents, particularly when parents are overly ambitious for their offspring. A young man of 17, a junior in high school, came to see me recently for educational and vocational advice. I asked him what were some of the things he had thought he might like to do for a living. He replied, "Go to college." When asked why, he said, "My mother says you can't get a job without a college education. My brother is in medical school." "Are you like your brother?" I asked. "No," he replied. "He's a brain. He wants to read books all the time and he never wants to go out with the guys." Further questioning revealed that this young man had never in his life read a book all the way through and had never received a mark higher than "C" in high school. He had barely average intelligence and very poor scholastic aptitude, and he hated to study. He spent his spare time working in a garage, enjoyed his work, and apparently gave satisfactory service. It was necessary to interpret the test results directly and meaningfully both to this young man and to his mother, pointing out to them that neither his interests nor his aptitudes were along academic lines, and that he would function far more adequately in a manual or mechanical field. The young man accepted the interpretation with relief, his mother with annoyance.

Even with a behavior problem, direct interpretation of a client's behavior to him may sometimes be effective. Recently, when a student was in danger of being expelled from school because of his belligerent, difficult behavior in the classroom and his open resistance to all authority, his guidance counselor, to whom he had previously revealed his hostile feelings toward his parents and his resentment of their harshness, restrictions, and punishments, reflected back to him his expressed feelings toward his parents. He then said to the boy, "You are angry at your parents but you daren't show your anger to them so you are taking it out on the school and saying all the things to your teachers that you would like to say to your parents. Maybe they will throw you out of school for it, and then you will really be getting even with your parents since it means so much to them to see you get through school." The student replied by complaining that the teachers were unfair to him and blamed him for things he didn't do. The counselor agreed that it might be so and interpreted it as the usual reaction to someone who is always in trouble and unpleasant. After interpreting the youngster's behavior to him as self-limiting and self-destructive, the counselor was able to establish better rapport with him, and his behavior gradually began to improve.

In most instances, interpretation of this sort would be considered too abrupt and direct, but in this case, the hunch of the counselor was correct. A less directive approach to the high-school or college students who present behavior or personality problems is generally more effective. These different approaches are discussed mainly for the purpose of stressing the importance of flexibility on the part of the counselor—the importance of being willing to modify his technique so that it will best suit the individual needs of a particular client or patient.

As mentioned earlier, the purpose of interpretation is to promote insight—to help the individual to understand himself so that he can live a happier life and deal more effectively with his problems. Perhaps the two most important things to remember in interpretation are timing and purpose. The counselor should know when to give an interpretation and when to withhold it, for an interpretation given too late may be useless and one given too early may be ineffective and may even delay insight because it is rejected by the client. The counselor should also know why he is giving an interpretation and should have some definite purpose in mind when he gives it. The purpose should be to help the client gain insight on some particular point or reaction or feeling, not to show off the counselor's superior skill or knowledge or to enable him to "play God." Unless the client is ready to and can accept interpretations offered, these interpretations may create resistance and damage the counseling process.

It is only when a client has been in counseling for some time and knows for sure that his counselor is really sincere in his efforts to understand and to help him, that he may be able to tolerate wrong interpretations. When a wrong interpretation occurs, it is usually more conducive to rapport if the counselor admits his error. At this point it might be well to note too that one of the major causes of misinterpretations is countertransference, something of which every counselor should be aware. Perhaps a cardinal rule for the counselor should be, "When in doubt, don't." If a counselor has any doubt whatever about whether he should give an interpretation, or if he is at all uncertain of his interpretation, it is better not to risk interpretation. The inexperienced counselor also would be wise to avoid attempting to give interpretations for the promotion of insight.

In most therapies the growing tendency seems to be to give fewer content interpretations and to be extremely cautious in giving them. Rogers (1942, 1951) feels that it is important to avoid giving interpretations of behavior based on the counselor's judgments, but rather always to interpret the expressed feelings of the client. In other words, interpretations should be reiterations of those feelings which the client has already expressed during the counseling session, not those which the counselor may know but which the client has not himself expressed. Also, in reflecting back the patient's feelings, it is generally more effective and acceptable to him to use his own terms and symbols. However, if the patient will not accept an interpretation even when these terms are used, it is better to let the matter drop, for interpretations should never become a subject for argument.

In discussion, a client will often discover unconscious meanings for himself without the interpretation of the counselor or will spontaneously see the application of insights in new areas. According to Rogers (1942), if the patient does not make such discoveries, it is the counselor who has the insight, not the client. A skilled counselor usually has a pretty good idea of the problem and of much of the dynamics involved after an interview or two, but it would serve no good purpose to interpret these things to the client at this time because, in all probability, he would not be ready to accept them emotionally, and intellectual insight alone is insufficient for therapy.

When a client has been in therapy or counseling for a short time, he usually begins to make his own interpretations of his feelings, attitudes, and reactions, relate them to past experiences, and even interpret his dream material if his counselor gives him an opportunity to do so. When interpretations and insights are offered spontaneously by a client, they usually suggest a better understanding of the self than when they are given by the counselor. It is particularly good if this spontaneous interpretation, indicative of self-understanding, can be brought about in working with adolescents, since these youngsters are often quite resistive to accepting interpretations from others. For many adolescents, a too direct interpretation, especially in the early stages of counseling, may be rejected because it smacks too much of the very authority they are resisting.

Summarizing briefly: (1) The nature of interpretation will vary with the matter to be interpreted and the person to whom it is to be interpreted. (2) Interpretation of a student's intelligence, aptitude, intellectual strengths and weaknesses, and behavior should, in most cases, be given to his teachers directly and in meaningful terms which will enable the teacher to understand him better and aid him in effecting a better adjustment. (3) Interpretation of these same things to the parents of a client may require greater tact and a less direct approach.

(4) Interpretations of a student's aptitudes for the purpose of educational or vocational planning should be presented to teachers, parents, or clients directly, clearly, and in simple, understandable terms. (5) Less directive approaches, with opportunities for the client to make his own interpretations, are generally more effective when dealing with personality or behavior problems. (6) Interpretations by the counselor should generally be a reflection back to the client of his expressed feelings, attitudes, or reactions, rather than a reflection of what the counselor may know or surmise about the patient. The counselor should be careful to time his interpretations so that he gives them when his client is ready to accept them. Finally, (7) the counselor should know why he is giving an interpretation, and generally this purpose should be to help the client gain insight on some particular point, reaction, or feeling.

# 30. Values in Counseling

RAYMOND J. McCALL

## The Meaning of Values

Any decision that one thing is better than another, or desirable or undesirable in itself, is a value judgment. By the same token, in the most general sense, a value is anything (person, object, activity, or condition) that men regard as worthwhile or preferable to other things. In this sense the term embraces everything that is valued, from the summum bonum to the next meal. Yet the values that are of greatest moment to the psychologist, and for which we usually reserve the term, are neither the transcendentals of philosophical wisdom nor the temporary goods for our recurrent appetites. They are rather those long-range or penultimate goals, on the relative importance of which people differ and by relation to some of which they tend to guide their day-to-day choices, for example, wealth, prestige, service, knowledge, beauty, comfort. Our values are for us the principal components and instrumentalities, practically speaking, of the good life as we see it.

Because each of us is at least a little bit different from anyone else, and because each of us sees himself and the reality around him at least a little bit differently from anyone else, our penultimate goals or values are amazingly diverse, however much we may share the same human nature and however much we may pursue a common end such as self-maximization.

## Pertinence of Values to Counseling

Common elements and differences in the conception and implementation of values are singularly important to the clinical and counseling psychologist. The very existence of what we have come to designate as the counseling or psychotherapeutic relationship would seem to be dependent on a similarity between counselor and counselee in attitudes toward truthfulness, confidentiality, concern for human well-being, and respect for human dignity, and this similarity certainly implies some common value orientation. But there is also, I believe, a differentiality in value attitudes between counselor and client that is even more important for the understanding of the counseling or psychotherapeutic function. Perhaps this difference has more to do with implementing and harmonizing, rather than with defining, values, but its clarification and resolution nevertheless constitute, as I see it, the very axis of the counseling process.

## Psychological Effectiveness as a Value

The difference in question is partly summarized by the client's implicit or explicit question: How can I resolve the conflicts that beset my life and make progress toward the goals of happiness and self-fulfillment that I seek? However clear the ultimate goals may be, he says in effect, the penultimate goals or values are organized badly and pursued ineffectively. What seems to be in question here is the psychological implementation of the individual's general life plan, and this implementation itself becomes then the supreme psychological value. Though often referred to as "mental health" or "psychological adjustment," the underlying notion is poorly conveyed by medical and biological metaphors and might be better designated as psychological effectiveness. This term is the one I prefer, and I shall mean by psychological effectiveness a condition of the psychic apparatus, of the powers of cognition and motivation, that enables the individual to move effectively toward, or offers no psychological impediments to, his ultimate goals in life.

Clearly, the notion of psychological effectiveness must be intimately related to a general ethical theory of what it is that is ultimately right and desirable for men to seek. "Effectiveness" is an instrumental rather than a terminal concept, and implies a further end for which or toward the accomplishment of which effectiveness may be predicated. At the same time, it would be presumptuous for the psychologist to suppose that the good life or human well-being as such is exclusively or even principally psychological in nature, and it is a misconstruction of psychological effectiveness to lose sight of its instrumental nature. The psychologist has no special competence in the realm of absolutes or ultimates. Like all practical scientists, the clinician or counselor is concerned with proximate (or at most near-ultimate) ends, and it is in this perspective that the ideal of psychological effectiveness must be viewed. Perhaps one can say that the concept of the good life that harmonizes most readily with the notion of psychological effectiveness should be broad and inclusive rather than narrow and exclusive, and that a philosophical concept of an ultimate goal such as "maximal self-actualization" seems prima facie to accord better with the instrumentality of psychological effectiveness than would, say, a concept like "spiritual perfection" or "esthetic creativity."[1] Nevertheless, it is important to note that this issue is a philosophical one on which the psychologist can speak with no authority; and if someone insists that as far as human good is concerned, considerations of a psychological nature are entirely secondary in spiritual or esthetic perfection, there is no psychological way of refuting him.

Now, though the psychologist can claim no philosophical expertise, by the very fact that he identifies himself as a counselor or psychotherapist, he does claim some kind of authority in the area of psychological effectiveness, some ability to help the client resolve his psychological conflicts and move toward self-fulfillment. Thus, even the client-centered therapist must, on the premises of his own system, acknowledge that he considers himself to have a deeper awareness than the individual does of the individual's own power of effective self-

---

[1] The concept of maximal self-actualization may be only a latter-day version of Aristotelian excellence (*arete*), but since it is removed from the Olympian heights of metaphysical utterance and transposed from its absolutistic frame of reference to something closer to a probabilistic system of coordinates, it should not be altogether offensive to the contemporary mind. Though I disagree pointedly with the position of M. Brewster Smith (1961) that the humanist and the theologian have no greater competence than the psychologist or social scientist in this area, I recognize the advantage that anthropological sophistication and a historical perspective offer us, as well as the advantage accruing from our exposure within a democratic and pluralistic society to a great variety of value systems. It is thus easy for us to recognize the self-defeating and illusory character of many socially condoned practices and institutions, such as the Kwakiutl potlatch and the separate-but-equal schools of the South, without assuming the absolute validity of our own culturally sanctioned system of values. And though psychologists and other social scientists are often woefully deficient in logical and philosophical sophistication, the applied psychologist as a thinking man has an obligation to make his value system with respect to psychological effectiveness as explicit and as evidenced as it is possible for him to make it.

determination toward constructive living, and a deeper appreciation of the interpersonal conditions that enhance this power. If indeed the psychotherapist is not sufficiently versed in the nature and determinants of psychological effectiveness to be able to assure the client that the latter has a better chance of achieving this value with the counselor's help than without it, both his ethical and his logical posture are weak, for then the counselor is worse than a salesman without a product; he is a specialist without a competence.

One may argue that it is only a working or pragmatic grasp of the ideal of psychological effectiveness that is necessary to the practical clinician or counselor. In this regard, it would seem, the psychological practitioner has a right to expect the psychological theorist to provide him with a conception of psychological effectiveness that is logically organized, empirically referenced, and clinically relevant. On the whole, needless to say, this reasonable expectation has gone unrealized, despite the efforts of a handful of psychologists[2] to come to grips with the problem. In the brief space I have available, I would like to sketch the outline of a theory of psychological effectiveness, hoping that it will demonstrate two of the three criteria for such a theory, namely, logical organization and clinical relevance, and that it will provide the possibility, if not the actuality, of empirical reference.

## The Components of Psychological Effectiveness

To the extent that the effectiveness we seek to describe is psychological, it must pertain in some way to knowledge (cognition, perception, awareness, understanding) or to motivation (conation, desire, appetency, emotion, affect). Let us then designate these two general requirements of knowledge and motivation as cognitive adequacy and

---

[2] In their often quite different ways, Erich Fromm (1947), Marie Jahoda (1958), Abraham Maslow (1954), O. H. Mowrer (1961), and E. J. Shoben (1957) have been working toward a conceptual clarification of the components and determinants of the good-life-psychologically-speaking, while Jahoda (1958), M. B. Smith (1959), and W. A. Scott (1958) have suggested various strategies for linking this largely philosophical conception to techniques of research. It is logically and semantically unfortunate, in my opinion, that most of these authors have identified the relevant concept by the spurious and confusing label "mental health" without indicating that this label is a mere concession to clinical (especially psychiatric) usage and the pervasively enduring myth that all psychological abnormality is "mental illness." While employing many of these authors' formulations, we shall adhere to the more defensible term "psychological effectiveness."

motivational organization respectively, and proceed to specify each as precisely as possible. In schematic outline here are the major components of psychological effectiveness as I view them:

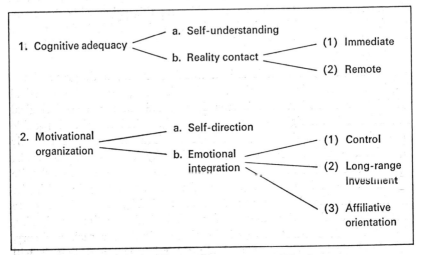

Fig. 1. Components of Psychological Effectiveness

## Self-Understanding

Self-understanding is sometimes referred to as insight and implies correct apprehension of that inner source of psychological functioning, awareness, feeling, and striving, of the locus of hope and hurt that we call the self. This self may be considered from various perspectives. In the first place, there is the real self, the total personality as a biological, psychological, and social entity as it exists in itself, independent of any perception of it, whether our own or that of others. Then there is the perceived (or phenomenal) self, the self as experienced from within, the self that we ourselves apprehend but that is hidden from the direct awareness of others. Finally, there is the so-called external (or social) self, a partial revelation of both the real and the phenomenal self, and hence from which certain characteristics of the inner self and the real self may be reasonably inferred.

Self-understanding may be said to be adequate when the self as understood by the individual corresponds to, or at least approaches, the self as it is. This self as understood is not identical with the phenomenal or experienced self, since it is more a matter of inference than of direct experience. All that we ourselves perceive directly and explicitly are states and activities of the self, not the self as an entity. Some of these states and activities are closely related to our body, like the pain of a sore finger or a headache, the sense of effort and exhilaration in skiing, or that complex of intense feelings we designate as sexual. Others are manifestive of a more mental or psychic aspect of the self, such as a feeling of apprehension about our ability to accomplish a task, a resolution to control our temper, a sudden realization that some goal or value is very important to us, and a recollection that this used not to be characteristic of us. In a sense, the awareness of the self is presented in these pains and joys, efforts and anxieties, evaluations and memories, since they are experienced as our own, while the continuity of our memories makes us feel sure that we are the same individuals who had similar but yet different experiences months and years ago. But the self, viewed as a continuous and abiding whole —bodily and mental, individual and social—is a construct rather than a given, implicit in our every experience and easily inferred from experience, but not itself immediately or explicitly experienced.

We are certain that the self *is,* but what it is is not so readily determined, because the self is complex as well as elusive, subject to development and to deterioration, and because understanding of the true self may, strangely, conflict with the very powerful motives of self-defense and self-enhancement. Thus virtually all great thinkers of the past and present are agreed that there is much in the inner life of man that is irrational and infantile and that he ordinarily strives to keep hidden not only from others but from himself. Moreover, the root of many of our most salient dispositions may be buried in early and forgotten experiences or in our biologically and unconsciously determined temperament, so that even when we know that we have this or that trait, we may have little idea of why we have it.

For these and many other reasons, adequate self-understanding can be acquired only slowly and with an effort that is generally irksome and often upsetting. Even when once acquired up to a certain point, this understanding may be subsequently rendered inadequate by changes occurring in the self with age or in response to new experiences or altered circumstances. It is small wonder, then, that Socrates' injunction "know thyself" remains for most of us a counsel of perfection, and that the search for adequate self-understanding is never-ending.

Yet difficult as it may be, a relatively high degree of self-understanding is indispensable if one is to adapt his behavior to his genuine needs, develop his true potentialities, actualize his real self. And there is no doubt that a conspicuous failure of this kind of self-insight is characteristic of many types of psychological ineffectiveness or abnormality. Self-understanding may not be enough to assure psychological effectiveness, but the latter is certainly impossible without it.

### Reality Contact

Reality contact means accurate registration of the external world, especially the world of other people and the institutions (like family, schools, police, courts, churches) and class distinctions (such as those based on work, sex, authority) that people have created and in and through which they function socially. Reality contact is not entirely separable from insight or self-understanding, since the self is not only engaged in the world but enmeshed with it, developing its distinctive reality in interpersonal interaction in various institutional settings, often incomprehensible apart from these settings and yet itself contributing to their character. Though our adjustment to them is always through interaction with other individuals, institutions and class divisions are the most permanent features of the world of social reality, so that in maintaining reality contact we must understand others not only in their individual make-up but—perhaps more importantly— also in their social functions or roles. Such role appreciation, or the ability to see things simultaneously from the viewpoint of the other individual and in institutional perspective, is enormously difficult, for it is not a matter of simple experience but of complex inference regarding the personal motives and social capacities of others, derived from behavior that is often anything but transparent in its design.

Correct perception of others requires also an accepting and unprejudiced attitude toward them, a willingness to suspend judgment or correct initial impression in the light of later experience. Moreover, since both we and other people change in ourselves and in our roles, reality contact, like insight, must reflect these changes. The adolescent who expects others to attend his needs like an infant's, the grandmother who anticipates from her grown family and from her grandchildren obedience of the kind exacted earlier from her children, the retired executive who continues to give orders, are common examples of people who are psychologically ineffective in the measure of their failure to maintain reality contact in a world of changing interpersonal relations. These examples are, of course, representative of only minor distortions, while marked and apparently uncorrectable disturbance of reality contact is a reliable indicator of the most severe form of psychological abnormality, psychosis. Whatever the range of example, the principle should be clear: Since each of us must strive for self-realization in a culturally structured world in cooperation and competition with others, if we do not register correctly this world of individuals and institutions, we are psychologically blocked from the possibility of self-fulfillment.

There is an impersonal aspect of reality contact that should not be overlooked, and this aspect we may call cognitive attunement to the distant in time. In a general way at least, a man has to plan for his whole life, although many goals are remote and are to be obtained only serially. The individual who is cognitively in touch only with the present and gives no thought to the future is so obviously out of contact with the reality of life as it has to be lived (and with the future dimension which his intellectual powers should enable him to anticipate) that there should be no need to labor the point of his psychological ineffectiveness. Clinicians among us will think of the simple schizophrenic who has no idea of what he'll do with himself when released from the hospital, or the sociopath who lives in an eternal present—remote, alas, from the eternal present in which the theologians tell us Divinity dwells—as conspicuous examples of failure to maintain contact with the temporal dimensions of reality, the secular trend of human life. Vocational counselors, too, will be thoroughly aware of the many people who expect to work for a living but manifest little understanding of the need to select a job well suited to their abilities and to plan and prepare themselves for it. Such persons will drift into jobs opportunistically and short-sightedly and remain unfulfilled and unhappy in them, and literally never see any connection between their work and their self-fulfillment.

## Self-Direction

Self-direction is the first of the appetitive components of psychological effectiveness, all of which I have subsumed under the heading of motivational organization. Since the goals of human endeavor and the appropriate means thereto are not supplied by an unerring instinct, man must either direct his behavior himself or accept the direction of others. In infancy and early childhood man's dependence leaves him little choice, and even in adulthood his social nature and continuing need for others demand conformity to social rules and a willingness to work toward general goals approved by the various groups with which he identifies. At the same time, development from infancy on is characterized by an increasing capacity for independent judgment and choice. The individual grows in his ability to act on his own and to seek common and approved goals in particular ways dictated by his own special talents and interests. Thus, for example, our culture expects a man to work for his living, but whether the job he takes is one well suited to his abilities and one for which he has planned and prepared himself, or one into which he has drifted with careless opportunism, or one which has been dictated by his father's ambition or his mother's hopes, is not culturally determined. The same may hold for other significant areas of development and self-expression.

There is no doubt that one's limited abilities and the opportunities provided by one's society may markedly narrow the field of choice, yet in a highly developed, pluralistic, and mobile society like our own, the individual's range of possible choices is, granted only a certain modicum of ability, truly enormous. In the American economy and culture, for example, not only are there more than 40,000 identifiable occupations for one or more of which the individual may become eligible; but, in principle at least, a man may marry whom he pleases (or not, if he chooses), become a beatnik or a Rotarian, a Democrat, Republican, or dissident of the Left or Right, a Roman Catholic or a Unitarian, a fundamentalist or an agnostic, an orthodox Jew or a Zen Buddhist, an esthete or a philistine.

At the same time ours is also a society in which pressures toward conformity are great. For the individual, its pluralism may mean only the presence of a great number of social groups, each one trying to mold him in some way different from his native cast; and while the forms of democracy may encourage the individual to make choices for himself, his failure to meet expected norms of behavior (or even of dress or hair style) will nonetheless frequently result in severe criticism. The conformist ideal is further reinforced technologically by mass production and rapid distribution of consumer goods, and by the virtually instantaneous communication of information and recommended attitudes via the so-called mass media (radio, television, and the press). In an ingenious experiment, Asch (1952) has demonstrated that the constraining force of group opinion can under certain circumstances cause an individual to reject the evidence of his own eyes.

As a consequence, then, of social pressure to "see things in a certain way," it may be all but impossible to see them any other way or to react to them independently, especially if the things to be seen are not immediately experienced but are evaluated inferentially from a limited sampling. Consider, for example, the heroic degree of intellectual and motivational independence required for a Mississippian or an Afrikaaner to behave toward a Negro in a very different fashion than do other Mississippians or Afrikaaners. Self-direction remains therefore, like self-understanding, a difficult and only partly achievable ideal. It is a paradoxical and typically human asymptote toward which we move as we become increasingly conscious of the many factors that serve to prevent our reaching it.

## Emotional Integration

Emotional integration implies first of all control, the habitual subordination of emotions like fear and anger, impulse and aversion, eagerness and despair to the judgment of reason. As Aristotle and Plato long ago clearly saw, adherence in day-to-day conduct to any program of self-improvement is impossible without the control of aberrant impulses and of the emotions generated by the partial or short-term good. Yet control by itself is not enough, since sustained adherence to any life plan is equally impossible without emotional investment in the long-range goals of such a life plan. One must be not only convinced intellectually of his ideals but also emotionally committed to them, and the lack of such commitment or emotional investment is precisely descriptive of the condition which the sociologists designate as anomie. It is the fusion of the emotional with what may be described philosophically as the ultimately rational that most of the great religions of the world have sought to convey to mankind, and it is the absence of this fusion that Jung (1933) has described as the lack of religious orientation in the soul of modern man.

In the last analysis, emotional integration therefore requires not just temperance and fortitude (control) but affective transcendence, the incorporation of emotional responsiveness and vigor with a philosophy of life. The disposition to invest one's farthest goals with a motivational power sufficient to overcome the lure of the immediately present may thus make control easier, as control may make affective transcendence possible. But it is not only emotional control and emotional transcendence that are mutually reinforcing and implicative. The cognitive and the motivational elements in psychological effectiveness, though distinct, are interdependent. Nothing is thus more disruptive of reality contact nor effectively preventive of self-understanding than uncontrolled emotion. The fear-ridden man starts at every shadow and knows nothing but his own terror; the angry man finds hostility in an innocent gesture and shows little or no insight into his own irritability; and we are all prone to distort the world and our own self-concept through the prism of our hopes and fears and resentments. Yet the individual cannot emotionally invest in distant goals if he is not cognitively attuned to them, nor can he readily control his emotional response to an unknown object. But self-direction demands transcendence of the present both cognitively and emotionally, for when the individual is stimulus-bound, it is the stimulus rather than the self that directs behavior. One may surmise, therefore, that mutual interdependence is to some extent characteristic of all aspects of psychological effectiveness, that one could not be markedly deficient in one component without all of the others suffering to some degree at least.

The final component of emotional integration is affiliative orientation. If the individual's motives and decisions are prompted only by his own advantage, without consideration or regard for others, he in effect denies the reality of his own dependence. Thereby he enacts a pattern which, if made general, could result only in the destruction of organized living and of his own well-being in any sense. It is not difficult to agree that the individual must be cognitively socialized, that is, he must recognize the necessity of social rules, even when they work to his own disadvantage, because without such rules an adequate life would be impossible for people in general. Cognition, however, is clearly not enough, for in practice the conflict between individual advantage and social good can result only in the triumph of the former, unless the individual's emotions can be brought to bear on the weak (or social) side of the conflict. This social activity can occur only by force of powerful threat and fear or by way of affiliation and love. Psychologically speaking, fear has an important role in the economy of the psyche, but strong fear is dystonic and disruptive of psychic balance, destructive of insight or self-understanding, incompatible with self-direction. Only affection toward others and loyalty to the group can painlessly mitigate self-seeking. The social existence—the only mode in which man can develop his powers adequately—would be seen as an intolerable burden were it not for our liking of and our joy in others. Long-term self-interest may require socialization, but only affection can efficaciously motivate it.

Since self-direction is a significant component of psychological effectiveness, the latter would demand independent, rather than dependent, affiliativeness. The dependently affiliative are the "other-directed" of

Fromm (1947) and Riesman (1950), the "organization men" of Whyte (1956). With them the motor of socialization is insecurity rather than affection. They have internalized the "thou shalt not's," and are governed in their conformity largely by fear of cultural sanctions. The independently affiliative, by contrast, are ruled more by good sense, good will, and affection than by insecurity. They are not necessarily indifferent to or totally unafraid of social disapproval, but they are less obviously and less pervasively governed by it. They can conform to the spirit of the law without being obsessed by its letter. They seem to recognize the "slippage" in all social direction and the arbitrariness and even the stupidity of many social regulations, but for the most part they go along tolerantly with silly rules and human foibles because they like people, want to be able to continue to manage their own lives in society, and recognize that even an imperfect regulation ought generally to be obeyed if the whole concept of social order and the whole context of human association are not to be rendered meaningless.

## Summary and Conclusion

Even though the concept of psychological effectiveness as sketched here represents an ideal, an asymptote that can never be quite reached, it seems to me that something like it not only can be employed meaningfully in counseling, but also must be employed if the process is to be maximally effective. The person functioning in productive relation to this ideal understands himself and appreciates others not only as individuals but also in their institutional roles. He is cognitively attuned to the temporal dimension of human life and formulates long-range plans to guide his present and future actions. He is emotionally integrated and controlled; yet he does not lack in affective resonance or drive with respect to distant purposes but rather, is committed emotionally in keeping with his intellectual understanding. He is self-directed, yet affiliatively oriented and warmly regardful of others.

The interrelation and interdependence of the various components of psychological effectiveness make it unlikely that one could manifest extreme variation in one component without thereby showing deviation in others. Some degree of variation from one component to another is certainly likely in view of differences in capacities, temperamental dispositions, upbringing, and circumstance. Thus the creatively gifted are more likely to be self-directive than affiliative; the temperamentally fearful more readily affiliative than the temperamentally irascible;

the highly intelligent introvert more insightful than the dull extrovert; the pampered child less regardful of others than the child who has learned to share, though both may have similar temperaments and intellectual endowments. We cannot, therefore, think of the correlation between the components as approaching unity, but we may nevertheless formulate the working rule that marked deficiency or deviation in any one of these components is manifestive of psychological ineffectiveness and at least potential abnormality. Because there is no absolute standard of acceptable degree of deviation, there is likely to be some disagreement whether a given amount of defect or imbalance is indicative of ineffectiveness or abnormality in a given case. With this qualification in mind (which can only be removed by empirical studies on relative scales of measurement somewhat in the manner of an IQ test), we may venture to say that an individual is psychologically ineffective to the extent that he significantly.

a. Lacks insight or self-understanding

b. Is incognizant of the reality of other persons either as individuals or in their institutional roles

c. Is unmindful of the future

d. Shows other-directedness, a failure of spontaneity and autonomy

e. Is emotionally unstable or uncontrolled, lacking in frustration and stress tolerance

f. Is emotionally unintegrated and uncommitted with regard to distant goals and his life plan

g. Lacks affiliative orientation or warm regard for others

How the counselor or psychotherapist should endeavor to help correct these aberrations or to reinforce the related positive values is, of course, another question. But that he must to a large degree operate in close and conscious concern for them, I at least cannot doubt.

# 31. A Philosophy for Guidance and Counseling

## FRANK M. BUCKLEY

For a paper of this kind dealing with a practical philosophy for guidance and counseling, it might be best to move along from one step to the next with a minimum of formality and academic appurtenances. This informal approach is partly due to what at first was an implicit, and more recently has become a conscious, reaction to the straitjacket appearance that organized presentations may sometimes give to what we all hope would be a free pursuit of the truth as we see it in our lives, in our work, and in our field of study.

With this caution in mind, let us look over some of the major developments and emphases in the field of guidance and counseling during the past half century. In the beginning of the counseling movement, our attention was focused on guidance as a phase in the discovery of individual differences. A little later it became a matter of matching talents with tasks, involving a sharper focus on educational and vocational guidance. In the 1930's we came to see a strong emphasis on the relationship of the individual to society and to the broader environment as they reflect the major mechanisms of adjustment. Still more recently, we have come to focus on adapting in more flexible and dynamic equilibrium to life and to life situations. From this recent focus has emerged the important and remarkable work in the study of the process of vocational choice.

And now, most recently, comes the dawning recognition that fundamental to all of these earlier and necessary steps and parts of our work is the understanding of the central role of the individual's relationship to other persons within the context of effective social and cultural forces. In other words, we have clarified what has come to be called the transactional aspects of relationship and the movement toward self-actualization in terms of what may be regarded as characteristically and distinctively human development. Since each one lives in a world of personal meaning, in addition to meanings that are common to others in our culture, it is not possible to understand our world without a close look (especially today) at the nature and range of a variety of special cultural factors. It is these factors that very often affect the meaning and the satisfaction and the self-actualization that a person seeks when he enters the world of study or work or of family life.

Consequently, it is not unimportant to ask ourselves—since most of us are involved in direct day-to-day guidance and counseling work with others—what it is that our counselees are fundamentally looking for. What do they expect on a deeper level? And why is it that they seek assistance from us or from others? Even a preliminary answer to these questions pushes us to inquire on a deeper level, on a level which is in a sense beyond psychology, beyond biology, and beyond physics—in other words, on a metapsychological, metabiological, and metaphysical level. Questions on the philosophical level are important and central if today we are to engage in our work more effectively.

What are some of these basic philosophical questions that the daily confrontation with our counselees leads us to face in a variety of altered forms? They certainly include the following: (1) What is the nature of man? What does it mean to be human? What is human existence? (2) What is the nature and purpose of the universe and of the world in which he finds himself? (3) What is man's relationship to the world, and does this relationship itself enter into the nature of his existence as man? (4) What is freedom? What is human freedom? What are the limitations of this freedom? (5) What is duty and obligation? Is man bound by "should's and ought's"? Is he responsible? (6) What is knowledge, and what are the criteria and limits of valid knowledge? What are the appropriate and acceptable methods of pursuing knowledge, scientia, modern experimental science, philosophy, or philosophy as science?

To attempt any exposition of the varied answers to these deep and complex questions is not the purpose of this short presentation. Needless to say, answers to these questions lie in the realm of general philosophy, which encompasses the accumulated lore of over 2,000 years of human thought. But we are concerned with these kinds of questions and issues in our work; and we come most closely to reexamining them when we engage as we must from time to time in any considered approach to the understanding of personality. Theories of personality constitute the major link between general philosophy and contemporary understanding of the structure, dynamics, and development of personality. Hall and Lindzey (1957), in their analysis of the significant elements that must be considered in any adequate attempt to fathom personality, have pointed among others to the following:

Its relation to empirical phenomena;
Its recognition of purposive and teleological qualities;
Its dealing with the unconscious determinants of behavior;
Its relationship to the process of learning;
The recognition of continuity of behavior;
Its dealing with holistic qualities;
Its recognition of uniqueness;
Attention to aspects of the psychological environment;
Recognition of group behavior and group determinants including the social and cultural factors;
The problem of selfhood, or the self-concept, and of subjectivity.

Any attempt to bear in mind these central elements and their interdependence in developing a theory of personality calls for, it would seem, immense sensitivity and observation, and inevitably leads to the central philosophical questions which have been raised above unless one deliberately prescinds from them. Therefore, it is interesting to note in the history of modern psychology how the major scientific traditions have dealt with these problems. For purposes of order and conciseness, we can think of the major modern traditions as three: (1) the positivistic tradition; (2) the psychoanalytic tradition; and (3) the existential tradition.

We are all well aware that the positivist tradition has insisted on the reduction of all observations to data which are directly and empirically observable and which can be reduced to manageable, quantitative terms. As such, positivism teaches us how to be exacting and careful and cautious in our observations and conclusions, but this virtue has been purchased at the price of literally pulling man to pieces; that is, of studying parts and segments of personality rather than the total unified being. The psychoanalytic tradition, on the other hand, has reached to a deeper and less discriminable level through a search of the unconscious—its structure, forces, and expression. Psychoanalytic thought, however, has continued to view man as an adjusting mechanism in his perennial task of managing the tyrannical forces of id and superego, and the determining forces of heredity and environment.

It is my considered point of view that only existential thought, in the broadest sense of this term, leaves room for the more adequate understanding and integration of the various elements in the complex unity of the total person. As such, it may be able to provide newer and deeper clarifications and avenues to further understanding that can lead to productive developments in our everyday work of guidance and counseling.

It is not my intention here to attempt any description of the development and varieties of existential thought. Most of us are aware of the differing and sometimes even opposed points of view of existential writers like Kierkegaard, Heidegger, Jaspers, Sartre, and Marcel. Yet there is to be found in all of them a commonly shared recognition of what constitutes the distinctive characteristics of human existence. Though sometimes phrased in differing forms, the philosophies of different existential thinkers are each concerned with the following, which may be considered fundamental points of agreement and principles of operation in existential and phenomenological thought: (1) awareness of the depersonalizing and alienating forces of modern technological thought and society; (2) emphasis on understanding man as distinguished from explaining him; (3) recognition of everyday human experience as the starting point; (4) insistence on seeing man in his situation (in time and place—Dasein) and that situation always in its totality; and (5) core emphasis on what constitutes the vitally human and on the primary place of meaning in human existence as each individual struggles to grasp this meaning for himself.

Gordon Allport gives another way of summarizing the common existential concern:

To sum up, there is a tendency among existentialist writers to seek for one basic intentional theme in human life. A fairly wide range of proposals is the result—and yet the varied proposals seem for the most part to be complementary and concordant, not in actual opposition. Man is inherently restless and anxious, desiring both security and freedom. He strives to counter his condition of alienation by seeking a meaning for existence which will cover the tragic trio of suffering, guilt, death. By making commitments he finds that life can become worth living. Along the way he enhances his own value experiences. If necessary he will sacrifice his life in order that some primary value can continue to be served. He is capable of taking responsibility, of answering by his deeds the questions life puts to him. In this way he rises above his own organic and spiritual urgencies, and achieves true self-transcendence. Although different writers place emphasis on different parts of this formula, the picture is consistent (Allport, 1961, p. 560).

We may note in this brief look at central existential emphases that several things stand out which we do not find in prior psychological traditions, and which may have a critical bearing upon our capacity to deal with the problems, in whatever various guises and forms, of modern youth and modern man. For one thing, anxiety is viewed as a direct derivative of the human experience, and as a natural and continuing outcome of finding oneself in an ever-changing and threatening world. "Die Angst der Kreatur" of Kierkegaard is a probing analysis of this continuing anxiety state; it is something which does not arise only as a product of the threat of inner instinctual forces or of challenging outside elements.

Another notable new note is the confrontation of, and acceptance of suffering, hardship and death as inescapable components of being human. This approach is a far cry from the implied expectations of continuing and improved efficiency, productivity, and pleasure that are central in the positivist and analytic traditions. Finally, there is the reemphasis on human freedom, the assertion that man is not entirely determined, that he is never more human, as Tillich says, than when he is making a decision, and that he consequently is a fundamentally responsible being. These recognitions and the concomitant attention paid to the here and now and the recognition of man's capacity to transcend both his experiences and himself, and thus to find a deeper meaning for human existence, go far beyond any other contemporary school of thought in psychology and open the door to a metapsychological recognition of spiritual values and the central role of religion in man's life and fulfillment.

Let us stop here for a moment to ask ourselves—supposing that existential insights are most thoroughly attuned to the totality of human experience and can be solidly buttressed by empirical and phenomenological evidence—what particular value has this philosophy for me as a counselor, as a priest, or as a parent or teacher? What changes or modifications would such a point of view have upon the counseling approaches and the guidance activities that we engage in? In other words, is it possible to translate existential principles into successful action? These are legitimate questions, since there are some counselors who feel that a given philosophical point of view may make no difference at all in practice. We do need a great deal more empirical research in order to find the right answers. However, we already have sufficient evidence to suggest several practical applications.

To begin with, the existential counselor, while versed in positivist and analytic contributions, would no longer view the counselee as someone who is the pawn of forces beyond his control. He sees a person who at the very least has the power and the capacity to take a stand, even in the face of otherwise ungovernable forces, and thus can assert his freedom. In other words, freedom of thought and action is restored; it is no longer an illusion or fiction. Such an attitude will permeate the whole context of one's relationship with his counselee.

Again, the existential counselor is more highly sensitive to those features of contemporary living which do directly enter into each man's existence. He is aware of the continuing growth of scientism and of the technological society with its increased sense of alienation. He is thus able to recognize such elements as they become manifest in the guidance or counseling situation, and can then help the counselee to recognize, accept, and attempt to deal with them. Also, the existential counselor is ever mindful that each counselee must clarify his own perception of reality, which is to say, his own phenomenal world, and must attempt to deal with this reality in a here-and-now manner as he integrates his own phenomenal world gradually and more congruently with the real world.

Another major feature of the existential approach certainly ought always to be an openness of mind, guided by the phenomenological principle that if one stops, looks, and listens with sufficient patience and with sufficient attention to reality, reality will begin to unfold itself. Such openness of mind precludes the arbitrary acceptance of any particular system of explanation of personality or of any particular type of technique; the counselor's attitude remains open at all times to the actual person and his perceptions, and to the unique situation. In other words, the differences in practice that can ensue from an acceptance of existential principles are due to a difference in (1) objectives and (2) the specific attitudes of the counselor.

VanKaam, in his treatment of this subject, elaborates further upon the desirability of certain attitudes. According to him, the attitudes of the counselor in this existential relationship would be especially characterized by (1) creativity, (2) acceptance, (3) gentleness, and (4) sincerity. He develops these implications further in the following passage:

Obviously much harm can be done by a counselor when his perception is distorted by the premature introduction of theoretical explanations. The existential counselor will penetrate first into behavior as it manifests itself and only then ponder how existing scientific theories may illuminate this behavior without distortion, or how scientific theories should be corrected, expanded, or renewed in order to keep in touch with behavior as given in reality today. Theories of personality and psychotherapy should supplement rather than supplant existential understanding. The existential counselor should draw on the rich fund of insight called science of psychology which is a collection of intellectual contributions by numerous enlightened theorists of behavior. But his prudent selection from this treasure-trove of theoretical explanations should be illumined by real behavior as it manifests itself in his clients. His primary commitment is to existence, not to a theory about existence, even an existential theory. His existential openness for the communications of his counselee will enable him not only to spot the relevant theoretical explanation but also to adapt it to the concrete situation or even to improve it on the basis of his observation. In the last case he may possibly enrich the treasury of psychology so that others after him may have more knowledge available. It should be his wish, however, that his successors will neither abuse his ideas for the distortion of data nor substitute his observation for their own existential perception. It should be his hope that they may be more sensitive to behavior than to his explanations about behavior, that their ears may not be deafened by the noise of theories, and that their eyes may not be blinded by expositions in journals, books, and papers, even if they happen to be his own (Mosher et al., 1965, pp. 77–78).

In terms of practical outcomes of such a point of view successfully applied, we may hope to achieve in varying degrees such modifications of attitudes and behavior as reveal a strengthening of the counselor's capacities:

a. to live meaningfully in the present; to deal with the here and now, in terms of satisfactory personal relationships and satisfactory work, and in terms of future-oriented meanings and goals;

b. to more truly communicate with oneself and others; to be able to express oneself (to be oneself) and to listen to others (to let others be themselves);

c. to participate; to more truly share, to experience an abiding sense of equality as a person, to give and receive; to love;

d. to live with problems, without undue accompanying feelings of frustration, anger, or anxiety;

e. to live with human anxiety ("Die Angst der Kreatur"), that is, to accept limitations of all kinds as an integral part of being human;

f. to accept, when inescapable, suffering such as boredom, depression, or fatigue as authentic components of human existence and, hence, as values; and finally,

g. to become "engaged," accepting responsibility for one's action (not blaming other persons or events) and thus to achieve real commitment to values and purposes.

# 32. Two Case Studies in Counseling

PAUL J. CENTI

ALEXANDER A. SCHNEIDERS

## Counseling the Anxious Adolescent: The Case of Tom
(PAUL J. CENTI)

Tom was originally referred to the Counseling Center by the Dean of the college. At this time he was just beginning his sophomore year. In his freshman year Tom was enrolled in the pre-med program, and, although he found the program difficult, he did achieve an average of slightly better than C.

After a month as a sophomore, Tom came to the conclusion that the pre-med program was too difficult, and, in an interview with the Dean, he indicated that he was uncertain of his choice of medicine as a career; that he had chosen the program without seriously reflecting on his choice.

In a meeting of the Dean with Tom and his parents, it was decided that Tom should withdraw from school for a year in order to separate himself from the pressures of school work and to appraise his situation more carefully. It was recommended that he make an appointment at the Counseling Center to determine on a career choice which could be pursued when he returned to college the following September. Thus Tom first came to the Counseling Center for vocational guidance.

### The Initial Counseling Sessions

When Tom came for his first session with the counselor, he appeared highly tense and apprehensive. His eyes, which he seldom fixed on the counselor, were heavily lined. He sat nervously moving his hands and feet. During the first interview, the counselor emphasized the wisdom of the decision to leave school, attempted to relieve the feelings of failure which undoubtedly accompanied Tom's decision to leave, and encouraged him to return to school the following September.

The initial interview brought out the following facts: Tom was 18 years old, lived in a nearby state with his mother, father, and a younger brother. His mother was a social worker and his father a fireman. The younger brother was an average student in high school but an outstanding athlete, and also played varsity baseball and football. Tom also participated in a number of other school activities and had dated once or twice. During his freshman year in college, however, he did not participate in any activities, nor had he dated. He had gone to one dance but had become very tense and had left. He considered trying out for the football team but gave up the idea because he felt that he had little chance of making it. He became increasingly anxious on tests and when he had to speak in class.

The test protocol showed College Board scores of 545 for Verbal and 503 for Mathematics. Entrance tests indicated that he scored below the tenth percentile in Vocabulary, Speed of Comprehension, and Level of Comprehension, and at the thirteenth percentile on the English Expression test. National norms were used for criteria. The counselor suggested that Tom's deficiencies in vocabulary, reading, and English probably affected his performance in college and on the College Board tests, and that as a result his potential was probably higher than the CEEB scores indicated. Tom was urged to complete the reading-improvement program and a remedial course in English before he returned to college the following year.

Tom was then scheduled to take vocational tests, and the results were discussed with him during a second interview before he left the college to return home. Test data indicated science and medicine to be his best choices. Nevertheless, he decided to change from the pre-med program to one which would leave open the greatest number of vocational opportunities. The Edwards Personal Preference Schedule, completed at the same time, indicated high manifest needs for Deference, Order, Autonomy, Abasement, and Aggression, and low manifest needs for Achievement, Affiliation, Dominance, Change, and Heterosexuality. The results indicated that Tom showed a tendency for self-criticism and feelings of inferiority, a need to defer to the judgment of others, and at the same time a need to be independent of other people in making decisions, a need to have things organized so that they run smoothly, and a predisposition to hostility and aggressiveness toward others. The results also indicated that Tom had no great need to achieve or accomplish something of significance, nor a need for change in activities or experiences.

Because Tom planned to leave the next day, it was decided to defer a discussion of the significance of the Edwards Preference scores until the following September. On leaving, Tom confirmed some of the indications of the Edwards scores by stating that he had, from the beginning, felt that the pre-med program was probably the easiest program at the college. He had received this impression not from the program itself but from his feeling that he was lucky to get into college in the first place and that he would not have been permitted to enroll in any but an easy program. He seemed surprised and disbelieving when the counselor told him that the pre-med program was probably the most difficult program in the school. Before leaving, Tom agreed to return to the Counseling Center during the following September.

Tom returned to the Counseling Center in October of the following year, at which time he indicated that he was again having difficulties with his studies and that he was considering dropping out of school permanently. He was now enrolled in the Bachelor of Science in Social Science program. He indicated that he felt his problem was neither academic nor vocational, but that it was actually a fear of socializing with girls. This problem was discussed further in subsequent sessions with the counselor.

### Background Factors

In high school Tom was self-conscious and shy with girls, which he attributed to the fact that he did not play varsity football until his senior year. He played varsity baseball, but baseball received little publicity in the school. The student body showed little enthusiasm for the sport and gave little attention to the players, whereas the varsity-football players received a great deal of attention, especially from the girls. As a senior, Tom tried out for the football team and made it, but he continued to feel awkward and ill at ease in the presence of girls and continued to avoid them as much as possible.

In his first year in college, Tom did not socialize at all with girls. He kept telling himself that he did not need to, but he felt "social pressure" to date girls. Other male students were continually talking about girls and dating them. Many had steady girlfriends. Now he was beginning to wonder if he were "normal." He felt that if he really had a need to date girls, he should be able to force himself to do so.

He had indicated that he left school the previous year not because of academic pressure but because of his problem with girls and the pressure to date. He felt this pressure so intensely that he had begun to avoid the company of boys. He felt that any contact with boys would lead inevitably to talk of girls and dating. He also felt that if he left school he would be able to socialize more and his problem would disappear. During the year out of school, however, he did not socialize at all.

In a subsequent interview Tom began to talk about his brother, who was now on the high-school football team and receiving considerable publicity for his brilliant play. Tom was very much interested in his brother and returned home every weekend to watch him play. He indicated, too, that he went home as often as possible in order to be close to his home and parents. He wondered if his interest in his brother's football playing and his desire to be at home were possible indications that something was wrong with him. He said he often felt dejected on Monday morning because of the thought that he had a week ahead of him before the next Saturday.

He talked, too, about his father. His father had been an outstanding football player in high school and was still known and respected in his community for his football prowess. Football had been and still was his father's greatest interest. He attended every high-school football game and was very proud of Tom's younger brother. The conversation in the home centered almost exclusively on football. Every game was planned in advance and discussed during the week that followed it.

Tom talked of the pressures he had felt to participate in sports, especially football. His father always supplied him and his brother with all the equipment needed to participate in the major sports. Tom recalled wanting to quit the football team in high school because his studies were suffering but changed his mind after talking to a friend of his father who told him that his father would be greatly disappointed if he quit the team. He recalled, too, the frustration he felt as a baseball player. He was captain of his team and played rather well. Yet he received little publicity and always felt that baseball was never as important to his father as football. He said, too, that his father had not asked him about his college grades in some time, but that when he did ask, Tom would become angry because it showed him that his father had no faith or trust in him. Tom then volunteered the idea that perhaps his brother contributed to his problem, that he would not be so tense and anxious if his brother were not playing football or if he were doing poorly on the team. Tom repeatedly said that if he could have been outstanding as a high-school football player his life would be better now.

In these sessions Tom indicated that he could not talk easily to his father, who was critical and impatient with him. He had criticized Tom's baseball playing and, in a joking way, criticized his lack of socializing with girls, topping this off by calling Tom "queer." His father constantly complained that Tom would not listen to him. Yet Tom hesitated to do anything that would reflect on his mother and father. He would not drink or even enter a bar for fear of scandalizing them.

### Analysis

Obviously, in the case of Tom, there were a number of inextricably interwoven conflicts and frustrations which caused anxiety. Some of the conflicts are quite common among adolescents. The fear of socializing with girls and the social pressure to date are familiar phenomena on the college campus. In Tom's case the anxiety resulting from his social immaturity led him first to avoid contact with fellow students, then to leave school for a year, and finally to seriously consider dropping out of college altogether. It led him also to question his morality. He said, "If I really had the need, I should be able to force myself to date girls," and his father added to the problem by calling him "queer." His anxiety caused him to return home each weekend and to spend time with his parents as a spectator at high-school football games, when his fellow students would normally be dating girls. It also sent his thoughts back to high school and to his failure to play well as a football player and thus to lose his chance to be popular with girls.

The conflict between independence and affiliation is also present in Tom's case. The need to be independent of his parents had already emerged. Evidence of this need can be seen in Tom's insistence on paying for his own clothes, in his questioning of his desire to return home as often as possible, in his performance on the Edwards Personal Preference Schedule, and in his father's statement that Tom never listens to him. Yet his need for the security of the home is revealed in his desire to return home each weekend.

Obvious, too, is the conflict between success and fear of failure. In Tom's case, it is more complicated than usual. Tom came to college with feelings of inadequacy; he felt lucky to get into college and found it hard to believe that the pre-med program was one of the most difficult. He came to college striving to succeed. His grade average at the beginning of counseling was slightly better than C, which would create little self-esteem. He began to doubt whether he was bright enough to do any better and then started to withdraw from contact with fellow students.

Even if he were outstanding, he did not anticipate that his father would show any great pride in his achievement. His father was not a college graduate; his self-esteem was derived from success on the high-school football team, and thus he valued success in football above success in studies. He showed little or no interest in Tom's work in school, a fact confirmed in a talk with the mother and father. As a result, Tom was pursuing a goal which he felt had little value in his own home, and he began to question the value of a college education.

This conflict led him to think more and more of his high-school years. College students who are failing or doing poorly and consequently receiving little self-gratification and esteem often return in their thoughts to their high-school successes. In Tom's case, however, thoughts of high school were not all happy. As already noted, in high school Tom was less anxious because his lack of socializing with girls was more acceptable. Also, he did participate in school activities (including baseball and football) and did rather well in his studies. Yet he was anxious because he was not outstanding in football and because he received little praise or publicity for his baseball playing.

The conflict wtih his father was a serious one in Tom's case. The father's intense preoccupation with football and the attention he gave to Tom's younger brother could only leave Tom with feelings of inferiority and rejection. His attempt to gain acceptance can be seen in his trying out for the football team and staying with the team even when it began to interfere with his studies; in his returning home each weekend to become part of his father's interest in football and his brother's success; in his stated intention of trying out for the college football team; and finally, in his fear that drinking and going into bars might bring scandal to his parents.

There was also hostility, hostility toward the father and toward the brother; and in addition, there was guilt stemming from his hostility and from his feelings of envy toward his brother. Finally, there was some evidence for the repression of sexual impulses in his fear of frequenting bars and drinking, in his fear of dating girls, and in certain responses to items on a sentence-completion test and in his figure drawings.

## Counseling Approaches

Counseling with Tom took many forms. During more than twenty sessions, the counselor discussed with Tom the question of his normality in heterosexual adjustment, the effects of social pressure, the problem of social immaturity, and the means of overcoming shyness and developing relationships with fellow students and girls. Problems in adjusting to college, factors important to academic achievement, the effect of anxiety on performance, the reaction to poor performance or failure, and the development of the self-concept and its influence on behavior and on interpreting reality were considered. Also, the causes of conflicts with parents, how to understand parents, and approaches to be used for gaining greater freedom and responsibility were brought into the discussions.

The counselor attempted to help Tom to develop insight concerning his problems and the possible etiology of his symptoms, feelings, attitudes, motivations, and ego defenses. He tried to create an atmosphere in which Tom would feel free to talk, one which was more permissive and accepting than Tom found at home. He provided an opportunity for Tom to overcome his feelings of loneliness and to release his tensions by talking about his problems, doubts, attitudes, and uncertainties. And he gave Tom a chance to ventilate his feelings of hostility toward his brother and father and to accept these feelings with less guilt and self-criticism.

Through positive transfer the counselor presented views and values contrary to those of Tom's father and tried to instill in him the desire to do something about his problem and to try out tentative readjustment plans for coping with his social immaturity, his conflict with his parents, his poor academic achievement, and his feelings of inferiority.

The counselor also provided a great deal of support and encouragement. He attempted to bolster Tom's self-regard by giving him assurance with regard to his normality, his academic potential, and his ability to cope with his own problems. And finally, he attempted to manipulate the environment through a long discussion with Tom's parents. He indicated to them how they might be contributing to Tom's problems and how they might help Tom to overcome them.

*Outcomes*

What were the results of counseling? In the final sessions, Tom showed far less anxiety and an increased self-confidence. The basic conflicts still existed but they were not as severe. His feeling of inadequacy continued but he was showing a greater capacity to act. There was a rededication to his studies and a greater initiative in making contact with people his own age. He began taking dancing lessons and joined a parish group of young people. In his conversation, there were far fewer disparaging self-references and self-comparisons with others. He was beginning to dream less of success and to think more realistically of the means of achieving goals. There were indications of more self-control being exerted over everyday experiences.

Three signs, perhaps, pointed more definitely to a better adjustment. He began going home on weekends with less and less frequency. During his last semester's work in school he received excellent grades: one A, two B+'s, and three B's. In commenting on his school work, he said, "I've got something to go to school for now." During one of his final sessions with the counselor, in response to a question, he indicated these three wishes: (1) to succeed academically in college; (2) to develop happy and pleasurable relationships with boys and girls; (3) to find a worthwhile vocational goal in life.

## Counseling the Sexually Confused Adolescent
(ALEXANDER A. SCHNEIDERS)

The concept of sexual confusion can mean a number of things, but whatever its particular meaning in a particular context, we can be sure that it applies to a great many teenagers. What with the numerous and pervasive physical, emotional, social, and other changes of the adolescent period, plus the upsurge of sexual drives themselves, plus the influence of environmental and cultural factors, it is a wonder that more adolescents do not become sexually confused.

Sexual confusion can mean uncertainty regarding one's sex identity and the role or roles one is expected to play in the drama of adolescent life, and later on of adult life. This confusion is not an uncommon experience for adolescents, as many counselors and psychotherapists will testify. But it is probable that the majority of teenagers manage to reach adulthood with a fairly clear idea of themselves as men or women and of the roles they are expected to play. Sexual confusion can also refer to the uncertainty the adolescent experiences regarding the meaning of sex for him or her as an adolescent, the relation of sex to future roles, the relation of sex to accepted canons of morality, the nature of the sex drive and of sex behavior, and the limits that one should observe in sex behavior and relationships.

This kind of sexual confusion is most common among teenagers, if not actually universal. In view of the fact that many adults are uncertain about the role of sex in their lives, experience considerable embarrassment, shame, and guilt in connection with sexual behavior even in marriage, and find it extremely difficult to discuss sex especially with their own children, it is not at all surprising that some adolescents should become confused in their efforts to cope with this complex problem. It is this complexity of sex, its intermingling with practically every other facet of human life and personality, and its deep meaning for the future roles that the adolescent is expected to play, that makes it easy for the teenager to become confused in this area. Also, of course, there is the fact that the puritanical and Jansenistic attitudes in our American culture tend to stamp all sex and sexual behavior with the quality of sinfulness and wrongdoing. In addition, the adolescent cannot easily avoid being confused by the paradoxical attitude of society toward sex, with its strict moral codes on the one hand, forbidding almost any form of sexual expression to the teenager, and on the other, implicitly or explicitly condoning sexy movies, salacious novels, public nudity, and public immorality. As counselors, we must take all of these facts and circumstances into account if we are to help the teenager cope with the sex problem.

Following is the case of a young girl, whom I shall call Francy, who was a freshman in college at a private girls' school and who was referred for counseling by the Dean of the college because of "emotional upset."

## The Case of Francy

When first referred for counseling, Francy was an attractive dark-skinned, 18-year-old freshman from an Italo-American background. She was of average height, with a trim, well-dressed figure, and a flashing smile that belied the emotional conflicts she was experiencing. Francy was the youngest of three girls and the third to attend college in her family. Her father was a professional man of considerable standing in the community, and her mother had been a school teacher. The father was a lonely and somewhat discouraged man because of marital disappointment, and the mother had undergone psychiatric treatment some years before, with a diagnosis of obsessive-compulsive neurosis. The relationship between the mother and father was not particularly good, but there had never been an open break. Part of the difficulty in the relationship revolved around sex relations. Francy loved both of her parents, but she tended to identify more with her father than with her mother, although there was no confusion in sex identity. Francy knew that she was physically attractive, and she was not above using physical charms for purposes of gaining attention.

Francy's chief complaint revolved around feelings of guilt and shame and a somewhat pervasive scrupulosity that reminded the counselor immediately of the mother's neurotic structure. Let Francy tell the story in her own words:

"You know, doctor, I'm all mixed up about certain things, especially sex, sin, how to act toward boys, and my relation to God. I suppose it all revolves around sex actually. When I go out with a boy, and I let him put his arm around me, or hold me close, or kiss me, I just don't know how to react. It's all very pleasant and exciting, but at the same time I get these awful feelings of shame and guilt. I feel that I have let God down, and that I have no business praying to Him, going to church, or even receiving the Sacraments. This scrupulosity thing can really bug me. Sometimes I feel horribly guilty even when I let a boy hold my hand or give me a brief good-night kiss.

"That's what really confuses me about sex. I haven't the faintest idea of what I can do, what I can't do, what is only a small sin, what is a mortal sin, when I have passed over the border as it were from acceptable behavior to unacceptable behavior and so on. Why is petting wrong? Is a short kiss all right and a long kiss wrong? Why is it wrong to enjoy physical contact of any kind? What is wrong with sexual pleasure? How can it be wrong when you're single and all right when you're married? Didn't God invent sex, and if He did, what is wrong with it? Are sexual thoughts wrong always? Is it wrong to desire something that is so natural and attractive? These, and a thousand other questions like them, have bothered me ever since my junior year in high school. And the worst of it is that no one has come up with any satisfactory answers."

Here we have a typical instance of the sexually confused adolescent. This attractive girl was torn by guilt and shame and degraded by self-loathing and self-rejection. At the same time the promise of sex lured her on with irresistible attraction. At times she was on the verge of forsaking her moral and religious values and abandoning herself to sexual freedom and libertinism. Devoutly religious, she sometimes wondered how she could reconcile the surging needs within her body with her fervent commitments to God. She wondered, too, how the raw facts of sex and its unwanted companions, guilt and shame, could be fitted into the framework of love and marriage. Such conflict is sexual confusion in its starkest form, and its unhappy victim cries out for understanding and relief.

What do we do in a case like this? How does the counselor help the client resolve the paradoxes and contradictions posed by clients like Francy? Is the counselor equipped to deal with such confusion, or is this problem primarily in the area of moral theology?

Fortunately, Francy was an intelligent girl, with some sophistication regarding the realities of sex and anxious to resolve the difficulties that she was experiencing. In a surprisingly short time, she abandoned her scrupulous attitude and began to accept sex as a part of reality. She learned how to divorce sex from the concept of sin, while retaining her moral safeguards against sexual misconduct. Her attitude toward God brightened considerably, and her religion took a new lease on life. She now feels that she has fitted sex into the pattern of her life independent of destructive feelings like guilt and shame. This sort of therapeutic development does not happen too often, but when it does it is striking testimony of the effectiveness of therapeutic counseling.

# PART VII

## *Counseling the Adolescent*

▲▲▲▲▲▲▲▲▲▲▲▲▲▲▲▲▲▲▲▲▲▲▲▲▲▲▲▲▲▲▲▲

# 33. Identifying Problems for Counseling

## EDWARD V. DAUBNER

The literature of psychology and guidance is replete with studies and discussions of the range and classes of young people's problems. Most of the classifications are sociological-environmental in nature; that is, they categorize problems either on the basis of the locus or phase of social activity in which the problem occurs or with regard to the aspect of environment with which the problem is associated. Other and less frequently used classifications are more psychological in nature, grouping problems on the basis of factors within the person himself.

What I propose to do in this paper is: first, to present some typical examples of the two types of groupings; second, to evaluate briefly each type; and third, to draw some conclusions regarding the value of such classifications for the practicing counselor.

## Sociological-Environmental Classifications

Let us first look at some categorizations which employ sociological-environmental rubrics. One of the most widely quoted of this type is that by Williamson (1939, pp. 180ff). Based on twelve years of clinical experience at the University of Minnesota during which he counseled approximately 10,000 high-school and college students, Williamson's grouping of the problems of youth falls into five main categories:

1. Personality
2. Educational orientation and achievement

3. Occupational orientation
4. Financial
5. Health

Subgrouped under personality problems are: social maladjustment, speech adjustment, family conflicts, and discipline. Under the heading of educational orientation and achievement Williamson lists: unwise choices of courses and curricula, unequal scholastic achievement, insufficient scholastic aptitude, ineffective study habits, reading disabilities, insufficient motivation, overachievement, underachievement, and problems of superior students. Occupational orientation subsumes: uncertain occupational choice, lack of vocational choice, discrepancy between interests and aptitudes, and unwise vocational choice. Financial problems include self-support in school and college and student placement. Under the heading of health, Williamson distinguishes between problems arising from illness and poor health and those stemming from physical disabilities. As might be anticipated from the number of subheadings listed, Williamson rates problems of educational orientation and achievement as the most frequently occurring type.

The problems of approximately 1,900 high school students in St. Louis were studied by Pope (1943). She had each student describe his problems in an essay. A total of 7,103 were identified and grouped into six areas similar to Williamson's:

1. Study-learning relationships
2. Occupational adjustment
3. Personal adjustment
4. Home-life relationships
5. Social adjustment
6. Health

Pope's results indicated that, by far, the largest percentage of problems for both boys and girls in every grade was in the area of study-learning relationships. Study attitudes, educational guidance, physical conditions, habits of study, marks, and grades were also mentioned frequently. Problems of occupational adjustment ran a poor second, but, as might be anticipated, were mentioned more frequently in each succeeding grade from nine to twelve. The problems most frequently mentioned in the area of personal adjustment were feelings of inferiority and superiority. While only 3 per cent of the boys and 2 per cent of the girls mentioned health problems, Pope reported an increase in concern over sex matters in the upper grades. Although the differences were slight, the percentage of boys who mentioned problems in the areas of study-learning relationships, occupational adjustment, and health was higher than that of girls. The percentage of girls was higher in the areas of personal and social adjustment. Boys and girls were equally concerned about matters pertaining to home life, social adjustment, the future, money, religion, and health and development.

In contrast with the findings of Williamson, social problems were reported most frequently, with school and home-life problems a distant second and third, in that order. More than twice as many girls as boys were concerned about social and home-life problems. Girls mentioned school problems slightly more often than boys. However, problems concerning the future and health and development were listed by three times as many boys as girls.

In a study of guidance in 611 elementary schools in nineteen states, Huslander (1954) reported that in kindergarten and first grade, personal-emotional problems were most numerous, whereas educational problems were few. There were some social problems, but, of course, no vocational problems. In grades two, three, and four, personal-emotional and social problems continued to predominate; however, educational problems began to increase in frequency. In grades five to eight educational problems joined personal-emotional and social problems as being most frequent, with a noticeable increase in the incidence of vocational problems.

Sociological classifications such as those of Williamson, Pope, Lewis, and Huslander tend to raise more questions than they answer. How do we know that a problem which Williamson classifies as educational or social would be so labeled by Pope or Lewis? Since the investigators themselves freely admit this difficulty (Williamson, 1939, p. 186), what do these discrepancies do to the confidence which we are justified in placing in the reported results? Certainly, some of the obvious discrepancies in these results are undoubtedly due to discrepancies in classification.

Assuming for the sake of discussion that everyone is in agreement about which problems should go into which categories, of what profit is this type of sorting to the counselor? Three students may report that they are experiencing difficulty in concentrating on their school work. All three would be classified as having problems of educational adjustment. But, what is the real value of this pigeonholing? For the first student, lack of concentration may come from anxiety; for the second, it may be due to poor health; and for the third, it may stem from lack of good study habits. Since the problems of the three students are obviously quite different, what has been gained by labeling them all as problems of educational adjustment?—certainly nothing, as far as helping these students cope with their difficulties. Any counselor who would attempt to handle all three cases in the same manner would be guilty of poor practice, to say the least. It is difficult to understand how any practice in guidance and counseling can be justified if it does not contribute to the all-important goal of helping the troubled student.

To take another example, few students report just one problem; most mention several (Bordin, 1946, pp. 174–175). A student may indicate that he does not like school, that he has trouble making friends, that he has trouble making up his mind about the future. Such a student would be classified as having problems in three categories—educational, social, and vocational. But how does this labeling help the counselor in counseling? Again, the answer is that it doesn't. Suppose a second student reported the exact same complaints. They would be placed in the same three categories. But the first student's problems might all arise from a single cause, whereas the second student's problems might all proceed from quite a different cause or, what is much more likely, from a complex of causes. Again, nothing has been gained in helping the student since the counselor must obviously handle each case in a different manner. Classification of problems which cannot be justified on the basis that it helps the counselor to help the student is, at best, a waste of time and effort.

Categorizing problems by means of environmental factors is admirably illustrated by the late Arthur Jones in his frequently revised classic of guidance literature, *Principle of guidance* (1951, pp. 57–61). Operating on the premise that there are typical conditions out of which problems develop, he groups these conditions into eight general areas:

1. Health and physical development
2. Home and family relationships
3. Leisure time
4. Personality
5. Religious and church affiliations
6. School
7. Social
8. Vocational

Under each general area is listed a variety of specific conditions, ninety-nine in all, out of which problems are likely to arise.

For example, under the heading of social factors, Jones lists such conditions as antisocial tendencies, rebellion against authority, unreasonable parental restrictions on friendship with the opposite sex, and low ideals of civic responsibility. In connection with school, he mentions ineffective study habits, feeling of boredom, fear of failure, and inordinate preoccupation with extracurricular activities. Included under home and family relationships are parental domination and neglect and unwholesome physical, social, and moral home atmosphere. Under personality, Jones places such so-called environmental conditions as delusions, emotional instability, and lack of aggressiveness! No attempt is made to indicate which classes or which specific conditions are the most frequent occasions of problems.

Aside from the fact that some of the specific conditions listed are obviously not at all environmental in nature (for example, delusions, fear of failure, rebellion against authority), and that some of the conditions could have been placed just as logically under another general heading (for example, unreasonable parental restrictions on friendship with the opposite sex could be listed under the heading of home and family relationships instead of social), such a system of classification gives the writer the uncomfortable feeling that problems are regarded as fundamentally and entirely environmental in origin. Hence, guidance and counseling are a matter of studying the person's environment to determine what conditions are giving rise to problems in his life and then of taking the necessary steps to eliminate or change these conditions. For example, if a student is experiencing difficulties with a certain teacher, his schedule is rearranged so that he does not have this particular teacher in class. Now, there are some human problems which unquestionably have their basis in environmental conditions. A child who is underweight, continually tired, and sickly from lack of nourishment caused by parental neglect or dire poverty has an environmental problem, and the only way that it can be resolved is by modifying the child's environment. However, not all problems are of this kind. Sometimes, the source of difficulty does not lie entirely in the environment, but wholly or partially within the person himself. In the case of the student who is having difficulties with a teacher, the source of trouble may not reside in the student-teacher relationship viewed objectively, but rather in the student's attitude toward the teacher. In such a case, manipulation of his environment is futile. If the student believes that the teacher "has it in for him," even though objectively this may not be the case, nothing will be gained by changing him to another teacher because the real problem, the student's attitude, has not been dealt with. Instead of changing his environment, he must be helped to gain a better understanding of himself, with the hope that as he achieves greater insight, he will effect a change in attitude. The counselor who uses an environmental classification would do well to heed Jones's own words of warning: "The center of each problem lies in the individual . . ." (1951, p. 58).

The use of problem check lists represents a special case of grouping problems on an environmental-sociological basis. Probably the most widely known and used instrument of this kind is the Mooney Problem Check List (Mooney and Gordon, 1950). Published by the Psychological Corporation, it is available in four forms: Adult, College, High School and Junior High School. The device consists of a series of statements such as the following:

Poor complexion or skin trouble
Having less money than my friends have
Not being allowed to use the family car
Embarrassed by talk about sex

In the high-school form, there are 330 such items grouped into eleven areas:

1. Health and physical development
2. Finances, living conditions, and employment
3. Social and recreational activities
4. Courtship, sex, and marriage
5. Social-psychological relations
6. Personal-psychological relations
7. Morals and religion
8. Home and family
9. The future: vocational and educational
10. Adjustment to school work
11. Curriculum and teaching procedures

The student is asked to read through all the statements once and underline those problems which are troubling him. He is then requested to read over the underlined statements and circle the ones which are of greatest concern to him.

Although the Mooney Problem Check List has been employed in

many investigations of the problems of youth, time permits mention of only one. Mooney himself studied the problems of about 600 high-school students in Asheville, North Carolina (1942). The results revealed that students tended to have constellations of problems in certain areas. The highest number of students reported constellations in the areas of vocational and educational future (90); finances, living conditions, and employment (87); and adjustment to school work (87). Roughly grouped, in second place were personal-psychological relations (63) and health and physical development (55). Social and recreational activities (36) and curriculum and teaching procedures (32) occupied third place. The areas with the fewest constellations were social-psychological relations (24); home and family (18); courtship, sex, and marriage (17); and morals and religion (14).

Another instrument of the same kind as the Mooney Problem Check List is the Youth Inventory, published by Science Research Associates and "constructed under the auspices of the Purdue University Opinion Poll for Young People, with the cooperation of more than 100 high schools, and over 15,000 teen-agers throughout the country" (Remmers and Shimberg, 1949, p. 1). The Inventory consists of 298 statements and questions similar to those in the Mooney instrument. According to the Examiner's Manual, the Inventory was administered to thousands of students in all parts of the country. The results indicate that the concerns of young people can be classified into eight major divisions. The eight categories listed in order according to the mean number of items checked in each category by the students in the normative group are shown in Table I (Remmers and Shimberg, 1949, p. 12). The specific

### Table I

**Eight Categories of Problems in the SRA Youth Inventory***

*Listed in order, according to the mean number of items checked in each category by the students in the normative group.

(*Source:* Remmers and Shimberg, 1949, p. 12).

| Categories | Mean Number of Items Checked |
|---|---|
| 1. After High School | 12.05 |
| 2. Getting Along with Others | 10.04 |
| 3. About Myself | 9.42 |
| 4. My School | 7.38 |
| 5. Boy Meets Girl | 6.64 |
| 6. Things in General | 6.36 |
| 7. My Home and Family | 5.76 |
| 8. Health | 3.94 |

items in each area which are checked most frequently are indicated in Table II (Remmers and Shimberg, 1949, pp. 15–18).

Certain limitations should be kept in mind when problem check lists are used to classify problems. First, the problems reported are those about which the student is concerned at the moment. Experience teaches that what is particularly bothersome at one time may be of little moment at another. Problems tend to change as the student passes from one stage to another. For example, Pope (1943) found that problems of occupational adjustment as well as concern over sex matters were mentioned more frequently in each succeeding grade from nine to twelve.

### Table II

**Items in the SRA Youth Inventory, Checked by Thirty Per Cent or More of the Students in the Normative Group**

(*Source:* Remmers and Shimberg, 1949, pp. 15–18).

---

*My School*

1. I have difficulty keeping my mind on my studies.
2. I wish I knew how to study better.
3. I wish I could be more calm when I recite in class.
4. I would like to take courses that are not offered in my school.
5. I feel sleepy in class even when I've had enough sleep at night.
6. I have difficulty keeping my mind on what goes on in class.
7. I would like to get some practical work experience.
8. I have difficulty expressing myself in writing.
9. I have difficulty expressing myself in words.

*After High School*

10. What are my real interests?
11. What shall I do after high school?
12. For what work am I best suited?
13. How much ability do I actually have?
14. I would like to know more definitely how I am doing in my school work.
15. I want to know more about what people do in college.
16. Should I go to college?
17. How shall I select a college?
18. Can I get into the college of my choice?
19. Do I have the ability to do college work?
20. What courses will be most valuable to me later on?
21. What career shall I pursue?
22. What jobs are open to high school graduates?
23. How do I go about finding a job?
24. Am I likely to succeed in the work I do when I finish school?

*About Myself*

25. I have trouble keeping my temper.
26. I worry about little things.
27. I can't help daydreaming.
28. I often do things I later regret.
29. I feel that I'm not as smart as other people.
30. I worry about tests.

*Getting Along with Others*

31. I want people to like me better.
32. I wish I could carry on a pleasant conversation.
33. I wish I were more popular.
34. I want to make new friends.
35. I need to develop self-confidence.
36. I want to learn to dance.
37. There aren't enough places for wholesome recreation where I live.
38. I get stage fright when I speak before a group.
39. I don't have a (girl) (boy) friend.

*Boy Meets Girl*

40. I seldom have dates.

*Health*

41. I want to gain (or lose) weight.
42. I want to improve my posture and body build.
43. I want to get rid of pimples.

*Things in General*

44. How can I help to make the world a better place in which to live?
45. I'm worried about the next war.
46. What makes people selfish or unkind?

Second, it should be remembered that the data obtained from the use of such check lists will vary considerably from one part of the country to another, according to the sex of the respondents, from rural to urban and suburban areas, according to socioeconomic level, from one ethnic group to another, and, even from one intelligence level to another. For example, girls have been found to have more problems than boys, and with increasing age the number of girls' problems increases, whereas for boys the number decreases. Girls are more likely to be concerned about marks, grades, teacher criticism, family relationships, social adjustment, and personal appearance. Boys tend to be more troubled about finances, vocational plans, health and physical development, and conflicts with parents. Students of low intelligence tend to report many more problems than those of high intelligence, and the problems of the low-intelligence group center around personal adjustment, emotional maturity, and self-acceptance.

Third, the possibility always exists that students may falsify their responses. It is naive to assume that the problems reported by students are necessarily their real concerns. Anyone who has had experience in counseling knows that the initial difficulties mentioned by the student are rarely the ones which really promoted him to seek counseling. Rather, they are likely to be trial balloons which the student uses to see how the counselor will react and to judge if it is safe to bring up more serious matters. Such presenting problems are apt to be respectable. A student who has a sex problem does not walk into the counselor's office and blurt it out. He is usually embarrassed to admit he has a sex difficulty, because he has been conditioned to believe that "nice" people do not have such troubles. Since he wants the counselor to think he is "nice," he usually begins by bringing up some "safe" problem, such as not doing well in school.

Hence, it is probably wise to interpret the results of studies of student problems based upon check lists and other self-report devices with considerable caution. It is difficult to accept as factual these results of studies which supposedly show that high-school and college students are much more concerned with problems of educational adjustment than they are with those concerning heterosexual relationships, courtship, sex, and marriage. A study by Holman (1955) seems to confirm this suspicion. In an investigation of the attitudes of adolescents toward seeking help with personal problems, she found that although young people are willing to discuss problems which are "safe" and relatively impersonal, they are reluctant to ask counselors and teachers for help with more personal problems, such as boy-girl relationships.

As we review the various classifications of problems mentioned previously, we are struck with the fact that what we really have been talking about up to this point are not problems but symptoms. When a student reports that he feels uncomfortable in a group or that he feels as though he cannot talk with his parents, he is defining symptoms, not problems.

Psychologically, a person has a problem whenever he is blocked in striving for a goal or when he is frustrated in his attempts to satisfy a need. The block or frustration may arise from some factor within himself or in his environment or in both. Symptoms are misdirected attempts to overcome the block or frustration or, if you prefer, faulty efforts to adjust to an uncomfortable situation. The bright youngster who earns all "A" grades and who is the answer to every teacher's prayer but who is not accepted by his peers is frustrated in regard to one of his basic psychosocial needs. This unsatisfied need is his problem. It may manifest itself in many ways. For example, he may give up trying to gain acceptance and withdraw into his own subjective world, or he may try to win approval by deliberately playing dumb in order to get lower grades if he thinks that his high grades are preventing him from being accepted. These are his attempts to overcome his frustrations. These are his symptoms, the indicators of his problem. Since it is axiomatic that we must not treat symptoms, there is a real danger that the counselor may be misled into mistaking symptoms for problems when using instruments like problem check lists or student-written essays in which they express their concerns.

### Psychological Classifications

This brings us to the second kind of classification mentioned at the beginning of this paper—one based not on social and environmental conditions but on factors within the person himself. Since a problem has been defined as the frustration of a need, one logical way of grouping problems based on factors within the person is according to his needs. Although there are countless statements of needs—children's, adolescents', and adults', any one of which would do nicely, depending upon the level on which the counselor is operating—Maslow's hierarchy of needs seems to be quite satisfactory for all purposes (Maslow, 1954, pp. 80–98). The grouping of needs is referred to as a hierarchy because, according to Maslow, needs are emergent; that is, when the needs at one level are satisfied, another and higher level emerges to motivate the person. Upon satisfaction of these needs, a still higher level emerges, and so on. Listed in the order of their emergence, these needs are:

1. The physical needs for food, sex, activity, and the like.
2. The need for safety, for a peaceful, orderly, predictable world.
3. The need for belonging and being loved, for close and affectionate relationships with others.
4. The esteem needs for self-respect, as well as the respect and appreciation of others, based on one's own accomplishments.

5. The need for self-actualization, for the full realization of one's potential.

6. The need to know and understand the world.

7. The aesthetic needs for beauty and harmony.

Whenever satisfaction of one of these needs is blocked, the person experiences a problem. The ways in which he attempts to get around, through, or away from the block will be manifested in his symptoms. The factors which produce the block in the first place are the causes of the problem.

One trouble with identifying problems by means of needs is that there is a tendency to overextend the concept of needs. There is a tendency to confuse needs with wants. A need is something which is necessary to physical well-being, psychological integration, or both. A want is something desired, craved, or wished. Every need is wanted, but not every want is needed. If a person is hungry, he craves food; but he may want a million dollars and still not need it. In the former case, if he cannot get food to satisfy his hunger, he has a real problem. In the latter instance, the person can get along without that much money, and if he learns to do so (and most of us do), he does not have a problem. If we categorize problems by means of needs, care must be exercised that we do so on the basis of real needs and not pseudoneeds.

Individuals in a particular culture are expected to do certain things of which they are capable by virtue of the fact that they have reached a certain stage of development. Although individuals differ in their rate of development, there is sufficient similarity among different developmental patterns to determine which tasks a person should ordinarily be able to perform at different ages. Such tasks are called developmental tasks. If a person is able to accomplish the tasks appropriate to his age, he will meet with happiness, success, and social approval in his present stage of development and will be prepared to tackle the tasks of the next developmental period. On the other hand, failure to perform these tasks will lead to unhappiness and social disapproval in the present period, as well as difficulties in performing the developmental tasks of later periods.

For children of school age, the developmental tasks are:

1. Widening the self-concept to include membership in social groups other than the family and neighborhood playmates.

2. Learning to function in peer groups.

3. Breaking the habit of total dependence on adults.

4. Learning one's sex role.

5. Developing physical skills in games and sports.

6. Learning the ordinary concepts necessary for effective functioning in daily life—time, distance, quantity, manners, cooperation, duty, work, and the like.

The onset of adolescence presents the individual with new tasks. In our culture these tasks are:

1. Developing new and more mature relationships with one's peers of both sexes.

2. Learning to accept one's role as a male or female.

3. Learning to accept one's physical assets and liabilities, and to make good use of one's physique.

4. Increasing one's independence and responsibility for self.

5. Achieving increasing financial independence.

6. Developing an interest in and making plans for one's future occupation.

7. Preparing for marriage and family life.

8. Developing the skills and concepts necessary for civic competence.

9. Developing behavior patterns which are socially and morally acceptable.

10. Developing a philosophy which will be a guide to a happy, productive, satisfying life.

Since all children and adolescents in our culture are faced with the necessity of accomplishing these appointed tasks, and since the failure to master them results in unhappiness and maladjustment, they offer the counselor another convenient means of classifying problems on the basis of factors within the person himself. It should be noted carefully that because all children and adolescents are confronted with developmental tasks, and because the working out of any task involves a certain amount of frustration, even when the task is eventually mastered, all children and adolescents will experience some problems in connection with developmental tasks. Such problems, however, are normal and should be distinguished from abnormal ones. Thus, an adolescent's resistance to adult authority is a normal and usual part of his attempt to achieve greater independence and self-responsibility, but if such resistance has not abated by the time he reaches twenty-five, it probably indicates an abnormal situation. The fact that boys want to play only with boys at a certain period of their development is quite normal.

If, however, at age nineteen or twenty, a young man wants only the company of other young men, it should cause the counselor to think twice about the course of his heterosexual development.

This is probably as good a place as any to call attention to the unpleasant fact that some adults—parents, teachers, counselors, clergymen—confuse normal behavior (normal, that is, in view of what can be expected at various developmental stages) with that which is abnormal. To state it simply, they see and create problems where they really do not exist. Conversely, and somewhat ironically, they are usually unable to detect problems that actually do exist. The teacher who regards Tony as one of his problem students because he speaks up in class and gets into brawls on the playground, and the principal who rewards quiet, retiring, studious Charles for being the outstanding student in the school, despite the fact that he has no friends or companions and never takes part in any activities with his classmates are typical examples of both situations. In one well-known study (Wickham, 1928), a number of teachers were asked to rate different kinds of undesirable conduct among the children in their classrooms in order of relative seriousness. Several psychiatrists and mental hygienists were then asked to rate the same kinds of behavior. The ranking by teachers from most to least serious was:

1. Immorality, dishonesty, and transgressions against authority.
2. Violations of orderliness in the classroom and lack of application to school work.
3. Extravagant, aggressive behavior.
4. Withdrawing, recessive behavior.

Mental hygienists and psychiatrists ranked the same kinds of behavior as follows:

1. Withdrawing, recessive behavior.
2. Dishonesty, cruelty, temper tantrums, and truancy.
3. Immorality, violations of school-work requirements, and extravagant behavior.
4. Transgressions against authority and violations of orderliness in the classroom (Wickham, 1928, p. 130).

In his conclusion, the author states: "Attacking types of conduct are regarded by teachers as the most undesirable forms of behavior, while many unhealthy tendencies of withdrawal and dependency are not recognized as symptomatic of maladjustment" (Wickham, 1928, p. 181).

While it may sound facetious, one of the main sources of problems of children and adolescents are people—more specifically, adults who fail to understand them. For example, the elementary-school teacher who lacks comprehension of a child's need to vent his energy in physical activity will have many children in his class whom he regards as problems because of their restlessness. The father who demands unquestioned obedience will regard his adolescent son's occasional attempts to challenge his authority as a serious problem, simply because he does not understand the youth's need to assert himself. Teenage girls chatter continuously and giggle almost as much. Such behavior may be difficult to put up with in the classroom, but it can scarcely be considered problem behavior. The question that might be raised in such instances is: who has the problem, the youngster or the adult? Referring again to the previously mentioned study on teacher ranking of behavior problems, the author observes that

. . . teachers' reactions to the behavior problems of children are largely determined by the direct effect which the behavior produces on the teachers themselves. Insofar as the behavior attacks the teacher's moral sensitiveness, personal integrity, authority, and immediate teaching purposes, it becomes recognized as a problem in behavior; insofar as behavior is agreeable to teachers, respects their authority, fits in with their teaching purposes as well as their ethical beliefs, it is considered desirable behavior (Wickham, 1928, p. 181).

Just change the word "teacher" to "adult," and the moral becomes immediately obvious and generally applicable.

## Conclusion

Let me state clearly that I am not in complete sympathy with attempts to classify the problems which students bring to the school or college counselor. The reader has probably surmised this approach already. Classifications are assayed, ostensibly, for the purpose of diagnosing the student's difficulty, so that the counselor may take the necessary steps to help the student deal with his problem. Such a diagnosis is usually centered in the counselor; that is, it is his view, his perspective, his notion of what the client's problem is. I am not opposed to diagnosis in counseling, since obviously someone, either the counselor or the student, must figure out what is bothering the student if anything intelligent is to be done about it. But I am opposed to the counselor taking full responsibility for such a diagnosis, not primarily because the counselor's diagnosis may be incorrect—although that is certainly an ever-present and considerable risk—but rather because it interferes with what we consider to be the fundamental purpose of counseling, that is, to help the student achieve a better understanding of self and consequently to assume greater responsibility for his own life.

When the counselor is busy trying to diagnose the student's problem and fit it into some preconceived classification, he is not likely to be listening perceptively to what the student is saying. He is likely to be concentrating on the way the problem looks to him, which is unimportant, instead of attempting to perceive how the problem looks to the student, which is all-important. As long as he is concentrating on his perception of the problem, the counselor will be unable to lead the student to a more realistic perception of himself, based upon the student's own insight into his difficulties. It is only when the student has achieved such insight that he will take the necessary steps to improve his own situation. Counseling which does not point toward helping the student assume responsibility for understanding himself and for initiating his own course of action fosters dependency, and as such, is a pernicious practice.

Classifying problems is a legitimate, worthwhile activity for those who write about guidance and counseling. It is probably a good exercise in academics. I question, however, whether classification serves any useful purpose for those who are engaged in the practice of helping students. Human problems are highly individual matters, and, even though they may look alike and thus be classified alike, they are different, if for no other reason than that they are the problems of different persons. As such, they cannot be treated in the same way. What, then, is the purpose of trying to classify them?

# 34. The Problem of Confidentiality

DESMOND P. McNELIS

Confidentiality is a problem. When given a secret by somebody else, we have to fight a natural urge to share it with a third person. The human mind seems to treat a secret just as the flesh deals with a foreign body. There is an internal reaction to it leading toward its rejection or elimination. We are familiar with such phrases about secrets as, "I'm dying to tell someone," "It's eating me up," "If I don't tell someone I'll bust." What motivates such inclination to share is not too clear, but one could guess that as most secrets (certainly in the counseling situation) deal with what is considered wrong, shameful and dark, or forbidden, the content is bound to resonate with repressed feelings, desires, and impulses of the listener, who then seeks vicarious satisfaction in relating the material to someone else. When a child discovers that his little brother has stolen the cookies, he delights in telling his mother about it, implying, "I also wanted the cookies but I didn't steal them."

It is well-recognized that children are very poor at keeping secrets. If we don't want to spread confidential matter around we keep it from children. Inability to keep a secret is childish and immature. Keeping a secret requires a maturing of the ego, and inability to do so indicates a weakness of the ego boundary. We are not surprised, then, to find that many psychotics have a markedly diminished capacity to keep anything private. It is salutary for you and me working in the field that we do have this capacity to keep a secret and that we remind ourselves to be mature and adult in dealing with confidential information. But a counselor's failure to keep a secret can be rationalized. On the pretext of teaching, or of being scientific, or of speaking anonymously, or even worse, of being amusing at the expense of our client, we can frequently manage to get rid of a secret with a clear conscience. Counselors, therefore, should establish clear principles of their own on the question of confidentiality. A very good principle to have is to talk about the client as if he were listening to your conversation about him. The more conscientious you are in this matter with your client, the more trust, confidence, and cooperation you will receive from him. You cannot help but convey in your attitude and manner the respect you have for him.

If you are in training and under supervision, and the client's communications are, by the nature of the situation, going to be passed on to another, your client should know this and should consent freely to it. It is all too easy to presume that the patient understands that what he tells you will be shared with your supervisor, or the team, or others. It is surprising how seldom the client really anticipates this transfer of information.

The client may give general permission for you to pass on information, but may treat certain items with reserve and ask specifically that these items be kept completely confidential. In this case you are morally obliged to keep this particular information from others. This, of course, poses a difficulty with inexperienced counselors because the secret information may hold the key to the general understanding of the patient and be of extreme value to the supervisor.

The biggest conflicts in the counseling situation arise on the question of confidentiality in relation to authority figures, especially to parents or guardians and teachers or superiors. I mentioned earlier that we don't expect children to keep secrets. Somehow, inversely and perversely, we seem to feel that the young are not deserving of confidentiality. The temptation to tell a mother of the revelations of her young child is particularly strong, and yet nowhere is the presence of trust and confidence more important. At our outpatient child-guidance clinic at the Seton Institute, the psychiatric residents treating the children never meet with the parents. Contact with the parents is maintained through the social worker alone. This arrangement has been developed from the experience that when the child knows that his doctor is talking to his parents he automatically believes that the doctor is betraying him to them and the result is usually the child's distrust and resistance and suspicion of adults in general.

You who counsel young people in schools and colleges have learned that their difficulties are principally with authorities, parental and academic; and you as counselors have to be—if not on the side of the angels—at least perceived by the clients as being incommunicado with the authorities. It is not sufficient to do unto others as you would have them do unto you. A piece of information that at first seems perfectly neutral and innocuous, may in fact be of exquisitely painful importance to the client. There is a classic case in psychoanalytical literature of a girl under analysis who gave a very lurid and lively personal history but whose major conflict lay in the fact that as a child she had had tuberculosis and this, in her particular culture, was her most horrible stigma; and yet she conveyed the information most casually. You might meet a student who feels the same way about menstrual cramps, or angry thoughts, or jealousy of a sibling—something that to you has not the same emotional meaning. You have to make sure that you see these matters from the client's point of view.

If one were asked to name the essential ingredients of the psychotherapeutic, guidance, or counseling situation, the answer would be interest, understanding, and the creation of confidence. A client's problems have to be listened to attentively. Only with continued interest and concentration can patterns, trends, conflicts, and behavior be understood. Only in being understood, and in being interesting as an individual to the counselor, can the client enter into the deeper area of trust and confidence.

Eric Erikson, in his book *Childhood and society,* regards basic trust versus basic mistrust as the first of the eight ages of man, and the achievement of basic trust as the first and the most fundamental requirement to the development of hope, mental health, and happiness. Basic trust is achieved by the infant through exposure to the understanding interest of mother and father, leading to consistent behavioral attitudes on their part toward the child.

It is well to remember that anyone sufficiently troubled to seek professional counseling already feels sensitive, vulnerable, and less than complete. The human being derives a great deal of his security, individuality, and sense of ego integrity from his realization that he has sole possession of many private thoughts and feelings—secrets that are part of his ego. Again, it is not surprising that in the disintegrated psychotic a very commonly expressed idea is that everyone can read his mind. The sense of personal loss and damage produced in the psychotic by this feeling creates in him immense anger, anxiety, and even terror.

One might compare the human individual to a pyramid; the broad base of this pyramid represents the common internal and external experiences shared with everyone; for example, the power of movement and sensation, the experience of appetites and satisfactions, and the like. In a narrower, higher plane there are still many common though less universal denominators, such as race, sex, age, culture, and education. At the peak of the pyramid, giving a final form to the whole structure, are the entirely individual experiences, internal and external, psychic and physical, which make the individual, at least to himself, truly an individual. It is this individual area we attempt to breach when we invite the client to share his confidence. And not unnaturally, we are met with a great deal of ambivalence from the client when we seek his confidence. Certainly, the greater the suffering of the client the more willing he is to expose his innermost self. He judges, rather correctly, that his conflicts are most likely to have arisen in the most private regions of his psyche. On the other hand, one frequently meets tremendous resistance to the process in patients who are markedly insecure or who are aware of a threatened disintegration of their egos.

We can imagine that no important confidence is ever given to the counselor unless the client has already identified to some degree with him—already coopting him, at least in part, as part of his own ego. The client is, in a way, still talking to himself, but now to a self presumed to be stronger and wiser than the original. As a practical point, when the client has doubts about the integrity of the counselor and directly asks about confidentiality of communications, he should be told directly that what he says remains a sacred trust. Whenever the client seeks more and more reassurance, it is useless to confirm yourself further; it is more helpful to say that you cannot verbally prove your integrity to him, that he will have to trust you if you are to help him, and then to comment on his marked anxiety on this point and perhaps have him attempt to explain his anxiety to you.

The law in regard to confidentiality deserves to be mentioned. In law the related term is "privileged communication." By definition, privileged communication is a right existing only by statute, whereby a patient may bar his doctor from testifying about his medical treatment and the disclosures which are an integral part of it. Privilege, when it exists, is a legal right belonging to the patient and not to the doctor. There are four basic criteria which must be met to justify privilege: (1) the communications must originate in a belief that they will not be disclosed; (2) the element of confidentiality must be essential to the full and satisfactory maintenance of the relation between the parties; (3) the relation must be one which, in the opinion of the community, ought to be sedulously fostered; and (4) the injury that would inure to the relation by the disclosure of the communication must be greater than the benefit thereby gained for the correct disposal of litigation.

In Maryland there are several areas of privileged communication defined by statute. Deriving from the old common law of England, communications between husband and wife and between lawyer and client are privileged. Privilege has also been established for many years for the accountant. Television, radio, and newspaper reporters have privilege with reference to their sources of news or information. In a bill enacted in 1957 privilege was established between priest and penitent.

Both the Hippocratic Oath and the American Medical Association Code of Ethics insist that a physician not reveal his patient's secrets; however, the American Medical Association Code of Ethics allows disclosure when it is required by local law. The law of the state of Maryland may require revelation in court of a patient's confidence to his doctor.

Governor Tawes of Maryland recently vetoed a bill passed by both houses of the legislature creating the status of privileged communication to the information passing between a patient and psychiatrist. His veto of this bill was encouraged by opposition to the bill from the State Bar Association, which argued that the bill went too far and that it was an infringement on their search for complete truth in court; and the bill was opposed by the Maryland Psychological Association, which argued that it did not go far enough because it did not include psychologists. Strangely enough, the bill was backed by the nonpsychiatric physicians of the state although they were not included in its provisions.

In no state of the union is there legislation to provide legal privilege for communications to social workers or guidance counselors. The function and purpose of the establishment of privileged communication are (1) to provide sanction to the silence of witnesses in court; (2) to establish the fact that the privilege belongs to the client and that the client then has the authority to waive the privilege, thus releasing the professional person from the sanction; and (3) to provide a means of erecting ethical standards in various professions. The likelihood of student counselors being involved in legal conflicts regarding confidentiality is minimal.

In our present-day culture, the problem of invasion of privacy— privacy of thoughts and confidential personal facts—is looming larger and larger. To avoid security risks, applicants for certain government jobs have for some time been obliged to undergo searching psychological and psychiatric examinations, involving broad private revelations by the candidate. It has also been the fashion in business and industry in recent years to subject aspiring executives to the same sort of screening. The material gained in such examinations is used to label the applicant as suitable or unsuitable for the job or for promotion. If the applicant refuses the examination, he is in most instances considered disqualified at the outset. In seminaries and novitiates for the religious life the same trend is apparent. It is probable that, with the increasingly intense competition for college entrance, applicants here too will some day be required to undergo psychological testing to help judge their suitability for entrance.

Granted that these principles are generally accepted, certain "side effects" are apt to arise which are not so desirable. First, there is created for people in general the implication that privacy is a diminishing privilege, that our society—particularly our educated and professional society—is suggesting that our psyches will have to yield the excessive coveralls of secrecy of the Victorian period and be allowed only a psychic bikini. Secondly, there is likely to be a diminished respect for privacy and confidentiality in general. Thirdly, the judgment of one's own integrity, stability, and worth is being taken away from the individual and put into the hands of psychologists and psychiatrists. The message seems to be clear that no man can any longer be his own judge. Finally, there is the fact mentioned earlier that ego strength is greatly bolstered by the possession of one's own secrets and privacy. If we think of ego strength as the glue which holds the whole personality together, then the processes of modern civilization which I have been describing generally tend to dissolve some of the adhesive qualities of that glue, and we all are a little less securely integrated. The increasing incidence of emotional disorders in this country may be a reflection of this fact.

It is the duty of the professions that concern themselves with mental health—psychiatrists, psychologists, social workers, and counselors in all fields—to counteract this trend by their own devotion to and respect for the confidentiality of their client's revelations. The trend toward diminished confidentiality should be resisted at all times. Nothing confirms one's qualifications as a counselor more than the seriousness with which he guards his client's secrets. If any professional person in this field treats confidences lightly and has little sense of ethical obligation, he should not be in the field. Such a person is probably indulging his own neurotic needs in his profession and has little or nothing to spare for the needs of his clients.

Technically, all material disclosed by the client is confidential, but there are degrees of confidentiality, and there are situations where confidentiality is forfeited by the client. In certain situations permission is freely given by the client to disclose confidential matter. There are, in addition, some situations wherein confidentiality may be ignored, even in the face of strong objection and direct sanction against disclosure by the client. I was recently told of a student counselor who was informed by a nineteen-year-old girl of a suicidal attempt that no one was aware of and of more recent thoughts of self-destruction; but because this girl told her counselor that she did not want anyone to know of this attempt because "they" would send her to a psychiatrist, the counselor kept her secret. A week later the girl killed herself.

It is easy, of course, to be wise after the event, but obviously this counselor was handed a situation that his training did not equip him to handle alone. Besides, the girl in all probability really wanted him to pass on the communication. But most important of all, in this instance the reduction of risk to the girl's life was a more important consideration than the principle of confidentiality.

There are other situations wherein confidentiality must be forfeited by the client. In such situations the client should be told, "If you do not communicate this information yourself, I will have no alternative but to pass it on"; or, "If you continue to do this, I will have no alternative but to inform the authorities." For example, if a high-school student informed you that he was taking drugs and that he belonged to a drug ring in the school, the preservation of the common good should take precedence over the principle of confidentiality.

Regarding the degrees of confidentiality, it is obvious that certain pieces of information are utterly neutral; for example, a student states that she had measles at the age of five. It may not be common knowledge, but obviously there is no expectation by the client that it will be treated as a secret. On the other hand, a child may state that his parents never have time to help him with his homework, and he may definitely not wish the parents to know that he made this complaint about them. We can use this example to illustrate the fact that although one has to keep information confidential, conidentiality does not prevent using such information. In talking with this child's parents later, the counselor can easily induce the parents to give the same information without any breach of confidence.

There are other instances in which the client will freely, spontaneously, and openly desire that the confidence be shared with others.

In fact, as we all know from experience, many students come to the counselor for the main purpose of using him as a mediator with parents or teachers.

However, there are more delicate situations where considerable skill in making a choice between silence and disclosure is required. Here is an example. A fifteen-year-old ninth-grade girl is referred to the counselor by her teacher because her grades are dropping without apparent reason. In the course of inquiring about her study habits, the counselor learns that her parents go out often in the evenings, and the girl, an only child, is left alone. When alone, she studies a little, watches television, and drinks—not much, not enough for the parents to notice any reduction in the liquor supply, but her drinking has continued for the period of a year. Here we need all the knowledge and experience possible to arrive at the right decision. In the final analysis, our conscience must be our guide.

When I started working on this paper I looked up the word "confide" in the dictionary. It is one of the beautiful words of the English language. It means to show trust by imparting secrets; to tell in the assurance of secrecy; and it comes from the Latin, *confidere,* which means to trust absolutely. This is what our clients expect of us.

# 35. The Personality of the Counselor

JOHN R. McCALL

Are counselors born or made? This is a moot question. Some persons do seem to be born with just the right qualities, but all agree that even these so-called "born counselors" can improve through supervision and training. Before studying the personality of the counselor, we should explore briefly the nature and aims of counseling and some critical aspects of the counseling relationship.

Counseling is a face-to-face relationship by means of which something should happen to the counselee and also to the counselor. The aims of counseling are to help a student to adjust more adequately to his situation, to change the situation where it needs to be changed, and to grow as a person through better relationships with God, self, family, friends, and other significant persons. By its nature counseling should be a temporary arrangement. In the counseling process the student learns to cope with present problems, but through increased personal insight he should also become better able to face up to himself, to figure things out, and to learn to handle future problems with less difficulty. Otherwise, counseling can become a crutch.

Let us now consider some important aspects of the counseling relationship. First, the counselor is engaged in helping others in a professional capacity, but more important than his counselor's role is his role as a person. The counselor is a human being with personal weaknesses and problems of his own. This means that the counselor as a person should continue to develop the capacity to grow.

Second, the professional counselor is an expert in helping others, but he has no magic solutions. His technical training can be helpful only if there is also present a continuous effort on his part to grow in self-knowledge. The counselor should be gaining in self-knowledge as much as the students he counsels. If the personality of the counselor does not remain flexible and ready for growth, techniques of counseling become ludicrous. The counselor has the obligation not of being perfect but of continuing to increase his self-understanding and his awareness of strengths and weaknesses. This is done in and through the counseling relationship.

Third, each student whom we counsel is a unique expression of human nature—a unique incarnation of God. Respect for the worth, the dignity, and the uniqueness of the individual is the keystone of counseling. This attitude or philosophy alone makes sense out of counseling techniques. The student in my office is like all other students, like some other students, and really and truly like no other student.

When a counselor uses the same techniques indiscriminately as if all students were the same, he becomes a charlatan. This practice is one of the difficulties with following one school of counseling too closely. When techniques take precedence over persons, we run the risk of being charlatans. In good counseling the practice is just the reverse. Each student is a unique expression of human nature. The textbook never applies exactly. We can't plan perfectly. Each counseling session is a voyage into the unknown.

Finally, counseling is a workshop for both the student and the counselor. We practice counseling, and the growth that ensues should lead to better personality integration in both the student and the counselor. Neither the student nor the counselor should be the same after the counseling sessions have been completed.

What kind of personality should the counselor have or at least be working toward? The counselor should be a relatively mature person—a person with flexible strength, one who is able to work and to love adequately. One occupational hazard in school counseling is that most of us who go into this field are teachers—book people, who are rational, reasonable, and methodical. There is a strong tendency in us to be overly intellectual in our approach to counseling.

Some intellectual training for counseling is indispensable, but it is never enough. There is no direct correlation between the number of counseling books we read and our success in starting or maintaining a counseling relationship. Somehow the heart—the emotions—have to come into this relationship. The "educated heart" is necessary if we are to be accepting and understanding counselors.

The counselor must have a relatively warm personality. He must have the ability to relate well to other persons. Spiritual growth, personality growth, and growth in counseling ability always involve an increasing emotional warmth which makes the counselor capable of widening the range of persons with whom he can relate in a warm personal way.

The counselor must have a clear picture of self, a well-formulated identity. A personal identity is necessary for any relationship, but it is of paramount importance for counseling. In the counseling process there are two persons, each in his own rowboat. The rowboats can and must come close together. They float together in the same troubled waters, but each person, counselor and student, must have a boat of his own and stay in it. The analogy of a fishing ship grounded off Norway is a good one. As the tide goes out, the ship may well be broken on the rocks. Another fisherman lashes his ship to the one floundering and they ride out the change in tide. Then the ships are freed. There is a sharing of the plight but no loss of identity for either one.

The personality of the counselor must be able to sustain a certain amount of the maternal. Jung says each of us is composed of two components, a masculine animus and a feminine anima. In a man the animus predominates, but not to the exclusion of the anima. In a woman the opposite is true. Both a man and a woman counselor must be able to tolerate the maternal in self. A man who is unsure of his sex identity finds it too frightening to be considered a mother figure by the student. Likewise a woman counselor who is afraid of the maternal in herself may feel uncomfortable in the counseling situation and may continually try to be logical. Unfortunately, there is little or no logic in feelings.

The counseling situation is often analogous to the mother-child relationship, at least in the early interviews. How do we react when some students treat us as mother figures? Some counselors panic, others seem to love it. The first group is liable to structure too much too soon; they explain too much about the relationship. The second group allows the dependency to be built up too much; they encourage the mother-child relationship.

The counselor should be able to tolerate being a mother figure since he knows it is a projection of the student. In four or five visits the relationship can and should change and become more realistic. In the beginning the student in need of help may project onto the counselor a mother image with all that it means—omnipotence, omniscience, and a host of other qualities the counselor does not possess. The counselor need not protest too strongly. How did our mothers get over the image of omnipotence and omniscience we had projected onto them? They waited, and we grew up. They did not have to tell us they were not omnipotent; we found that out for ourselves. So does the student in counseling. When he no longer needs to see us as omnipotent, he no longer casts us in this role.

The counselor must have a sanforized personality that can tolerate stretching and shrinkage. He must be comfortable while the student sees him as nine feet tall. He must be happy when the student begins to see him as five feet five or five feet ten. This changing attitude of the counselee is another reason why the counselor needs to have a fairly clear picture of self without too much distortion.

The counselor should have a personality relatively free from anxiety. All persons, counselors included, go through periods of greater or lesser anxiety. It is a part of living. If we wait until we are anxiety-free before we counsel, it will be too late—we will be dead. However, some people have such a high level of anxiety that it interferes with the counseling relationship. How high is too high? If the counselor can prescind from his own anxieties sufficiently to build a good relationship with the student, his level of anxiety is not too high. This level is easily determined. If the counselor can put the student at ease and help him build a relationship in which he can lower his defenses, the counselor is not too anxious.

One of the best qualities a counselor can bring to his work is a sense of calm. The counselor can grow in this respect and learn to handle his own anxieties in such a way that they do not interfere with his counseling. As we grow in our counseling ability and learn to face our own problems, we can learn to forget ourselves, raise our level of activity, and spend less time and effort on self. Like pain, anxiety goes on even while we are busy.

The personality of the counselor should be mature enough to tolerate the destructive forces that are in all men. The anger, jealously, hostility, and aggression that are part of every personality are also a part of the counselor. Often in counseling sessions we see a student expressing these negative feelings. If we can accept these negative forces as a part of ourselves, we are much better able to accept the student who is temporarily storm-tossed by these powerful emotions.

On the other side of the ledger, the counselor should be able to tolerate the wonderful positive forces for growth in himself and in the student. The love, tenderness, and other positive forces in each one of us are also present in the student. These qualities are closely related. To acknowledge one's anger and hostility is to make one able to acknowledge his love and tenderness. Good counseling allows a person to free the constructive forces, both natural and supernatural, that are in all men.

The counselor's personality might be best characterized by the virtue of selflessness. His main function is to listen—probably the hardest human activity of all. It means to let another person have the center of the stage. He must increase; I must decrease. To listen and to leave oneself out is selflessness, and at times it is heroic. The more the counselor listens, accepts, tries to understand, the more mature he becomes. The number of words we speak is in inverse ratio to the quality of our counseling. Nonverbal communication is much better than excessive verbalization.

The good counselor has a consciousness that retains all past experiences. Research on creative persons reveals that they often speak of having had a difficult childhood. In reality their childhoods were not much different from the average. What is different is that they can make available to their consciousness the painful experiences of their early life.

If the main function of the counselor is to be warm, accepting, and understanding, we can see that it is easy to accept some students, for they seem to be very much like us. What, however, do we do with the students who are foreign to our personalities? The mature counselor is not revolted or disgusted by such persons. His own experience of being rejected, bogged down in vice, caught in the web of self-defeating behavior, help him to empathize. Nothing that is human is foreign to him. The availability of our own past experiences is a great help in counseling. It is the sign of a mature person. Block out childhood, and you regress to childhood and remain a child.

The good counselor can be alone—even enjoy being alone at times. He has inner resources and doesn't need to be constantly involved with others. Only if we enjoy and treasure our own privacy will we be willing to respect the privacy of the student. The student may prefer to be alone at a given time, not yet ready to communicate. If we decide beforehand that the student should be able to express his problems to us right now, in half an hour, and he cannot, we get angry at him for not playing the game.

The good counselor has a personality which is capable of nonverbal communication. How does the counselor show that he thinks the student has dignity and worth? This feeling is ordinarily conveyed through action rather than words. Liza Doolittle said, "Don't talk to me about love—show me!" We make a person comfortable, hold a chair, know his name—a thousand little things that say without words: I respect you, I like you, I value you as a person. The counselor is the host. His first concern is the student and his problem; the student cannot be selfless and thoughtful of the counselor just now. After hours of counseling he begins to see the counselor as a person.

In counseling something happens in a nonverbal way which is good. Go back in your own experience to several important interviews in your life. You had something bothering you. One after another people gave you the brush-off, the pat answer. Then you met someone, and you sat down and talked for half an hour with him, and in that period you began to see things clearly and to make your own decision. As you look back on that experience you feel a deep sense of gratitude that will stay with you the rest of your life. What did the person say? You don't remember, because it was mostly communication of a nonverbal type

The good counselor has a sense of humor. In a $100,000 study made at the Menninger Foundation in Topeka on the selection of medical students for psychiatry, one of the main findings was this: if the student had a good sense of humor he would probably be successful in psychotherapy. The same can be said of the counselor. One of the prime requirements is a sense of humor and the ability to laugh at the things we love and to go on loving them—especially ourselves.

The good counselor is capable of loving, and as he counsels he becomes more and more able to love. The relation between good counseling and the qualities of love are exemplified clearly in the life and work of Christ. He chose the qualities which would best reveal him. He left aside everything that would impress us—prestige, power, strength, wealth, nobility of race. Instead he chose love, tenderness, simplicity, weakness, fidelity. Those who do not love the poor, who are revolted by the sick, the wounded, and the dying; and those who do not love the misfits of the world are not capable of being good Christians or good counselors.

There is a risk that at a certain age we set the limits and determine for all time the extent of our love for others. We become too worldly-wise. We diagnose too well; we set up limits. But this way is not the way of real love. Love is being father and mother. To love someone is to summon him into life; to believe and to have hope in him always. A child really grows only when someone loves him. No one develops properly except in response to the love of another. Jesus loved Mary Magdalene to purity. He made up for all those who had not loved her enough. We condemn a person to sterility by refusing to love him. If someone did not love you, you could not have become the person you are.

Love is not blind. It is perfect lucidity. There are only two blindnesses: believing that people are bad, and believing that people are all good. Love is truth and lucidity. Each person, student, and counselor is stunted in growth if there is a lack of sufficient love. Through love a good counselor makes the counselee feel faith and confidence in himself. When we love, we hope for the loved one; but when we judge, we limit our confidence in him. When we limit the student to what we know of him, we reduce him to a cold perception and we cease to love him. If we do not love him, we cannot really help him. In counseling we try to love, imperfect as we are. We dare to love in a world that does not know too well how to love.

# 36. The Teacher as Counselor

EDWARD V. DAUBNER

Long before the advent of organized guidance services in education, adolescent pupils sought counsel from their teachers. Even though many modern secondary schools have special counseling personnel on their staffs, adolescents, on occasion, still go to their teachers for help with various kinds of problems. Whether or not this state of affairs is desirable has been and is presently a controversial topic among educators, psychologists, and other professional people who are charged with the guidance of adolescents. While teachers continue to counsel their pupils, to a large extent blissfully ignorant of the storm raging about their heads, school administrators, guidance experts, and others hotly debate the propriety of this practice.

Stated simply, the argument revolves around this question: Can a person function as a teacher at one time and a counselor at another without experiencing a conflict of roles? Or, to put it more pragmatically: Will the attitudes, responsibilities, duties, and expectations of a teacher interfere with his effectiveness when he attempts to function as a counselor? Obviously, such a question is quite germane to our topic. If teachers, precisely because they are teachers, cannot counsel effectively, then this practice should be discontinued immediately. If there are certain conditions which are necessary for teachers to counsel successfully, then such conditions should be clearly enunciated.

Before plunging more deeply into this controversy, let us make certain that we are thinking and talking on common ground. By a teacher, I am referring to a person who is engaged full time in instructing pupils in one or more subjects of the school curriculum—English, history, physical education, or other subjects. Such a person may counsel pupils voluntarily, or he may be assigned to counsel by the school administration. Although in some instances he may be allowed some time free from his instructional duties for counseling, in most cases he counsels on his own time, whenever he can fit it into his busy day.

By counseling I mean a personal, face-to-face relationship between two people in which the counselor, by means of his special knowledge and competencies and through the counseling relationship itself, provides an experience in which the counselee can achieve a better understanding of himself, his environment, and his relationship to his environment through a process of psychological self-exploration. The counselor provides a permissive, understanding, psychologically non-threatening atmosphere wherein the counselee is able to examine and perceive himself as the kind of person he really is without fear of criticism, evaluation, ridicule, or rejection. The counselor exerts every effort to convey to the counselee that he is concerned with understanding and accepting him and not with passing judgment on him. In such a climate, the counselee is able to learn and accept new things about himself. As a result, he realizes his potentialities more fully and becomes capable of dealing more adequately with his environment. Aside from establishing the relationship and creating the proper atmosphere, the counselor's task is not to do something for or to the counselee, but rather to make it possible for the counselee to do something for himself—to exercise self-direction.

If we accept this concept of counseling, and it is one which is quite generally accepted, many of the personal conferences which teachers have with individual pupils are not really counseling interviews, even though they are commonly so labeled. Most of these conferences—in which the pupil is given information of an educational, vocational, or personal nature; in which the teacher suggests, advises, urges, exhorts, or warns the pupil to follow a particular course of action; and in which the pupil is given encouragement, sympathy, or a piece of the teacher's mind—most of these instances are not counseling as we have defined it. I do not mean to imply that teachers should avoid doing such things. Certainly, there are times when pupils need information and encouragement. There are even times when they can profit from advice, suggestions, warnings, preaching, and sympathy, although their value is far less than is usually supposed. Some wit has observed that the worst vice is advice; and another has declared that it is only safe to give advice when you are certain the other person will not follow it! The important thing to note is that when teachers, or counselors for that matter, engage in such practices, they are probably not counseling.

**Some Basic Propositions**

With this brief clarification of terms in mind, we may now return to the question of whether a teacher can function effectively as a counselor. The answer as one might expect is not a simple yes or no, but a series of conditional propositions which I hope to delineate in the balance of this paper by examining some of the difficulties which teachers-counselors face.

Any discussion of the teacher as counselor must consider the factor of time. To teach well one must devote his full time and energy to teaching. A part-time teacher cannot be a good teacher. This is more true today than ever. The demands which current education makes on a teacher are far greater than those of fifty years ago. Only those who have taught in an elementary or secondary school can fully appreciate the expenditure of time and effort which modern educational curricula, methods, and mounting pupil loads require. If teachers counsel pupils, they must perforce do so principally at the close of the school day, after their mental and physical energies have been drained by the day's teaching. Counseling, too, is a task which makes severe demands on the counselor. To counsel well, one must be mentally and physically rested; one must be at ease, relaxed, and above all, alert. Teachers who attempt to counsel pupils after a strenuous day of teaching are fatigued. Counseling performed under such adverse conditions is not likely to be effective. Weary teachers do not make good counselors. Although some teachers may reach the end of the day with greater energy reserves than others, it is difficult to understand how any teacher who has just finished a full day in the classroom can have the energy and alertness to counsel well.

Contrary to popular belief, one cannot counsel effectively by merely having the desire to help people with their problems. Certainly, the urge to help is important as a motivational condition, but it is not of itself sufficient. I know that to many people counseling is somewhat analogous to kissing; most everyone does it at one time or another, and, furthermore, almost everyone feels fully qualified to do it! Be that as it may, one who would counsel well needs certain specialized knowledge and skills which are not normally possessed by everyone, not even by highly educated persons. I call your attention, for example, to the body of knowledge a counselor must have in the areas of testing, occupational information, and the dynamics of human behavior, and to the skills involved in establishing and maintaining a deep and understanding relationship with another person. Such knowledge and skills are not the birthright of everyone, and they are not likely to be possessed by a teacher unless he has undertaken some specialized education in psychology and counseling. To the extent that teachers are lacking in these qualifications, their participation in counseling should be both limited and cautious.

I think this is the logical place to consider how personal differences among teachers affect their ability to counsel. Although there is no generally accepted personality pattern considered necessary for a counselor to be effective, and although there is only limited and tenuous research evidence available regarding the specific personality traits considered desirable in the counselor, most authorities in counseling have definite notions of the personal characteristics which they regard as necessary counselor qualifications.

There is practically unanimous agreement, for example, that a counselor should have a deep, sincere, abiding interest in people. This interest should not be abstract, such as a philosopher, sociologist, or psychologist might have, but it should be interest in this and that individual person. The counselor's interest should not be restricted to the so-called conventionally "nice" people, but should include even those who are commonly regarded as being "bad" or undesirable. For the teacher who would counsel, this requirement might mean that his interest should include the pupil whose sex behavior is deviant, or the pupil who is making life miserable by his antics in the classroom, or the student who belongs to the "great unwashed."

Almost all of the experts agree that a counselor should have a genuine respect for the intrinsic worth of each person. Again, this respect is not to be confused with a philosophical or theological respect of human nature in general (even though such a view may underlie his respect) ; rather, it is a practical attitude toward individual human beings. Moron or genius, paragon of virtue or habitual sinner, physically attractive or repulsive, each pupil must be regarded by the teacher who would counsel as worthy of his finest efforts. Each commands the same interest and respect. The problems, plans, and goals of the "dead-end kid" are no less important and merit no less attention from the counselor than those of the college-bound youngster from the right side of the railroad tracks.

The consensus among authorities is that the counselor must be tolerant of human foibles and ambiguities. He does not condone them; he accepts them for what they are—the fruits of fallen human nature.

To be able to accept, he must be the kind of person who is more concerned with understanding human behavior than with judging it. For example, when the teacher who would counsel is confronted with a pupil who has been disrespectful, who has failed to measure up to his ability, or who has stolen, his approach should be one of trying to determine the cause of such behavior, rather than of blaming or punishing the pupil. For many teachers, including Catholic teachers, who have been raised in and infected by the extreme moralism of our strongly Calvinistic milieu, this attitude may be extremely difficult to adopt.

There is complete accord that to be successful, a counselor must be the kind of person who radiates genuine warmth and friendliness. He must be one who naturally reaches out to others, who is not cold, forbidding, or distant in manner, who is easy to approach and converse with, and who invites the confidence of others, not by asking, but simply by being the kind of person he is. This trait is not something which can be play-acted, a role which can be assumed or dropped at will. Any sham is certain to be eventually detected and resented by the counselee. Although it is conceivable that a teacher might, by assiduous practice, acquire this trait, it is not a likely occurrence; either he is or he is not this kind of person.

The above should make it amply clear that some teachers might be handicapped in counseling because they lack certain requisite personal qualities. The point has been raised that everyone ought to possess such traits of friendliness and acceptance. These qualities are an ideal, and we can scarcely quarrel with it; but in practice they do not always exist, a fact with which we must reckon.

To be successful in the classroom, a teacher must be, to some degree, an authority figure. He is largely responsible for determining the knowledge, understanding, and skills which pupils will acquire and for seeing to it that they undergo the required curricular experiences whether they like it or not. He must evaluate how much each pupil has learned in comparison to other pupils. He must judge whether a pupil's conduct is "good" or "bad," conducive to learning or not. He must correct the pupil if he makes a mistake in learning, and, occasionally at least, he must discipline a pupil if his conduct is out of order. Such an authoritative posture is necessary for successful teaching, but it is quite inimical to effective counseling.

To counsel well, a teacher must permit and encourage freedom of thought and expression, as well as self-determination in action. It is the pupil who must decide what he wishes to talk about and what course of action he wants to pursue. The teacher's fundamental task is to communicate understanding and acceptance to the pupil. By this I mean that he must convince the pupil first, that a sincere attempt is being made to understand how the pupil perceives himself and his world and his feelings about them; and second, that the pupil is unconditionally accepted as a person worthy of respect and help regardless of his shortcomings and weaknesses. Obviously, such common, acceptable teaching practices as prescribing what the pupil will talk about, when he will talk about it, and what he will say about it; evaluating the correctness or goodness of his thoughts, words, and actions; and imposing discipline to regulate his behavior are completely at odds with what is expected of a teacher when he attempts to counsel. Instead of exercising authority over the pupil, the teacher—when counseling—must rigorously divest himself of it.

It follows then that a teacher will be successful as a counselor of adolescents to the extent that he will be able to disassociate himself from an authority role. Experience indicates that this task may be a difficult one. As a teacher, he has a tendency to dominate, control, order, prescribe, manipulate, evaluate, and sanction. As a counselor, he must eschew such tendencies entirely and concentrate instead on being permissive, nonprescriptive, nonjudgmental, and noncoercive. A teacher may perceive this yielding of authority as psychologically threatening to his own security in the classroom. He may feel, for example, that if he permits a pupil to express hostile feelings about him or some other authority figure, he is undermining his status as a teacher. But for successful counseling, this yielding of authority is exactly what is necessary. The teacher must learn to listen rather than talk. He must encourage the pupil to say what he really thinks and feels, not what he thinks the teacher wants to hear. He must learn to reflect the pupil's attitudes and feelings, rather than to criticize or evaluate them. He must learn to listen to the pupil's story, instead of telling the pupil what he thinks the problem is and what should be done about it. He must allow the pupil to direct his own affairs instead of making decisions for him. In short, he must abandon his role as one who leads and takes charge of pupils and assume the role of one who works with the pupil to help him become self-directive. This last statement leads us logically to the fifth difficulty which teachers face when they attempt to counsel.

When working in the classroom, teachers tend to think of helping the pupil in terms of doing something for or to the pupil and his environment. If a pupil is suffering in his school work because of poor home environment, the teacher attempts to effect a change in his home conditions. If a pupil is experiencing a personality clash with one of his teachers or classmates, the teacher may take steps to manipulate the pupil's school schedule so that he has little or no contact with this person. If a pupil cheats on examinations, special efforts are made to arrange the testing conditions so that he is unable to cheat. I do not mean to imply that such manipulations may not be desirable or even necessary at times. However, unless we are willing to reject the idea that "the fault, dear Brutus, is not in our stars, but in ourselves. . . ," we must recognize that a manipulative approach does not always strike at the core of the pupil's problem. Sometimes there is absolutely nothing a teacher can do about changing a pupil's environment, and sometimes changing the environment is not the best solution even if it is possible. In such cases, the only feasible course is to help the pupil understand his situation, as well as his attitudes, feelings, and other personal factors which may be contributing to it, with the hope that as he achieves greater insight, he will effect changes in himself which will result in a more satisfactory adjustment to his exigency. Teachers who would counsel must learn that the help which is afforded in counseling is basically not the kind in which the pupil's environment is manipulated, but rather the kind which enables the client to reach a deeper understanding of himself and his conditions and thereby to initiate his own measures of coping with his problem. To hew to this line will be difficult for some teachers, since their previous experience as well as their compassion for those in trouble exert strong pressure on them to do something more concrete and tangible for the pupil, a temptation which they must learn to resist.

Although it is true that in modern education we talk much about individual differences among pupils, and the teacher is exhorted from all sides to tailor his work in the classroom to fit the particular needs, abilities, interests, and characteristics of individual pupils, the fact still remains that in everyday practice, he regards the pupil, fundamentally, as a member of various social groups, such as ninth-grade class, the student body of the junior high school, the industrial-arts department, the lower middle-class social stratum, a certain church, or other groups. This attitude is to be expected, as one of the aims of formal education is to teach the pupil to become a worthwhile member of the various societies in which he must function both as a child and as an adult. As a result, teachers tend to regard the development of pupils from the standpoint of how well they are comforming to various group norms. Consequently, the teacher's efforts to develop the pupil's individuality are always tightly circumscribed by the objective of group conformity. The teacher is likely to look with favor on the pupil's differences only insofar as they do not conflict seriously with accepted group limits.

The teacher who would counsel is likely to approach the pupil in the same way. If he does, however, he will be negating one of the basic purposes of counseling. In counseling we are concerned with the pupil not primarily as a member of a group, but as an individual. It is not an either-or proposition, but a matter of emphasis. If a teacher would be true to the principles of counseling, he should not ask himself whether a pupil's attitude or contemplated action would be in conformity with this or that group, but whether the attitude or action would promote the healthy development of this particular person. Sometimes healthy development proceeds along the same lines as group conformity; sometimes it does not. When it does not, the teacher must be prepared to allow and encourage the pupil to exercise his individuality. By virtue of their education and their experiences, teachers are prone to be conformists rather than individualists. Hence, some who attempt to counsel find allegiance to the pupil's individuality a difficult pill to swallow. If they are unable to overcome this difficulty, their effectiveness as counselors will be seriously hampered.

Finally, one of the obstacles which teachers face when they attempt to counsel is that presented by the set of expectations about teachers which adolescents have built up over the course of their school careers. Even though a particular teacher may have an impartial respect for the worth of each pupil regardless of who he is or what he has done, even though he may be tolerant and understanding instead of judgmental and has learned to listen more than he talks, even though he may be able to keep confidences and does not attempt to run other people's lives, even though he may be this kind of person, the pupil may be so conditioned by his previous contacts with teachers of another kind that he fully expects this teacher to be biased, to be unable to see the pupil's point of view, to reject and condemn him, and to tell him what he should do. Expectations of this kind may cause the pupil to enter the counseling relationship in a suspicious, wary, antagonistic, or even hostile frame of mind. Although these attitudes may not be fatal to productive counseling, the teacher may need many interviews to overcome them. If the teacher has little skill in counseling, he may never be able to change the image which the pupil has of him.

## Conclusion

To conclude, I would not say that teachers should not counsel, but I am convinced that they face many serious obstacles when they do try to serve as counselors of adolescents. Of course, some teachers may be able to overcome these obstacles and to counsel effectively. Such teachers should be encouraged to continue counseling. Those who find most of the difficulties insurmountable should not be required to carry on with this type of work. Under no circumstances, however, should these teachers be made to feel that they are somehow lacking or at fault because they cannot counsel successfully. Both teaching and counseling are honorable professions, but they are not the same; and I am quite convinced that relatively few people are able to engage in both successfully. Certainly no one, without exception, should try to counsel within the framework of his role as a teacher. To do so is to court failure, if not disaster.

# 37. The Administrator as Counselor

PAUL J. CENTI

▲▲▲▲▲▲▲▲▲▲▲▲▲▲▲▲▲▲▲▲▲▲▲▲▲▲▲▲▲▲▲▲

The title of this paper carries the implication that various difficulties are presented by the situation in which a school official or administrator also serves as a counselor, and that there is perhaps something contradictory in the two roles which one individual is asked to play. The importance of the question need not be emphasized. It is obviously important on theoretical grounds. Can the administrator counsel effectively? It is important, too, for the practical reason that in many Catholic and public high schools counseling and administrative responsibilities are now invested in the same person.

There is also the implication that the problems which exist are unique to the administrator who attempts to counsel, that they arise when one person is both administrator and counselor. I am not therefore concerned with the administrator who helps the student to solve immediate problems by providing information or advice, but rather with the one who enters a true counseling relationship with a student, one who attempts to help a student to overcome certain limiting personality factors and to achieve improved adjustment and self-realization. Nor shall I be concerned with the problem of administrators who are not qualified to counsel. I shall assume he is qualified by training and experience for counseling, and that he is reasonably mature and well-adjusted.

Again, I shall not be speaking of all administrators. The administrative roles of some counselors do not negatively affect their work. Among such administrators are admissions officers and directors of placement. The administrators with whom I am concerned here are those who hold line positions of authority and whose responsibilities may include the discipline of students. Finally, I shall not deal with related questions of whether any counselor in an educational institution is ever actually free from the authority role, and whether he is ever regarded by students as being a counselor only and not as an instrument of administration. It is obvious to all of us that psychological counseling in an educational setting is not the same as counseling in a clinic or in private practice. The factor of authority permeates both college and high school and as such influences the counselor's work and the counseling program.

### The Perception of the Counselor

What, then, are some of the problems peculiar to the administrator-counselor in his attempt to help students? A student approaches any counselor with a mental set which affects to a considerable degree his relationship with the counselor during the counseling sessions. It affects the degree of his involvement in the relationship and his perception of all that takes place in counseling. This perceptual bias may be favorable or unfavorable to the counselor. It is partially determined by the student's attitude toward people in general or toward counselors in particular, but it is much more influenced by the counselor as a person. The student also expects certain outcomes from counseling. The factors which affect these perceptions and expectations are the counselor's personality, his reputation, his status in the institution, and the degree of familiarity between counselor and student. It is with the counselor's status that we are directly concerned since the administrator-counselor is an authority figure. Positions involving authority or disciplinary functions may, it is thought, interfere with counseling procedures because students are unwilling to bring their problems to an authority figure. Any good which the counselor does is in danger of being perceptually overshadowed and his acceptance by the student body weakened if he must also administer discipline.

Positions involving authority may also adversely affect counseling by preventing the confidence necessary to a counseling relationship. Effective counseling requires that students feel free to speak openly without fear of censure and to see the counselor as one who is sincerely interested in helping them with their problems. Administrators are not always seen in this light.

The administrative title, whether it be "principal" or "dean," suggests authority and implies institutional responsibility. As such, it may make students reticent to speak freely or may even make them suspicious. The knowledge that the administrator has responsible authority over students, and perhaps has even disciplined other students for the infraction of rules, may make the individual student unwilling to accept him in his role as counselor and thus destroy his effectiveness in counseling. The Code of Canon Law acknowledges this same difficulty in its prescriptions that Superiors or Masters of Novices do not serve as Confessors unless freely sought by their subjects. Also, Spiritual Directors in seminaries have little or nothing to do with discipline. The same problem is reflected in the present concern of college administrators for the priest who also serves as a disciplinarian. At some colleges, for example, priests are being replaced by upper classmen as corridor prefects in residence halls, while the priests function solely as spiritual counselors.

The difficulties presented by the conflict of roles may be lessened after initial counseling sessions, and especially if the administrator is skilled in establishing rapport. Nevertheless, no matter how skilled the counselor or how appealing his personality, he is perceived as an authority figure and this perception remains a part of the relationship. Perceptually, a person's role cannot be easily separated from his personality.

It sometimes happens, too, that students involved in infraction of the rules are referred to an administrator-counselor. The student may arrange an appointment with the counselor, feeling compelled to do so because of the perceived administrative role of the counselor; or if he volunteers to enter into a counseling relationship, it may be because he sees this as the lesser of two evils, to be preferred to disciplinary action. Both situations are not particularly conducive to effective counseling. Being forced into the counseling relationship will likely cause the student to become antagonistic or even hostile. Effective counseling requires that the student wants help with his problem and that he comes to counseling voluntarily.

### The Administrator-Counselor

The perception of roles by the counselee is only one of the factors affecting the counseling relationship. It is quite possible that no one person can do complete justice to two or more roles. Holding an administrative position is usually a full-time job in itself, and by the same rule being a high-school or college counselor today requires maximum time and effort. If a person must play both roles, there is danger that one may overshadow the other, so that one or the other is slighted. In such situations, the role slighted is likely to be the counseling function because it is more easily set aside than the administrative responsibilities. The administrator often has difficulty in devoting the time necessary to intensive individual counseling, regardless of his interest or ability.

There is real danger, too, that the modus operandi of the administrator will be carried over into the counseling relationship. The administrator usually operates by making decisions, giving orders, or issuing directions. He is a person who expects obedience. These characteristics have little place in the counseling process. Certainly we can expect that the counselor who also has an authoritative role will become authoritarian in his relationship with his counselee. Yet it is generally agreed that criticism, reprimands, or impatience seriously interfere with effective counseling. The question is, therefore, can the administrator-counselor keep separate the two roles to which he is assigned? Can the roles of counselor and administrator be operationally separated?

This question is not easy to answer. The points of view usually associated with the administrator and the counselor are radically different. Administrators are more interested in the overt behavior or misbehavior of students, whereas counselors are more interested in the dynamics of behavior, the inner sources or frustration and conflict from which the behavior stems. In the counseling situation, too, counselees may be encouraged to express such feelings as anger; but such ventilation of hostility may well be interpreted by an administrator as evidence that disciplinary action is necessary.

There are additional problems for the person who has the dual responsibility for maintaining discipline and counseling at the same time. What sequence should be followed? Should counseling precede or follow discipline? Is discipline at all necessary when counseling is successful? By putting discipline first the counselor endangers both rapport and success in counseling. Further, if counseling is successful, it would seem that discipline is unnecessary. Yet the counselor may be forced by outside pressures or by the requirements of his office to discipline the student. Otherwise it might appear to the student body that misconduct has gone unpunished, a situation that would have adverse effects on the school's discipline.

Inherent in this duality is one of the most perplexing problems with which the administrator-counselor is confronted—that of conflicting loyalties. As an administrator, his primary loyalties are to the school, and it is his responsibility to carry out school regulations and policies. As a counselor, his primary allegiance is to the student, and his primary concern is to the integrity and welfare of the counselee. The Religious who serve as administrators are often caught in a similar duality whenever parental appeals for students are directed to them as Religious rather than as school administrators.

Persons in dual roles of this kind may often become involved in certain ethical problems. Everyone agrees that counseling must not be used as a means of gathering facts about students, of obtaining a confession to be used for disciplinary purposes. Yet, during counseling, information is often revealed which may suggest disciplinary action. The counselee may reveal that he or other students are violating certain rules and regulations. In this situation the administrator-counselor finds himself caught between his responsibility to the school and his concern for the students. The problem here is similar to that of the full-time counselor who is assigned to serve on academic committees which must evaluate and pass judgment on students whom the counselor has accepted as counselees.

Additional problems may arise when the administrator-counselor is also a priest. Hagmaier and Gleason (1959, pp. 40–45) point up some of the difficulties of the priest who attempts counseling. The priesthood is perceived by many persons as the embodiment of authority and primarily associated with instruction or admonition. The priest is expected to have all the answers to the problems presented by penitents or clients. Moreover, in the presence of the priest, people are anxious to show their best behavior, not their worst. Furthermore, the priest is handicapped in counseling because he spends so much of his time instructing, urging, persuading, and other exhortatory activities which may carry over into the counseling relationship. Indeed, just because he is a priest, there are times when he must be didactic and must admonish his client. His whole life is a commitment to authority, and therefore he may unconsciously expect the same commitment from the counselee. This expectation of obedience is strongly supported by the belief of some clergy that they have all of the essential answers, and thus they tend to react negatively when a counselee rejects their advice or the solutions offered.

## Some Positive Effects of Dual Roles

So far nothing has been said of the possible advantages of being both an administrator and a counselor. With regard to the last role discussed, that of the counselor who is also a priest, it should be pointed out that the role of counselor is one which the priest has held from time immemorial. He is typically perceived by his penitents as a counselor, and this perception instills confidence in students to approach him with their problems. They may feel less hesitant to talk freely because they know that the priest has dealt with similar problems many times and that whatever is revealed will be held in strict confidence.

There may even be advantages for the counselor who is also required to function as a disciplinarian. If nothing else, he has an opportunity to learn much more about the student who is referred to him for disciplinary reasons, and therefore he is in a position to administer discipline more objectively. In addition, since punitive discipline is seldom conducive to self-discipline, and since it is not based on the conflicts from which the misbehavior stems, the counselor-disciplinarian is in the unique position of being able to understand and cope with underlying causes of misbehavior. If things go well, he can provide counseling before and after disciplinary action. Also, there is always the additional possibility that the perception of the counselor as an authority figure may be supportive of the counseling relationship for students who react positively to authority.

Finally, the administrator-counselor is in a unique position to help provide an environment which will *prevent* problems from arising, and thus to promote the mental health of the student body. He can focus the attention of other personnel on the needs and problems of the students. Through the force of his position, he can influence the administration, faculty, and students to a wider acceptance of the counseling program, and he can provide effective leadership in the development of adequate counseling services.

## Some Practical Suggestions

In the foregoing discussion there are several implications of practical value for the administrator-counselor. First, he should attempt to dissociate himself from his authoritative role as much as possible. He may do this by avoiding an administrative title which is too imposing or forbidding or by avoiding the use of signs which label him and his office as an arm of the administration. In addition, he can locate his office apart from other administrative offices and avoid such obvious symbols of authority as a large desk, plush carpets, or heavy furniture. He should always work toward avoiding the reputation of a disciplinarian by engaging in as many nondisciplinary functions as possible.

The more the administrator-counselor is known to the student body personally, the less forbidding will be his administrative role.

Second, the administrator-counselor should not force any student into counseling nor permit anyone else to do so. Third, he should explain to the student who comes to him for counseling the responsibilities involved in his dual roles. The student should understand that the purpose of counseling is not to pass judgment on him but to help him with his problems. As always, the student should be given the choice of seeking counseling elsewhere; but if he chooses to continue in counseling, the administrator-counselor should occasionally remind the student (as well as himself) of his dual roles and responsibilities.

Fourth, the administrator-counselor should strive to create an atmosphere which is nonthreatening to the student, one in which he will feel free to communicate with the counselor. The counselor's attitude should be an accepting one, free of criticism; and if discipline is necessary, he should explain his action to the student while making clear his interest in and concern for the student as a counselee. Fifth, the counselor should provide enough time for counseling so that the student will not feel that he is being hurried, or be made to feel guilty about taking up time that the counselor should be devoting to other duties. The student should feel that the time in the counseling session is his and his alone, and therefore the counselor should not be interrupted during counseling sessions for administrative purposes.

Sixth, the administrator-counselor should always be ready to make a referral to a full-time counselor when he feels that the student is in need of help which he himself cannot provide because of limitations of time or of competency. Perhaps, to avoid role confusion, referrals should be made to persons in parallel capacities. The priest-counselor might well refer the counselee to another priest for Confession, or the administrator-counselor might refer the student to another administrator for answers to questions regarding administrative policies.

Seventh, in all situations the welfare and integrity of the student should be the administrator-counselor's primary concern. All records of interviews should be held in strictest confidence. They should not be used without the student's permission even when their use would help the student. No other person should be contacted concerning the student, or any action taken without his permission. Needless to say, the bonds of confidentiality may be broken—just as in situations with any professional counselor—when the counselor feels that there is serious danger to the student, to another person, or to the common good. Even in such situations, however, action should not be taken without first attempting to secure the student's permission.

Finally, in order to avoid creating any misunderstanding or difficulties with other administrators and teachers, the administrator-counselor should make known just what policies will determine the counseling function in the school. This rule is especially important with respect to the confidentiality of information secured through the counseling process. If these several suggestions are carefully observed, the school administrator should be able to function as a counselor.

# 38. The Professional Counselor

ALEXANDER A. SCHNEIDERS

This particular symposium on roles and relationships in counseling was conceived as an effort to help various key persons involved with the teenager to define their respective roles. It is a rather widely accepted truism in counseling philosophy that inadequate role definition, role confusion, or role diffusion are bound to leave adverse effects on the counseling relationship and the counseling process. Similarly, role mixture or complexity is likely to stand in the way of effective progress in the counseling situation.

A number of questions arise immediately in this connection. Is it ever possible, for example, for the teacher to be an effective counselor, especially of students in his own class? By the same rule, and even more to the point, can a priest, minister, or rabbi function effectively as a professional counselor? There are quite a few opinions on both sides. Many Protestant ministers are highly trained in the profession of counseling, and would certainly argue that their role as clergymen does not prevent them from doing effective counseling. The same is true of many rabbis. There are some Catholic priests—notably Reverend William C. Bier, S.J., a professional psychologist certified by the State of New York—who would argue most strongly that the primary business of the priest is to bring souls to God, and not to heal the mind or to mend the personality of the penitent. Bier argues that when these two aims are mixed together, both of them suffer, and the hapless client is victimized by this mixture of roles.

This is an issue not easily settled to everyone's satisfaction, but I can say from my own professional experience that many of my clients have reported that they could not accept the clergyman as a professional counselor. This attitude is particularly true of Catholics, who regard the priest as a confessor and therefore as a judge and find it impossible to divorce this role from the person himself. It is not easy, especially for young people, to think of a priest as a counselor who is supposedly accepting and nonjudgmental when one knows that he is at the same time a confessor. Unfortunately, this difficulty of dissociating one role from the other is heightened by the fact that the clergyman very often wears a distinctive garb which makes it perceptually impossible to think of him as anything other than a clergyman. In some few instances, clergymen have donned a layman's attire for this reason.

These difficulties apply with equal force to other groups whose primary roles are quite different from that of the counselor. The dean of men or the dean of women in a college or a university often finds it quite difficult to maintain a counseling relationship with students. This aspect has already been thoroughly discussed by Dr. Centi in his paper. But, in a more general sense, there are difficulties that stem from the counselor's identification with a group or organization. Religious, for example, are often shunned as counselors because of their identification in the mind of the student with authority figures or with an authoritarian organization. The counseling situation must be entirely free of the threat of discipline, punishment, or reprimand; and these qualities are often identified with certain groups of people. Unfortunately, this impression is often strengthened by the members of such groups who find it impossible to be accepting and permissive, and whose so-called counseling is laced with veiled threats, rejections, moralizing, and incessant advice giving. Such persons should beware of the counseling relationship because they often do more harm than good. Because of their own personal characteristics or limitations, some people simply cannot accept or countenance rebellion, sinful behavior, sexual anomalies, laziness, unruly conduct, or other signs and symptoms of maladjustment. Their moralistic heckles bristle at the first recital of such behavior deviations, and they begin to think immediately of disciplinary measures, reprisals, high-sounding principles, or moralistic straitjackets. You can easily test the presence of such characteristics by insisting to such a person that lying is as much an "adjustment" as it is an immoral act, or that rebellion against authority is simply one way in which the teenager is trying to find his way to maturity. The person with an authority complex will immediately insist that you are the one who needs the counseling more than the rebellious teenager.

Does this viewpoint leave room only for the professional counselor in the high school or college situation? Are teachers, administrators, and Religious of all kinds automatically disqualified for the counseling role? While the professional counselor is prone to give an affirmative reply to such questions, on the ground that the business of counseling should not be entrusted to amateurs any more than teaching or the ministry should, such exclusion would create a great many difficulties. Everyone knows that there are not enough counselors to go around, and with the exploding high-school and college population the situation promises to become worse rather than better. There is no way in the world to meet these needs of our teenagers without the help of auxiliary personnel.

Moreover, it could be argued that all persons, including the professional counselor, are to some extent disqualified for the counseling profession because of their own limitations, biases, prejudices, or lack of knowledge and skill. In other words, a particular teacher may be in a better position to help a teenager in trouble than would a professional counselor. Many such counselors (and teachers also) are themselves the fathers or mothers of teenagers, and therefore their relationship with the counselee will be conditioned by their own experiences, relationships, conflicts, and disappointments. As we have seen, the counseling process involves an intimate interpersonal relationship between two people that sparks an interplay of feelings, experiences, and perceptual reorganizations that deeply involve both parties to the relationship. Psychoanalysts have identified this sort of interplay as transference and countertransference, a concept which constitutes one of the most useful insights that the analysts have contributed to counseling theory. These involvements no counselor can escape; or if he does escape them, nothing will happen in the counseling process. The effective counselor knows that such relationships will develop and is ready to exploit them for the deeper purposes of counseling.

It is at this point that we begin to understand the role of the professional counselor in the high-school or college situation or in private practice. His role is seen to differ sharply from that of the amateur counselor. By reason of his training and his experience, the professional counselor should possess or acquire the knowledge and the skills that are needed to help others with special problems and that no amateur counselor could be expected to possess. How could an ordinary teacher be expected to recognize incipient psychosis? How could she learn how to identify and interpret significant symptoms? What would she know about the essential dynamics of guilt or scrupulosity? What does the ordinary guidance counselor know about the pathology of inferiority? How many teachers or administrators are acquainted with the dynamics of transference and countertransference in the counseling relationship? What does the ordinary teacher know about peer-group relationships, the shifting dynamics of adolescent behavior, the dynamic implications of family position, or the basic relationships between needs and feelings? How can the teacher be expected to develop the acceptance, the permissiveness, and the objectivity that counseling requires? How many persons are equipped by reason of their noncounseling profession to prescind from value judgments or from moralizing in a person-to-person relationship? These, and a hundred other questions like them, point up the importance and the necessity of professional counseling. Every school system should have access to the services of a professional counselor or therapist, whether his speciality be in the area of psychology or psychiatry. Invariably, the teacher and the administrator encounter problems that they can neither comprehend fully nor cope with effectively, and such problems should be referred to a person who is professionally trained for this type of work.

At this point let us make a distinction that we have deferred making for too long already. This is the distinction between guidance and counseling. In the course of their training, numerous teachers and administrators will acquire a certain degree of competence in dealing with human problems at the guidance level. There are countless teenage problems of this sort—problems that a wise and intelligent teacher, principal, or dean can handle with considerable skill. Not all human problems are embedded in a neurotic or psychotic substructure. Nor are all of them of a deeply pervasive nature or traceable to early traumatic experiences and relationships. In numerous instances all that the teenager needs is the opportunity to share his experiences, feelings, or hopes with a sensitive and discerning person. In other instances, what he needs is for someone to open up new vistas of thought, to clarify perceptions, to suggest a new approach to a baffling situation. There is a great deal of room within the panorama of teenage events for guidance, advice, or just plain sympathetic listening. And in these arenas of human problems the teacher and the administrator can play very important roles. But they must also be ready to spot more serious difficulties which may require counseling and therapy. They must be alert to danger signs and symptoms. They must be prepared to make a referral whenever such a referral is necessary. In many instances the teacher and administrator can be the bridge by which the teenager crosses over to counseling and therapy—and to a healthier personality.

# 39. The Psychiatrist's Role in Guidance and Counseling

DESMOND P. McNELIS

The role of the psychiatrist in guidance can be summarized as supervisory. Most psychiatrists have a built-in belief that psychotherapy, as they conduct it, is a superior product to that purveyed by psychologists, pastors, or counselors. Counseling would seem to be regarded as a palliative, supportive exercise which the psychiatrist regards many times with a patronizing air.

The psychiatrist is willing to supervise, in fact he seems to feel it his moral duty to leave no counselor unsupervised, and his supervision is apt to be slanted towards restraining the overeager and overenthusiastic counselor so that he won't get into areas beyond his competence, that is, in areas belonging to the psychiatrist; and the psychiatrist is sometimes also inclined to undervalue the positive factors in the counseling situation.

Now it is true that any client with an emotional problem who seeks a counselor's help is producing for his consideration a situation, a conflict, or behavior that has roots and ramifications that go beyond the usual, logical, conscious aspect of things. Moreover, the communication itself is delivered not only through logical verbal channels but also through nonverbal and other unusual modes as well. In other words, the interaction between the counselor and the client is modified by the unconscious influences not only of the client, but sometimes, unfortunately, also by the unconscious influences of the counselor.

The unconscious reveals itself in psychotherapy and counseling through five principal ways: slips of the tongue, free association, dreams, body language, and the counseling relationship. Through these manifestations we, and through us the patient, become aware of previously unknown forces affecting his life. It is one of the purposes of counseling to avoid the area of the unconscious. The counselor ordinarily is not equipped to cope with these matters by virtue of his lack of specialized training and supervised experience in this area. The counselor cannot avoid being exposed to it, and he may well be able to understand quite a lot of it, but there should be no effort on his part to interpret it, to remark on it, or to discuss it with the patient. Let us now elaborate on some of these five unconscious manifestations in more detail.

First of all there is the transference relationship, which involves the transfer or displacement by the client onto the counselor of feelings towards, and his concept of, some significant figure in his past life. The significant figure is usually a parent, and he frequently reacts to the counselor as if he were his father or mother. As a consequence, the counselor finds himself the object of reactions from the client that may be entirely uncalled for in his own right. The counselor may, and often does, exist in the concept of the client as an omnipotent, all-loving, lovable, nurturing (or conversely) a threatening, rejecting, and hateful person. These transference reactions have to be taken for what they are and are not to be taken personally. One of the most useful techniques of the psychiatrist in psychotherapy is interpreting the transference situation to the patient and having him see and understand the perpetuated, childlike attitudes that color his adult interpersonal reactions. Interpreting the transference is not in the realm of the counselor, but he should be aware of the possibility of a similar process in himself, directed toward the client—a situation which is known as counter-transference. Also, the client might report dreams he has had, but no attempt should be made to interpret them either, although again the counselor may well see significant meaning in the dream of which the client seems unaware.

By body language we mean all the ways that the soma or the physical organism can express the content and especially the unconscious content of an individual's mind. The term "body language" would then include anything from facial expression, body posture, and mannerisms to actual organic physical disease, which is the area of study known as psychosomatic medicine. Any emphasis on a repetition of physical complaints should warn the counselor that he is dealing with something beyond his field of knowledge.

This brings us to a most important question. In what circumstances can one decide that he should not be counseling a particular client and should instead refer him to a doctor, a psychiatrist, or another counselor? First, if the counselor feels that the client is seeing him unrealistically, if he has intense feelings for the counselor, either positive or negative, the counselor is involved in a transference situation with the patient. Second, if a marked proportion of the client's complaints are physical, for example, headaches, tiredness, stomach pain, dizziness, and the like, then counseling is not the appropriate approach. Third, any awareness of disturbance in the client's thinking, a feeling that he has some peculiar ideas, that he has attitudes beyond ordinary understanding, that he has eccentricities of thought or behavior that are abnormal —for example, an expressed feeling that everyone is against him or that he feels people can read his mind—should signal that we are dealing with a mentally sick person who should be referred. Fourth, any feeling in the counselor that his own personality has come up against something very distasteful or anxiety-provoking may necessitate ending the relationship. Fifth, the counselor should be alert to the possibility of abnormal depression in people who come for help. If a youth is sad and unhappy and cannot attribute this to any circumstances in his recent life; if he persistently downgrades himself; if he is sleeping badly; if he expresses hopelessness about improving, and especially if these symptoms are combined with vague physical complaints, then the counselor might prevent a suicide if the client is sent to a doctor as soon as possible, and he might literally kill the client with sympathy if he holds onto him.

Presuming then that the counselor has decided that he cannot help this person who needs psychiatric help, how does he inform his client? The counselor may come to his conclusion in the first five minutes of contact, but that is not the time to mention it. If the client is going to accept advice about referral, he must be made to feel that he has had a fair hearing. It is well to be frank, honest, and fairly direct with him. The counselor can admit that he has encountered a problem beyond his competency, that there are things going on in the client that the counselor does not understand, and that a psychiatric consultation would be of great help.

It is probably acceptable to most people to describe psychiatric treatment as a process of getting to know yourself better with the help of another person. It is more effective to be definite about the need for psychiatric treatment than to be tentative about it. The client may, of course, not accept advice about referral, and this is his privilege, but if the client refuses psychiatric treatment, one should not allow him to continue in counseling once the counselor has decided against it. One may also find himself in circumstances where the patient is not psychiatrically ill but there is no rapport, in which case the counselor should consider making a referral.

Counselors do difficult work and their skills are tested just as much as those of the psychiatrist. Like psychiatrists, they accept emotionally troubled people. They offer their time, attention, interest, privacy, confidentiality, and most importantly their respect. They reserve judgment on their client's worth, and strive hard to develop an understanding of his difficulty. They endeavor, temporarily at least, to forget their own needs and to focus exclusively on the needs of the client. They avoid the big pitfalls, primarily the error of giving advice. As we know, the good counselor leads the client to formulate and to follow his own good advice; and secondly, he avoids the ridiculously human error of trying to be liked, to be nice, to be likeable and to be wise in every instance.

The main problem for counselors, as for psychiatrists, is to maintain a continuous awareness of the personal quirks and idiosyncrasies that can enter into and distort the counseling relationship; to insure continually that it is the needs of the client that are being attended to and not one's own. If the counselor is sure that the focus of his efforts and interests is the client's needs, then the quality of his counseling may well be of the highest order and will compare favorably with that of any related discipline.

# 40. Significant Literature on Adolescents

ROBERT J. McALLISTER

ROSE MARIE DICKSON

EDWARD V. DAUBNER

## Literature on Adolescents for Parents
(ROBERT J. McALLISTER)

My first reaction to this topic was a rather negative one, and in spite of the fact that I have pursued it in some depth for this discussion, my reaction is still generally negative. This stems from the fact that I am somewhat dubious about the personal value derived from reading books in the mental-health field.

Undoubtedly, I have my private prejudices in this area. I have been influenced by the number of patients I have seen whose interest in psychological literature has added to their confusion and anxiety. One of the few rules I give to patients in treatment is to avoid books and magazine and newspaper articles relating to mental health or disease. In addition, I ask them not to watch TV shows such as *The Eleventh Hour* and *Breaking Point,* as well as *The World Beyond* and *The Twilight Zone.* These admonitions are particularly important for the suggestible teenager, although I have recently seen two adults whose illnesses were greatly influenced by programs they had seen on *The Twilight Zone.*

I do not have any professional opportunity to assess the value which healthy individuals may derive from personal readings in psychology. If there are those who obtain benefit from handbooks for self-analysis, they are naturally not seen in psychiatric practice. The successful ones must be found outside the psychiatrist's office.

There is another cogent argument against the value of reading to understand personal problems. Students of the psychological sciences, including psychiatrists, social workers, and psychologists, are not notably helped in solving their own personal emotional problems by the diligent pursuit of their studies. It is not an unusual experience in treating such people to have them acknowledge their complete inability to apply basic mental-health principles to their own lives. The personality growth which students in this field develop comes through personal supervision or the teacher-student relationship. I think it is safe to say that they gain little insight into their own emotional problems, and even less understanding of how to cope with them, from reading alone, even though this same study may give them a keen ability to understand and to help others.

For these reasons there is considerable difference between discussing literature on teenagers for counselors and teachers and literature on teenagers for parents. Of course, the literature for parents has as its purpose an improved understanding not of themselves but of their teenagers. Yet the problems of sons and daughters intimately involve parents. For the student in the mental-health field, general principles may come easily and provide deep understanding of neurotic interaction in marriages, pathologic parent-child relationships, and unhealthy response to needs on an individual basis. These principles can be applied to patients, clients, students, or counselors, as the case may be. Application to oneself or to better understanding of one's spouse, one's parents, or one's children is difficult. In situations where one is deeply involved, whether through countertransference or family ties, the objective application of mental-health principles fails. It is for this reason, more than for any medical ethic, that a psychiatrist would not treat a member of his own family or even a good friend.

Most parents who read the literature on teenagers can, I have no doubt, see the basic soundness of the principles involved. To apply these principles to their own teenager who is failing in school, going unbathed for long summer days, stealing from stores, refusing to go to confession and communion, or answering rudely every time he is spoken to can be a trying and tiring process.

There is yet another reason why I oppose giving books to parents to answer their problems. I fear that we in the mental-health field often undermine the courage of parental devotion, weaken the dedication of parental purpose, and impair the adequacy of parental thought. Books on this subject are usually full of so many platitudes that they must make the average parent doubt his basic ability as a parent. I suspect the average parent reading such books has one of two choices. He can deny the applicability of these principles to himself and his children, as is commonly done by students in the mental-health field. Or he can become so concerned about the need to apply these principles and about his own negligence and inability, that he is plunged into anxiety and insecurity and then communicates his new confusion to his teenagers.

Now, after having given all the reasons why parents ought not to read books on adolescence, I shall briefly discuss some of the books they might read. There is one type of book which I think the parents of adolescents definitely ought to have and to use. These are books on sex information and education. There is one particular paperback that I find most suitable, for it contains schematic drawings of the male and female reproductive systems, drawings of the union of egg and sperm and the development of the fetus, and finally, drawings of childbirth. In the area of sex education, it is most important that some visual aids be used to give adolescents a legitimate view which is not sexually stimulating, but which does much to assist their understanding of a complex phenomenon. The book I have in mind is *Accent on purity,* by Father Joseph E. Haley, published by Fides.

The number of books available to parents concerning adolescents is rather astonishing. In a regional public library of Prince George's County, there are approximately eighty volumes. When I consider that one volume might be confusing I shudder to think of the results if they read on and on. These books range all the way from badly conceived, naively presented, poorly written handbooks with so-called helpful hints to rather erudite, technical tomes which present, for example, the application of psychoanalytic principles to the understanding of adolescence. Such is the book by Peter Blos entitled *On adolescence,* published by The Free Press of Glencoe.

There were two books among this large selection which are a good representation of what might be profitable to parents. The first of these is *Patience and fortitude, the parents' guide to adolescence,* by a psychiatrist, Graham B. Blaine, and published by the Atlantic Monthly Press.

Dr. Blaine's book might have particular appeal for the parents who are moderately well educated and expect more than the "Dear Abby" approach to life's problems. His own stated purpose is to deal with what is known and "leave out the speculations of the specialists." He is also careful to explain that parents should not be blamed for all the problems of their children. His words would certainly be comforting to parents whose anxieties bring them to such reading.

As psychiatrist at University Health Services at Harvard and Radcliffe, Dr. Blaine is oriented toward school problems and perhaps overweights the book with his many pages on underachievement, reading problems, school phobias, and the like. On the other hand, this is certainly one of the most prominent areas of parent-adolescent conflict. His comments on the importance of a developed conscience and the stabilizing influence of religion are gratifying.

But all is not perfect. In his discussion of underachieving Blaine suggests six possible reasons, ranging from the need to fail to subtle rebellion. Yet one question remains: How could a parent reading this book arrive at the specific emotional difficulty underlying his son's or daughter's underachievement? On the other hand, the author's discussion of the lazy adolescent is an excellent one.

The second book which I would like to mention is *How to live with your teenager,* written by a psychologist, Dorothy W. Baruch, and published by McGraw-Hill. This is light reading. It has occasional cartoons and catch phrases which are boxed on the page. It is a book better suited to the less educated parent who might slow to a halt in heavier reading. While it is presented in a somewhat casual fashion, it contains a great deal of good material.

Dr. Baruch obviously means to stick with the "feeling" side of human nature and does a good job of it. She emphasizes the need for parents to recognize their own feelings and to be honest with their teenagers about them. She should have a medal for her persistence in maintaining that the most important requirement for healthy adolescent development is to feel worthwhile.

Her discussion of sexual material leaves something to be desired. She finds herself out on the limb in allowing a great deal of freedom with regard to masturbation and then begins the hazardous climb down to the solid earth in advising sexual control in dating practices. However, many of her psychological points are well taken, especially regarding parental attitudes toward sex. Unfortunately, her light approach to the topic of teenagers runs aground when she discusses oedipal conflicts. Some of her statements are certainly more than most parents could follow or swallow.

With limitations, both of these books are good. Another book which

I would like to mention briefly is for the parent who is the product of extensive Catholic education and is deeply concerned about his teenager's religious needs. This book is written not for parents but for educators. However, its insightful approach to the crises of faith that occur in adolescence makes it a book which could be helpful to the Catholic parent of deep personal conviction who might tend to demand too much of teenagers or lose touch with the realities of teenage psychology out of devotion to the realities of faith. This book is *Crisis of faith, the religious psychology of adolescence* by Pierre Babin, published by Herder and Herder (1963). The major theme of this book can be expressed in the following quotation, which might also be the theme of a study such as ours:

Woe to those who preach only a black Christianity, symbolized by death and flight from the world! They are unfaithful to the Resurrection of Jesus and to the hope of youth. Besides, no one will listen to them (p. 197).

### Literature on Adolescents for Teachers
(ROSE MARIE DICKSON)

Selecting books that have value for teachers in their work with adolescents is not an easy task, considering the number of publications that roll daily from the presses. This paper, then, in no way proposes to give a survey of readings in this area. Rather, it will examine a few books that appear to have something to say to teachers—books that will help teachers grow in their understanding of adolescents.

Once the selections were made, assembling them into a unified presentation posed a problem. My approach to this difficulty has been to group the books in three categories: those that give some insight into how the adolescent sees himself, those that present the adult view of the adolescent, and those that examine the problem of discipline from both points of view.

#### How the Adolescent Views Himself

Turning our attention to the first group, let us look at *High school students speak out* by David Mallery (1962). Too infrequently, in assessments of the strong points and weaknesses of education, is the student himself consulted. Applying the student's point of view is precisely what Mallery's book attempts to do. Students from eight high schools located in the New England, Middle Atlantic, and Midwest regions were interviewed. Though the interviews were informal and students were encouraged to speak freely on a wide range of topics, Mallery was seeking answers to two main questions: "What happens to a student as a person as he goes through an American high school today?" and "What impact, if any, does the school have on his life and his thinking?" (Mallery, 1962, p. xiii).

The most revealing section of this book is Part III, "Teachers and Teaching." Such chapters as "The Way a Teacher Teaches" and "Mr. Smith and the Shop Kids" give insight into what students want and appreciate in their teachers. Chapter 24, "An Emerging Picture," serves as a good summary of the volume.

*The adolescent views himself* by Ruth Strang (1957) makes a significant contribution to understanding the problems of growing up from the teenager's point of view. Strang focuses on "the manifold ways in which adolescents perceive themselves in the psychological, social, and physical setting in which they are growing up" (1957, p. vi). Her data represent ten years of research on adolescents' views and feelings about themselves in addition to information gathered from observation and interviews of hundreds of teachers, counselors, and administrators.

Chapter 3, "Developing an Adequate Self-concept and Philosophy of Life," gives comprehensive treatment to the problem of achieving identity. Interpreting the self-concept as having four dimensions, Strang defines its dynamic nature and development. One of the most valuable contributions of this book is its emphasis on what adults—whether parents or teachers—can do to help adolescents scale the hurdles to maturity.

### How the Adult Views the Adolescent

Switching our attention to the second section, I would like to recommend for reading *Emotional problems of the student* by Graham Blaine, Charles McArthur, and twelve contributing authors (1961). Though this volume derives its existence from psychological and psychiatric case studies of Harvard University students, there is much of interest here for the high-school teacher. Some of the emotional problems discussed are unique to the college setting; however, most of them have their roots in earlier periods. Such chapters as "Distinguishing Patterns of Student Neuroses," "Problems Connected with Studying," and "Student Apathy" describe the types and causative factors of problems that teachers in high-school settings often encounter.

As the title implies, the emphasis is on the abnormal. And though one may think the abnormal receives too large a share of the spotlight since most students do not deviate seriously from the normal, two points are significant about this book. The first is the insight it provides into the ticklish distinction between true neurosis in adolescents and problem behavior that is phase-like. The second is the book's discussion of the encouraging results that can occur when proper referral facilities are available. Many of us feel that college psychiatry is in many ways unique. It is not psychoanalysis nor is it simply counseling. Blaine and McArthur's volume does much to clarify its role in both academic and therapeutic settings.

Luella Cole and Irma Hall's *Psychology of adolescence* (1964) has become a classic in the study of adolescents. The sixth edition is comprehensive in its treatment of all aspects of growth and development, both deviant and normal; the latest research from sociology, medicine, education, and psychology gives unusual depth to the volume; and it is practical in its application of psychology to education in such areas as curriculum, personnel work, social life, emotional problems, and teacher-pupil relations. Teachers will be especially interested in Part Six, in which these applications are described. Also of note in this section is a description of the high-school population in terms of ability range and dropouts. "Emotional Problems in the Schoolroom," Chapter 24, deals effectively with symptoms of disturbances that every teacher will probably face at some point in his career. These signs of emotional difficulty are spelled out in terms of behavior that should be easy for teachers to identify. Also worthwhile are the materials on mental health in the classroom which deal with the teacher's personality, his own personal problems, and characteristics of good and poor teachers.

R. M. MacIver has edited a book entitled *Dilemmas of youth in America today* (1961). This volume attempts to give adults a renewed insight into some of the particularly pressing problems which confront the youth of our generation. Several chapters are devoted to the difficulties that often arise from the family. Harold Taylor focuses on the pressures exerted on American youth which have resulted from recent developments in other parts of the world. Pressures for conformity and pressures against intellectuality are discussed by Charles Frankel and Walter Metzger. These are just a few of the many provocative problems that *Dilemmas of youth* offers for consideration.

### The Problem of Discipline

Beginning his volume with a discussion of adolescent identity, Wittenberg stresses the role of the ego, the group, and social identity in his book *Adolescence and discipline* (1959). The author explains why an understanding of the developing ego is essential in a discussion of discipline (1959, p. 17):

> The final goal of all our efforts at home, in school, and in the community, is to achieve a strong and healthy ego inside the personality, an ego that can cope successfully with the instinctual demands and the superego forces. Once the individual has achieved this ego balance, he has developed healthy inner discipline . . . In other words. ego balance, healthy self-discipline, and the ability to enjoy life to the fullest are identical.

From this beginning Wittenberg goes on to discuss what adults can do to help adolescents develop discipline through the use of examples from the home, school, camps, and work settings. Part III, the most detailed section, develops ideas for adults in assisting young people to achieve inner balance by giving ego support.

For those of us working with adolescents, penetrating insight can be gained from the section on meeting our own needs as opposed to meeting those of our students, as well as learning something of the limits of our rights and abilities. This book, along with those already described, can be of significant aid to the teacher interested in the problems of adolescence.

### Literature for Counselors of Adolescents

(Edward V. Daubner)

My task is to review some important literature on the counseling of adolescents. The most difficult part of such an assignment is to make a selection from among the many publications on this topic which have appeared in the last twenty-five years. The three works which I have chosen are: *Counseling adolescents,* by E. G. Williamson; *Counseling and psychotherapy,* by Carl R. Rogers; and *The work of the counselor,* by Leona E. Tyler. I would like to emphasize that in addition to these three there are, literally, a hundred or more others which might well merit your attention, not to mention a host of articles to be found in professional journals, such as the *Personnel and Guidance Journal, Journal of Consulting Psychology, Journal of Counseling Psychology, The Catholic Psychological Record,* and others.

The rationale for my selection is briefly this: in my opinion, the works I have chosen are eminently representative of three contrasting approaches to counseling. Williamson's book, *Counseling adolescents,* is a revision of Part One of his previous work, *How to counsel students,* published in 1939, which was one of the earliest and most detailed descriptions of clinical counseling as it operates in a school or college setting. It is also an accurate presentation of what has become known as the directive method of counseling. Rogers' work, *Counseling and psychotherapy,* appeared three years after Williamson's *How to counsel students* and proceeded to shake the counseling world to its foundations by presenting an entirely different approach known as client-centered, or more familiarly, nondirective counseling. It immediately precipitated a widespread and sometimes acrimonious controversy between the adherents of the directive and nondirective schools, which has not entirely subsided even to the present day. Tyler's *The work of the counselor* is significant not only because it is one of the best attempts at a reconciliation of these two disparate points of view, but because it is concerned, primarily, not with detailing a particular theory of counseling, but rather with the *process* of counseling, that is, with what clients and counselors do, say, think, and feel in the counseling interview itself. It is not that the other books are not concerned with such matters, but rather that they are more oriented toward the delineation of a unified theoretical approach to counseling.

Suppose we maintain our historical perspective, and first take a closer look at Williamson's work. In the interest of brevity, I will attempt to summarize the first four chapters of *Counseling adolescents* (Williamson, 1950) in the following comments. In this part of the book Williamson shows the importance of counseling in education, as well as its relationship to formal education as a whole. His thesis—that counseling is a means of personalizing and individualizing the educational process, of providing some assurance that the development of the whole personality of the students will not be neglected in favor of a one-sided intellectual development—is beyond cavil. However, in substantiating his thesis he tends to indulge in overstatement and questionable history, to say the least. For example, the unsophisticated reader is apt to get the impression that man is an irrational animal on the one hand (Williamson, 1950, pp. 13, 14), and on the other, that there is a fundamental opposition between education for intellectual development and education for the development of the whole person. Neither proposition, of course, could be further from the truth. Precisely how he could bemoan overemphasis on intellectual development in one breath and characterize man as an irrational animal in the next is something that only God and Williamson knew at the time the book was written. Probably, now only God knows! To state it simply, the reader is cautioned to take Williamson's philosophizing in these first four chapters with a generous dose of salt (Williamson, 1950, pp. 31ff, 79ff).

The next five chapters constitute the heart of the book, and it is here that Williamson explains his theory. Counseling is defined as "that part of personnel work in which a counselor helps the client to marshal his own resources, the resources of an institution and of the community, to assist the client to achieve the optimum adjustment of which he is capable" (p. 209). Clinical counseling is "the application of the methods of science, experimental, statistical, and conceptualizational, to the process of human adjustments" (Williamson, 1950, p. 109).

Williamson emphasizes an objective, scientific study of the adolescent, his environment, his problems, their causes and their solution. The method of clinical counseling is patterned after the method used in medicine—analyze the patient and his symptoms; diagnose his illness and its causes; prescribe the indicated treatment; and follow up the patient to verify that the diagnosis was correct and the treatment effective.

As applied to clinical counseling, the method involves six steps (Williamson, 1950, pp. 101ff):

1. Analysis—the gathering of pertinent data about the student and his environment through the use of available records, various types of tests, rating scales, observations, autobiographies, and other evaluation and assessment devices. This information is necessary to understand the student adequately.

2. Synthesis—the organization and summarization of the data from analysis in an orderly fashion to project the student's assets, liabilities, adjustments, and maladjustments in bold relief.

3. Diagnosis—the identification of the student's fundamental problem and its causes. The central importance of this step in Williamson's theory will be discussed later.

4. Prognosis—the prediction of the future course of events should the student follow this or that course of action.

5. Treatment—the steps taken by the client and the counselor to help the student achieve a better adjustment or solution.

6. Follow-up—the contacting of the student at a later date to determine the correctness of the diagnosis and the effectiveness of the treatment, and to assist him in facing any new problems.

Certain fundamental concepts underlie this approach to counseling: First, it is assumed that the counselor, like the medical doctor, is a highly trained specialist who because of his training and experience is able to do something for his client which he is unable to do for himself. The counselor's role is to analyze the student, diagnose his problem and its causes, and decide what must be done to remedy the situation. True, Williamson hopes that the student will take an active and co-operative part in this process, but it is the counselor who is responsible for taking the initiative, both because of his training and experience and because he believes most students cannot do these things for themselves in an objective, impartial, scientific manner (Williamson, 1950, pp. 180, 224, 229ff).

Williamson's second basic idea is that counseling is, primarily, an intellectual exercise, on the part of both the student and the counselor. Naturally, Williamson acknowledges the existence of emotional problems. However, he seems to imply that the treatment of such problems is accomplished by means of curative counseling or therapy, which he distinguishes from noncurative or clinical counseling (Williamson, 1950, pp. 107–110). It is the latter with which he is primarily concerned, and in this type of counseling, it is the task of the student and the counselor to apply rational, problem-solving methods to the student's difficulties. Williamson believes that if a student has sufficient knowledge about himself and his situation, if he knows which choices are open to him and the consequences of each, if he knows which goals are best for him and what are the best means of reaching these goals, he will inevitably make the right decision. By the time Williamson reaches the end of his explanation of clinical counseling, he is willing, apparently, to extend its use even to the treatment of emotional problems. One cannot help but note a contradiction here. If, as previously stated, Williamson believes man is essentially an irrational animal, how is it possible for him to place such great faith in a student's ability to reach and accept a purely rational conclusion about what he must do to make an optimum adjustment (Williamson, 1950, pp. 279–281)?

A third concept, which seems to flow naturally and logically from the first two, is the great significance attached to *diagnosis*. The counselor needs as much valid and reliable information about the student as he can obtain, but what is even more important, he must know how to interpret this information. According to Williamson, "diagnosis is a process in logical thinking or the teasing out from a mass of relevant and irrelevant facts, of a consistent pattern of meaning and understanding of the student's assets and liabilities" (Williamson, 1950, p. 179). The art of diagnosing is the heart of clinical counseling: it is the principal difference between clinical and ordinary counseling. Unless the counselor can fit the facts together in a meaningful manner so as to understand the student and his problem and its causes, he is engaging in nothing more than generalized listening and advising. Without careful and correct diagnosis, the treatment of the student's difficulty may be inappropriate. In other words, the successful resolution of the student's problem is largely, if not wholly, dependent upon accurate diagnosis. Improvement in counseling depends upon improvement in diagnosis (Williamson, 1950, pp. 102, 208, 239–240).

A fourth idea, which again seems to proceed logically from the previous ones, is the active and dominant role assigned to the counselor. It is this facet of clinical counseling which earns it the appellation of directive counseling. Throughout the entire process, it is the counselor who does the leading. He decides what information is needed and how it should be obtained. He pieces the information together and arrives at a diagnosis and a prognosis. He suggests solutions and means of achieving them. He takes the initiative in attempting to motivate the student. He decides whether the student has set proper goals for himself. It is true, however, that Williamson does admonish the counselor to help the student take as much responsibility for his own affairs as possible, to enlist the active participation of the student in every step—analysis, diagnosis, and treatment, *"insofar as he is intellectually able* and willing to do so." He also advises *that there are times when the counselor must move in and take over* if the client is unwilling or incapable of doing for himself, or if he makes a faulty diagnosis, or if he decides upon a poor program of action. In fact, Williamson believes that the need for this kind of assistance constitutes the primary reason for the existence of counseling (Williamson, 1950, p. 180).

Possibly the best way to summarize Williamson's position is to characterize it as "interference counseling." Interfering is used here as a synonym for intervening or interposing. The counselor actively and purposefully steps into the student's life space, surveys it, decides how it needs to be reorganized, and helps the student carry out the reordering. This task is accomplished by giving him or helping him to acquire needed information; by assisting him to interpret the information correctly (correct, that is, according to the counselor's views); by helping him explore optional goals and means of attaining them; and by suggesting, encouraging, advising, and persuading him to make a choice which, in the counselor's eyes, seems most likely to result in a better life style for the student. Finally, counseling, as Williamson understands it, is essentially a personalized, individualized learning situation in which the counselor teaches the student to apply the scientific method of problem solving to the conduct of his life. As in all teaching-learning situations, the learner must take an active part, but it is the teacher who figures most prominently in deciding the goals which the learner must pursue and the best means of achieving them (Williamson, 1950, pp. 219, 281).

As mentioned previously, Rogers' *Counseling and psychotherapy* (1942) was published just three years after Williamson's *How to counsel students,* and its impact was amazing, to say the least. Practically all counselors in schools and colleges were committed, at least nominally, to the method described by Williamson. I say nominally because at this time formal counseling was still something new on the educational scene. Hence, very few counselors were trained or knew enough about counseling theories and techniques to have any predilections concerning their relative merits. Shortly after Rogers' book appeared, controversy between the informed adherents of the two methods filled the air.

Inevitably, counselors in schools and colleges were attracted by the argument and took sides. The principal beneficial effect was not so much that counselors adhered to one side or the other, but rather that they began to study and to think more about their counseling.

From the very outset, Rogers differs sharply from the directive approach. "Effective counseling," he says, "consists of a definitely structured, permissive relationship which allows the client to gain an understanding of himself to a degree which enables him to take positive steps in the light of his new situation" (Rogers, 1942, pg. 18). Basically, this approach means that the personal relationship in the interview between the student and the counselor is of paramount importance. It is by means of this relationship that the student will engage in psychological self-exploration which will result in new and richer understanding of himself which, in turn, will motivate him to change his life pattern in the direction of becoming more fully the person he is capable of being.

The counselor's principal task is the building of such a relationship. It is a unique relationship, quite different from any social bond the client has experienced before (Rogers, 1942, pp. 85–86). Rogers characterizes it first as a warm, friendly, responsive relationship, in which the student clearly perceives that the counselor has a positive regard for him. Second, it is a psychologically permissive, nonthreatening relationship, in which the student is free to talk about all those hidden and forbidden feelings, attitudes, impulses, and other personality aspects which cannot be broached in ordinary conversation. Third, although it is a permissive relationship, it also has definite limits in regard to time and action. "The student is free to keep an appointment or break it, to come on time or to come late . . ." and to sit in silence for the entire time of the interview if he pleases, but he may not have more time than called for in the original schedule. He may shout, pound on the desk with his fists, stamp his foot on the floor, but he may not attack the counselor personally or destroy the furnishings in the counselor's office. These limits, according to Rogers, are "one of the vital elements which make the therapeutic situation a microcosm in which the client can meet all the basic aspects which characterize life as a whole, face them openly, and adapt himself to them" (Rogers, 1942, p. 89). Fourth, it is a noncoercive relationship in which no pressure of any sort in the way of suggestion, advice, threat, warning, or any of the usual devices is used to persuade the student to follow one course of action rather than another (Rogers, 1942, pp. 87–90).

In such a situation, the student discovers for himself that he can drop all those psychological defenses which he normally uses to justify his behavior. For example, he can stop being the nonconformist, the bully, the clown, or renounce whatever role he needs to assume to cover up his sense of inadequacy. In such a situation, the student can face himself and evaluate himself, because he has no need to defend himself against attack. In such an atmosphere, he gains new insights which become the bases of self-initiated, positive, growth-producing behavior (Rogers, 1942, pp. 40ff, 90). By insight, Rogers means "new perceptions of relationships previously unrecognized, a willingness to accept all aspects of the self, and a choice of goals, now clearly perceived for the first time" (Rogers, 1942, p. 216).

The counselor creates this kind of relationship by his warmth and responsiveness; by making reflective statements which recognize and

municate these attitudes to the student. "Acceptance involves primarily two things—first, a willingness to allow individuals to differ from one another in all sorts of ways, and second, a realization that the ongoing experience of each person is a complex pattern of striving, thinking and feeling" (Tyler, 1961, pp. 24, 25). Acceptance involves neither approval nor disapproval of the student, but respect for his worth as a person, regardless of any particular pleasant or unpleasant facet of his personality. By understanding Tyler means that the counselor must try to enter the student's world as much as possible, not to tell him what is wrong with it or how it needs to be reorganized, but simply to see it as the student sees it, to perceive it, not as it appears to the counselor but as it looks to the student. Hence, for Tyler, *counseling is not a verbal skill, but rather a perceptual skill* (Tyler, 1961, pp. 28, 29, 44, 218).

What a counselor says and does is not nearly as important as what he perceives. What has happened to the student is not nearly as important as his attitudes toward his experiences, and it is these attitudes which the counselor must try to perceive if he is to understand the student. "The main skill a counselor must develop," according to Tyler, "is that of communicating his understanding of what the client is trying to express" (p. 29). To learn this skill, odd as it may seem, the counselor must learn *to listen*—to listen perceptively and to respond, not to the facts which the student is relating, but to the feelings and attitudes in which the facts are embedded. This skill is difficult, but the student's progress will depend in large measure on the counselor's ability to perceive and clarify the student's feelings about his experiences (Tyler, 1961, pp. 29ff, 217ff).

Tyler attaches special significance to the first interview, even if it may be the only one that the counselor will have with a student. The goals of this first interview are three: first, to lay the foundation for a warm, friendly relationship with the student; second, to open up the psychological realities in the student's life, that is, to provide opportunities for him to talk about and face up to his feelings and attitudes, which is done not through the use of probing questions but through reflective statements; third, to structure the situation for the student. By structuring Tyler means giving the student an idea of what counseling is and is not, what it can and cannot do for him. Of these three, the first is most important and should take precedence over the other two (Tyler, 1961, pp. 53–56, 57). Nancy's case provides an example:

. . . 17 year-old Nancy who has been expelled from high school for truancy and defiance spends all of the first counseling hour telling the counselor what a fine person she (Nancy) is, and how the world misunderstands her. . . . Sore as she is from much buffeting around by the rough winds of experience, she must know the healing that comes from being sure of a friend whom she can trust. . . . In this case, both the planning (structuring) and the opening up are sacrificed to enable the relationship itself to be built on a sound basis (Tyler, 1961, pp. 57–58).

An attitude which shows the student that he is welcome, cared for, and received and respected as someone of value regardless of his shortcomings; a relationship built on sincerity, honesty, and frank-ness—these are the keynotes of successful counseling.

Analysis and diagnosis, stressed by Williamson and shunned by Rogers, are accorded a middle-of-the-road position by Tyler. The use of tests, records, or other analytical devices is justified, but only to the extent that they can help the counselor perceive how the student looks at his life, and only if the information obtained from them is interpreted to the student in such a manner that he clearly understands the implications for his particular situation (Tyler, 1961, pp. 72, 86, 106, 131ff). Extreme caution should be exercised that such information is not used by the counselor to prejudge the student. Diagnosis, as an exercise in labeling or pigeonholing students, is a waste of time because psychological problems are not analogous to disease entities such as cancer or appendicitis. Underachievement, for example, may take many forms, and may be the result of many different combinations of factors for which no standardized treatment is known. Hence, it is futile to diagnose one student as an underachiever and another as having a problem of vocational indecision. The only value in diagnosis is when it is used to form a developmental picture, a working image of the student. Such a picture of the student must be based not upon the counselor's ability to adopt an external, objective, third-person viewpoint, as Williamson advocates, but rather upon the counselor's perceptions of how the world looks to the student (Tyler, 1961, pp. 60, 61, 63).

For Williamson, the role of the counselor is to teach the student to apply scientific problem-solving methods to the conduct of his life. For Rogers, the counselor's task is to create a relationship in which the student's innate tendency for growth can assert itself. For Tyler, "The counselor's role is to stimulate and facilitate the natural developmental processes—to enable them to operate more efficiently than they do by themselves—the same way that a gardener encourages the growth of plants in his care" (Tyler, 1961, p. 295). In other words, Tyler views counseling as a way of furthering the student's development, rather than a means of teaching him something or of curing him. Such developmental counseling emphasizes the discovery and exploitation of the student's natural strengths and a bypassing of his weaknesses, rather than a complete restructuring of his personality. Stress is placed upon what the student can do with the resources he has at his disposal, rather than what he must do to reorganize his life (Tyler, 1961, pp. 213–215). For example, Jim's stuttering has caused him to feel so inadequate socially that he has resorted to overaggressiveness and defiance to bolster his sagging feeling of self-worth. Developmental counseling, instead of trying to help him reshape his self-concept, concentrates on helping him understand that he has untapped assets which, if properly used, can lead to a much more satisfying life.

Let me leave you with this thought. You are probably pondering which of these authors you should imitate. Do not bother yourself. Available research indicates that success in counseling depends very little on the counselor's theoretical orientation—directive, nondirective, or psychoanalytic. It does show, however, that the attitudes and feelings of the counselor toward the client are of much greater significance. Counselors who are warm, friendly, permissive, interested, and accepting are perceived by clients to be more helpful than those who are cold, uninterested, distant, and judgmental (Rogers, 1958). Apparently, as Tyler observes (1961, p. 239), the kind of person the counselor *is* means much more than what he *does* as the result of his preference for any particular school of counseling. Insofar as the nondirective approach has caused counselors to be more conscious of such matters, it has made a monumental contribution. If you would improve your counseling, therefore, look to yourself. What you *are* clamors so loudly in the student's ears that he scarcely hears what you say or do.

# PART VIII

## Principles of Mental Health
## and Mental Hygiene

▲▲▲▲▲▲▲▲▲▲▲▲▲▲▲▲▲▲▲▲▲▲▲▲▲▲▲▲▲▲▲▲

# 41. The Concepts and Dynamics
# of Mental Health

ALEXANDER A. SCHNEIDERS

## The Practical Significance of Defining Normality

Some time ago there was a story in *The New York Times* relative to what is known as the Mid-town Manhattan Project, in which was stated that only about 22 per cent of people in this study could be classified as normal. Twenty-three per cent were found to have such serious symptoms that treatment was necessary, and the remainder were found to have symptoms of varying degrees of severity, but not disabling. These data have serious implications for the study of mental health and support other empirical findings relative to the incidence of mental disorder and maladjustment. They certainly indicate the need for a careful definition of normality (Schneiders, 1965b).

From a purely practical standpoint, it is clear that teachers, parents, and counselors need to have some idea of what normality and mental health mean. The image of the so-called normal person influences our judgments, our expectancies, and our behavior toward others. Similarly, our concepts of abnormality, mental illness, and such phenomena as neurosis, eccentricity, and queerness prejudice our thinking about people and our actions toward them. To know what is normal and healthy, or what is abnormal and unhealthy, is basic to our differentiations of adolescent behavior, whether in the home or in the classroom.

Moreover, a clear concept of abnormality helps us to identify disturbing symptoms and thus to institute the right kind of help or to make the necessary referral. For counselors, school psychologists, and psychotherapists particularly, clear thinking in this area is of particular importance to the interpretation and the evaluation of both symptoms

413

and behavior. It is required for a proper diagnosis and particularly for differential diagnosis. It is obvious that the label of schizophrenia could lead a counselor far astray in his work with a client if it happened that the person was not at all schizophrenic. We recognize, of course, the limitations inherent in conceptualizations that are too rigid. We must always be careful not to create conceptual molds and to force our children or clients into them. Conceptualizations of this kind, leading to labeling, can often stop clear-headed thinking and adequate diagnosis.

Before tackling the concept of normality, let us ask some basic questions about normality and mental health (see Deutsch and Fishman, 1963). I will answer these questions as I proceed, and I trust that the answers will give the reader a better perspective regarding normality. To the question, "Is there a truly normal person?" the answer is no, just as the answer would be no if we were to ask whether any human person is perfect. However, if we qualify the question a little bit and ask, "Are some persons relatively normal?" the answer would be yes. The second question stems from the first one, and the answer is obviously yes: "Is everybody abnormal in some degree or at some time?" For the same reason that no one is absolutely normal, it follows that, human nature being what it is, everybody will run into some behavior or mental difficulty at some point in his life.

If we ask, "Is normality the same thing as adjustment or mental health," or "Is maladjustment the same thing as abnormality?" the answer is no in both cases. This means that a person can be relatively normal and still suffer some maladjustment, or that some people are in the strict sense abnormal without being maladjusted. These distinctions will be clarified more fully later on in this discussion. Two other questions that we hear quite often have to do with the incidence or prevalence of psychological difficulties and symptoms. We often hear the question, "Is it true that we are all neurotic to some degree?" and also, "Are outstanding or creative persons generally abnormal?" To both of these questions we would have to answer yes. In the course of coping with reality demands and daily problems we are not likely to escape the development of some neurotic symptoms. By the same rule, outstanding or creative persons deviate from the normal quite naturally, and often to a noticeable degree.

Finally, we should answer the question, "Does normality indicate a rigid conformity or mediocrity?" The answer here is no. In fact, there are times when rigid conformity tends strongly toward the abnormal.

Of one thing we can be sure and that is that all neurotics, psychotics, and other persons suffering from some form of mental disability are abnormal, deviant, maladjusted, or ill. In the *best* sense of the term, normal implies an adequate, healthy, adjusted personality.

## The Many Faces of Normality

It is clear that normality wears many faces. When we examine carefully the origin of the concept "normal," the first difficulty we encounter is that of isolating acceptable norms, standards, or criteria in terms of which to evaluate behavior or mental life. Some people like to emphasize healthiness, others good adjustment, and still others effective interpersonal relationships. All of this is complicated by early medical and legal influences on the idea of normality. The physician refers to normal blood pressure, or normal ranges of body temperature, or normal childhood diseases. The legal expert uses his own particular bases for deciding what is normal and who is responsible for a person's behavior (Senn, 1950).

Going far back into the history of human thought, we find strong ethical and religious influences at work. Ethics itself is defined as a "normative science." It describes what ought to be and attempts to develop basic principles for right conduct. Much of our thinking in psychology and psychiatry reflects this ethical influence because we too have decided on what ought to be in the area of behavior. It is obvious, of course, that the development of ethical principles and codes has been strongly affected by different religious systems. The science of ethics and the practice of religion have always gone hand in hand, especially since it is religion that offers adequate sanction for the principles of morality.

The development of science and scientific methodology has also given the concept of normality a new facet. As distinct from the ethical principle of what ought to be, science offers a statistical-group concept of normality, which is derived from what people do, rather than what they ought to do. The standards of normality here are determined in large measure by the reactions and behavior of particular groups. This statistical concept of normality offers a great deal of trouble because it is generally assumed that what is "normal" is also "natural," and this notion has led to many difficulties. Thus, it is "normal" for most children to develop dental caries, run the gamut of childhood diseases, and rebel against parental authority when they reach adolescence. But none of these things is particularly good or desirable. From this view the healthy, obedient child would be abnormal.

There are in fact many behaviors which, from a statistical point of view, would have to be regarded as normal (especially sex behavior), but that might be quite objectionable from an ethical or social point of view. The social-ethical concept of normality would of course differ from this statistical interpretation and would tend to interpret as normal that which is socially beneficial or ethically correct, regardless of empirical studies that show what people actually do. In contrast to these notions, we must emphasize that normality must leave room for individuality, since it is possible to establish individual as well as group norms. For example, it may be normal for one person to smoke a pack of cigarettes a day and distinctly abnormal for another person to smoke three cigarettes a day. In other words, in order to interpret behavior adequately, we have to know something about the individual's personal history. Without this knowledge, we may completely misjudge his behavior.

There is finally the medical concept of normality, disease, and health. The contrary of this is the pathological concept of abnormality. From the medical point of view it is normal to be healthy and abnormal to be sick. By health is meant not only the absence of disease and disease symptoms, but the possession of those qualities of mind and body that enable the person to function adequately and efficiently and to be as productive as his talents permit. The healthy person possesses the energy and the stamina that are required for his work and that enable him to meet the demands of reality and the problems of daily life in a resolute and effective manner. The presence of a disease process and the symptoms associated with disease, tend to preclude this type of performance.

## A Psychological Concept of Normality

The medical concept of normality and health comes close to what is best described as the psychological concept of normality. This concept, as we will see, is quite different from the statistical-group concept of normality and from the social-ethical concept of what is normal. It is most closely related to the idea of mental health. In this view, a person is psychologically normal when he fulfills certain criteria for mental health. These criteria include such qualities as self-insight, self-acceptance, a healthy attitude toward self, adequate contact with reality, good moral and social attitudes, a wide range of interests for work and play, and adequate interpersonal relationships. To the extent that any person fulfills these criteria he can be described as both mentally healthy and as psychologically normal.

These ideas and criteria are derived in large part from the concept of the nature of man. In this sense, psychology—in attempting to define normality—closely resembles ethics in its attempt to define morality. A study of the nature of man tells us how he ought to behave, not only in an ethical but also in a psychological sense: human beings ought to sleep well, to relate effectively to other people, to cope adequately with reality, and so on; they ought not to have recourse to symptoms and maladjustive responses in order to cope with problems. In this attempt to define what is normal and mentally healthy, psychology assumes the form of a normative discipline (Schneiders, 1954).

### Normality and Adjustment

I have already indicated that the concept of normality and adjustment do not convey exactly the same meaning; nor can we equate abnormality and maladjustment. Adjustment is essentially a process involving behavior or internal response, whereas normality is a quality of the personality or of its behavior. Adjustment is an effort on the part of the individual organism to cope with the demands of reality, with conflicts and frustrations, and with the stresses and threats and problems of daily life. When this adjustment is effective, it contributes a great deal to normality; and by the same rule the more ineffective or distorted it becomes, the more it detracts from normality. As behavior becomes more symptomatic (rather than remaining reality-bound), the person becomes more seriously maladjusted. Thus maladjustive behavior tends toward the abnormal, although it must be emphasized that some degree of maladjustment can exist without labeling the person abnormal. For example, a student can be poorly adjusted to the demands of school work without being abnormal. Moreover, as we have already seen, abnormality only means a deviation from some norm, and since this deviation can be in the direction of a desirable response or characteristic, it may at times be a creditable quality. Thus intellectually brilliant persons deviate in considerable degree from the normal—but in a desirable direction. Their abnormality is an asset.

It is helpful to think of both adjustment and normality as constituting a continuum that extends from one extreme of behavior to another. On this continuum we can arrange all kinds of behavior from that which is quite adequate, well adjusted, and normal to that behavior which is severely maladjustive, abnormal, and pathological. Between the two extremes will be found all those behaviors that we would characterize as mildly disturbed, disabling, neurotic, psychotic, and psychopathic. Here too we can find room for the well-known adjustment mechanisms such as rationalization, sublimation, sour grapes, compensation, repression, and egocentrism. It must be understood that in setting up such a continuum we are dealing with behavior, not with capacity. We have just seen that certain deviations in capacity may be quite desirable, whereas deviations in behavior are generally undesirable (Schneiders, 1965)

### General Conclusions

What I have tried to emphasize here is a positive concept of normality that is based upon a realistic concept of human nature. Normality is not something that is statistically determined by empirical investigation, nor by group attitudes or behaviors. It is a positive psychological quality which distinguishes the healthy-minded and effectively responding person from one whose behavior or attitudes are inadequate to the demands of reality.

The same thing can be said with respect to the concept of mental health (Nunnally, 1961). While freedom from disabling symptoms and from negative feelings is a helpful introduction to mental health, there are also more positive qualities that bespeak mental health, such as productivity, enjoyment of work, mental efficiency, emotional control, the capacity to love and be loved, a healthy realism, a deep sense of humor, self-acceptance and self-love, physical stamina and energy, and a sound, workable scale of values. These, and other qualities like maturity, are always part and parcel of the mentally healthy personality (Senn, 1950). These qualities are the basic criteria by which we can evaluate good adjustment and mental stability whether we are working with children, adolescents, or adults.

### The Dynamics of Mental Health and Adjustment

This study of mental health was begun with the general problem of its nature and definition. The stage was set for the discussion of related problems by defining what is understood by mental health, both in the positive and in the negative sense, and by relating these concepts to the qualities of adjustment and normality, emphasizing the importance of an interpretation of normality that would avoid the morass of statistical confusion that is found in many places.

Basic to an understanding of mental health and adjustment is an analysis of their dynamics. This problem has to be studied very carefully to determine why it is that some people pass through the vicissitudes of childhood and adolescence with a relatively healthy, integrated mind and with adequate and useful behavior patterns and interpersonal relationships that seem to enrich their lives, whereas other people emerge from adolescence with wholly inadequate personalities. What is it that disrupts mental equilibrium and the process of adjustment? Why is it that some people cannot cope with reality, or with the demands, stresses, and threats of daily living? These people cannot work out their own destiny, nor can they strive consistently for the goals they have set for themselves.

These are the questions I want to answer. Here we encounter the important problem of the causes (dynamics) within the individual that contribute to mental disorder. I use the term dynamics with somewhat the same meaning it has in physics, although the usage is only analogous. And, in much the same way that the atomistic chemistry of the nineteenth century gave way to the dynamic physics of today, the earlier atomistic psychology changed to the dynamic psychology and psychiatry of today, particularly under the influence of Freud. There were many persons besides Freud in the fields of medicine, psychiatry, and psychology who contributed to this development, including his disciples, Adler and Jung. Today, any roster of such persons would include Karen Horney, Harry Stack Sullivan, Carl Rogers, and many others who have contributed greatly to our knowledge of the impelling forces that determine human behavior and that promote mental health or undermine it. When, therefore, we refer to behavior dynamics or dynamic psychology, we are talking about the forces, tendencies, impulses, needs, drives, instincts, desires, wishes, feelings and emotions, attitudes and interests, goals and incentives that cause or condition human behavior and interpersonal relationships.

I deliberately mentioned a number of these tendencies in order to avoid the error of oversimplification of human motivation. Watson made the mistake of reducing all motivation to a stimulus-response equation, and Adler oversimplified the situation in his theory of inferiority. Freud also is guilty of oversimplification in his dynamic theory. If the range of dynamic factors is empirically or existentially broader than some theory proposes, then we should be careful not to limit our thinking by the theory. Without getting into theoretical arguments, I simply want to point out that the range of human dynamics is quite broad: it extends from the organic or even tissue level of the organism through the level of sensory drives that man shares in common with the lower animals to the level at which man can talk about goals, values, and ideals, things that exist only for an organism endowed with rationality.

## The Mechanisms of Behavior Dynamics

Borrowing an idea from Freud and psychoanalysis, let us keep in mind a basic principle of dynamics, namely, that at any particular level—except the purely rational—these dynamic tendencies may operate unconsciously in such a way as to distort behavior or cause serious maladjustment. In other words, we assume that some dynamic factors operate without the knowledge of the person himself and are expressed in the symbolic formulation of dreams, fantasy thinking, symptom formation, mental disorder, and psychological mechanisms. These are typical ways in which unconscious factors influence psychic reactions or behavior.

The presence of unconscious factors does not mean that at all times we are subject to unconscious influences. I am simply recognizing the fact that at times we do things without knowing why we do them. As Freud said, the business of psychotherapy is making conscious what is unconscious, bringing into conscious awareness material that is influencing or disturbing the individual. Here we may remind ourselves of another basic principle of behavior dynamics which is that in the development of behavior there is a fundamental economy that guides its course. The organism tends toward the most effective utilization of behavior response, and this type of utilization is exactly what we very often find in the analysis of behavior, particularly abnormal behavior. Thus, behavior economy requires that the individual short-circuit the drive into a type of activity that will reduce the strength of the drive and the tension which it creates. In following this economy, he may do all sorts of unusual things. Let us take a simple example. If a boy or girl in class is bored by the teacher's description of the Holy Roman Empire, what will he do to overcome the frustration and the tension that he feels? We know from experience what he does. He stares out the window and mentally transports himself to some faraway place that is much more exciting and therefore gratifying to him. This is the well-known daydreaming mechanism. Here we see the economy of behavior expressed very clearly. The person escapes the boredom of the classroom situation without ever leaving his seat. He transports himself on the magic carpet of imagination, and "to heck with the Holy Roman Empire!"

We all do some daydreaming. The older person stares at television, which transports him from the living room to the stimulating arena of the nightclub or the ludicrous situation created in "I Love Lucy." This escapism is accomplished through the medium of imagination and identification, and we use it with novels and movies as well as with television. Escapism is a simple example of the manner in which the organism copes with drives and needs, and the frustrations or conflicts to which they give rise.

### Behavior Dynamics and the Concept of Drive

At the very roots of the dynamics of human behavior and personality formation are certain fundamental drives for which I shall use the term "thrust." If the reader has ever taken a jet plane he knows what thrust is. In about three seconds you are traveling at 400 miles an hour some 5,000 feet off the ground, and that's real thrust. In my view there are certain basic goals or thrusts in human nature that transcend individual motivation such as needs and drives but utilize the dynamics of these drives. There is an inherent thrust toward growth, maturity, and adulthood, which means that if the organism is left entirely to its own devices, the thrust would still exist. True, this thrust would not operate as well if the child did not have a home and family and the care, support, and love which they provide. The child needs this external support. But the basic thrust is there, and we are referring to this thrust toward maturity when we say, "He'll grow out of it." Allow this thrust to operate, and the child will reach adulthood on his own. Maturity is a natural goal that is built into the makeup of the organism.

There is also a second basic thrust and that is toward self-actualization. To actualize one's self is to activate personal capacities and to create or discover a self that is distinctively one's own. This self-actualization is what writers like Rollo May are referring to when they refer to the search for self. And we very often hear people use such phrases as "I finally found myself." A strange statement, and yet one that is very meaningful. And in counseling or psychotherapy we often find that this search for self is the client's basic problem. He doesn't know himself and has literally never found himself. However, there is always a basic thrust toward self-actualization, and it is this thrust that gets blocked by neurotic and psychotic development.

The third basic thrust within the organism, and one closely allied to self-actualization, is the thrust toward self-identity, individuality, and independence. If the reader has ever lived or worked with adolescents he will have seen this thrust at work. Adolescents want and crave self-identity. They also crave individuality even though they have a strong tendency toward conformity, but only conformity at a particular level and toward certain things. More basic is the thrust to find out who they are and what they are and where they are supposed to be going. Finding self-identity is one of the biggest problems of adolescence and also one of the most important tasks of the adolescent period.

There is a fourth basic thrust which we can recognize very readily, and that is the thrust toward socialization. This is the tendency to become social and to fully realize the privilege of being social; to establish interpersonal relationships, enjoy friendships, and organize get-togethers; and to work successfully with other people. Socialization— or the development of adequate personal relations—is what Harry Stack Sullivan emphasized in so much of his professional writing. We are not, as Rousseau held, just animals who become socialized by being a part of society. There is within us an innate drive toward socialization, something that the organism is endowed with.

Finally, in my view the organism is also endowed with a basic thrust toward health. I do not accept the principle that there is a disintegrating force within the individual, whether we call it a death instinct or a self-destructive tendency. There are persons who manifest self-destructive tendencies and actually manage to destroy themselves. Self-destructive tendencies certainly exist in suicides, and to a lesser degree in the drug addict, the alcoholic, or the motorcycle speedster. However, because some people develop pathological tendencies toward self-destruction, it does not mean that such tendencies are universal. The evidence suggests, on the contrary, that the organism has a powerful thrust toward health, and it is this thrust that we must take advantage of in trying to help young people. In my view, nobody wants to be sick, in the sense that sickness is a value or a goal to be desired. Even the person who utilizes the "flight into illness," who adopts illness as a means of coping with reality, is not doing so because he wants to be ill, but simply because he wants what illness will bring. He is using illness as a means, not as an end.

Accepting this thrust-toward-health concept is important because we can then approach people with a more positive attitude, since in our view it is natural to be healthy. The idea that suffering is something to be accepted with total resignation—"this is my cross and I must bear it"—is a doubtful philosophy. Let us remember that the greatest Healer of all spent his public life healing people and set a definite pattern for us to follow. He made the blind to see, the deaf to hear, and even raised people from the dead.

### Needs and the Dynamics of Behavior

Having identified the basic thrusts, we can now determine what provides the energy for these thrusts and what are the more important dynamic factors of behavior. Quite apart from psychological or psychiatric theory, we can see in the behavior of all persons the influence of basic needs. A need represents a deprivation within the organism of something actually required, and from this deprivation a strong tendency develops which functions as a drive toward some thing, quality, or experience that the organism requires for its survival, its integrity, or its health.

Everyone is aware of such needs. Why do we need food? Simply because without food we will die. The same thing is true of liquid, rest, air, and other basic requirements. These things are so obviously necessary that we don't even think about them; but they represent very real needs and without their adequate gratification the organism will not survive. This is why hunger, thirst, and the need for rest are so dynamic.

Physical needs and their powerful energy clearly indicate how dynamic motivations can be. Can this dynamism happen at other levels of motivation? We know clinically that there are people who die mentally from lack of love. Here of course we are speaking of psychological needs and their deprivation, some of which function at the psychical level in much the same way that physical needs function at a physical level. If these needs are not gratified adequately, at the right time and in the right way by the right person, then the organism is in trouble.

This interpretation applies not only to affection or love, but also to belonging, acceptance, security, independence, and self-identity, each one of which is dynamically oriented toward mental health. Here we encounter the essential dynamics of mental illness. In simple terms, if there are two children in the same family, and one child is loved completely and wholesomely by his mother and the other is rejected, the one has a good chance of growing up healthily and the other one an equally poor chance of doing so. Frustration of or conflict with psychological needs is related to mental health in the same way that physical needs are related to physical health.

In addition to these needs there are social needs which are related to and provide the energy for the thrust toward socialization that I mentioned earlier. These needs are not as dynamic as others, so that if they are frustrated a person is not likely to become mentally disturbed, as is the person whose psychological needs are deeply frustrated. Thus social needs do not have the same relationship to personality growth, although frustration of these needs can lead to social maladjustment. These needs include participation, social approval, conformity, and communication.

The three categories of physical, psychological, and social needs prompt the question whether there are also spiritual needs within the personality, that is, tendencies to establish some kind of a meaningful relationship with a reality other than ourselves. Does the organism need a relationship with God or some higher power? Does it need a relationship, belief, or faith that will give meaning to life? Here we encounter the problem of the relationship between religion and mental health. Only if there are real spiritual needs can the proposition hold that religion is basic to mental health. This relationship is the one to which Carl Jung referred when he said that of his thousands of patients there was not a single one whose basic difficulty did not center around a philosophy of life. In other words, people require a system of values, or, what is very similar, the adequate gratification of spiritual needs.

Taking all such needs into account, what do they represent theoretically? The answer is simple: they reflect the nature of man himself, the ontology of his being. Man is physical and therefore has physical needs; he is psychic and therefore has psychological needs; he is by nature social and therefore has social needs; and he is spiritual and therefore has spiritual needs. It is because of these different facets of human nature that these needs exist; and the needs are, therefore, innate. They are not inherited nor acquired. We learn a great deal about these basic facets of human nature and the needs that spring from them through our experiences in counseling disturbed and abnormal people. There is, for example, the deeply neurotic, obsessive-compulsive person who has to wash his hands fifty times a day because of the contamination that he feels. Or there is the person who is always ill even though there is nothing organically wrong with him. What has happened in these cases with reference to basic needs? Obviously, the needs of these people are not adequately fulfilled.

### Need Interference and Mental Health

What is it that stands between a person's needs and their gratification? There are four factors involved, which we may pair together for purposes of simplification: conflict and frustration, and stress and threat. In other words, when basic needs—like love, sex, acceptance, or conformity—impel us in certain directions, they often come into conflict with the moral or social order, or are blocked by circumstance or by some factor within ourselves. Thus a single girl may have a strong need for sexual fulfillment, but she may also have strong moral principles, and thus the two forces come into conflict with one another. If she cannot cope with this conflict, trouble will result.

Let us recognize that there is nothing wrong with conflict or frustration in itself. Everybody experiences these two hindrances to human gratifications. If a person learns how to handle conflict then it will cause no difficulty. But what if he does not know what to do when conflict arises? He cannot stand the thought of sexual behavior because it frightens him. He then makes use of a mechanism—one that Freud described so clearly—the mechanism of repression. Take the example of a young boy, fourteen or fifteen years of age, who has never done anything wrong sexually. He has never masturbated and has never petted with a girl. He has not had any impure thoughts and has not indulged in sexual fantasy. Nor have there been any homosexual contacts. This boy is good and pure, but he is also probably neurotic. Any boy of this age who does not encounter some kind of sexual experience, particular thoughts, dreams, and fantasies, is likely to experience sexual difficulties. We must understand that there is nothing wrong with these sex experiences in themselves; it is only the poor handling or control of sexual experience and behavior that leads to immorality.

We can think of frustration in the same way. Everybody experiences frustration throughout each day of his life. Frustration occurs whenever a need cannot be gratified because of circumstances. But this normal frustration is not the same thing as neurotic frustration. The person who is deeply frustrated assimilates the frustration and then shows it in his behavior. Therefore, frustration tolerance is very important; it is a technical name for the rational deferment of the gratification of needs until such time as they can be legitimately gratified. The adolescent boy and girl experiencing sexual drive must defer the gratification of sex in order to avoid moral wrong. However, they should defer the gratification without repressing the drive. But when a person cannot cope with frustration, he is likely to develop symptomatic behavior.

The same principles apply to stress and threat. There are many stresses in our daily lives and ordinarily we survive them. We think of a mother standing at the sink washing the dishes, with a little child pulling at her dress for attention; the phone is ringing, someone is knocking at the door, the husband is late for dinner, and one of the children has a messed-up diaper. Certainly, this mother is experiencing stress. Stress occurs when a person is badgered by many demands at the same time, as we see so clearly in the case of a soldier in actual combat. Here stress can reach an extremely high point and cause a disastrous psychological reaction.

Stress is therefore closely related to threat, and sometimes it reaches the point where there is actual threat of serious injury or death. And when stress reaches a certain point, as Selye has indicated in his research, the individual begins to break apart. Anyone can suffer a breakdown, even though the point of stress tolerance varies with the individual's level of integration and adjustment. We clearly see the effects of stress and low stress tolerance in the hysterical person, who literally flies to pieces under the influence of stress. The same is true with respect to threat. We are threatened by many things, including impoverishment, death, loss of a job, or ill health. Threat, like stress, varies with the personality of the individual. If a person is already anxious, threat will produce a much more pronounced effect than if he is emotionally well-adjusted and mentally healthy.

These four factors define the path to normality and mental health, or to abnormality and mental illness. If a person learns in the course of development to cope successfully with conflict and frustration, or with stress and threat, he will likely mature and become a well-adjusted adult. Let us note, therefore, that there is nothing in the dynamics of human needs that causes the difficulty. Needs are simply natural tendencies toward things that are required. But when needs are distorted, under- or overdeveloped, or twisted by the mismanagement of conflict and frustration or of stress and threat, one is likely to encounter psychological difficulty. Poor reaction to these factors results in the formation of defensive mechanisms and the symptomatic behavior of the neuroses and psychoses, all of which are simply ways of solving human problems. Just as the schizophrenic solves his fear of reality by escaping into a dream world, so the normal person will stabilize his relationship to reality by work, play, healthy interpersonal relationships, or by finding a purpose in life that will support him in his various efforts.

## Needs, Feelings, and Mental Health

The dynamics of human needs is complemented by other factors that are important to mental health and that result from the manner in which a person copes with needs, conflicts, and frustrations. I refer to human feelings and emotions, which are also dynamic in their influence on behavior. Let us use a simple example to illustrate this point. A girl, twenty-five years old, is highly neurotic with a strong compulsive component in her psychological makeup. During the course of psychotherapy we discover that when this girl was very young she was rejected by her mother so that the need for affection was never gratified. She has never felt love, nor has she learned how to love others. As a result, from early childhood she has felt bad, evil, and rejected. When such a person feels that she is evil, what happens? She develops guilt—a deep, unconscious, pervasive guilt that reaches out to everything that she does. And how does one get rid of this guilt? One way would be to wash one's hands repeatedly, and here we encounter the mechanism involved in the hand-washing compulsion. This compulsion is a defense against guilt; the behavior, even though bizarre, is quite understandable.

In the course of human development the range of feelings increases to a great extent, and in some instances these feelings are deeply negative and self-destructive. Hostility, hatred, envy, jealousy, inferiority, inadequacy, insecurity, and similar feelings are all negative and destructive. These feelings are generated in people who are deeply frustrated, who cannot resolve basic conflicts, who feel unwanted and unloved, and whose other needs are poorly gratified if at all. Healthy people have healthy feelings; they are part of their makeup. They see all of the tomorrows as possibilities for further self-realization. They like people, they enjoy things, they have fun, and they are optimistic. They have a zest for life. Unhappy and unhealthy people, on the contrary, are just the opposite. They are chronically beset by conflicts and frustrations and always feel threatened by stress and threat. Their feelings are negative rather than positive in character. Their whole outlook is pessimistic. For these reasons, joy and a sense of humor are characteristically lacking; they clearly distinguish the normal, happy person from one who is maladjusted or neurotic. Feelings are the barometer of mental health and of mental illness.

# 42. Mental Health and the School

## LEO H. BARTEMEIER

At the outset it is essential for us to understand that all human behavior has meaning and purpose. The knowledge of this fact has been well established for the past fifty years, and although it is of practical value for people in all walks of life, it is especially useful for everyone engaged in the teaching profession. It helps us to understand the difficulties encountered in the learning process. It affords understanding as to why children behave or misbehave, and it makes it possible for us to understand why some teachers always exert a wholesome influence on their pupils and why other teachers find it so difficult to secure the cooperation of the children in their classrooms. The knowledge to which I am referring has also made it possible for us to understand why some people enjoy wholesome relations with each other, and why others find it so difficult to get along with their contemporaries or with persons in authority.

Our knowledge about human behavior and human relations is the chief concern of psychiatrists and clinical psychologists, of psychiatric social workers, and of sociologists and anthropologists. Clinical psychologists work with psychiatrists in mental hospitals and with psychiatrists in private practice, and their services are highly useful to all organizations interested in guidance, counseling, and treatment. Both psychiatry and clinical psychology have contributed extensively to general and special education, from nursing school to graduate school, and are deeply concerned with all problems of maladjustment and mental illness.

### Defining Mental Illness

Mental illness includes a number of afflictions which vary from the disorders which are only partially disabling to those which are totally incapacitating. The majority of mental illnesses do not require hospitalization, and the persons who suffer from them are able to remain with their families and to continue with their occupations.

The common belief that the mentally ill are all stark mad, violent, or dangerous is a misconception. Only a small fraction of all the mentally ill are dangerous to themselves or to others, and with proper treatment many of these patients recover and are again able to lead useful lives. It is also untrue that those who speak of suicide or threaten to destroy themselves will not do so. Every remark pertaining to self-destruction needs to be regarded seriously. It is erroneous to think that all those who suffer from mental illness have lost control over their minds. Anyone who would visit the patients in a mental hospital would observe that the greatest number of them are rational, logical, intelligent, and that their behavior is altogether conventional. Who, then, are the mentally ill?

It is a significant fact that those who suffer the most serious mental afflictions are not qualitatively different from ourselves. The difference is a quantitative one, and it is necessary to understand that we are only more or less mentally healthy. No one is in complete control of himself at all times, even though it may be pleasant to entertain such notions. In everyday life there is much of our behavior that is irrational and beyond our conscious control. Everyone is liable to behave in ways which are far from one's best intentions. Many accidents, for example, are of this character. We often tend to protect our self-esteem by the false belief that another person, or a specific circumstance, or a situation was responsible for our having injured ourselves or someone else. We show, however, that we know that an accident was a self-destructive experience when we remark, "I cut my finger," "I broke my arm," "I bumped my head," or "I sprained my ankle." These familiar remarks reveal the awareness of personal responsibility for accidents suffered.

Many people wish to pay attention to what a lecturer is saying, but despite their best efforts their minds wander into daydreaming and thinking about other matters. It is in moments of inattention that we have accidents or make mistakes in reading or writing. Our moods vary from day to day, in various degrees of cheerfulness and sadness. Everyone has experienced periods of elation or depression, and everyone at some time in life has thought of suicide, or of harming one's self, or of killing someone else. No one, on retiring for the night, can invariably be certain of falling asleep promptly or of how well or how poorly he will sleep. No one can know in advance whether he will dream or walk or talk or engage in other activities during sleep. Everyone has difficulty at some time or other in distinguishing what is real from what is unreal—whether something was dreamed or whether it was experienced while awake. These are but a few of the numerous examples which show that we have only more or less control over ourselves, and that we are only more or less mentally healthy, and that no one of us can maintain complete control of our mental activities and our behavior. We reveal ourselves to others to the best of our abilities, and in doing so it is necessary to hide much that we know about ourselves, because we all wish to be respected and to have the approval of others. We know relatively little about ourselves, however, and those who know us will also know many facts about ourselves of which we are wholly unaware. These facts are more or less unpleasant, and we hide them even from ourselves. Many of us have less confidence in ourselves than the degree of confidence which other persons have in us.

One of the fascinating facts about the emotional life is that when human beings undergo experiences which they cannot tolerate, they may regress to earlier periods of development. When his life is threatened, the opossum becomes motionless. When darkness overtakes a man walking in the forest, he has the opportunity to turn back and retrace his steps. When we become severely fatigued after a long day of work, we turn away from the world and go to sleep. In doing so we regress to early periods of development. When we are able to recall our dreams, we find that they are often senseless, not in keeping with our daytime experience, and irrational, foolish, silly, or frightening. In our dreams we regress to primitive ways of thinking. Our dreams are the way our minds work during sleep, and our minds never cease operating in sleep although on awakening it seems to us that the reverse must be true. If someone has heard us talking in our sleep we deny it because we remember nothing, and it seems that it cannot be true. When we ask the other person what we were talking about in our sleep we are usually told that what we were saying was completely unintelligible, that it was gibberish. Little children of two and three years sometimes speak a primitive language all their own which is equally unintelligible to themselves and to their parents. This language is thought to be inherited from uncivilized ancestors.

When some adults experience crises which have greater psychological impact than they can tolerate, they automatically regress to previous levels of emotional development. These regressions are recognized as various forms of mental illness requiring hospitalization.

Following childbirth, for example, some women regress to that stage of human development in which there is no distinction between the self and the not-self. They suffer acutely from the conviction that those around them know what they are thinking and can read all their thoughts; and they know nothing whatever about having given birth to a child. As one observes them it is evident that they are severely withdrawn from the reality of their lives. But we know that little children are much the same. They believe their parents know what they are thinking, and they too have not yet developed a sense of reality. Upon recovery, women who become mentally ill after childbirth liken their illness to a bad dream.

The mechanism of regression operates beyond the conscious control of every individual. It is something which happens *to* us. It is not something which we bring about through our volition. Its occurrence cannot be predicted. It is an automatic protective measure or device which prevents the total disorganization of our personalities. Early hospitalization and early psychiatric treatment of women who succumb to mental illness following childbirth often result in successful cure within three or four months, and many of them are restored to living again with their families. The psychology of women is more complex than that of men, and this is probably the reason why a larger percentage of women develop serious mental disorders requiring hospital treatment.

In even the most severe illnesses, however, there are always some mental faculties which remain healthy. No one ever becomes mentally ill throughout one's self. In addition to this fact it has always been known that during mental illness there are forces within every sick person which are operating toward recovery. This self-healing is most clearly discernible in many of the depressive conditions which disappear spontaneously. These mental depressions may incapacitate the person for weeks or even months, but recovery from them occurs without medical treatment. It is also well known that there are many people in the community who, though they suffer from mental disorders, are nevertheless able to continue in their occupations and to live with their families.

All these facts tend to show that it is incorrect to think that anyone ever *loses* his mind. It may be that for a time they suffer from a lack of control over their feelings or of their customary control over their rational thinking, but even those who suffer the grave forms of mental illness never lose their mental faculties. Their faculties are misplaced temporarily but can always be regained.

## Detecting Mental Illness in Schoolchildren

Little children—those in kindergarten and in the first grades—have far less control over themselves than older children. In fact, until the age of five years, children are so unmanageable in their behavior that the educational system does not permit their entry into school until that period of their development. The Church does not regard them as responsible for their behavior until the age of seven. They are still more irrational than rational, and they are too much under the influence of their primitive, uncivilized impulses to conform to the conventional behavior required in the classroom. They may be healthy in terms of their chronological development and have reasonably healthy parents; they are just not old enough to have acquired control over themselves so as to be amenable to the educational process.

The signs and symptoms of mental illness are already evident in some children before the age of five years. Some of these children are mentally retarded, and their retardation is the result of inheritance or acquired influences in their relations with their parents. Other children become quite withdrawn from reality, or they have been so intimidated that they become the so-called model children who never misbehave and who always do everything that is expected of them. They are never naughty, and they are, unfortunately, the delight of school teachers, who do not recognize that they have become too terrified to ever misbehave in the classroom or in their relations with their superiors or other children. It is a sad mistake on the part of teachers not to recognize that these children whose behavior has been portrayed as a model for the behavior of other children as sorely need to liberate their aggressive behavior as other children already manifesting signs of mental illness.

In our culture, we have overemphasized the importance of human intelligence and have failed to understand that human emotions are of greater significance. We know many children, for example, whose mental retardation is the result of emotional deprivation or emotional conflict. The better schools for the training of the mentally retarded are well acquainted with this knowledge. Any number of children with intelligence quotients of fifty or over have been able to develop their native intelligence level of performance after a year of residence in wholesome environments. This is but a single example of how intellectual activity may be smothered by influences in family life. We are all familiar with the fact that when we are worried, when we feel depressed, or when we are excited, we cannot think as well as when we are more composed, in a good mood, and untroubled. Unintentional damage to the development of intellectual potentialities is said to begin in infancy and the period of babyhood. These statements do overlook the instances of inherited mental deficiency. However, the concept of inherited deficiency is generally overemphasized because maladjusted teachers tend to perpetuate this type of thinking. We need to recognize that if we had less intelligent but better-adjusted teachers in our schools, the educational process would be a happier and more wholesome experience for many children.

Some of the individual maladjustments of school teachers are related to the emotional atmosphere in the school. We need to consider that a low quality of morale among the teachers in the school is usually due to a poor quality of leadership by those in charge of school administration. We may speak, therefore, of schools that are sick, as well as of schools that are healthy. This problem is one of group psychology, now well recognized everywhere. A school principal who suffers a chronic physical illness, or who for other reasons is unfit to function as a parental surrogate to the teachers in the school, unknowingly and unintentionally prevents them from functioning wholesomely and effectively with their pupils. Situations of this kind are equally familiar to psychiatrists and clinical psychologists who have worked with industrial organizations. In manufacturing, in department stores, in fact in any type of business, it is obvious that the emotional failures of management are often responsible for dissatisfaction among employees. We are all familiar with the fact that universities, colleges, manufacturing plants, and hospitals are as excellent as the persons who manage them. Children in school not only reflect the attitudes of their parents but also the attitudes of their teachers who, in turn, reflect the attitudes of school principals in the same way that workers in industry reflect the attitudes of management.

## Emotional Growth and Development

We tend to think of human personality in terms of the total reactions of a child or adult to the various interpersonal and other situations he encounters. These total reactions represent the final outcome of three components which contribute to mental functioning. The first component of personality is seen in the infant who is under the domination of his instinctual strivings. As we meet him, we know that he wants something from us. He seeks our attention, our approval, our affection. He seeks gratification of hunger, the comfort of being held. He seeks relief from pain or cold; he wants something from everyone he meets. He seeks only from others, and we expect nothing from him in return by way of appreciation or gratitude. We know he is yet too little and too young. Our own pleasure and satisfaction derive from our personal feelings of usefulness in his behalf and from our affection for him. We know that infants cannot receive too much affection; that they cannot be spoiled.

The human being develops from infancy through babyhood, and during childhood a second component in personality formation is developed. We speak of this component as the ego, meaning the "I" or the "self." Soon after the acquisition of language, the baby is liable to refer to himself as though he is speaking about someone else. He says, for example, "Robert wants drink." He refers to himself by the name his parents have been calling him. A little later he refers to himself as "me," and only then does he come to use the personal pronoun "I." This gradual development of the sense of reality, or of the distinction between the self and the not-self, or of the recognition of personal identity is a process about which parents and nursemaids are often more familiar than teachers. It will be seen later, however, how important consideration of this development is for understanding the transformations in personality which take place in childhood, in adolescence, and in adult life.

The third component in personality formation is spoken of as the superego, a prohibitive instrument which functions like, but is different from, our concept of conscience. The superego can be described very briefly as the incorporation within the child of the prohibitions of his parents.

The harmonious functioning among the three components of personality is regarded as an ideal condition of mental health. Whenever these three distinctive components of personality are in conflict with each other, we have the condition of intrapsychic conflict or neurosis. To be afflicted with intrapsychic conflict means to be neurotic. We distinguish between different kinds of neuroses. If the intrapsychic conflict is mild, the person may still be regarded healthy. However, an intense intrapsychic conflict partially or completely immobilizes a person in following his occupation and gives rise to difficulties in his relations with other persons.

School children are often reported by their teachers as being capable of doing much better work than reports indicate if they would only try. It cannot be said, however, that the laziness which is thereby implied, and for which children are criticized by their parents, is a justifiable accusation. We know that good teachers do not consciously intend to make accusations against children because they themselves are frustrated in their efforts with them, and we are equally certain that many teachers sincerely believe that if children would try harder they would do better. The fact that they do not do better, however, is not to be ascribed to laziness. It is rather due to lack of motivation or to some temporary physical condition; or it is a reflection of parental attitudes or the teacher's own lack of enthusiasm for her work.

The child psychiatrist and the clinical psychologist who examine many children find a marked difference between the levels of children's intellectual abilities and their actual accomplishments. The results of their examinations show the presence of the internal emotional conflict I have been attempting to describe. The more teachers understand the psychological health or ill health of their pupils, the more intelligently will they word the monthly reports which parents usually take so seriously.

What has been said about school children who are already suffering from various manifestations of neuroses is also applicable to many adult patients in mental hospitals. The psychological examinations of these patients frequently show a discrepancy between their intellectual development and their actual performance. As they improve under treatment and their conflicts become diminished, their psychological-test performances also improve.

School teachers often observe that the child who presents specific behavior problems in the classroom may later become more compliant, more obedient, and generally better behaved. Such observations confirm the scientific observations that emotional disorders in children may appear and disappear at various levels of their chronological development.

It is also a matter of common observation that some teachers always encounter more behavior problems with their pupils than other teachers do with the same group of children. Whenever this occurs we can only conclude that unknowingly and unintentionally the teacher who experiences repeated classroom difficulties has somehow initiated them or provoked them, and that the children are reacting to the emotional maladjustment of the teacher.

The education of children is one of the noblest of all the professions. The Church has always emphasized the importance of quietly reviewing with one's self one's daytime activities on retiring for the night. This principle has always been referred to as the nightly examination of conscience. All school teachers who are dedicated to their vocations would do well to review their behavior with their pupils, as well as with other teachers, each night before going to sleep. A self-examination has been found to be an excellent device for improving individual daytime behavior. The wisdom of the Church with regard to the nightly examination of conscience can be relied upon not only for the original purpose for which it was designed, but also for the purpose of providing better educational opportunities for children.

The transition from home to school at the age of five is accomplished easily and with much pleasure by children whose emotional development is in keeping with their chronological age. Such children look forward with eager excitement to the day of starting school. Other children with the same intellectual endowment and of the same chronological age are retarded in their emotional growth and are either unable to leave their mothers and must return home with them, or they can only start school with their mothers present and make the transition from their mothers to their teachers gradually and painfully.

Five-year-old children who leave their mothers easily as they enter school and whose emotional development is in keeping with their age are able to enter into school life with attentiveness and can learn readily. Children for whom the entry into the first grade is an emotionally painful experience are more concerned about the separation from their mothers and are thinking more about them than whatever may be taking place in the classroom. They are unable to be attentive or to participate in the class activities, and they have little zest for learning. They are emotionally retarded. They are unhappy and only gradually achieve interest and attachment to their teachers and to other children. When these same children are sent to summer camps for the first time, they experience the same painful separation from home that they underwent when they began school. When they marry they remain more attached to their mothers than to their mates, and the boys are usually found unfit for military service. Their mothers have not changed.

The children who have average or superior intelligence and sound physical health but suffer failures in emotional growth and development are the children who often develop mental illnesses in their adult lives. They are prone to develop these illnesses when they experience the crises which are associated with living. The same crises which percipitate mental disorders in these persons will not bring about personality disorganization in those whose emotional development has been wholesome. A young married woman, the mother of two children, suffered a severe mental depression and attempted suicide within two months after the death of her mother. The loss of her mother was the crisis that brought about her depression. In this depression she suffered insomnia, loss of weight, and loss of interest in her husband, in her children, and in her own personal hygiene. Life without her mother was unbearable. She was hospitalized and treated successfully. She appeared to have made a complete recovery, but a year later when her husband lost his position and was unemployed for several weeks, she became morose again and required professional care by the family physician, who was able to assist her in recovering emotional balance without the necessity of a second hospitalization. This young woman lives with an emotional handicap. This is commonly described as emotional immaturity. Her mother was never able to free her daughter from herself, and her daughter always remained more a part of her mother than a free and independent person.

This thumbnail sketch of the life of a mother and her daughter portrays a disaster in human development that begins at the time of birth. To regard this disaster as the sole responsibility of the mother would be a serious mistake, because the tragedy grew out of the mother's deprivation of love in her relations with her husband. When a woman is not loved by her husband she often tends to seek the love from her child. She does so quite unknowingly and without recognizing the damaging effect on her child. She cannot cling to her husband, and out of her personal emotional need she clings to her child.

What has been described is characteristic of many mother-child relationships, and every school teacher has become familiar with children whose emotional life has been stunted in the manner I have been describing. The mothers of these children are so possessive that their children can never achieve a natural aggressiveness and a sense of self-reliability. It needs to be emphasized, however, that the mothers of whom I am speaking are not to be blamed or criticized. Their abnormal attachments to their offspring are only secondary to the failures in emotional development of the men whom they have married. The fathers of emotionally immature children exercise a minimum of influence in the lives of their children, and the histories of these families usually show that the mother was the more powerful influence and that the father was more like a shadow in the lives of his children.

## Human Instincts and Development

In any discussion concerning emotional growth and development, it is advisable to recognize the inherited forces and their influence on human development. These forces are inherited through the germ cells of the parents and are present, therefore, from the time of conception. We speak of these forces as the human instincts. Instincts are present in all animal life. They are observable and familiar to everyone and are spoken of as the creative and destructive forms of behavior: the self-preservative or life instinct and the destructive or death instinct. The life instinct includes the sexual instinct and the instinct to propagate the human race. It includes the love of self, the love of others, and the creative impulse, which may express itself in painting, in sculpture, in music, in drama, or in any of the other aesthetic and artistic expressions. The death instinct or the destructive impulse, though also present at birth, is not apparent in infancy and can only manifest itself after some muscular development and coordination, after which it shows itself in hostility to others either in phantasy or in action. In wholesome development the destructive impulse is expressed in socially acceptable and useful forms of work and play.

We are basically creatures of instinct or impulse, and it is only through years of training and development or acculturation that we become civilized and able to live comfortably with other human beings. The veneer of our civilization is, however, very thin, and our uncivilized animal instincts always threaten to break through in our behavior with others.

During infancy and babyhood the human being lives entirely under the domination of the instincts, especially of the self-preservative instinct. The infant wants what he wants when he wants it. He wants no delay, tolerates no frustration, and becomes livid with rage if his needs are not immediately satisfied. He lives solely for himself. He is amoral, asocial, and completely primitive in his behavior. He has no shame and no sense of disgust. In the beginning and for many months after birth he does not distinguish himself from his surroundings. He does not know that which is himself and that which is not himself. Only gradually does he come to develop the sense of reality and to acquire the ego or "I" faculty.

Primarily, however, the infant sleeps, eats, and eliminates like the animals, and for the first months of life these activities comprise his total behavior. He does not distinguish his mother's breast as something apart from himself and only gradually does he discover his fingers, his toes, his navel, and other parts of the body. Only through the influence of training does he learn not to bite, scratch, or strike others. Only after the first years of training does he become housebroken and learn to eat with knife and fork and spoon and not with his fingers. Only gradually does he learn to rise from all fours and assume the biped posture, and only gradually does he acquire adult speech.

Children love themselves and no one else until about the eighth year of life. This self-love is essential for human growth and development. Unfortunately, some fathers and mothers unknowingly arrest their children's emotional development, and many persons continue to love themselves and no others throughout their lives. Children whose emotional development proceeds healthily develop attachments to other children, close, intimate relations with members of the same sex, and through these friendships they come to care as much for others as for themselves. It is a mistaken notion that everyone has the ability to love others, if by love we mean the ability to care for another person as much as or more than one cares for oneself.

It is an original necessity that one must love oneself first before one can come to love another, and it is essential to wholesome emotional living that one should always be able to love oneself, to have self-respect and self-regard. But the love of others, or giving more of one's love to others than to oneself, is one of the principal hallmarks of emotional maturity. In this connection we distinguish between lust and love. Being sexually attached to another human being may be one aspect of one's love for another person, but to feel nothing but sexual attraction to another is no different than what occurs between animals.

The sexual instinct in human beings is present from the time of birth and is manifested in the behavior of little children by the pleasure of nail biting and sucking, in the release of tension through defecation and urination, and in the pleasurable sensation derived from rubbing, scratching, or tickling the skin. It is important to understand that the pleasurable or erogenous zones of the body that are the object of infantile sexuality do not include the sexual organs and that they persist throughout life to the lesser extent. It is not until the age of five or six that the sexual organs take precedence over these areas. Teachers are frequently concerned about thumb sucking, nail biting, and masturbation, and do not ordinarily know how to manage these problems, which trouble other children far less than the teachers themselves. No specific advice can be given other than the principal one of disregarding, overlooking, and paying no attention to such incidences of behavior. Teachers who react with anger to situations of this kind among their pupils might do well to consider whether their reactions may not be evoked by their own frustrations and conflicts over similar problems at earlier periods in their personal development. Nail biting as well as masturbation are understood as devices for reducing tension in the children whose lives and life situations do not provide them with the satisfactions and the happiness they have a right to experience in their relations with their parents and their siblings. The more attention that teachers pay to these devices of unconventional behavior among their pupils, the more they tend to intensify such avenues of escape from tension. Punishment of the child is completely unjustified, induces humiliation, and lowers self-regard.

The first appearance of sexual feelings associated with the reproductive organs is about the age of five or six. They diminish and fade as children reach the age of six and seven, when the total behavior becomes more quiet, more relaxed; and this is the period in which children become more educable. It is not until the time of puberty around the age of eleven, twelve, or thirteen that the sexual life is again awakened. Adolescence has come to be recognized as one of the stormy periods of crises for both boys and girls, during which the lightning changes in behaviors and attitudes are confusing to many parents, to other relatives, and to the teachers in the school. These points have already been developed in the preceding papers.

# 43. Cultural Determinants of Mental Health

## ALEXANDER A. SCHNEIDERS

Chapter 41 concerned itself primarily with the nature of mental health and with the subjective factors that influence both mental health and adjustment. Particular attention was paid to the relationship between basic personality needs and mental health, but the influence of conflict and frustration and stress and threat was also studied. There was no intent to imply that the behavior of human beings is wholly determined by these factors. We saw in fact that there are many kinds of motivating influences, including ideals and principles, goals, attitudes, and values, which also play an important part in determining mental life and behavior. I referred briefly to the fact that a basic philosophy of life is essential in the development of a person's mental health and that this philosophy always involves personal values, attitudes, principles, and ideals. Thus if a person's motives, ideals, and goals are healthy, adequate, and realistic, the chances are that he will remain mentally healthy.

What I wish to do here is to develop some useful concepts regarding the conditions and determinants of mental health. In referring to the conditions of mental health, we have gone one step beyond the dynamics of mental health already referred to. We should also distinguish the conditions of mental health from its determinants. The former concept refers to a situation or matrix out of which something emerges. For example, there is the ancient phrase "a sane mind in a sane body." This aphorism implies that a sane body is a condition of a sane mind. If on the other hand we refer to the impact of family relationships on mental health we are talking about determinants. In other words, family relationships help determine the course of mental health.

Let us go back for a moment to the concept of stress and threat. Many persons collapse mentally under stress, that is, under events and forces that are going on in the world around them. This world includes not only the structure and influence of the family, but also of the school, the neighborhood, the community, the church, and the cultural pattern within which personality develops. Here we can include also the influence of religion on mental health.

Let us first study the conditions of mental health before we turn to its cultural determinants. The first of these conditions is heredity. While we know far too little about the relationship between heredity and mental disorder, and do not want to overemphasize its importance, there is evidence that some disorders seem to be influenced by family traits; and in diagnosis the facts of genetic etiology can be of considerable importance.

Perhaps an even more important condition of mental health is the constitution of the individual person, which would include both his physical and his psychic makeup. There is considerable evidence to suggest that in some individuals there is a strong predisposition toward the development of mental health or mental illness. We cannot identify these influencing factors precisely, nor can we precisely define the term "constitution." But we do know that people differ from one another deep within the makeup of their personalities. They have unique nervous and glandular systems, and these systems are important in setting the stage for the evolving psychic constitution. Thus some infants and children seem to be naturally happy—they cry very little and have a joyous disposition; whereas others are cranky and irritable, crying almost from the moment they are born. These facts force us to recognize the possibility of a constitutional predisposition toward the development of mental health and good adjustment or the development of their opposites.

A third factor which acts as a condition for good adjustment and mental health is physical health. Ill health tends to undermine good adjustment. Ordinarily, happy children are healthy children, and healthy children are happy. Then there are the children in our classes, our neighborhoods, or our families who are just the opposite of this type. They are always sickly; they have hay fever, or asthma, or head colds. They are always sucking their thumbs or biting their nails. They characteristically complain, "I don't feel good. I can't go to school today. I've got a stomachache." Many of them are psychosomatic when they are five years old. Children use psychosomatic symptoms much more frequently than we realize and thus indicate a tendency toward the development of neurotic disorder. Physical ill health, therefore, is either a precondition or a sign of mental ill health.

Fourth, there are the factors of development and maturation, both of which are important to good adjustment and mental health. If a person is to achieve adjustment, mental health, or normality in adulthood, he must develop in a healthy manner, and he must achieve maturity. Development is a basic condition that influences a person's life, especially in childhood and adolescence. Mental health is therefore an emergent—a quality of an individual human being that results from the proper functioning of basic conditions.

The second broad category of factors determining mental health and adjustment can be classified as environmental determinants. This group includes physical surroundings, the home and family, parent-child relations, the community in which the individual lives, the school, and the church. The third category, to be developed later, consists of cultural influences on the growth of mental health. In order to study these factors most effectively, I will set them within a context of the newer science of epidemiology, which will give us a clearer picture of how mental health and adjustment are determined by external influences.

In recent years a new approach has grown up within the framework of medical ecology which is referred to as the epidemiology of mental illness and mental health. Ecology, as you know, is the study of man's relationship to his environment. What does his environment do to him? How does it affect him? Medical ecology, then, is the study of this relationship within the framework of medical science. Psychiatrists especially are interested in the larger question: How does the individual react to his environment? What exactly happens to him under certain circumstances? The term epidemiology refers to the familiar phenomenon "epidemic." Thus epidemiology is the study of mental illness as an epidemic. There is a serious question today as to whether mental illness has reached the proportions of an epidemic. We know from the figures on mental illness that it is the most ravaging of all our diseases. It takes the greatest toll of human resources, and it costs society more than any other disease.

In a recent publication, *Epidemiology and mental illness* (Plunkett and Gordon, 1960), published by the Joint Commission on Mental Illness and Health, the authors say, "The relevance of epidemiology to mental illness may seem questionable at first glance, especially if one is accustomed to associating this discipline with the control of infectious disease" (p. ix). Later on in this book, the authors discuss the question of the infection of mental illness and its communication to others. The fact is that epidemiology is a science which studies the factors initiating and controlling the appearance of disease within populations and is destined to provide much of the information and guidance on which public-health authorities of the future will base their approach to the problem of mental illness. Anyone who questions the existence of an epidemic of mental illness in the United States should consider the estimate that there may be as many as 17,500,000 Americans who have psychiatric disorders serious enough to warrant treatment. This epidemic is of larger proportions than we have ever seen with regards to any other disease in this country.

The prevalence of mental illness is one of the principal reasons why epidemiology is developing at a rapid pace. It reminds us that "mental illness—perhaps more than any other scourge of humanity—is a by-product of man's social existence in a complex environment of his own making. Much, of course, can be gained by studying the pathological processes in the individual; but complete understanding can be approached only as mental illness is viewed in the light of man's eternal striving to adapt himself to the demands of his destiny" (Plunkett and Gordon, 1960, p. xii). This statement is a clear and precise picture of what is happening in the area of mental illness, and also in the thinking of men who are much concerned with this problem. During the past fifty years many studies have been made on extrapersonal factors that enter into the development and the genesis of mental disorder, and almost every possible factor or relationship has been explored.

This situation cannot be easily reduced to experimental or even to empirical investigation because there are countless persons who never come to anybody's professional attention and who do not enter into the statistical picture. They never see a doctor, a therapist, or a counselor. They manage to struggle through their difficulties and to live with their symptoms and behavior problems without coming to the attention of an expert. On the other hand, there are many persons who go to physicians with what seems to be a physical illness, but whose diagnosis shows that there is nothing physically wrong—unless theirs is a psychosomatic disorder developing out of emotional difficulty. It is estimated by the medical profession itself that 50 to 75 per cent of the people who come to them for medical treatment do not require their services. The problem is essentially an emotional one. You can well imagine what a staggering figure this amounts to.

Various investigators have tried to bring together all these statistics but, because of inadequate hospital and medical records, the failure of disturbed persons to receive help, and other reasons, the statistical picture of mental illness or psychological disorder is very inadequate. The important thing, however, is that all these different facets of the problem have been studied, including the relationship between urban living and mental illness, sex and mental illness, and race and mental illness, and the connection between nationality, church membership, and psychological illness. In each case certain lines of evidence have been found that help us gain a better understanding of how the disorder develops.

Some of these relationships are sex-linked. We know, for example, that there are more women patients than there are men patients, whatever the reason may be. Involutional melancholia is obviously linked to the menopause in women, although men are not free from this disorder. But no man has ever suffered a postpartum psychosis. There are also certain national characteristics. For example, suicide rates run higher among certain national groups than among others, particularly in the northern part of Europe. We know that depressive psychosis is more common among the Mediterranean peoples than among the northerners in Europe. Manic-depressive psychosis seems to be related in some way to the Jewish population, and alcoholism is a problem that is very common among the Irish. Schizophrenia is found more often among Nordics than among the Mediterraneans.

Admittedly, these linkages could be biological or hereditary, which would push us back into endogenous factors again. Or they could be familial in character. No one knows the complete answer to these questions, but we do know that there are certain relationships that must be taken into account in trying to understand mental disorder and how it happens. All such questions are a part of the problem of epidemiology and help us understand where the epidemic comes from. Whatever the magnitude of the problem, with the tremendous incidence of mental disorder in the United States, we will have to continue to work hard to understand what exactly is happening to the American people.

The statistics available are staggering in their implications. According to reliable sources, one out of every ten or twelve people will spend some time in a mental hospital in their lives. One out of every twelve children born each year will sometime during his life suffer a mental illness severe enough to require hospitalization. These figures were published in 1952, and since then the figure has gone up to some extent. Patients in mental hospitals make up in any one day almost half of all the patients in all the hospitals in the United States. Each year 250,000 new patients are admitted to mental hospitals, and at least 200,000 are seen each year in psychiatric clinics.

During World War II about 900,000 men between the ages of 18 and 37 were rejected from military service because of mental illness or other personality disturbances. Another 460,000 were discharged from the service because of mental illness. In addition, there are almost 2,000,000 serious crimes committed each year, and these crimes are committed by maladjusted people. Fifty thousand persons are addicted to narcotics; there are about 3,800,000 problem drinkers in the United States, and 950,000 of these are chronic alcoholics. Each year 17,000 people commit suicide. And for every four marriages each year in the United States there is one divorce, and these figures do not take into account all the separations and family breakdowns that occur outside of divorce. And finally, there are 265,000 children between the ages of 7 and 17 who are brought into Juvenile Court each year, and this figure is constantly rising.

The picture is of course very disturbing, but we need to know these facts so that we know what we are up against when we talk about mental illness and mental health. We should ask ourselves some very very serious questions: What exactly is happening to society? Is the world changing in such a way that mental illness is inevitable in many people and that our uphill fight against mental illness is essentially a losing battle? It is well known that we need at least an additional 25,000 psychiatrists and 40,000 psychologists to cope with the problem. It is actually an uphill climb, and it will continue to be so as long as there is a growing change in the cultural pattern. All of us have heard reference to the existence of universal anxiety; and we all know that the core of mental disorder is intense anxiety. Some people cannot manage their anxiety and thus develop various behavioral mechanisms and symptoms in order to cope with it. Is there actually such a universal condition? Is something happening to our world that causes a general reaction, a deep feeling of anxiety, so that people no longer feel secure and are chronically frightened?

We certainly know this: the world has changed radically since 1910, and in many ways. During the past fifty years we have gone through two major, threatening, destructive wars, not counting minor skirmishes. Notice the term "threatening." We have already seen that threat of intense kind is one of the things that can throw a person off balance and can push him over the brink into mental disorder. During these fifty years we have also experienced the effects of a devastating depression, effects that left a serious impression on many people who are alive today. If a person's means of livelihood is taken away from him, he is deeply threatened, and many people destroy themselves by suicide or react with mental illness to this type of situation.

During the Second World War we invented the atomic bomb, which threatened complete annihilation of all peoples, and now of course we are faced with even more destructive weapons at the disposal of those committed to destruction. These are serious threats to our well-being. Many persons who seek counseling will tell you very frankly how frightened they are by the threat of total destruction. They are of course insecure and anxious people to begin with, but they are reacting to external events.

In addition to these more obvious threats, we also have experienced during the past fifty years a serious breakdown in our moral, religious, and social values. Family life has suffered serious disruptions, and we have seen already that one out of every four marriages is broken by divorce each year. This situation is bad enough, but the effects of divorce are even worse. Separation, desertion, divorce, and death disrupt the lives of the children who later on will enter into marriage. And most of them will disrupt the lives of their own children because of their neurotic inclinations, and thus we have an unending wave of psychological disruption. Children cannot grow up healthily without parents. If here and there you see someone who manages to grow up successfully after the death of one or both of the parents, he is the exception and not the rule.

There are many other things that have been happening to make people less secure, less certain of themselves, less sure of their values and goals, all of which create anxiety. Anxiety is the reaction to uncertainty and insecurity. When one feels that he cannot cope with reality, with his work, with his children, with interpersonal relationships, or with God, then he feels unsure of himself and insecure. He then experiences anxiety and tends toward the development of neurotic or psychotic symptoms or maladjustment.

The attack against this serious problem cannot be psychiatric or psychological alone. The psychiatrist could work twenty-four hours a day, every day of the week, and still never be able to cope with the problem. Therefore, the attack must also be sociological, educational, and religious. Teachers, clergymen, sociologists, and social workers must join forces with the psychiatrist and psychologist in their attack on mental illness.

One of the factors that has gained unusual attention in recent years because of this very problem is religion. Does religion offer us a hope for coping with mental disorder? Is religion conducive to mental health? Is the injunction to pray harder, to go to the Sacraments more often, and to turn to God a valid instrument for promoting mental health, peace of mind, and peace of soul? There are many persons who think that there is real value in religion for the development of mental health. Many psychologists, psychiatrists, and clergymen have been cooperating in various institutes throughout the country in an attempt to reach a better understanding of mental illness and to develop a better technique in working with persons suffering from some kind of mental disorder. Courses in psychology, psychiatry, and mental hygiene are being introduced into many seminaries in the belief that if the clergy can come to a better understanding of what is going on in the minds of people, they will be in a better position to help their parishioners. In New York City the National Academy of Religion and Mental Health is doing good work in this area. And there are countless publications—books, pamphlets, and articles—coming off the presses each year on this topic. In other words, there is a highly concerted effort involving some of the best minds of the country directed toward the mental-health problem.

The relationship of religion and mental health creates a strange paradox. If we take the facts just as they are, we can make a strong case for the value of religion and a strong case against it. One cannot rely wholly on the proposition, "Religion is a positive force in influencing mental health." Teachers particularly should keep in mind that religion does not of itself function as a positive force whenever we think it does or whenever we want it to. Here we have to be very careful. In many instances, a well-meaning teacher or mother, using the concepts of religion to control the behavior of children, has done more harm than good.

Let us first take a look at the negative aspects of religious influence. If religion contributes to mental health, we would certainly like to know whether those people who have devoted their lives to the service of God, including ministers, priests, nuns, and rabbis, experience mental disorders. If anybody should be free of mental disorder by reason of their dedication and vocation and also by the graces of God, or if anybody should have peace of mind, it should be the persons who are closest to God. Unfortunately, the fact is that these persons are no more free of mental disorders than are people in the general population. All of the empirical studies on this problem have demonstrated that mental disorder is as common among the religious as among the general population. Religion of itself, therefore, does not provide a guarantee of mental health. In addition, many lay persons who are devoutly religious, who go to church and pray regularly, receive the Sacraments, and are otherwise religiously active are often disturbed. They cannot seem to "pray themselves out" of the morass of mental difficulty. In fact, their anguish and anxiety are often deepened by the failure of religion to produce the effects they expect.

There is also the fact that formal religion can be the source of many conflicts, frustrations, and threats. Religion has much to do with generating disturbing and damaging feelings, particularly the feeling of guilt. The guilt that neurotics often feel in relation to their religion is of fantastic proportions, leading to shame, self-rejection, and degradation, which every psychologist recognizes as part of many psychological disorders.

Let us now look at religion and mental health from a positive viewpoint. Certainly, to the extent that religion gratifies basic emotional needs, promotes the feeling of being loved and accepted and of being worthwhile, and offers the promise of the security of eternal salvation, it is salutary to mental health. In other words, when religion promotes different aspects of mental health, it also promotes the psychological well-being of the person. There is no question whatever that religion, in the best sense of the term, is one of the most powerful instruments for mental health that is available.

The trouble is that, in their use and misuse of religion, in their frantic effort to gain peace of mind, people have failed to realize that religion undergoes a developmental process just like everything else; and that in the course of time there is an accretion of all sorts of feelings, habits, ideas, anxieties, and fears with respect to religion and the values that it represents. But we must understand that religion in the best sense of the term is not a developmental accretion of feelings and habits; it is a spiritual force that has to get to the soul of the individual before it can produce the desired effects. Unfortunately, standing between the graces of God and this spiritual soul is the psyche of the individual with all of its accretions; and very often religion is not able to do the work that it is capable of doing in promoting mental health until something—counseling, psychotherapy, self-understanding, self-insight, or conversion—peels away these accretions.

# 44. Basic Principles of Mental Hygiene

ALEXANDER A. SCHNEIDERS

The several approaches to problems of adjustment and mental health—mental hygiene, guidance, counseling, and psychotherapy— are closely allied. They have several aims in common, and often the principles of mental hygiene are put into practice in the counseling or therapeutic situation. It is helpful to think of the various factors that influence an individual for good or ill as arranged along a continuum that extends from his earliest experiences through various stages of growth and development to the other extreme of the continuum that includes counseling and psychotherapy. In other words, if we ask ourselves, how did this person who is mentally healthy and well adjusted get that way, and how did this other person who is maladjusted or mentally ill become ill, we see that the process began in the earliest moments of the person's life, not excluding the prenatal period. Growth and development start immediately when the organism is conceived. And when it emerges into the external world, other processes begin to influence him, such as training, conditioning, and education.

Of these factors, training is one of the earliest to influence the growing organism. For example, we begin toilet training early, and we also train the child in habits of cleanliness, eating, dressing, and so on. This training leads to the development of necessary habits by which the person is better able to meet the demands of reality. We then introduce discipline, a factor closely related to training; but discipline goes one step beyond training. As the child grows older, we introduce formal education, which begins ordinarily with kindergarten or nursery school and continues through grade school, high school, college, and graduate school. Education is different from training, just as training is different

451

from discipline, but they are closely allied. Education is a means whereby a person acquires many of the skills necessary to his adjustment, such as reading, writing, and spelling, and by which he also acquires knowledge. From this education he achieves a great many of the necessary facts, information, ideas, values, attitudes, and interests that are important to adjustment and mental health.

If all these forces of experience, training, discipline, and education, along with the continuous development of interpersonal relationships, particularly those within the family structure, were good and wholesome; if, in other words, the child had worthwhile experiences, a happy home life, good relations with his parents, firm and consistent discipline, and was trained in the right habits and attitudes, he should certainly develop a healthy, normal personality. But quite often something goes wrong. The child has a severe traumatic experience, the family breaks up because of the loss of the father or mother, there is poor parental discipline, or there is failure in development, and as a result the whole developmental process tends toward personality malformation. It is then that guidance, counseling, or psychotherapy may have to be added to education and experience.

As the child grows older and has to make decisions about school or career, we supplement the educational process with guidance. In this process we help a person think through a particular decision, provide him with necessary facts or ideas, and try to bring him to a point where the problem can be solved. But sometimes all of these things, including guidance, are not enough. The problem is deeper, more intense and disturbing, and the person may require counseling. If it becomes still worse, then psychotherapy may be indicated. These processes are not of themselves necessary, and there are a lot of people who have never had any counseling or therapeutic treatment. If the problem reaches extreme proportions and is not even amenable to psychotherapy, more stringent medical methods may have to be used, including shock therapy, drugs, or hospitalization.

Let us emphasize that these latter approaches to human problems are not of themselves necessary, and we would like very much to be rid of them. In a very real sense, every psychologist, psychiatrist, or psychiatric social worker would like to work himself out of a job. On the other hand, experience, training, development, education, discipline, and guidance have always been a part of human experience and growth because they are the natural means by which people reach maturity. Within this continuum mental hygiene can also be fitted. It is essentially a body of principles that are directed toward the maintenance or achievement of mental health and, of course, toward the prevention of mental illness. It is exactly equivalent to physical hygiene. If you want to be physically healthy you must practice certain principles of physical hygiene. You must eat correctly, get enough sleep, exercise, and rest in order to ward off illness and to promote health. Practicing physical hygiene is much simpler than the application of mental-hygiene principles because the dimensions of the human mind are not as well defined as are man's physical characteristics.

There is much we do not know about the nature, formation, and dynamics of the human mind. We have learned a great deal in the last one hundred years about behavior dynamics, but we are faced with the fact that many people who grow up in good environments still develop mental illness. However, the things we do know we can formulate as basic principles of mental hygiene.

Because there are different ways in which these principles may be applied, we should think of mental hygiene in terms of its different forms. The basic form of mental hygiene is preventative or prophylactic, which means simply that we will do whatever is necessary as parents, teachers, or counselors to set up situations in such a way that they will preclude the development of inadequate, immature, maladjusted, self-destructive, or symptomatic behavior. This principle is the most important one for mental hygiene. If we follow this principle early in the life of the child, we are much more likely to be successful in promoting his mental health. Sometimes the situation gets out of hand before the principles of mental hygiene can be put into operation. Parents may do the best they know how but it may not be enough, and the child begins deviating from the psychologically normal. He starts manifesting symptomatic or acting-out behavior, and the damage is done.

In such cases mental hygiene must become remedial or ameliorative. Then the principles of mental hygiene are directed against the existing behavior pattern, in exactly the same way that a physician prescribes a diet that acts against existing malnutrition in a child. The principles are the same as those directed toward the attainment of mental health, but in this case they are used against the existing problem. Let us say, for example, that a child is somewhat solitary in his behavior, showing tendencies toward withdrawal from other children. We think that perhaps if we send him to a boys' camp where he'll be with other children and get away from the influence of his parents, which is sometimes useful, he will have a chance to build friendships, relate to others, and draw away from his isolation. This action is ameliorative mental hygiene; and it might be the best thing we could do in such a situation.

There is also the method of supportive mental hygiene. Some persons outside the norm of mental health who undergo counseling or psychotherapy fail to develop a fully adequate personality. It may then be necessary to reinforce what has been achieved from time to time, and the approach is supportive rather than corrective. There may exist a strong tendency for a relapse to occur because the disorder has existed for some time. The patient himself is aware of this possibility, and thus there is always the chance that he will react again to pressures or conflicts as he did before. Here mental-hygiene principles are used to help the individual from sliding back into the abyss of symptomatic behavior and adjustment mechanisms.

These are the three basic forms of mental hygiene. But there is an even broader way of utilizing these principles which enables us to speak of the mental hygiene of the home, of the school, and of society. We have to recognize that there are communities that are sick, in which standards and practices are very poor and in which children are given carte blanche to do what they want to do. Not long ago in a wealthy county outside of New York City there was a teenage party which was completely unchaperoned and at which there was a great deal of drinking. There were about fifty local young people at the party, and very few of the parents knew where they were or what they were doing. Two of the boys got into a fight and one of them was killed. The community must accept responsibility for such tragic events. A community like this one is unhealthy, and there are many communities, particularly in large metropolitan areas, that are as unhealthy in their own way as are individuals. Imagine the moral tone of these communities where crimes such as murder and rape are common events more or less accepted by members of the community.

In some of these situations there is little that could be done except to destroy the slum areas and start from the beginning. This solution is being tried in urban renewal, which could be an effective form of mental hygiene. Certainly it is better, from the standpoint of mental hygiene, to live in a decent, clean home and neighborhood than in a dirty one. Studies of the relationship between the individual's adjustment problems and his physical environment show a definite connection. The more dilapidated and impoverished the neighborhood, the more likely is a person to develop behavior difficulties. Boys and girls with a record of truancy often state very simply that they couldn't stand it at home; that physically it was so disagreeable and painful to live in their environment that they had to get away.

We should therefore reorient our thinking about mental hygiene along broader lines. We must learn to apply mental-hygiene principles to the home, the school, and the community as well as to individuals. Often we find that the results of good counseling are completely counteracted by a return to the environment that had much to do with the original problem. Sometimes the only remedy for people whose difficulty resides in the home or in family relationships is environmental therapy. Many persons, after six months or a year of counseling, will leave unfavorable environments by their own decision and become much healthier people. In applying mental hygiene, therefore, we cannot limit it to a person-to-person counseling relationship or to a therapeutic relationship, but must apply it to those external situations which may influence the person very deeply.

The church is another agency which influences human behavior and can be utilized for mental-hygiene purposes. In Protestant communities particularly, the church is used quite effectively to create social situations for young people wherein they are given a chance to communicate with one another, establish healthy relationships, and promote social adjustment. This practice is good mental hygiene, and other denominations would do well to follow this lead.

In the same way that the church promotes social activities and adjustment, it often works to broaden the scope of sex education, and such programs are good mental hygiene. For a period of some years I participated in such a program, often lecturing to as many as 600 parents at a time on the principles of sex education and control of sex behavior, especially in adolescence. Programs of this kind are of course prophylactic mental hygiene directed toward the problems of sexual behavior and adjustment.

Let us digress for a moment into an area that many of us have wondered about. What about the nonreligious avenues to the "good life"? The good life is of course what we are all looking for; it is what we want for our children—a good, happy, decent, and productive life. Have psychology and psychiatry preempted what formerly belonged to the church, to morality, and to religion? Do we now go to a psychiatrist with our problems instead of to our priest or minister as we did previously? From time immemorial there have been two persons who were the haven of refuge for troubled and disturbed people. The first was the family doctor, to whom nearly all problems were taken for solution. He was the family confidant, the source of knowledge and wisdom, the person to tell us what to do in time of crisis. And the second one was the clergyman—the priest, the minister, or the rabbi— someone to tell us what was good and right and how to behave in such a way that we would no longer be troubled. And of course our religious practices provided a certain amount of mental peace. If we did something wrong, we could set our minds at ease by Confession or by using the other Sacraments to give us the strength we needed to face the difficulties, battles, and conflicts of life.

Has this approach been preempted by modern psychiatry? The answer is yes, to some extent, with the result that there has been considerable conflict between religion and psychiatry. We have all heard of the serious and sometimes bitter criticisms of psychiatry by representatives of religion. And others have lashed out against modern psychiatry because of its connection with Freud, whose emphasis on sex was coupled with a deterministic and materialistic philosophy. There have been many conflicts, but today there is a great deal more agreement among the helping professions. There is much less antagonism and suspicion and much more cooperation.

We must recognize that there is room in the area of mental hygiene for everybody concerned with human problems, for any specialist or member of the healing professions; and we must appreciate that these different avenues to the good life are closely allied. We can talk about principles of mental hygiene and argue that if one follows these principles he will get along well; he will achieve the good life. But we can argue just as forcibly that if a person develops the moral virtues to a high degree he will also achieve the good life. And if he realizes the theological virtues, he is even more likely to develop a noble life. Consider, for example, the quality of fortitude. Certainly, if a person develops the fortitude to stand up to the difficulties and problems of life it is unlikely that he will need a psychiatrist or other specialist. One has to be tough in order to meet the dangerous and threatening aspects of daily living, to get up from the ground as it were when the vicissitudes of life knock one down. This is the virtue of fortitude. Or an alcoholic can appeal to Alcoholics Anonymous in order that he may achieve the virtue of temperance.

This argument represents the moralistic approach to the good life. By the same rule, if a person practices his religion in a sensible, mature, and realistic manner; if he activates his relationship to God in a healthy manner, he is taking a giant step toward the good life. In other words, psychology, morality, and religion all offer us important means and principles for achieving peace of mind, happiness, good adjustment, mental health, and the good life. And of course none of these avenues should be left unexplored if we wish to use mental hygiene successfully.

The conflicts between these different approaches to mental health have been more apparent than real. Psychiatry, psychology, and moral theology are in their own way normative sciences. They tell us what we ought to do if we want to live a good and healthy life, just as civil law tells us what we ought to do if we want to be good citizens. Since there are these different avenues to mental health, and since there are different facets to human nature and to human problems, we should always keep in mind, when working with adolescents, the possibility of referral. If we are counseling a person who has a problem outside of our competence, then the method of referral becomes just as basic and just as important as any other method that may be used in helping young people. If a boy or girl comes to the counselor with a deep moral problem and the counselor does not regard himself as an expert in ethics, then perhaps the best thing to do is to refer the youngster to somebody who knows how to handle moral problems. If we can answer his questions and help him solve his problem, fine; but if the problem is outside our competence, referral is the proper method. Similarly, if the client has a religious problem and the counselor does not feel comfortable discussing religious problems with him, then referral to a priest, minister, or rabbi is in order. By the same rule, if a child is mentally sick and shows extremely disturbing symptoms, referral should be made to a psychiatrist or to some agency for proper treatment.

In working with people we observe that many of their problems are interlaced. As an example let us consider the serious and common problem of homosexuality. A youngster comes to a counselor, and after hedging around for a half hour or so, finally blurts out, "I think I am a homosexual." Now homosexual behavior is obviously outside the pale of accepted morality; it is behavior that cannot be tolerated morally; so in itself it is a moral problem. The client might say, "I went to a priest and he was very kind and understanding but he didn't help me. I still have the same problem and I thought maybe you could help me." Now, is homosexuality a moral problem? Yes, objectively it involves behavior that contravenes moral principles; but basically it is a psychological problem; and there are many sexual difficulties of this nature. Sometimes we will see promiscuity develop in a young boy or girl. We may react to this situation with a strong feeling of repugnance. "How immoral can youngsters get?" But on investigation we find that the girl involved is very lonely, seldom has any dates, and wants so much to be accepted by the group and by the young men in her group, that she becomes desperate for attention and love. She has no real interest in sex as such, but she knows that by making her gifts available to a young man, she can get some acceptance, some attention, something remotely akin to love. This problem is no longer a strictly moral one. It does have the quality of immorality in it, but the problem is basically emotional and psychological.

This psychological aspect of some human problems is important to understand. Unfortunately, it is something that many religious persons do not understand; they do not undertand that although these problems are objectively moral, subjectively they are emotional and psychological. Not long ago a husband was referred to me at the insistence of his wife. She related that she had found pornographic magazines under the mattress and that her husband was given to drawing sexual pictures. The situation sickened her and she wanted no more to do with him. We might think that here is an oversexed individual. He's looking at sexy magazines and drawing sexy pictures and casting lewd glances at the girl next door. But the truth of the matter is that this man was sexually impotent! Far from being oversexed, he was incapable of adequate sexual expression. His behavior was his way of proving to himself and his wife how powerful he was. This is the story of every Don Juan, the patient who makes love to every woman he meets. He has to prove his sexuality.

This is the way we have to "read" symptoms and behavior. We cannot take them at face value, but must try to understand the problem itself and to see if we have a religious or moral problem, or something quite different. We have all heard of and encountered scrupulosity at one time or another. Is scrupulosity a moral problem? It is not. It is a deeply emotional and psychological problem that is extremely resistant to therapy. The patient complains that he is always committing sin, or that he commits hundreds of sins every day. This may sound like immorality, but the problem is not a moral one at all and should not be approached in this way. What we have to do, therefore, is to determine the nature of the problem; and when it is beyond our field of competence we must find someone to whom the patient can be referred.

Let us now take a brief look at some of the basic principles of mental hygiene. The first of these principles has to do with physical well-being, which can contribute importantly to mental health. Children especially have to be watched carefully with respect to physical health. Sensitivity and anxiety can be symptoms of inadequacies in diet, rest, or exercise; once these inadequacies are corrected, much of the sensitivity and anxiety disappears.

Secondly, mental hygiene requires reasonable conformity to moral and social norms. Although everyone is prone to mistakes, there are persons who are flagrantly immoral and who show unmistakable signs of mental ill health. Normal, healthy persons try at least to adhere to moral norms and bulwark their behavior with religious and moral principles. Ideally, they conform to the moral law even though, being human, they fall into error quite often. On the other hand, those who care little about morality, who carelessly violate ethical codes, laws, and principles, risk mental illness because they are likely to feel deeply guilty, and there are few things more destructive than guilt. Nobody can tolerate guilt feelings indefinitely. This problem is clearly illustrated in the scrupulous person, whose guilt may bring him to the brink of serious mental disorder.

A third principle important to mental hygiene involves the development of self-control and self-discipline, without which mental health and adjustment are difficult to achieve. Also necessary is the development of mature independence. We see many young people twenty or twenty-five years old who are still deeply tied to the maternal apron strings; or, to use a more recent phrase, they are strangled by the umbilical cord of emotion that mothers often wind around their children's throats. The mother is usually the offender in this regard, not because the father is without fault, but simply because the mother is ordinarily with the children much more and therefore has more opportunity to develop and maintain this emotional dependence. This theme has been treated in a well-known book by Strecker, *Their mothers' sons* (1946). In a companion volume, *Their mothers' daughters* (1956), Strecker points out again how a youngster's independence is choked off by anxious, possessive parents. Dependence of this kind does not allow for real personal growth. As adolescents approach adulthood, they must become independent, particularly in the emotional sense. But they must also become independent in thinking and acting. They must think for themselves, and they must acquire the ability to make decisions, especially about the important things in their lives. Decisiveness is a quality of the mature mind.

Mental health requires also the development of self-knowledge, which is the beginning of a healthy self-concept and a wholesome attitude toward one's self. There must also be a continuing development—no matter on how small a scale—of the important moral virtues. We do not say that a person must be perfect, nor should he be caught in the web of perfectionism, which is a distortion of the principle of moral development. But he should always strive toward the goal of perfection, even though he realizes that he will not reach it. However, the person who takes this injunction too literally becomes a perfectionist. The dynamics behind this perfectionism is the same as that behind compulsive orderliness. Just as some persons overemphasize the injunction "Orderliness is heaven's first law," others will give too much import to the principle "Cleanliness is next to godliness." Perfectionism is an unmistakable sign of neurotic tendency

The achievement of mental health requires also the development of effective habits. Many years ago William James said that we should confine "to the effortless custody of habit" as many things as we possibly can to free the mind for more important things. And that is of course what the average person does. We carry on countless activities every day without even thinking about them. Some things require our close attention, and others we do habitually. But there are some people who fail to develop worthwhile habits and thus accomplish very little. Good habits are obviously important to efficiency, and efficiency is necessary to effective adjustment.

Mental health is dependent also on flexibility and adaptability, which might seem something of a paradox in view of the fact that I have just emphasized the importance of habits. And yet both things are necessary. We clearly see the lack of flexibility in neurotic people. They are rigid; they cannot adapt readily to new or varying situations. Things always have to be blueprinted for them, and they are uncomfortable without this blueprint. Adjustment requires flexibility, an ability to change when it is necessary. Young people especially must learn how to relax and to adapt the pace of daily activities to the demands of both body and mind for rest and change. They must create opportunities for the reduction of tensions that are a part of daily living.

There are many other principles that we could develop if time permitted. For example, a person must find the right vocation in life, one that is suited to his interests, abilities, and characteristics. Countless people are unhappy because they are in the wrong vocational field. Developing a realistic attitude and seeing the world as it really is are also basic to mental health. And there must be an expanding awareness of one's relationship to God and an activation of this relationship in everyday affairs. These are some of the basic principles of mental hygiene which, if applied to ourselves or to other people with whom we work, would certainly help pave the way to mental health.

## Mental Hygiene in the School

If we now shift our focus to that form of mental hygiene which is found in the school and which can be applied by teachers to good advantage, we can see that there are a number of things that can be done. But first let us clear the ground of any false ideas regarding the use of mental hygiene in the classroom. We should not think of the school as a laboratory of adjustment. It is not the place for nondirective counseling, psychotherapy, or group therapy, as some people seem to argue. The classroom is primarily a learning situation, and the business of the teacher is to teach, which is particularly true at higher levels of education. In speaking of the mental hygiene of the school, therefore, I am not falling into the trap that many educationists—following the line laid down by John Dewey—have created for teachers by their insistence that education is a life process and an exercise in adjustment. The primary business of education is the intellectual development of the student, even though it does involve learning experiences in other areas. A child learns some psychomotor skills, habits that are social in nature, and principles of a moral and religious kind. Thus, throughout the educational process he grows physically, morally, spiritually, and socially as well as intellectually; but such growth is not the main purpose of education.

Nevertheless, it is easy for the teacher to function as a "mental hygienist" without doing anything but being a good teacher. He can function this way because there is an intrinsic relationship between the learning process and mental hygiene, since learning is a mental process and will vary in direct proportion to the degree of mental health and stability in the pupil. Every teacher has seen this relationship at work. If, therefore, a pupil is troubled by anxieties or hostilities, conflicts or frustrations, symptoms or disruptive behavior, then certainly he cannot concentrate well and will find it hard to study, and the whole learning process is disrupted.

To develop this point further let us ask, "What role or roles is the teacher supposed to play?" First of all, the teacher is required to play the role of a custodian of truth and a communicator of knowledge and skills. When he does this he has already fulfilled a major part of his role. But his role does not end here, because certainly a teacher is often a source of inspiration for the total development of the pupil. He serves as a model of behavior and of interpersonal relationships, so that just by being himself he can have a salutary effect on the pupil. Not long ago one of my clients informed me that he was going to be a psychologist. He said, "I think that being like you and doing the work that you do is the most wonderful thing in the world." This reaction is obviously a typical transference phenomenon, but it does reflect the influence that a teacher or a counselor can have on persons with whom he comes in contact. The teacher can help his students a great deal by serving as a model of behavior, competence, and professional performance, and this kind of help is mental hygiene at its best.

Whether he likes it or not, a teacher is in part a parent substitute, a mother or father surrogate. In many instances a boy might spend more time with his teacher than he does with his own father, because his father is traveling, working late at the office, or is otherwise engaged in various activities. In some instances the teacher becomes a parent substitute in toto, and in these situations he can do a great deal of good in helping the young person formulate sound ideas and healthy attitudes.

In still other situations, teachers function as faculty counselors. Here the contact extends beyond the classroom and the occasional get-togethers after class, and the teacher has an excellent opportunity to put mental-hygiene concepts into practice in his developing relationship with the student. Thus, without consciously trying to use mental-hygiene principles, a teacher can, through his behavior and his relationships with his students, foster principles of character formation and personality growth. He can instill in the student ideas of honesty, integrity, fortitude, temperance, and other practical virtues. Like the life of Caesar's wife, a teacher's life must be above suspicion. He must possess personal and moral integrity; and students are quick to discover if this integrity does not exist. Possessing this integrity, a teacher can be a splendid model for the young person.

What other characteristics should the teacher possess? Like the counselor and therapist, he ought to be mentally healthy and well-adjusted. If not, he is going to have adverse effects on the lives of his pupils. He must also have a genuine liking for children. There is nothing more irritating than to hear teachers talk about the monsters they have just escaped from and about what horrible creatures youngsters are. Why such people enter the teaching profession is something that is hard to understand unless of course they do so to vent their own hostility. Either that, or they are not competent to get into another field.

Unfortunately, there are quite a few teachers who fit into this category. They hate their pupils, and they are certainly not qualified by any standard to influence the lives of children. Students know if a person likes to teach, and readily spot the teacher who is in the business of education because he is not qualified for anything else. One has to believe in the profession, and that it is worthwhile even if fifty out of every sixty students fail or drop out of school. Teaching is one of the noblest professions and can be utilized to great advantage for the welfare of young people. Christ himself was a teacher, and we should try to realize the dignity of this profession and convey to our students its full meaning.

The teacher who would have a positive effect on the adjustment and mental health of students must also possess self-discipline, since personal discipline is necessary if one is to discipline others. The irascible, angry teacher who loses his temper repeatedly on the slightest provocation cannot set a good example for his students, nor can he develop positive relationships with students, with other faculty members, with the administration for which he works, and with other persons who become a part of his life. The poor teacher is characterized by feelings of inadequacy, inferiority, and hostility; his irritations, conflicts, and frustrations prevent him from being a good teacher and from functioning as a model for his students. The effective teacher, on the other hand, promotes mental hygiene by creating a good atmosphere in the classroom. This atmosphere is enhanced to an important extent by using discipline effectively, but it is also stimulated by interest in the subject, by inspired teaching, and by a warm relationship between teacher and students.

Mental hygiene in the classroom can be furthered by promoting maturity in the students. The teacher should foster independence and should help the students to define goals for themselves, make positive decisions, and actualize their potentialities. The teacher should help the slow starter and underachiever so that they can develop some feeling of achievement, and he should function as a model of competence and achievement for all of the students. And finally, mental hygiene can be promoted by the teacher who takes the time to refer a student who is in trouble and needs special help to whatever person or agency can help him.

For the teacher to promote the adjustment and mental health of students, the school must also fulfill its responsibilities. The school must support the dignity of the teaching profession by providing salaries that enable teachers to live in dignity, and by providing the tools and accommodations that are necessary for teaching. Just as a poor neighborhood generates mental ill health, so poor school facilities generate discontent and ineffective teaching. The school must do everything it can to promote dignity and pride in the teaching profession, and it should foster healthy relationships among the faculty and between the faculty and the administration. It should do whatever is necessary to create a healthy, effective teaching climate.

If all these principles of mental hygiene are carried into effect in the home, school, and society, the adjustment and mental health of young people will be promoted to a gratifying extent.

# 45. Counseling for Mental Health

ALEXANDER A. SCHNEIDERS

The most direct approach for handling this topic is to determine first of all what goals a parent, teacher, or counselor would have in mind when counseling young people. And closely allied to the question of goals is the problem of the criteria one might use in determining the level of adjustment or mental health. Criteria make it possible to recognize mental health or mental illness since they can be applied to both conditions.

## The Goals of Counseling

Let us consider first of all the general counseling goal that one might have in mind, particularly if he is functioning as a professional counselor. Although many persons who counsel would not consider themselves professional counselors, it is good to start with a discussion of professional counseling because we can then modify our approach to suit individual needs. In general, the aim of counseling and of psychotherapy is the promotion of mental stability and emotional health by the reduction of inefficient or symptomatic behavior and its causes. This counseling approach is therapeutic as distinguished from a mental-hygiene approach, which is essentially preventative in nature. The goal can be expanded to include the promotion of adjustment, of personality integration, and of emotional stability, all of which are basic to mental health.

This approach is identical to the physician's. He must get at the causes of an illness or disease, and he is clearly aware how difficult it is to do anything effective at a purely symptomatic level. In counseling psychology and psychiatry, one must do the same thing, that is, get at the essential causes. Thus, in a typical situation, if a child is living in a home environment that is obviously damaging to him, it might be necessary to remove the child from this environment in order to reduce the symptomatic behavior. This method is referred to as environmental therapy. We see something similar in the work of Alcoholics Anonymous, where the unfortunate victim utilizes the environment and interpersonal relationships to reduce the degree of alcoholic addiction and to eliminate it. In this case the treatment is to a large extent symptomatic, but it is the best procedure that has been worked out so far.

Looking at the problem more specifically, in counseling for mental health we work toward the relief of tension that springs from unwanted conflicts, anxiety, guilt, hostility, inferiority, and other negative feelings that are destructive of mental health. Here is the place where both the teacher and the school counselor can do effective work. A boy or girl comes to the teacher and wants to talk about his or her problems, and the teacher, just by listening sympathetically and letting the student know that he is interested, can relieve a great deal of tension. The youngster might talk about an unhappy home situation and her poor relationships with her mother, and this ventilation of feeling brings considerable relief from tension. This aim or goal any counselor, teacher, or parent can achieve without much difficulty.

A second goal in this type of counseling would be to help a person, especially a young person, learn how to handle conflicts. This help is important because of the effects conflict has on need gratification. Here the teacher or counselor can do a world of good. Adolescents particularly cannot be expected to know how to handle conflict, and our job is to show them the inevitability of conflict and what should be done about it. Adolescents must learn that conflict is something that they can expect in the course of everyday experience, that it is not something bizarre or abnormal. When they encounter a deep moral conflict concerning their behavior, they may react destructively to the conflict, and the counselor can help them understand the nature of the conflict and how to resolve it. Learning how to handle conflict is everyone's responsibility. Similarly, the young person must learn how to cope with frustration. Young people are notoriously impatient; they don't want something a year or five years from now; they want it today or tomorrow. But they have to learn that frustration is an inevitable part of life. They must acquire the habit of tolerating frustration, or, to put it in terms we have used before, they must learn to defer need gratification.

Everyone must learn frustration tolerance. Youngsters must learn to tolerate frustration with respect to dating, coming in late at night, smoking, driving the family car, drinking, and any other behavior not appropriate to their age level and proscribed by parents or by society.

Unfortunately, the tendency of many parents today is to allow children to experience things that should be deferred until much later in their development. Dating at a very early age when youngsters are not yet fully aware of basic sex differences; driving a car before they have the judgment or skill necessary to handle such a destructive instrument; or drinking alcoholic beverages before they possess the maturity to cope with the effects of drinking are all instances of premature behavior that is lacking in frustration tolerance. Unhappily, the drinking problem among teenagers has increased precipitously in the last ten years, a problem which is largely the responsibility of parents. The social argument that "everybody is doing it" has nothing to do with the rightness or wrongness of behavior, and is an exceedingly poor criterion for determining what is right and what is wrong. It makes no difference what other people do; the only issue is whether something should be done; and if it should not be done for moral or social reasons or for mental-health reasons, it should be excluded. If parents do not possess the intestinal fortitude or the integrity to carry through on what they believe is right, they ought to give up the business of parenthood and turn the child over to someone who does.

A third basic aim of counseling for mental health is to help young people to develop insight into their own feelings and behavior and to understand why they feel the way they do. This is particularly true of adolescents because they are so often deeply confused. Adolescence is a period of widespread transition and hence a period of instability. As new feelings and experiences and strong impulses impinge upon their consciousness, they often become confused. They must learn much about their human nature and what is happening to them.

It is particularly important to give them adequate sex instruction, and this point requires emphasis because the great majority of people never receive such instruction. Adolescents need this instruction because without it they can become confused and develop many psychosexual problems. Typically, when a boy reaches adolescence without this necessary information and experiences such a thing as nocturnal emission, he doesn't now what is happening to him and then acquires his knowledge in a distorted manner from companions, from reading, and from other doubtful sources. Similarly, the girl begins to menstruate, and because she is ignorant of this natural function, the menstrual shock is of such proportions that she never fully recovers from it.

We must get away from the Jansenistic notion that sex is evil. We must learn to treat it objectively and to stop linking it to impurity and degradation in the minds of young people. We must examine our consciences carefully lest we do untold damage to children under our control. These youngsters need instruction rather than fear and threat, since instruction is the only secure antidote to the sexual conflicts that arise in later adolescence. Instruction is the only sure way to avoid sexual confusion.

Counseling for mental health can also be directed toward stimulating growth toward positive goals and personal integration. Admittedly, such stimulation is not easy to accomplish, but it can be done by helping young people to define their own goals, since goals help to determine personal integration. When a person has well-defined goals, when he knows what he wants to do and where he is going, his striving achieves much greater unity; in other words, he achieves integration. The person also achieves a higher level of growth and of self-actualization, processes in which young people especially need help. Through teaching and counseling we should also do whatever we can to increase self-acceptance and self-esteem. Young people especially have to learn that unless a person loves himself he will not be able to love anyone else. A person who hates himself and who is alienated from himself cannot accept himself and thus tends toward mental illness. This is what the Commandment enjoins us to do, "Love thy neighbor as thyself," and this authority is pretty good. Self-love is not to be interpreted as narcissistic love. When a person exclaims, "Of all my wife's relations I like myself the best," he is tending toward narcissism, which can be destructive. Narcissism undermines the achievement of mental health.

This type of self-love obviously is not what we are referring to. A healthy self-love is the opposite of narcissism. The neurotic hates himself; he cannot tolerate the kind of person he is, and therefore in counseling we try to get the person to accept himself and in that way lay the groundwork for self-love. This does not mean that the person should condone everything that he does. This is not the meaning of self-acceptance. One may reject the evil and the sinfulness in himself, but he does not reject himself as a person. Rejection of self is exactly what happens to the neurotic. We should do whatever we can to help young people to understand and to accept themselves, so that the forces of self-hatred and self-rejection do not get a chance to generate the defensive behavior patterns so often found in the neurotic.

In counseling young people we should also try to promote feelings of security and safety, because the feeling of insecurity is the beginning of the anxiety that is so widespread today. This psychological insecurity can be related to recent changes in our society, particularly to the breakdown of family life and the development of the welfare state. This development represents the "take care of me" and "the world owes me a living" attitude. This insecurity and welfarism is reflected strongly in the behavior of people. There are numerous men making no more than $5,000 or $6,000 a year who carry as much as $50,000 worth of insurance. They are the people who work themselves to death so that someone else can live from their insurance. While it is a good and provident thing to take care of one's wife and children, it would be much more sensible if the husband were to relax more, live longer, and in that way take care of the people dependent upon him. The insurance craze and the growth of the insurance business reflect the insecurity of people today. The difficulty is that many of us were so shocked and frightened by the economic setback of the depression that we went overboard in the other direction and supported the creation of all sorts of agencies designed to take care of the needs of everyone. Such welfarism is not necessarily a good thing. We should learn to stand on our own feet. An obvious aim in our counseling work with young people is to stimulate growth toward maturity, which is one of the biggest and most difficult counseling problems. And it is the lack of maturity that is reflected in welfarism.

Unfortunately, no one has ever told us how to promote maturity in young people, perhaps because maturation is inherent in the human organism. In Chapter 41 we referred to the thrust toward maturity as an innate quality, and that may be the reason why it cannot be imposed from the outside. We have all had some direct or indirect experience with the young boy or girl whose problems seem to revolve around immaturity. In such cases it is difficult to know exactly what to do, and even more difficult to convert the immature person into a more mature one. Every counselor has worked with people thirty-five or forty years of age who are still very immature and whose immaturity persists even after long periods of counseling. We are dealing here with a failure in development, and failures in development are extremely difficult to correct; but this difficulty should not deter us from doing what we can to stimulate growth toward maturity.

What should we look for as the criteria of maturity? Probably the most important criterion here is a sense of responsibility. The mature person is a responsible person. And responsibility is closely allied to another quality, and that is healthy interpersonal relationships. To become mature, people need to develop adequate and worthwhile relationships with other persons in their environment, a development that is directly related to the gratification of basic human needs. "No man is an island" is a quotation from John Donne and is most pertinent today. Man cannot live in isolation. He must have friends, and he must have a confidant to whom he can entrust his feelings and ideas. He must have someone he can talk to, play with, and relate to. This relationship is necessary to emotional stability, to good adjustment, and to mental health. In promoting good interpersonal relationships, we can make good headway in helping young people to achieve mental health. Very often a social director in a school does more to promote the adjustment of students than any other person. The right person can do a world of good for young people in helping them to grow socially, to relate to members of the opposite sex, and to learn to enjoy social activities. But young people have to be helped in many instances; they have to be drawn out of themselves if they are to achieve any social development.

Another basic goal of counseling is to help young people to move toward an adequate philosophy of life. Achieving this goal is no more a problem now than in earlier times, but it is certainly true that there are a lot of young people today who feel that the values passed on to them by their parents are not too reliable. Young people today often do not trust their elders because of the mixed-up world which they have inherited from the preceding generation. A recent book that deals with this problem is Pearson's *The conflict of generations,* which studies the conflicts between the older generation and the youth of today. As Pearson points out, there is not the same relationship between young people and parents that existed in previous generations. Young people state this difficulty very simply: "If this is the kind of world you people have created, we don't want any part of it." Such is their philosophy, and we have to help these young people to a better understanding of what the world and what reality are like and to help them formulate a workable philosophy of life. Without a sound philosophy, as Jung has said, there is no mental health.

While there are many more aims of counseling that for lack of space cannot be discussed here, there is one other that deserves particular mention, and that is to help youngsters organize their perceptions along realistic lines. The relationship between personal perception and the processes of adjustment and mental health has gained attention only in the last few years. Since adjustment and mental health both require an adequate orientation to reality, it must follow that our perception of reality will be important to these processes. We do not always perceive reality as it is, but as determined by our past experiences, our personal background, our needs, wishes, and unconscious tendencies. This knowledge is not a matter of theory but of fact. For example, a mother looking at her child does not see the same thing that other more disinterested people see. Similarly, when you look in a mirror you do not see a true reflection of yourself. Applying these facts to mental health, we can see that the neurotic or the psychotic person perceives reality in a distorted manner and therefore cannot adjust to reality as well as the normal person. His world is often a bizarre image of reality. We see this fact clearly illustrated in the paranoid patient who sees elements of diabolical significance in the simplest gestures or situations.

The normal child and the adolescent also perceive reality in an inadequate way, partly because they have not yet grown up and thus do not possess the knowledge or the experience required for adequate interpretation of reality. Our task, then, is to help people, especially those who are immature or on the edge of mental disorder, to organize their perceptions properly and to see reality as it actually is. All of us are subject to distortion to a degree, but in the majority of instances this distortion causes no problem. The moon appears small to the perceiver, and he cannot see it any other way, but this distorted perception does not disrupt the normal course of his life. But the same is not true of people who are strongly influenced by needs and feelings. For example, if a person is wracked by a deep feeling of inferiority, his perceptions are likely to be influenced by this feeling. The simplest remark or gesture is twisted into an insult or a rejection.

In the same manner, a person with pervasive hostility will see antagonism in the behavior of others no matter how innocuous their behavior may be. One of my clients, a young man twenty-three years of age, would tell me, "I don't trust anyone. The whole world is no darned good and that includes you. I hate my parents and you are just like them." This is typical of the way a disturbed person will react in terms of his feelings. Everyone is against him. If you say to such a person, "Why do you feel that way toward me? I thought I was trying to help you," he will say, "All you want to do is to build up your own lousy

ego. It makes you feel good to help me." Maybe this client is right,
but the important point is that he keeps seeing reality in a distorted
manner, and therefore he cannot adjust adequately or maintain mental
health.

## The Criteria of Mental Health

This discussion of the aims and goals of counseling and psychotherapy suggests another question: What are the criteria by which we can
judge the degree of mental health or adjustment? How can we recognize mental health or ill health in ourselves or in others? By criteria I
mean simply standards or norms by which we can determine the existence (or nonexistence) of any quality in a person. Among these criteria
for mental health perhaps the most prominent are self-knowledge and
insight. Here we can see immediately why criteria are closely related to
mental-health aims, since these criteria must be fulfilled for the achievement of mental health. Mentally healthy people do not react disas-
trously to every situation; they always have the ability to laugh at
themselves; and this capacity to laugh at one's self is a good sign of
mental balance. Thus objectivity and self-acceptance are good criteria
for identifying mental health. If, in addition, a person can also love
himself despite his limited qualities, then we have another criterion
of mental health.

Self-control and self-discipline are good criteria of adequate adjustment, and some persons would say that control is the most important
quality of all. Certainly without a measure of self-discipline there can
be neither healthiness nor happiness in this life. That is why it is so
important for teachers and parents to impose some discipline on the
lives of children, for without it they cannot develop to maturity. No
child can achieve self-discipline unless parents and others impose external discipline early in his life. I am not talking here about punishment, although there are times when punishment cannot be avoided.
Discipline refers to the order in a person's life, and we might remind
ourselves that "order is heaven's first law." This order does not mean
a compulsive orderliness such as is found in neurotic persons. There
are people who have to straighten every picture on the wall, who must
return three or four times to see whether a light has been turned off,
or who must perform the same ritual in the same way at the same time.
By contrast, a normal orderly life is one in which the behavior of the
individual is organized according to a reasonable pattern though at the

same time allowance is made for necessary adaptations. We do not get up at four o'clock in the morning to have breakfast, nor do we eat dinner in the middle of the afternoon. There is a rhythm in our daily behavior which corresponds generally with the natural biological rhythm of the body. We go to bed about the same time each evening and get about the same amount of sleep. This orderliness does not preclude adaptation whenever we must change the pattern of our daily lives to meet the exigencies of situations that arise.

The compulsive neurotic, on the other hand, is a person who, because of the disorder in his own personal life, tries to blueprint his life objectively by his compulsiveness. He figures that if he can keep everything arranged very neatly, his clothing stacked just right, everything immaculately clean, then life must be orderly. He must have order in his objective reality because of the disorder within himself. He is like the person who preaches morality ad nauseum, and then when you look into his own personal life you find that there is a great deal of immorality. Persons who make the most noise about morality are usually the worst sinners.

Another important criterion of mental health is personal integrity, and when we understand what integrity is, we can see that ordered self-discipline contributes a great deal to it. Integration means of course oneness, and that is why integrity is a part of mental health. The person who is mentally healthy is not only well-integrated but also possesses integrity, meaning that he always acts in one way. You can always depend upon him. Disturbed people, on the other hand, are always disassembled. They are moving in six different directions at the same time. Characteristically, they are conflicted, they are not sure of what they believe in, they are confused on social, political, moral, and educational issues, and they are ambivalent in regard to many important phases of life. This lack of integration and this ambivalence are developmental phenomena in which the failure of discipline and self-discipline have played an important part. The self-disciplined person contributes to his own integration and reduces his ambivalence by his orderly behavior.

A fifth criterion of the well-adjusted person that we can help young people to achieve is the development of well-defined goals and goal direction. This quality is very important for adolescents and is always found in healthy-minded persons. Goal-directedness is exemplified in the person whose life and behavior have a purposiveness that gives them special meaning. With this directionality it is much easier to maintain an even balance and avoid shooting off in various confused directions. Goals are closely allied to the scale of values we mentioned previously, since they are a special kind of value.

Responsibility and maturity also help us identify good adjustment. These factors apply more to adults than to young people since many youngsters will not have yet reached this point. But to be mentally healthy and adjusted, an adult person must think and act like an adult, and therefore must be mature. The true adult cannot afford to behave like an immature child, to cry for what he wants, to run away from home, to get depressed, or to refuse to accept things as they are. Immaturity is always betrayed in the person who acts like a child. One such person, a 26-year-old veteran, would throw himself on the floor and kick violently whenever his mother did not give him what he wanted. Similarly, the flight into illness, that is, the use of illness for personal gain, is typically immature.

Still another quality of maturity is adaptability, the capacity to assume and to play different roles as situations change and as demands vary. We play a different role in the classroom than we do at home, and we play a different role in church than we do in a social gathering. Adjustment means meeting the demands, conflicts, and problems imposed by life and reality in an efficient and healthy manner without personal cost to one's self. And since life changes all the time, day in and day out, and the people around us change, we have to keep adapting to changing situations. Our friends and relatives move away or die; we change our job; our children grow up and get married; or our husbands and wives grow old, less attractive, and less youthful than before. Things are changing all the time, and we have to be able to adapt to these changes. People should always develop their personal and social life in such a way as to maintain some independence. Otherwise, they are likely to be unable to adapt to loss when it occurs.

Good adjustment is further characterized by a wide range of interests in work and in play. This quality is important for coping adequately with daily frustrations. We indicated earlier that needs or drives are not destructive of adjustment or mental health, but that difficulty often arises when serious frustration occurs. One of the ways in which frustration is adequately handled, leaving aside for the moment frustration tolerance, is to have available substitute responses, so that one can turn in another direction when necessary and still get need gratification. If, therefore, a youngster finds it impossible to realize his ambition for medical school, it is quite possible to adopt a substitute goal such as chemical research, dentistry, or pharmacy.

In some instances there may be no substitute available, in which case a person may fall back on the mechanism of sublimation, which is itself a kind of substitution. Sublimation is defined as a redirection of the energy of a drive into another and acceptable channel or activity. Sex, aggression, and other such drives can be sublimated into various forms of useful or even creative activity. This substitution of vicarious activity can be effective in many instances. Gratification from movies, TV programs, football games, and the like is often effected through sublimation. In all instances there should be satisfaction derived from both work and play, another important criterion of adjustment.

Mental health requires also that a person have a healthy sense of humor. It is a notorious fact that unhappy, mentally disturbed, or neurotic people are quite deficient in this quality. They do not enjoy comics or comedy situations. Yet man is by nature a risible animal, just as he is a moral and social animal; and therefore the capacity to laugh and to enjoy humor is natural to man. Man has as much need for enjoyment as he has for physical or spiritual gratifications.

Another criterion of adjustment is an adequate orientation to reality, a requirement which fits in with the organization of perception that we defined previously. It is important to learn to see reality as it is. For example, if a person is incompetent, he should try to do something about it rather than blame others, rationalize his failures, or attempt to introject the qualities of other persons. Introjection is what characterizes the typical joiners, who join one group after another thinking that by doing so they can assume the qualities of the group. It is easy to see that this desire to introject another's qualities has deep roots in feelings of inadequacy or inferiority; otherwise the introjection would have no meaning.

A healthy orientation to reality is backed up by healthy attitudes— attitudes toward self, society, work, neighbors, racial groups, minority groups, religion, and the like. This criterion is in turn related to another, the need for mental efficiency. The well-adjusted person organizes his thoughts and experiences and can express them adequately, at least within the limits of his education. He can solve problems when they need to be solved and can dispose of his personal affairs in an effective manner. These qualities young people must acquire if they are to achieve maturity.

A healthy self-concept is another important feature of mental health, especially since it is required for self-identity. Young people particularly must learn how to develop a self-concept and to find out who they are.

As parents or counselors, we can help young people to identify themselves, and if there is serious failure in this area, they should be referred
to a professional counselor or therapist.

Finally, it is clear from everything that I have said that adjustment
and mental health require healthy feelings and emotions, as well as
freedom from disabling or symptomatic responses. This latter criterion
is a negative one, but also important from the standpoint of mental
health. We cannot permit ourselves, or the persons whom we counsel, to
fall victim to the anarchy of feelings (Schneiders, 1963). When anarchy
develops, reason is dethroned, and the unfortunate victim cannot use
his qualities of intellect and control to organize his life in a self-
disciplined manner. A person should at all times be aware of his feelings and act in such a way as to limit the influence of negative feelings
on his behavior or relationships. One can see that all such criteria
are similar to the conditions of mental health and are directly related
to the dynamics of mental health. The quality that we call mental
health emerges out of the conditions through a process of development,
and the criteria are means by which we can test the degree of mental
health. This is a complex affair simply because human nature itself
is very complex.

# References and Bibliography

▲▲▲▲▲▲▲▲▲▲▲▲▲▲▲▲▲▲▲▲▲▲▲▲▲▲▲▲▲▲▲▲

Aldrich, C. K. *An introduction to dynamic psychiatry.* New York: McGraw, 1966.

Allers, R. *The psychology of character.* New York: Sheed, 1943.

Allport, G. W. *Pattern and growth in personality.* New York: Holt, 1961.

Arbuckle, D. S. *Counseling: an introduction.* Boston: Allyn and Bacon, 1961.

Arieti, S., ed. *American handbook of psychiatry* (2 vols.). New York: Basic Books, 1959.

Asch, S. E. *Social psychology.* Englewood Cliffs, N.J.: Prentice-Hall, 1952.

Azner, R., and A. E. Bennett. "Pregnancy in the adolescent girl." *Amer. J. Obst. and Gynecol.,* 1961, *81,* 934–940.

Babin, P. *Crisis of faith, the religious psychology of adolescence.* New York: Herder and Herder, 1963.

Babin, P. *Faith and the adolescent.* New York: Herder and Herder, 1965.

Balser, B. H., and J. F. Masterson. "Suicide in adolescents." *Amer. J. Psychiat.,* 1959, *116,* 400–404.

Banary, R. S. *Youth in despair.* New York: Coward, 1948.

Barry, R., and B. Wolf. *Modern issues in guidance-personnel work.* New York: Teachers College, Columbia Univ., 1963.

Baruch, D. W. *How to live with your teenager.* New York: McGraw, 1958.

Baruch, D. W. *New ways in discipline.* New York: McGraw, 1958.

Berdie, R. F., ed. *Counseling and the college program.* Minnesota Studies in Student Personnel Work, 1954, No. 6.

Bertocci, T. A. *The human venture in sex, love and marriage.* New York: Association Press, 1951.

Bier, W. C., ed. *The adolescent: his search for understanding.* New York: Fordham, 1963.

Blaine, G. B., and C. McArthur. *Emotional problems of the student.* New York: Appleton, 1961.

Blaine, G. B. *Patience and fortitude, the parents' guide to adolescence.* Boston: Little, Brown, 1962.

Blos, P. *On adolescence.* New York: Free Press, 1962.

Bordin, E. S. "Diagnosis in counseling and psychotherapy." *Educ. and Psychol. Measmt.,* 1946, *6,* 169–184.

Bossard, J. H. S. *Parent and child.* Philadelphia: Univ. of Pennsylvania Press, 1953.

Buehler, C. *Der menschliche Lebenslauf als psychologisches Problem.* Leipzig: Hirzel, 1933.

Cantril, H. *The "why" of man's experience.* New York: Macmillan, 1950.

Cass, J. "What happened at Berkeley." *Sat. Rev.,* Jan. 16, 1965, 47–48, 66–69.

Cavanagh, J. R. "The failure of communication as a cause of marriage failure." *Bull. Guild. Cath. Psychiatrists,* 1963, *10,* 11–17.

*Christopher News Notes,* Apr. 1964, No. 135. New York: The Christophers, 1964.

Clear, V. Paperback pedagogy. *Sat. Rev.,* Feb. 15, 1964, 73.

Cole, L., and I. Hall. *Psychology of adolescence.* New York: Holt, 1964.

Coleman, J. C. *The adolescent society.* New York: Free Press, 1961.

Coleman, J. C. *Personality dynamics and effective behavior.* Fairlawn, N.J.: Scott, Foresman, 1960.

Curran, C. A. *Counseling in Catholic life and education.* New York: Macmillan, 1952.

Deisher, R. W., and J. F. O'Leary. "Early medical care of delinquent children." *Pediatrics,* 1960, *25,* 325–335.

Dempsey, D. "Summer is the time to take a giant step." *N.Y. Times Book Review,* May 10, 1964, 3.

Deutsch, A., and H. Fishman, eds. *Encyclopedia of mental health* (6 vols.). New York: Watts, 1963.

D'Evelyn, K. *Meeting children's emotional needs: a guide for teachers.* Englewood Cliffs, N.J.: Prentice-Hall, 1957.

Douvan, E., and J. Adelson. *The adolescent experience.* New York: Wiley, 1966.

Dugan, W. E. "The organization and administration of guidance services." *Rev. Educ. Res.,* 1960, *2,* 105–113.

Engel, G. L. *Psychological development in health and disease.* Philadelphia: Saunders, 1962.

Erickson, C. E. *The counseling interview.* Englewood Cliffs, N.J.: Prentice-Hall, 1950.

Erikson, E. *Childhood and society.* New York: Norton, 1950.

Farwell, G., and H. Peters, eds. *Guidance readings for counselors.* Chicago: Rand McNally, 1960.

Feder, D. D., J. F. Bishop, W. S. Dysinger, and L. W. Jones. *The administration of student personnel programs in American colleges and universities.* Washington, D.C.: Amer. Council on Education, 1958.

Fishman, L. " 'You're the critic' marks fifteen years." *Top of the News,* Oct. 1963, 61–63.

Flanagan, J. C., et al. *Design for a study of American youth: 1. the talents of American youth.* Boston: Houghton, 1962.

Fletcher, G. N. *What's right with our young people?* New York: Morrow, 1966.

Frank, L. K., and M. Frank. *Your adolescent at home and in school.* New York: Viking, 1956.

Freedman, M. B. *Impact of college.* Washington, D.C.: U.S. Gov't. Printing Office, 1960.

Friend, J. G., and E. A. Haggard. "Work adjustment in relation to family background." *Appl. Psychol. Monogr.,* 1948, No. 16.

Froehlich, C. P. "Counseling, its use and abuse." In G. Farwell and H. Peters, eds. *Guidance readings for counselors.* Chicago: Rand McNally, 1960, pp. 369–378.

Fromm, E. *Man for himself.* New York: Holt, 1947.

Gallagher, J. R. *Understanding your son's adolescence.* Boston: Little, Brown, 1951.

Gallagher, J. R., and H. I. Harris. *Emotional problems of adolescents.* New York: Oxford Univ. Press, 1958.

Gillespie, J. M., and G. W. Allport. *Youth's outlook on the future.* Garden City, N.Y.: Doubleday, 1955.

Ginsburg, S. W. *A psychiatrist's views on social issues.* New York: Columbia, 1963.

Ginzberg, E. "Toward a theory of occupational choice." *Occupations,* 1952, *30,* 491–494.

Gobetz, W. *New York Univ. Alumni Bulletin,* Apr. 1961.

Goldburgh, S. J., ed. *The experience of adolescence.* Cambridge, Mass.: Schenkman, 1965.

Goldfarb, W. "The effects of early institutional care on adolescent personality," *Child Develop.,* 1943a, *14,* 213–22.

Goldfarb, W. "The effects of early institutional care on adolescent personality," *J. Exp. Educ.,* 1943b, *12,* 106–129.

Greeley, A. M. *Religion and career.* New York: Sheed, 1963.

Greeley, A. M. *Strangers in the house.* New York: Sheed, 1961.

Grinder, R. E., ed. *Studies in adolescence.* New York: Macmillan, 1963.

Gruenberg, S. M., ed. *Our children today.* New York: Viking, 1952.

Gruenberg, S. M. *We the parents.* New York: Harper, 1948.

Hadley, J. M. *Clinical and counseling psychology.* New York: Knopf, 1958.

Hagmaier, G., and R. W. Gleason. *Counseling the Catholic.* New York: Sheed, 1959.

Haley, J. E. *Accent on purity: a Catholic guide for sex education.* South Bend, Ind.: Fides, 1948.

Hall, C. S., and G. Lindzey. *Theories of personality.* New York: Wiley, 1957.

Hand, H. C. *General education in the American high school.* New York: Scott, Foresman, 1942.

Harper, R. A. *Psychoanalysis and psychotherapy.* Englewood Cliffs, N.J.: Prentice-Hall, 1960.

Harris, I. D. *Emotional blocks to learning.* New York: Free Press, 1961.

Hawkes, H. E., and A. L. Hawkes. *Through a dean's open door.* New York: McGraw, 1945.

Hechinger, G., and F. M. Hechinger. *Teen-age tyranny.* New York. Morrow, 1963.

Hendrickson, R. C., and F. J. Cook. *Youth in danger.* New York: Harcourt, 1956.

Himmelweit, H. T., A. N. Oppenheim, and P. Vince. *Television and the child.* London: Oxford Univ. Press, 1958.

Hobbs, N. "Some notions about guidance." *Peabody J. Educ.,* 1952, *29,* 229–231.

Holaday, P. W., and G. D. Stoddard. *Getting ideas from the movies.* New York: Macmillan, 1933.

Holman, Miriam. "Adolescent attitudes toward seeking help with personal problems." *Smith Coll. Stud. Soc. Wk.,* 1955, *25,* No. 3, 1–31.

Horney, K. *Neurosis and human growth.* New York: Norton, 1950.

Huslander, S. C. "Assisting youth adjustment in elementary schools." *Personn. and Guid. J.,* 1954, *32,* 393–394.

Hussey, H. H. "Emotional problems of adolescents." *GP,* 1956, *13,* 74–78.

Hutchins, R. M. *The conflict in education in a democratic society.* New York: Harper, 1953.

Hutchins, R. M. *A conversation on education.* Santa Barbara, Calif.: Center for the Study of Democratic Institutions, 1963.

Hutson, P. W. "Vocational choices, 1930 and 1961." *Voc. Guid. Quart.,* 1962, *10,* 218–222.

Jahoda, M. *Current concepts of positive mental health.* New York: Basic Books, 1958.

Jenkins, G., W. W. Bauer, and H. Shacter. *Teenagers.* New York: Scott, Foresman, 1954.

Jones, A. J. *Principles of guidance,* 4th ed. New York: McGraw, 1951.

Josselyn, I. M. *The adolescent and his world.* New York: Family Service Association of America, 1952.

Josselyn, I. M. *Psychosocial development of children.* New York: Family Service Association of America, 1948.
Jung, C. *Modern man in search of a soul.* New York: Harcourt, 1933.


Kaufman, J. F. "Student personnel services in higher education." *Educ. Rec.,* 1964, *45,* 355–365.
Keller, F. J. "Same door wherein I went, a confession of faith in guidance as education." *Occupations,* 1953, *13,* 689.
Kelley, E. C. *In defense of youth.* Englewood Cliffs, N J : Prentice-Hall, 1962.
Kelly, A. *A Catholic parent's guide to sex education.* New York: Hawthorn, 1962.
Kelly, G. A. *The Catholic youth's guide to life and love.* New York: Random, 1960.
Kiell, M. *The universal experience of adolescence.* New York: International Univs. Press, 1964.
Klapper, J. T. *The effects of mass communication.* Glencoe, Ill.: Free Press, 1960.
Klineberg, O., and J. T. Klapper. *The mass media: their impact on children and family life.* Washington, D.C.: Television Information Office, April 21, 1960, p. 48e.
Knapp, D., and E. Denny. "The counselor's responsibility in role definition." *Personn. and Guid. J.,* 1961, *40,* 48–50.
Kostant, G. H. *A guide to skin care for teenagers.* New York: Rosen, 1961.
Kunkel, F. *In search of maturity.* New York: Scribner, 1955.


Landis, P. H. *Adolescent and youth.* New York: McGraw, 1952.
Lear, M. W. *The child worshippers.* New York: Crown, 1963.
Lee, M. L. "Counseling vs. discipline: another view." *Cath. Counselor,* 1963, *7,* 114–119.
Leighton, A. H., J. A. Clausen, and R. N. Wilson, eds. *Explorations in social psychiatry.* New York: Basic Books, 1957.
Lewis, O. Y. "Problems of the adolescent." *Calif. J. Second. Educ.,* 1949, *24,* 215–221.
Lindner, R. *Prescription for rebellion.* New York: Holt, 1952.
Lindworsky, J. *Experimental psychology,* trans. by H. R. DeSilva. New York: Macmillan, 1931.


Maccoby, E. E. "Television: its impact on school children." *Pub. Opinion Quart.,* 1951, 421–444.
McGowan, J., and L. Schmidt, eds. *Counseling: readings in theory and practice.* New York: Holt, 1962.

MacIver, R. M., ed. *Dilemmas of youth in America today*. New York: Harper, 1961.

Mallery, D. *High school students speak out*. New York: Harper, 1962.

Malnig, L. R. "The school counselor." In W. C. Bier, ed. *The adolescent: his search for understanding*. New York: Fordham, 1963, pp. 159–162.

Martin, L. *Students and the Pratt Library: challenge and opportunity*. Baltimore: Enoch Pratt Free Library, 1963.

Maslow, A. H. *Motivation and personality*. New York: Harper, 1954.

Mathewson, R. H. "Manpower or persons: a critical issue." *Personn. and Guid. J.*, 1964, *43*, 338–342.

Measham, D. C. *Fourteen: autobiography of an age group*. New York: British Book Centre, 1966.

Menninger, K. *Love against hate*. New York: Harcourt, 1942.

Miller, D. C., and W. H. Form. *Industrial sociology*. New York: Harper, 1951.

Mooney, R. L. "Surveying high school students' problems by means of a problem check list." *Educ. Res. Bull.*, 1942, *21*, 57–69.

Mooney, R. L., and L. V. Gordon. *The Mooney problem check list*, rev. ed. New York: Psychological Corporation, 1950.

Moore, T. V. *Personal mental hygiene*. New York: Grune, 1952.

Moser, C. G. *Understanding girls*. New York: Association Press, 1957.

Mosher, R. L., R. F. Carle, and C. D. Kehas. *Guidance—an examination*. New York: Harcourt, 1965.

Mowrer, O. H. *The crisis in psychiatry and religion*. New York: Van Nostrand, 1961.

Muuss, R. E. *Theories of adolescence*. New York: Random, 1962.

Myers, G. E. *Principles and techniques of vocational guidance*. New York: McGraw, 1941.


*National Decency Reporter*, Dec. 1963, *1*, No. 4. Cincinnati, Ohio: Citizens for Decent Literature.

Nixon, R. E. *The art of growing: a guide to psychological maturity*. New York: Random, 1964.

Nunnally, J. C. *Popular conceptions of mental health: their development and change*. New York: Holt, 1961.


O'Brien, J. *Sex-character education*. New York: Macmillan, 1953.

O'Brien, T. J. "Discipline and counseling: are they incompatible?" *Cath. Counselor*, 1962, *7*, 3–9.

Osborne, E. G. *Understanding your parents*. New York: Association Press, 1957.

Overstreet, H. *The mature mind*. New York: Norton, 1949.

Parsons, F. *Choosing a vocation.* Boston: Houghton, 1909.

Patterson, C. H. *Counseling and guidance in schools: a first course.* New York: Harper, 1962.

Patterson, F., ed. *The adolescent citizen.* New York: Free Press, 1960.

Pearson, G. H. J. *Adolescence and the conflict of generations.* New York: Norton, 1958.

Phillips, E. L., D. N. Wiener, and N. G. Haring. *Discipline, achievement and mental health.* Englewood Cliffs, N.J.: Prentice-Hall, 1960.

Plunkett, R. J., and J. E. Gordon. *Epidemiology and mental illness.* New York: Basic Books, 1960.

Pope, C. "Personal problems of high school pupils." *School and Society,* 1943, *57,* 443–448.


Raab, E., and G. Joeger. *Major social problems.* New York: Harper, 1964.

Rappaport, V. A., and B. M. Goldman. "The lonely student." *Educ. Rec.,* 1963, *44,* 223–227.

Reed, A. "Is guidance a racket?" *The Nat. Educ. Assoc. Proceedings, LXXVI,* 1938, 628.

Reiss, I. L. *Premarital sexual standards in America.* New York: Free Press, 1960.

Remmers, H. H., and B. Shimberg. *Examiner's manual, SRA youth inventory.* Chicago: Science Research Associates, 1949.

Riesman, D. *The lonely crowd.* New Haven: Yale, 1950.

Rogers, C. R. "The characteristics of a helping relationship." *Personn. and Guid. J.,* 1958, *37,* 6–16.

Rogers, C. R. *Client-centered therapy.* Boston: Houghton, 1951.

Rogers, C. R. *Counseling and psychotherapy.* New York: Houghton, 1942.

Ruesch, J. *Therapeutic communication.* New York: Norton, 1961.

Ruesch, J., and G. Bateson. *Communication: the social matrix of psychiatry.* New York: Norton, 1951.

Russell, D. H. *Children's thinking.* Boston: Ginn, 1956.

Russell, J., and A. Willis. "Survey of teachers' opinions of guidance services." *Personn. and Guid. J.,* 1964, *42,* 707–709.


Samler, J. "Automation: the threat and promise." In D. G. Miller and E. D. Swanson, eds. *Technological change and vocational counseling.* Washington, D.C.: Nat. Voc. Guid. Assoc., 1964, pp. 57–78.

Sattler, H. V. *Parents, children, and the facts of life.* Paterson, N.J.: St. Anthony, 1952.

Saul, L. J. *Emotional maturity.* Philadelphia: Lippincott, 1947.

Schneiders, A. A. *Adolescents and the challenge of maturity: a guide for parents and teachers.* Milwaukee: Bruce, 1965a.

Schneiders, A. A. *The anarchy of feeling: man's search for freedom and maturity.* New York: Sheed, 1963.

Schneiders, A. A. *Personality development and adjustment in adolescence.* Milwaukee: Bruce, 1960.

Schneiders, A. A. *Personality dynamics and mental health.* New York: Holt, 1965b.

Schneiders, A. A. "Psychology as a normative science." In M. B. Arnold and J. A. Gasson, eds. *The human person.* New York: Ronald, 1954, pp. 373–394.

Schofield, M. *The sexual behavior of young people.* Boston: Little, Brown, 1965.

Scott, W. A. "Research definitions of mental health and mental illness." *Psychol. Bull.,* 1958, *55,* 29–45.

Seidman, J. M., ed. *1 he adolescent.* New York: Holt, 1950.

Senn, M. J. E., ed. *Symposium on the healthy personality.* New York: Josiah Macey, Jr. Foundation, 1950.

Sheitzer, B., and H. Peters. *Guidance: techniques for individual appraisal and development.* New York: Macmillan, 1965.

Sheridan, B. C. "The war against smut." *Cath. Digest,* Jan. 1963.

Shoben, E. J., Jr. "Guidance: remedial function or social reconstruction?" *Harvard Educ. Rev.* 1962, *32,* 430–443.

Shoben, E. J., Jr. "Some problems in establishing criteria of effectiveness." In G. Farwell and H. Peters, eds. *Guidance readings for counselors.* Chicago: Rand McNally, 1960, pp. 574–580.

Shoben, E. J., Jr. "Toward a concept of the normal personality." *Amer. Psychologist,* 1957, *12,* 183–189.

Siebert, S. *Work with young adults.* Baltimore: Enoch Pratt Free Library, 1964.

Smith, M. B. "Mental health reconsidered: a special case of the problem of values in psychology." *Amer. Psychologist,* 1961, *16,* 299–306.

Smith, M. B. "Research strategies toward a conception of positive mental health." *Amer. Psychologist,* 1959, *14,* 673–681.

Sorokin, P. A. *The American sex revolution.* Boston: Sargent, 1956.

Strang, R. *The adolescent views himself.* New York: McGraw, 1957.

Strang, R. *Pupil personnel and guidance.* New York: Macmillan, 1940.

Strecker, E. A. *Their mothers' sons.* Philadelphia: Lippincott, 1946.

Strecker, E. A., and V. T. Lathbury. *Their mothers' daughters.* Philadelphia: Lippincott, 1956.

Sullivan, H. S. *The psychiatric interview.* New York: Norton, 1954.

Super, D. E. *The psychology of careers.* New York: Harper, 1957.

Super, D. E., et al. *Vocational development: a framework for research.* New York: Teachers College Bureau of Publications, 1957.

Symonds, P. M., and A. R. Jensen. *From adolescent to adult.* New York: Columbia, 1961.

Ticknor, W. E. "Education toward maturity." *Top of the News:* Baltimore, May 1964, 269–272.

Tooze, R. *Your children want to read: a guide for teachers and parents.* Englewood Cliffs, N.J.: Prentice-Hall, 1957.

Tyler, L. E. *The work of the counselor,* 2nd ed. New York: Appleton, 1961.

Valentine, C. W. *Parents and children.* New York: Philosophical Library, 1955.

vanKaam, A. "Counseling from the viewpoint of existential psychology." In R. L. Mosher, R. F. Carle, and C. D. Kehas, eds. *Guidance—an examination.* New York: Harcourt, 1965, pp. 77–78.

Warters, J. *Achieving Maturity.* New York: McGraw, 1949.

Warters, J. *Techniques of counseling.* New York: McGraw, 1964.

Waskow, A. *The limits of defense.* New York: Doubleday, 1962.

Weisner, W. M., and P. A. Riffel. "Scrupulosity: religion and obsessive-compulsive behavior in children." *Amer. J. Psychiat.,* 1960, *117,* 314–318.

Weitz, H. "The role of the guidance worker in the schools." *Personn. and Guid. J.,* 1958, *37,* 266–272.

Wharton, D. "The battle against mail-order pornography." *Reader's Digest,* Feb. 1964, 147–154.

Wheelis, A. *The quest for identity.* New York: Norton, 1958.

Whittington, H. G. *Psychiatry on the college campus.* New York: International Univs. Press, 1963.

Whyte, W. H. *The organization man.* New York: Simon and Schuster, 1956.

Wickham, E. K. *Children's behavior and teachers' attitudes.* New York: Commonwealth Fund, 1928.

Wilkes, E. T. *Family guide to teenage health.* New York: Ronald, 1958.

Williams, M. M., and I. Kane. *On becoming a woman.* New York: Dell Publishing, 1960.

Williamson, E. G. *Counseling adolescents.* New York: McGraw, 1950.

Williamson, E. G. "The fusion of discipline and counseling in the educative process." *Personn. and Guid. J.,* 1955, *34,* 74–79.

Williamson, E. G. *How to counsel students.* New York: McGraw, 1939.

Wittenberg, R. M. *Adolescence and discipline.* New York: Association Press, 1959.

Wittenberg, R. M. *On call for youth.* New York: Association Press, 1955.

Witty, P. A. "Children and TV: a sixth report." *Elem. English,* Nov. 1966, 469–476.

Wolf, A. M., and S. Szasz. *Helping your child's emotional growth.* Garden City, N.Y.: Doubleday, 1955.

Wrenn, C. G. "The ethics of counseling." *Educ. and Psychol. Measmt.,* 1952, *12,* 161–177.

Wrenn, C. G. "The fault, dear Brutus." In J. F. McGowan and L. D. Schmidt, eds. *Counseling: readings in theory and practice.* New York: Holt, 1962, pp. 561–572.

Wrenn, C. G. *Student personnel work in college.* New York: Ronald, 1951.

Wrenn, C. G., and D. L. Harley. *Time on their hands: a report on leisure, recreation, and young people.* Washington, D.C.: Amer. Coun. on Educ., 1941.


Zavalloni, R. *Self-determination,* trans. by V. Biasiol and C. Tageson. Chicago: Forum Books, 1962.

# Index of Names